SPACE COMMERCIALIZATION AND THE DEVELOPMENT OF SPACE LAW FROM A CHINESE LEGAL PERSPECTIVE

SPACE COMMERCIALIZATION AND THE DEVELOPMENT OF SPACE LAW FROM A CHINESE LEGAL PERSPECTIVE

YUN ZHAO

Nova Science Publishers, Inc.
New York

LIBRARY OF CONGRESS CATALOGING-IN-PUBLICATION DATA

Zhao, Yun.
Space commercialization and the development of space law from a Chinese legal perspective / Yun Zhao.
p. cm.
Includes bibliographical references and index.
ISBN 978-1-60692-244-6 (hardcover)
1. Space law. 2. International law--China. I. Title.
KZD1145.C475 2009
341.4'7--dc22

2008047099

Published by Nova Science Publishers, Inc. ✝ New York

Contents

PREFACE

This book will be the first English on space law written by a Chinese scholar. With the rapid development of space activities in China, many space scientist and lawyers are keen to know Chinese Legal views on policies and laws on space activities.

The book discusses new development of space law in view of the rapid development of space commercial activities from a Chinese legal perspective. The topics selected in the book reflect the author's teaching and research in space law at four different universities: Leiden University, Erasmus University Rotterdam, City University of Hong Kong and the University of Hong Kong. Six areas of space law issues have been selected: property rights, space registration and liability regime, launching services, telecommunications services, national space legislation and international space cooperation. All the topics are closely related to current Chinese space legislation and practice. When dealing with the above six issues, the author will first briefly discuss the current rules and practice at the international level, followed by in-depth analysis of Chinese situation.

This English book will be unique. Those who are researching on space law and/or in charge of formulating national space policy will be especially interested in the elaboration of Chinese attitude toward space commercialization and of the current Chinese space policies and laws.

I.H.Ph. Diederiks-Verschoor
May 28, 2008

Chapter 1

INTRODUCTION

Law provides basic means to regulate our daily life; it offers guidelines for human activities and defines illegal actions and possible penalties. In modern society, human beings will always need to check and rely on laws to decide their actions. As a result, lawyers and legislators are keen in developing new rules wherever and whenever new activities arise. This also holds true to the development of space law. The ultimate success or failure of the commercial space industry now lies in the hands of legislators, those that will determine and shape our regulatory environment, our law and our policy.[1]

We witnessed rapid technological developments in the last century, one of the distinct examples being the emergence of space activities. Significant progress in space technology has led to the successful event in 1957 when Sputnik I became the first satellite to orbit the Earth in outer space.[2] Since then, space exploration has become heated issues for international society. The States have regarded the ability to exploit outer space as one factor evaluating their national power.

Space legislation started soon after the launch of Sputnik in 1957 and has since then achieved great success in regulating space activities. Five space treaties drafted in the 1960s and 1970s provide important guidance to space activities. [3] These treaties (except one) have been well received by international society.

However, further development in space technology and world economy drastically changed the situation under which the space treaties were the adopted. Commercialization

---

1 C. Stott, Making Space Profitable: the Role of Law and Policy, China 2004 Space Law Conference Paper Assemble, at 19.

2 I.H.Ph. Diederiks-Verschoor, An Introduction to Space Law, 2 (Kluwer Law International, 2nd ed., 1999).

3 Treaty on Principles Governing the Activities of States in the Exploration and Use of Outer Space, including the Moon and Other Celestial Bodies, London/Moscow/Washington, done January 27, 1967, entered into force October 10, 1967; 610 UNTS 205; TIAS 6347; 18 UST 2410; UKTS 1968 No. 10; Cmnd. 3198; ATS 1967 No. 24; ILM 386 (1967) (hereinafter "Outer Space Treaty); Agreement on the Rescue of Astronauts, the Return of Astronauts and the Return of Objects Launched into Outer Space, London/Moscow/Washington, done April 22, 1968, entered into force December 3, 1968; 672 UNTS 119; TIAS 6599; 19 UST 7570; UKTS 1969 No. 56; Cmnd. 3786; ATS 1968 No. 8; 7 ILM 151 (1968) (hereinafter "Rescue Agreement"); Convention on International Liability for Damage Caused by Space Objects, London/Moscow/Washington, done March 29, 1972, entered into force September 1, 1972; 961 UNTS 187; TIAS 7762; 24 UST 2389; UKTS 1974 No. 16; Cmnd. 5068; ATS 1975 No. 5; 10 ILM 965 (1971) (hereinafter "Liability Convention"); Convention on Registration of Objects Launched into Outer Space, New York, done January 14, 1975, entered into force September 15, 1976; 1023 UNTS 15; TIAS 8480; 28 UST 695; UKTS 1978 No. 70; Cmnd. 6256; ATS 1986 No. 5; 14 ILM 43 (1975) (hereinafter "Registration Convention").

and privatization of space activities have become the main challenge for the existing space legal regime.

Recent developments in outer space signal the introduction of a new era in the rapidly developing field of space law. The 1998 Intergovernmental Agreement (IGA) provides the basic framework for establishing the International Space Station (ISS) and future commercial applications.[4] The successful trips of space tourists to the ISS, [5] using the ISS for a global advertising campaign, [6] etc., further justify the diversified commercial potential of the ISS. This trend is not the end of the story. The successful launch of space stations that support humans has inspired China to establish a Chinese national space station in the near future.

It is the primary purpose of this study to look into the new trend of space activities and its influence on the development of space law. In this study, the author makes use of his knowledge and experience in Chinese space legislation and practice for purposes of illustration.

The present study consists of seven parts. After a brief introduction, Chapter Two deals with property rights, more specifically, the understanding and application of the Common Heritage of Mankind (CHM) Principle and patent protection in outer space. The CHM Principle is of great importance to the formulation of space commercialization regime. It is time to seriously consider and realize the means and structure to allocate and use space natural resources in a fair and equitable manner. The concept of "International Space Authority" is introduced for the above purpose. Intellectual property protection remains a difficult matter in outer space. With space commercialization well in place, it is urgent to look into the matter to find out the way to protect intellectual property. This section introduces the concept of "space patent" and proposes a special regime to protect space patent.

The space treaties were drafted in the cold-war period; it is now time to examine the possibility for further development of the space treaties to accommodate the ongoing process of space commercialization. The Registration Convention and the Liability Convention were picked up for discussion in Chapter Three. Several areas have been identified for possible revision to accommodate the development of space commercialization.

Satellite launching services constitute the basis for further space activities. Three issues relating to launching activities are selected for analysis in Chapter Four: liberalization of satellite launching services (as a major issue facing current society), the use of Nuclear Power Sources (NPS) in launching services and the heated topic of space tourism. Space tourism is not an imaginative story any more. With several space tourists having been sent to outer space, it is now time to think about possible rules to regulate this new industry. This Chapter

---

[4] Agreement among the government of Canada, governments of Member States of the European Space Agency, the government of Japan, the government of the Russia Federation, and the government of the United States of America concerning Cooperation on the Civil International Space Station, January 29, 1998, Temp. State Department No. 01-52, CTIA No. 10073.000, available at 2001 WL 679938 (entered into force March 27, 2001).

[5] Anna Badkhen, US Tourist Arrives at Space Station: Tito is Greeted by Russians After Weekend Flight, *Boston Globe,* May 1st, 2001, at C4; South African Tourist Docks at Space Station, *L.A. Times,* April 28, 2002, at A10; Sean R. Mikula, Blue Helmets in the Next Frontier: The Future is Now, 29 *Ga. J. Int'l & Comp. L.* 531, 556-557 (Summer 2001).

[6] Henkel was the first company to use the ISS for advertisement: a set of Pritt gluesticks was tested by the cosmonauts under conditions of weightlessness and the experiments were filmed. Henkel later used the footage to produce TV commercials for the glue that works in space. See *World Wide Pritt—Space Proof Quality*, available at <http://www.prittworld.com/space_proof/index_hau.htm> (visited on October 15, 2004).

suggests several changes and improvements to the current legal regime to help promote the new industry.

Closely related to satellite launching is the issue of telecommunications services. The WTO and the ITU are the two main international organizations in regulating telecommunications services. The WTO focuses on the trade aspect, while the ITU on the technical side. Telecommunications services are the first area in space regime to be liberalized under the WTO framework. This Chapter analyzes the liberalization of telecommunications services under the Framework of the WTO and identifies areas for further liberalization. Closely related to the liberalization is the issue of national telecommunications regulators. This Chapter further examines the ITU's position in securing good national regulation practices and the relationship between the ITU and national regulators.

The last two Chapters take a closer look at space legislation and practice in China. With no new space conventions adopted after 1979, national space legislation becomes more and more important in space regulations. Chapter Six introduced the principles, means for national space legislation. This Chapter further gives an overview of China's present legal framework for space activities. Hong Kong, as a Special Administrative Region of China, has its own separate legal system. A separate section in Chapter Six is devoted to the discussion of Hong Kong's space law and its further development.

International space cooperation is especially important in space activities. China emphasizes the importance of international cooperation and has reached several bilateral agreements fro space cooperation. The China-Brazil space cooperation exemplifies China's determination to cooperate with any country, developed or developing, for the ultimate goal of peaceful use of outer space. This cooperation presents the best example for the South-South space cooperation. This Chapter introduces the above cooperation and suggests ways to improve the model of space cooperation.

Chapter 2

PROPERTY RIGHTS AND OUTER SPACE

1. REVISITING THE COMMON HERITAGE OF MANKIND PRINCIPLE

1.1. Introduction

For centuries, human beings have been viewing outer space as a source of inspiration. The launch of Sputnik-1[7] and Armstrong's walk on the Moon[8] marked the dawn of the space age. Technological developments have made exploration and use of outer space a reality. The race for accomplishment in outer space was a mark of the Cold War period. However, after the 1990s, the international political atmosphere fundamentally changed. Peace and Earth-bound development become main themes for State governments. The political change also substantially influenced the intended activities in outer space.[9] How to make full use of outer space in a peaceful way became the main concern of most space scientists, lawyers and practitioners. Outer space is replete with natural resources and the potential profits from the use of these resources justify commercializing outer space. The development of the legal regime for outer space rightly follows the evolution of space activities.

While national governments remain as the primary entities undertaking responsibilities in outer space, private groups are increasingly getting involved in space activities. Throughout the 1980s, the government of the United States encouraged private enterprises to take the lead.[10] The lure for non-governmental entities is certainly present: the potential for profit is great in outer space.[11] Yet, the ambiguity in the extant legal regime for outer space remains an obstacle for further involvement of private parties.

---

[7] Walter Sullivan, Course Recorded-Navy Picks Up Radio Signals—4 Report Sighting Device, *N.Y. Times*, October 5, 1957, at A1.

[8] John N.oble Wilford, A Powdery Surface Closely Explored, *N.Y. Times*, July 20, 1969, at A1

[9] Frans G. von der Dunk, Towards a European Space Agency, Mark II?, *Proceedings of the 35th Colloquium on the Law of Outer Space* 172 (1992).

[10] Anthony R. Filiato, The Commercial Space Launch Act: America's Response to the Moon Treaty?, 10 *Fordham Int'l L.J.* 763, 772 (1987).

[11] For detailed discussion, see Ty S. Twibell, Space Law: Legal Restraints on Commercialization and Development of Outer Space, 65 *UMKC L. Rev.* 589, 591 (Spring 1997).

The notion of States sharing a common interest in the exploration and use of outer space led the international community to declare outer space to be the "province of all mankind".[12] Some scholars have interpreted this to be the *functional and legal equivalent* of "common heritage of mankind (CHM)", [13] which was officially introduced to the mineral resources of the Moon (emphasis added).[14] The use of the two terms above rightly shows the concerns of the international community as a whole. However, the ambiguity and ramifications of those terms have left space law as one of the least stable and clarified areas of international law. No treaties offer guidance on how to implement the CHM concept in outer space.

Actually, it is not the only area where the CHM concept is used. In the United Nations Convention on the Law of Sea (UNCLOS), deep seabed resources are also defined as CHM. A regime was established to realize the purpose of the term.[15] Part one of this section compares the use of the term in the two regimes and discusses the feasibility of transplanting the model of deep seabed to outer space for the sole purpose of commercialization.

Part two discusses the term "common heritage of mankind" and its use in the two treaties: the Agreement Governing the Activities of States on the Moon and Other Celestial Bodies (Moon Treaty) and the UNCLOS. Part three addresses the establishment of the International Seabed Authority (Seabed Authority) and the realization of the purpose of the CHM. Part four suggests an International Space Authority (ISA) might be established, following the model of deep seabed. The ISA can create a stable governance regime for private activities in outer space that will be acceptable to both developed and developing countries. Based on the analysis of these parts, part five reaffirms the necessity and feasibility of the establishment of the ISA to accommodate the commercialization trend in outer space.

1.2. The Concept of "Common Heritage of Mankind"

More than any technical challenge, the lack of legal stability is the primary impediment to the commercial development of outer space.[16] There are no insurmountable technological

---

[12] See further Article 1 of the Treaty on Principles Governing the Activities of States in the Exploration and Use of Outer Space, Including the Moon and Other Celestial Bodies (hereinafter Outer Space Treaty), January 27, 1967, 18 U.S.T. 2410, 610 U.N.T.S. 205 (entered into force on October 10, 1967).

[13] The two terms, as applied in two different treaties for different purposes, cannot be used interchangeably. See B. Maiorsky, A Few Reflections on the Meaning and the Interrelation of 'Province of All Mankind' and 'Common Heritage of Mankind' Notions, *Proceedings of the 29th Coolloquium on the Law of Outer Space* 58-61 (1986). Nevertheless, the principles outlined in the Outer Space Treaty—for the benefit of all countries, free for exploration and use, on a basis of equality, free access, and not subject to national appropriation—form the heart of the CHM. Both terms share the following *functions* (emphasis added): apply to the exploitable space resources and protect the interests of technologically less advanced states. The CHM allegedly establishes a legal framework to implement the declaration in the Outer Space Treaty. See further Gijsbertha Cornelia Maria Reijnen, *The United Nations Space Treaties Analyzed* 96 (Kluwer, 1992); Sylvia Maureen Williams, The Law of Outer Space and Natural Resources, 36 *Int'l & Comp. L.Q.* 142, 145 (1987); Aldo Armando Cocca, The Advances in International Law through the Law of Outer Space, 9 *Journal of Space Law* 13, 16 (1981).

[14] See further Article 11 of the Agreement Governing the Activities of States on the Moon and Other Celestial Bodies (hereinafter Moon Treaty), opened for signatures on December 5, 1979, 34 U.N. GAOR Agenda Items 48, 48 at 1, U.N. Doc. A/RES/34/68, 18 I.L.M. 1434 (1979).

[15] Article 156 of the United Nations Convention on the Law of the Sea, opened for signature on December 10, 1982, U.N. Doc. A/CONF. 62/122, reprinted in 21 I.L.M. 1261 (1982).

[16] See generally Ty S. Twibell, Circumnavigating International Space Law, 4 *ILSA Journal of International & Comparative law* 259 (1997).

impediments to the exploitation of outer space resources. The restraints are imposed by policy, economics and law.[17] CHM was the chief source of confusion and uncertainty in the outer space legal regime. The use of this concept can resort to the Roman law theory of *res communis*, which was applied to community property that could not be owned by a person, a state, or a collection of states.[18] This concept was later applied to the Antarctica, the deep seabed and outer space.[19] However, the modern version has incorporated an additional element of reasonable use: *res communis* property still cannot be owned, but it can be used in an appropriate way to benefit mankind.[20]

There are five elements generally considered to be central to the modern application of the CHM concept: the area is not subject to national appropriation; all countries share in the management of the area; the benefits derived from exploitation of resources in the area must be shared with all regardless of the level of participation; the area must be dedicated to peaceful purposes; and the area must be preserved for future generations.[21]

Divergences exist concerning the detailed implementation of the CHM concept. The primary problems derive from its demand for a forced transfer of benefits in the name of equity and the legal uncertainty that this doctrine has engendered regarding private property rights and an international governance regime.[22] Developed and developing countries[23] hold totally different views towards the concept.[24] That is, the need to recover the invested cost and return a profit to finance future activities *vs*. an opportunity to correct past inequalities and to redistribute global resources and wealth. Accordingly, some scholars have concluded that the divergence results from a conflict between the efficient allocation of communal resources and equitable allocation of these resources.[25]

Various scholars have deeply discussed their understandings of the CHM concept.[26] The discussions during the drafting of the UNCLOS led to the adoption of the governance regime:

---

[17] Richard Berkley, Space Law Versus Space Utilization: The Inhibition of Private Industry in Outer Space, 15 *Wisconsin International Law Journal* 421, 428 (1997).

[18] Lea Brilmayer & Natalie Klein, Land and Sea : Two Sovereignty Regimes in Search of a Common Denominator, 33 *N.Y.U.J. Int'l L. & Pol.* 703, 706-707 (2001); L.F.E. Goldie, A Note on Some Diverse Meanings of 'The Common Heritage of Mankind', 10 *Syracuse J. Int'l L. & Com.* 69, 81 (1983); see generally L.F.E. Goldie, Title and Use (and Usufruct)—An Ancient Distinction Too Oft Forgot, 79 *AJIL* 689 (1985).

[19] Oscar Schachter, Philip Jessup's Life and Ideas, 80 *AJIL* 878, 894 (October 1986); Carl Q. Christol, The Moon Treaty Enters into Force, 79 *AJIL* 163, 164 (January 1985).

[20] Mahdi El-Baghdadi, The Seabed's Mineral Resources and the Conditions Affecting the Regime to Regulate Their Exploitation, 26 *Journal of World Trade* 88 (1992).

[21] Barbara Ellen Heim, Exploring the Last Frontiers for Mineral Resources: A Comparison of International Law Regarding the Deep Seabed, Outer Space and Antarctica, 23 *Vanderbilt Journal of Transnational Law* 819, 827 (1990); See generally Christopher C. Joyner, Legal Implications of the Concept of the Common Heritage of Mankind, 35 *International & Comparative Law Quarterly* 190 (1986).R.J. Rao, Outer Space: A Part of Common Heritage of Mankind, in V.S. Mani et al. (Eds.), *Recent Trends in International Space Law and Policy* 195-199 (1997).

[22] Kevin V. Cook, The Discovery of Lunar Water: An Opportunity to Develop a Workable Moon Treaty, 11 *Georgetown International Environmental Law Review* 647, 648 (Spring 1999).

[23] M.C.W. Pinto, The Developing Countries and the Exploitation of the Deep Seabed, 15 *Colum. Bus. L. Rev.* 30 (1980).

[24] Kelly M. Zullo, The Need to Clarify the Status of Property Rights in International Space Law, 90 *Geo. L.J.* 2413, 2424-2426 (July 2002).

[25] Christopher M. Petras, "Space Force Alpha": Military Use of the International Space Station and the Concept of "Peaceful Purposes", 53 *A.F.L. Rev.* 135, 151-152 (2002); Michael J. Finch, Limited Space: Allocating the Geostationary Orbit, 7 *Nw. Journal of International Law & Business* 788, 798 (1986).

[26] See for example, Eric Husby, Sovereignty and Property Rights in Outer Space, 3 *Journal of International Law & Practice* 359, 369 (1994); Heidi Keefe, Making the Final Frontier Feasible: A Critical Look at the Current Body of Outer Space law, 11 *Santa Clara Computer & High Technology Law Journal* 347 (1995).

establishment of the Seabed Authority.[27] This body undertook its duty from 1994 after several revisions of the original UNCLOS.

However, heated discussions did not lead to any substantial improvement in the legal regime accommodating the commercialization of outer space. Existing space law does not provide any guidance enabling the creation of an effective regime fostering commercial space exploitation.[28] Theoretical analysis did not come to any conclusion acceptable to all the parties.[29] Nevertheless, even with the unstable legal status in place, various parties, foreseeing potential profit, have started their own projects aiming at commercializing outer space. For example, the IGA provides a specific model for multinational cooperation among active participants without an overarching international legal and governance regime.[30] The United States has also executed a series of bilateral Memoranda of Understanding with Partner States concerning outer space activities.[31] With no clear-cut rules and regimes in place, the activities are carried out subject to Partner States' own interpretations. This is increasingly detrimental to the development of commercial activities in outer space. States can take actions at will and there are no defined rules governing their activities, which ultimately leads to the devastating result of a "gold rush" by space-faring states. Developing states will be totally left out of the game. Such a situation will fail to provide a predictable and stable environment which is necessary for the involvement of private entities, and will fail to win international approval.

While no theoretical framework can be agreed upon to govern the commercial activities in outer space, [32] states should adopt a pragmatic approach to deal with the issue. Simply put, they should start formulating a governance regime for the purpose of commercialization in outer space. Appropriate guidance could be formulated to accommodate the interests of different parties. Though some might argue that this approach is premature, the result is better than needlessly quarreling over the essentials of the concept. A good example has been set by the UNCLOS. States should follow similar steps and formulate a regime subject to further discussion and adoption.[33]

Based on the example of the deep seabed, it appears that CHM has lost much of its attraction for developing countries. The political and economic conditions that led to the UNCLOS have changed significantly. The treaties containing the concept of the CHM were argued vehemently in the politically tense atmosphere of the Cold War. The primary goal was to prevent the former Soviet Union and the United States from gaining a military advantage, rather than developing a regime that would support private development.[34] The end of the

---

[27] Article 156-169 of the UNCLOS.

[28] Heidi Keefe, Making the Final Frontier Feasible: A Critical Look at the Current Body of Outer Space Law, 11 *Computer & High Technology Law Journal* 357-358 (1995).

[29] Brian M. Hoffstadt, Moving the Heavens: Lunar Mining and the "Common Heritage of Mankind" in the Moon Treaty, 42 *UCLA Law Review* 575, 581, note 30 (1994).

[30] See generally Lara L. Manzione, Multinational Investment in the Space Station: An Outer Space Model for International Cooperation?, 18 *Am. U. Int'l L. Rev.* 507-535 (2002); Andrew D. Watson & William G. Schmidt, Legal Issues Surrounding the International Space Station, 7 *USAFA J. Leg. Stud.* 159 (1996).

[31] A. Farand, Space Station Cooperation: Legal Arrangements, in G. Lafferanderie & D. Crowther (eds.), *Outlook on Space Law Over the Next 30 Years: Essays Published for the 30th Anniversary of the Outer Space Treaty* 153 (1997).

[32] The Moon Treaty has achieved so far only a very little number of ratifications. Neither developed nor even developing countries had become parties to the Treaty. The CHM concept in the Moon Treaty has long been and still is subject to different interpretations by developed and developing nations.

[33] Grier C. Raclin, From Ice to Ether: The Adoption of A Regime to Govern Resource Exploitation in Outer Space, 7 *Journal of International Law & Business* 727, 739 (1986).

[34] Ezra J. Reinstein, Owning Outer Space, 20 *Nw. J. Int'l L. & Bus.* 59, 62 (1999).

Cold War and the adoption of a market-economy approach by most developing countries have pushed the idea of capitalism and the free market approach into the limelight.[35] Through years of discussions, most scholars believe that the CHM, while maintaining some policy significance, lacks the force of accepted international law.[36] A great number of persons even consider the concept as meaningless and lacking any practical value.[37]

While continuing upholding the concept of CHM, the free-market approach plays an important role in devising the regime for the deep seabed. Most scholars believe that only by making full use of the resources in the deep seabed rather than establishing a regime installing the commercial exploitation, can the living standards in all the Nations be effectively improved.[38] Acknowledging the benefits of commercial exploitation, all nations, developed and otherwise, have a basis to work together to find an appropriate resolution. Essentially, the same political and economic environment exists for outer space. A similar regime to that of the deep seabed could, thus, be possible for the exploitation of outer space resources. Consequently, the focus for now is to identify the legal mechanisms and political compromises that successfully resolved the CHM dilemma for the deep seabed and apply it to outer space. This is more efficient than developing new legal, economic, and political theories.

1.3. The International Seabed Authority

The Seabed Authority, established in 1994 under the UNCLOS, is an intergovernmental body.[39] It organizes and controls all mineral-related activities in the international seabed area beyond the limits of national jurisdiction.[40] Part XI of the Convention uses the CHM to preclude the deep seabed from national appropriation.[41] It is Part XI that has caused the most debate and is the principal obstacle to US ratification of the Convention.[42]

The Authority is responsible for licensing and regulating mineral exploration and exploitation of the seabed beyond the limits of national jurisdiction.[43] According to Part XI, a multinational mining company is created to participate in mining activities in competition with private companies licensed by the Authority.[44] Access to the resources is prohibited if not approved by the licensing authority.[45] Applicants are required to present two sites of

---

[35] Jonathan I. Charney, The United States and the Revision of the 1982 Convention on the Law of the Sea, 23 *Ocean Development & International Law* 279 (1992).

[36] Peter Malanczuk, Actors: States, International Organizations, Private Entities, in Lafferanderie & Crowther (eds.), *Outlook on Space Law Over the Next 30 Years: Essays Published for the 30th Anniversary of the Outer Space Treaty*, 32-33 (1997); Arthur W. Blaser, The Common Heritage in its Infinite Variety: Space Law and the Moon in the 1990s, 5 *Journal of Law & Technology* 79, 93 (1990).

[37] Joyner, *supra* note 15, at 198.

[38] Glenn H. Reynolds, Outer Space and Peace: Some Thoughts on Structures and Relations, 59 *Tenn. Law Review* 723, 731 (1992).

[39] *International Seabed Authority: From Wikipedia, The Free Encyclopedia*, available at <http://en.wikipedia.org/wiki/International_Seabed_Authority> (visited on August 3, 2004).

[40] *Id.*

[41] See specifically Article 136-137 of the UNCLOS.

[42] Charney, *supra* note 29, at 280.

[43] Article 156 of the UNCLOS.

[44] Article 170 of the UNCLOS.

[45] *Id.* See also Cook, *supra* note 16, at 680.

roughly equal value.[46] The Authority may reserve one site for its own use.[47] Furthermore, the Authority is empowered to collect fees from the licensees and to distribute funds in excess of that necessary to cover its operating expenses to developing countries.[48] Other provisions in the Convention include a decision-making process[49] and the transfer of technology to member states[50].

Part XI is the subject of heated discussion. The absence of customary international law on the particular question of mining resources from deep seabed[51] made Part XI of the Convention all the more important.[52] No doubt, the Convention acknowledges the CHM, [53] and the Authority is created to realize the purpose of the CHM.[54] However, the controversy exists concerning the level of control exercised by the Authority and its preferential treatment for developing countries.[55] Several provisions of the Convention were considered to deter the development of natural resources: the imposition of specific production guidelines and limits;[56] requirements of mandatory private technology transfer and benefit sharing;[57] the failure to give a valid decision-making role to the countries actively involved in the mining of deep seabed resources;[58] the failure to provide assured access to qualified deep seabed companies to conduct mining activities.[59]

Negotiations continued until the adoption of the 1994 Agreement relating to the Implementation of Part XI (seabed provisions) of the Convention.[60] The difficulties posed by the CHM are in the process of being successfully resolved. The original divergence between developed and developing countries was reconciled when voluntary multilateral agreements were reached by the developed countries and their mining companies in the 1980s and also by discussions initiated by the Secretary-General of the UN in the early 1990s.[61] While maintaining strong opposition before 1994 to the adoption of Part XI of the Convention, the US signed the new Agreement, enabling it to provisionally apply the seabed-related portion of the Convention and to participate in the work of the Authority.[62]

---

[46] Article 8 of the UNCLOS, Annex III.

[47] *Id.*

[48] Article 173 of the UNCLOS.

[49] Article 159 of the UNCLOS.

[50] Article 144 of the UNCLOS; Article 5 of the UNCLOS, Annex III.

[51] Patricia Minola, The Moon Treaty and the Law of the Sea, 18 *San Diego Law Review* 455, 459-460 (April 1981).

[52] Cook, *supra* note 16, 681-682.

[53] Article 136 of the UNCLOS.

[54] Article 157 of the UNCLOS.

[55] The US and the European Community were both against Part XI. For discussions, see further James L. Malone, The United States and the Law of the Sea, 24 *Va. J. Int'l L.* 785, 786 (1984); Michael Hardy, The Law of the Sea and the Prospects for Deep Seabed Mining: The Position of the European Community, 17 *Ocean Dev. & Int'l L.J.* 309, 314 (1986).

[56] Article 6-7 of the UNCLOS, Annex III.

[57] Article 5 of the UNCLOS, Annex III.

[58] Article 159 of the UNCLOS.

[59] Charney, *supra* note 29, at 286; Heim, *supra* note 15, at 828.

[60] Agreement Relating to the Implementation of Part XI of the United Nations Convention on the Law of the Sea of 10 December 1982 (hereinafter the Annex), 28 July 1994, reprinted in 33 I.L.M. 1309 (1994). The Annex entered into force on July 28, 1996.

[61] Charney, *supra* note 29, at 287; James H. Andrews, US Changes Tack on Ocean Treaty, *Christian Sci. Monitor*, May 18, 1994, at 8.

[62] Marjorie Ann Browne, *Law of the Sea: the International Seabed Authority—Its Status and U.S. Participation Therein*, September 16, 1996, available at <http://www.ncseonline.org/NLE/CRSreports/Marine/mar-22.cfm?CFID=16587223&CFTOKEN=99935987> (visited on October 18, 2004).

While reaffirming that deep seabed and its resources are CHM, the new Agreement establishes rules and procedures governing the exploitation of those resources, which rightly resolve the concerns of developed countries. The following summarizes the important changes in the new Agreement.

First, a consensus-based decision-making process took the place of the one-member, one-vote system. Representation on the Council is evenly distributed among different categories of members. Only when consensus is not possible, should the decision be made by a two-thirds majority vote.[63] Second, a market-oriented approach was adopted to resolve the issue of technology transfer. The application fee and the annual fees are reduced.[64] Developing countries can obtain technology on fair and reasonable commercial terms.[65] Production ceilings are abolished. Third, the Agreement provides that subsidization or any other discriminatory practices shall not be applied in the development of deep seabed resources.[66] Furthermore, fifteen-year timetables, instead of five-year, were provided for the approval of proposed exploration work plans, thus providing economic certainty for investors.[67]

The modifications adopted in this Agreement are relevant to the discussion regarding outer space, which has characteristic similar to the deep seabed. This similarity forms the basis for employing the model and style of deep seabed governance to outer space. The improvements in the new Agreement are considered in the discussion on formulating a governance system for outer space.

1.4. Establishment of the International Space Authority

Realizing the commercial potential of outer space is an issue in need of urgent resolution. It is important to devise a regime for the exploitation of outer space by reaching a balance between protecting the profits of relevant exploiting entities and serving the interests of humankind.[68] While previous discussions focused on the theoretical framework of the CHM concept, it is the purpose of the present writing to focus on establishing a governance regime based on the successful example of the Seabed Authority. Discussions concerning the use of CHM will continue, just like the situation regarding the deep seabed: heated discussions continued even after the Seabed Authority was established and commercial activities began. Nonetheless, the existence of a stable governance regime can, as in the case of the deep seabed, enhance the confidence of space investors and promote further development of commercial space activities.

The deep seabed and space share the following similarities: they have potentially valuable natural resources; they both require high technology and sufficient financial backing for exploration; and activities in the two areas should be carried out for the benefit of all humankind. The main difference between them is their geographical locations. However, this will not require significant or substantial impact on the final rules and the regime adopted

---

[63] See further Section 3 of the Annex.
[64] Section 8 of the Annex.
[65] Section 5 of the Annex.
[66] Section 6 of the Annex.
[67] Section 2 (5) of the Anex.
[68] David Tan, Towards a New Regime for the Protection of Outer Space as the "Province of All Mankind", 25 *Yale J. Int'l L.* 145, 193 (Winter 2000).

governing space activities.[69] Space law has therefore, been largely influenced by factors similar to the deep seabed.[70]

The Moon Treaty did not create an international regime, but it requires that States parties to the agreement do so "as such exploitation is about to become feasible".[71] Witnessing the rapid development of outer space activities, it is time for space lawyers to take a pragmatic approach. Theoretical discussions are beneficial to the clarification of the CHM concept. However, commercial activities will proceed and will not wait for the final resolution of the issue. It is thus all the more important to start devising a regime as required by space commercial activities. Commercial projects had actually started before reaching the final stage of the ISS: the sending of the space tourists to the ISS meant even more for the future.[72]

1.4.1. Guidelines

The original text of the UNCLOS on the deep seabed was not well received in several aspects.[73] Only after making several amendments did the governance regime for the deep seabed receive wide acceptance. It is thus important to bring the disputed issues to notice before formulating a similar regime for outer space. No doubt, the CHM is the underlying principle guiding the formulation of these rules.[74] Several guidelines should be further formulated for better implementation of the CHM.

First, the proposed ISA should have a Council consisting of a wide and balanced representation in the decision-making process. Similar to the Seabed Authority, representation on the Council should consist of thirty-six members, and be distributed as follows: four from the largest consumers or importers of products; four from among the largest exporters of products; four from among those States that have made the largest investments in preparation for commercial activities in the area; six from developing countries; and the rest selected to achieve equitable geographical distribution.[75] Consensus shall be the primary mechanism in decision-making. Where consensus is not possible, then a decision should be made by a two-thirds majority of the Council.[76]

Second, technology transfer to developing countries should not be obligatory. Modern technologies represent invaluable assets that must be equally protected by existing laws governing intellectual property rights.[77] The entities, having worked, risked, and spent money on research and development, should be allowed to maintain their technologies and retain any

---

[69] The rules and the regime for both areas share the same purpose: to create a stable and equitable legal environment where the financial risks are tempered and property rights are protected. Governance regimes for both areas can provide economic incentives necessary to promote and sustain the development of commercial activities. Accordingly, economic and equitable considerations are most important in devising a governance regime.

[70] Husby, *supra* note 20, at 362.

[71] The Moon Treaty, Article 11, para. 5, 18 I.L.M. at 1438. It provides that " States Parties to this Agreement hereby undertake to establish an international regime, including appropriate procedures, to govern the exploration of the natural resources of the Moon as such exploitation is about to become feasible."

[72] See generally R. Thomas Rankin, Space Tourism: Fanny Packs, Ugly T-Shirts, and the Law in Outer Space, 36 *Suffolk U.L. Rev.* 695-716 (2003).

[73] Edith Brown Weiss, International Environmental Law: Contemporary Issues and the Emergence of a New World Order, 81 *Geo. L.J.* 675, 704 (1993).

[74] *Supra* note 33.

[75] See further Section 3 (15) of the Annex.

[76] Section 3(2), (3) of the Annex.

[77] Hoover, Law and Security in Outer Space from the Viewpoint of Private Industry, 11 *Journal of Space Law* 122-124 (1983).

profits from them.[78] Developing countries should obtain technology at market price, but the price should be fair and reasonable. Other ways can be formulated to promote the transfer of technology to developing countries, such as establishment of joint ventures with developing countries. Furthermore, as a balance to benefit the exploring entities and States, rules regarding economic assistance to developing countries, especially to those having been seriously affected by the commercial activities in outer space, should be formulated. A special fund can be established to assist economic development in these countries; the funds can be levied from payments received from contractors', including the exploring entities', voluntary contributions.

Third, a free-market approach should be adopted. Formerly, national governments have been the main body responsible for space activities. Government regulation has resulted in a poorly managed space industry with little accountability for failures.[79] When private entities become increasingly involved in this field, a free-market approach has been called on. As claimed by Fountain, a free-market approach bolstered by the legal certainty inherent in a system that provides defined property rights would do much to energize the stalled development of the space industry.[80] Exploitation of outer space resources should thus be based on commercial principles: anti-competitive practices, such as subsidization and discriminatory treatment should not be permitted on the process of commercializing outer space. Important rules in the World Trade Organization (WTO) concerning liberalization of relevant markets, such as the principle of national treatment[81] and rules on monopolies and exclusive service providers[82], should also be applied.

Fourth, closely related to the last point, transparency in granting access should be advocated. Transparency measures, as an important mechanism of both reassurance and verification when linked to cooperative obligations, serve to demonstrate peaceful intent, good faith and ongoing compliance with the rules.[83] Basically, commercial ventures will be the most important vehicles for future space activities. Equal access to outer space resources should be well available and guaranteed.[84] Procedures for approval of new applications should be in place. The availability of accurate information on space resources is also vital to the success of exploitation. Accurate information can enable private entities to plan their efforts, deploy assets effectively, reduce costs and risks.[85] Thus, transparency and easy access to information relevant to space exploitation should be provided.[86]

Fifth, the proposed body should try to balance the interests of exploring countries and developing countries.[87] The Outer Space Treaty establishes that all nations, on the basis of equality and without discrimination, are free to explore and use outer space; Exploration and

---

[78] *Id.*, at 118.

[79] Lynn M. Fountain, Creating Momentum in Space: Ending the Paralysis Produced by the "Common Heritage of Mankind" Doctrine, 35 *Conn. L. Rev.* 1753, 1774-1775 (Summer, 2003).

[80] *Id.*

[81] See Article 17 of the General Agreement on Trade in Services (GATS), April 15, 1994, reprinted in 33 ILM 1168.

[82] See Article 8 of the GATS.

[83] Nina Tannenwald, Law versus Power on the High Frontier: The Case for a Rule-Based Regime for Outer Space, 29 *Yale Journal of International Law* 363, 419 (Summer 2004).

[84] See Article 1 of the Outer Space Treaty.

[85] See for example, Sergio Marchisio, Remote Sensing for Sustainable Development, in Lafferanderie & Crowther, *supra* note 25, at 348.

[86] See further International Law Association Resolution 1/2002: Space Law (2002).

[87] See Article 9 of the Outer Space Treaty.

use must be for the benefit of all countries, irrespective of their economic or scientific development.[88] However, in view of the fact that only a few nations have the ability to carry out space activities, the proposed body should offer exploring countries efficient guidance and impetus to develop their programs and conduct their activities in space.[89] The point here is to balance equity and efficiency.[90] While addressing the economic development of developing countries, an equitable and efficient governance regime should also be able to guarantee a sufficient return on investments[91] and enough profits for exploring entities in successful space activities.[92] Failing the latter can deter commercial activities in space. To promote fairness and maintain control, it is advisable to limit the years of the continued use of resources. Once the initial period expires, the private entity can apply for an extension of its license. On the other hand, the system of payments to the body should be fair and reasonable.[93] The level of payments shall be based on several factors: the investment made, profitability, the environment affected; the economic situation of affected States, etc. For this purpose, a special Finance Committee should be established to oversee financial issues. The body should monitor the development of outer space activities, establishing the level of payments in proportion to the scope of outer space activities.

Finally, while acknowledging that economic gain is the primary purpose for developing space resources, the proposed body should offer the opportunity to create a new paradigm that avoids past conflicts and promotes peace.[94] Ideally, space activities should be carried out in the interests of maintaining international peace and security.[95] Peaceful use of outer space, being the basic principle in international space law, should be upheld.[96] Particular attention should be paid to illegal activities, such as terrorist activities, that might be carried out in the name of commercialization. Furthermore, as provided in the Outer Space Treaty, States should pursue studies and conduct exploration of outer space so as to avoid harmful contamination and also adverse changes in the environment of the Earth.[97] Accordingly, the body should promote a co-operative environment for commercialization, reduce environmental impacts on Earth and protect the terrestrial environment.[98]

---

[88] Article 1 of the Outer Space Treaty.

[89] James S. Trimble, The International Law of Outer Space and Its Effect on Commercial Space Activity, 11 *Pepperdine Law Review*, 521, 530 (1984).

[90] This point was made in the context of geosynchronous orbital slots, but it applies equally to many other outer space resources. See M. J. Flinch, Limited Space: Allocating the Geostationary Orbit, 7 *Nw. J. Int'l L. & Bus.* 798 (1986). It also applies to the deep seabed. See Marietta Benko & Kai-Uwe Schrogl, Article I of the Outer Space Treaty Reconsidered after 30 Years, in Lafferanderie & Crowther, *supra* note 25, at 69.

[91] Robert Rachlin, *Return on Investment Strategies for Decision-Making* 2 (1987).

[92] Lawrence L. Risley, An Examination of the Need to Amend Space Law to Protect the Private Explorer in Outer Space, 26 *W.St. U.L. Rev.* 47 (1998-1999).

[93] Carl Q. Christol, Commercial Uses of Outer Space: Highlights of American Policies, 10 *Annuaire de Droit Maritime et Aerospatial* 348 (1989); Carl Q. Christol, The Common Heritage of Mankind Provision in the 1979 Agreement Governing the Activities of States on the Moon and Other Celestial Bodies, 14 *International Lawyer* 429, 473 (1980). Private entities need attractive return on their research and development investment. See Richard A. Posner, The Material Basis of Jurisprudence, 69 *Ind. L.J.* 10 (1993).

[94] Reynolds, *supra* note 32, at 726.

[95] Article 3 of the Outer Space Treaty.

[96] Fountain, *supra* note 73, 1761-1762.

[97] Article 9 of the Outer Space Treaty.

[98] We should avoid a regime that will ultimately mirror the over-exploitation of resources and environmental havoc we have wreaked on Earth. See further Fountain, *supra* note 73, at 1760.

1.4.2. Formulation of the Space Authority

Several approaches have been suggested as institutional models for an ISA. They range from one similar to the Seabed Authority, to one that is more scientifically and technologically oriented to one that would serve as a subsidiary body under the International Civil Aviation Organization (ICAO).[99] So what style should be adopted? The basic purpose of the proposed body is to have jurisdiction over development and exploitation of outer space resources for the benefit of all humankind.[100] An international authority will result in a more equitable distribution of benefits than will a private enterprise regime, which conversely might create a monopoly over space resources and exclude other public and private entities.[101] It is, thus, advisable that the body be an international governmental authority to which all countries can be members.

The UN is institutionally weak and incapable of enforcing any mandate;[102] while maintaining responsibility in a wide range of activities, it cannot respond effectively to resource development on celestial bodies.[103] Nevertheless, the UN is the body maintaining an important position in procuring the benefits of the international society. Therefore, it is necessary for the proposed body to have a relationship agreement with the UN. Considering similar political, economic and legal backgrounds, formulation of a body similar to the Seabed Authority is an appropriate means to reach a balance among developing and developed countries.

Two organs, the Assembly and the Council, can be established under the proposed ISA.[104] In the Assembly, all the members would be represented. It will formulate policy, elect officers, and approve budgets and rules. The Council elected by the Assembly, would be selected according to a formula ensuring equitable representation of countries from various groups. The Council is the executive body and responsible primarily for the administration of the space activities regime.

As discussed above, a Finance Committee can be established to take the role of financial and budgetary arrangements, including the draft financial rules, regulations, procedures of the organs, the financial aspects of the Authority's work, assessed contributions of the Authority's Members, project application fees and renewal fees, and most importantly, the level of payments (possibly in the form of tax) from exploring entities. The fees collected would be the Authority's primary source of income, covering its administrative costs, budgets for public research and other activities.[105]

Taking the model of the Seabed Authority, a Legal and Technical Commission can be instituted, consisting of persons with appropriate qualifications relating to exploration,

---

[99] Rao, *supra* note 15, 205-206; see also Gennady M. Danilenko, The Progressive Development of Space Law: New Opportunities and Restraints, in Tania Zwaan *et al.* (eds.), *Space Law: Views of the Future* 106-107 (1988); A.S. Piradov, Creating a World Space Organization, 4 *Space Policy* 112 (1988); V. Vereshchetin & E. Kamenetskya, On the Way to a World Space Organization, 12 *Annals Air & Space L.* 337 (1987).

[100] G.A. Res. 1348, 13 U.N. GAOR Supp. (No. 18) at 5, U.N. Doc. A/4090 (1958).

[101] Fred Kosmo, The Commercialization of Space: A Regulatory Scheme that Promotes Commercial Ventures and International Responsibility, 61 *S. Cal. L.Rev.* 1055, 1080-1082 (1988); see also Berkley, *supra* note 11, 437-438.

[102] Berlin & L.I. Tennen, The Role of the United Nations in Colonization of Outer Space, or Chicken Little was Right, *Proceedings of the 19th Colloquium on the Law of Outer Space* 215 (1977).

[103] Moses Moskowitz, *The Roots and Reaches of United Nations Activities and Decisions* 8 (1980).

[104] The Authority could have a secretariat. See Bruce Stockfish, Space Transportation and the Need for New International Legal and Institutional Regime, 17 *Annals Air & Space L.* 359 (1992).

exploitation and processing of resources, environmental protection, and economic or legal matters relating to outer space. This Commission will undertake the task of supervising exploration and commercial activities, assessing the environmental impact of such activities and making recommendations on environmental protection in outer space.[106]

A licensing system should be instituted.[107] An entity planning to exploit outer space resources should submit its proposal to the Authority and the Authority should have the power to decide on granting the request or not. The decision should be made based upon previously-determined criteria. A license could be renewed or revoked. No permanent property rights would be conferred by the license. Only the resources exploited by the licensed entity would come under its exclusive control.[108]

The ISA would operate by contracting with private and public corporations and entities authorized to conduct specific activities and exploitation in outer space. The detailed tasks and duties of the ISA can follow the example of the Seabed Authority, subject to relevant modifications according to the specific situation in outer space.[109]

1.5. Conclusion

Outer Space and its resources have been widely considered as Common Heritage of Mankind. The concept of CHM *per se* has resulted in serious discussions. The ambiguous term is argued to be the obstacle to the commercial use of outer space.[110] In the absence of definite property rules and an enforcement authority, there is likely to be chaos in the commercialization of outer space. Both developing and developed countries recognize the importance of a stable regime fostering the exploration and development of outer space.[111] Some scholars have rightly suggested that it is time for scientists, engineers, lawyers, and management experts to develop a workable set of guidelines for space commercialization.[112]

A pragmatic approach is proposed in the present section. The progress made on the UNCLOS led to an improved understanding of the CHM and suggests that the differences between developing and developed countries can be reconciled. While leaving the theoretical discussion of the term unresolved, formulation of an international body to address the use of outer space resources can begin. Whatever form it takes, the body should be able to address and further the common, equitable interests of the developing countries (the non-space powers), and the interests of developed countries (the space powers).[113] The proposed

---

[105] See for example, The 1998 Intergovernmental Agreement Concerning Cooperation on the Civil International Space Station, Article 15.

[106] See for example, *id.*, Article 14, para. 4-5.

[107] See further ILA Resolution 1/2002: Space Law.

[108] Allen Duane Webber, Extraterrestrial Law on the Final Frontier: A Regime to Govern the Development of Celestial Body Resources, 71 *Geo. L.J.* 1427, 1453-1454 (1983).

[109] See further Section 1 of the Annex.

[110] Kosmo, *supra* note 95, at 1067.

[111] Webber, *supra* note 102, 1432-1433.

[112] Eilene Galloway, Status of the Moon Treaty, *Space News*, August 3-9, 1998, at 21-22; Bin Cheng, The Commercial Development of Space: The Need for New Treaties, 19 *Journal of Space Law* 17, 43 (1991).

[113] Harminderpal Singh Rana, The "Common Heritage of Mankind" & The Final Frontier: A Revaluation of Values Constituting the International Legal Regime for Outer Space Activities, 26 *Rutgers L.J.* 225, 250 (Fall 1994).

governance regime will try to encourage the beneficial aspects of property rights and formulate rules that discourage conflict and predation.[114]

While following the example of Seabed Authority, this section proposes the establishment of International Space Authority. The commercialization of outer space is no longer a fantasy. There is an urgent need to take a practical look at the issue and formulate feasible rules and organs to guard against taking the wrong direction. Humankind has taken the first tentative steps laying the technological foundation for commercial expansion. The challenge lying ahead is to build on the existing technological foundation and create the appropriate legal regime that will support and encourage this expansion.

2. Patent Protection

2.1. Introduction

The outer space, once solely monopolized by the States, is under drastic change. More and more private entities are interested in outer space. The rich natural resources, the abundant commercial opportunities and the potential profits from outer space have been known to the public and private entities are taking practical steps to exploit the benefits. The rapid development of space technology has also offered the possibility of private participation in space activities. The commercialization of outer space is developing into a new stage.[115]

Intellectual property rights are based on a "strict territorial" approach. National rules concerning intellectual property protection do not extend beyond national borders. However, the concept of territorial sovereignty does not exist in rules regarding space activities. As clearly defined in the Outer Space Treaty, outer space is not subject to national appropriation and free use shall be carried out for the benefits and interests of all countries.[116] While it is not easy to reconcile these two different approaches, protecting intellectual property rights arising out of space activities is vital to the sustainable development and commercialization of outer space. It will be devastating to space development were private entities to lose their interests and enthusiasm in space activities.[117]

The importance of the International Space Station (ISS) can never be overestimated. It provides an ideal environment in outer space to carry out important long-term tasks and facilitates scientific experiments which may result in inventions and new products. The ISS provides a starting point for the present discussion on the protection of intellectual property rights, in particular the protection of patents.

The present section examines patent protection in outer space, comparing the international Patent legal framework for space-related activities and proposing a viable regime for the protection of the so-called "space patent". Part 1 provides a general overview

---

[114] Glenn Harlan Reynolds, International Space Law: Into the Twenty-First Century, 25 *Vand. J. Transnat'l L.* 732 (1992).

[115] See Dan K. Burk, Application of US Patent Law to Commercial Activity in Outer Space, 6 *Santa Clara Computer & High Technology Law Journal* 307 (1991).

[116] Outer Space Treaty, Article 2.

[117] Anna Maria Balsano, Intellectual Property within Public International Research Organizations: The Example of the European Space Agency, *The Proceedings of the 36th Colloquium on the Law of Outer Space*, IISL 3 (1993).

of the subject matter and Part 2 provides a detailed analysis of the application of the current concept of patent to inventions from space activities. Part 3 will be devoted to a discussion of the United States (US) and the European Space Agency (ESA) regimes for use, transfer and ownership of patents.

The 1998 Intergovernmental Agreement (IGA)[118] is a good example to show the international efforts of cooperation in intellectual property protection. Part 4 will analyze relevant provisions in the IGA and show that in view of its restricted application to the ISS, it is necessary to develop a special regime for the protection of space patents. Part 5 elaborates on the establishment of a special regime and the improvements to be made in view of the special nature of space patents. This section concludes that space patents are special in many different ways and that a special regime for space patents will be meaningful in many aspects. Potential interested parties can be assured that private entities are encouraged to take part in the process of space commercialization and that the international society is determined to secure the profits from investing in space activities.

Hong Kong is at the moment not an active participant in space activities, except those related to telecommunications services. However, as Special Administrative Region, Hong Kong is at an advantageous position to be involved in future space projects initiated by Mainland China. Hong Kong is determined to be the regional hi-tech center and outer space is no doubt an excellent field for future consideration. For this reason, Hong Kong patent system will be constantly referred to during the discussion and suggestions will be offered to improve the present situation so that Hong Kong can well fit in the present space age.

2.2. Substantial Requirements for Patent Protection

According to the World Intellectual Property Organization Model Law for Developing Countries on Inventions, the term "patent" is defined as an idea of an inventor which permits in practice the solution to a specific problem in the field of technology.[119] Not all inventions are patentable. Three substantial requirements should be satisfied for an invention to enjoy patent protection: novelty, inventive step and industrial application. It is important to see how to apply these three requirements in outer space. The third element of industrial application is easy to satisfy as long as the invention can be made or used in any kind of industry actually or constructively.[120] Such invention need not be perfect or incapable of further improvements to constitute actual industrial application.[121] The requirement is satisfied if the invention is useful and operable by providing a tangible benefit.

We need to look further into the first two elements, which are closely related. It involves a two-step analysis. First, what is considered as "novel" compared with the prior state of art? Secondly, what is the degree of inventiveness to satisfy patentability?

---

[118] Agreement Among the Government of Canada, the Governments of Member States of the European Space Agency, the Government of Japan, the Government of the Russian Federation, and the Government of the United States Concerning Cooperation on the Civil International Space Station, January 29, 1998.

[119] World Intellectual Property Organization, Model Law for Developing Countries on Inventions, available at <http://www.wipo.int/eng/general/ipc/manual/manual1.htm> (last visited May 14, 2006).

[120] Patent Ordinance (Cap. 514), s. 97.

[121] Office of Technology Licensing, University of Florida, Invention and Inventorship to Potential Investors, available at <http://www.rgp.ufl.edu/otl/inventorship.html> (last visited May 10, 2006).

Novelty is determined in reference to existing knowledge of the invention. The Patent Ordinance of Hong Kong adopted the term "state of the art" to determine the degree of novelty: an invention shall be considered to be new if it does not form part of the state of the art.[122] It must not be fully anticipated by a prior patent, publication or other knowledge within the public domain. This ordinance further defines the time factor in determining admissible state of the art: before the deemed date of filing of an application for a standard patent for the invention or, if priority was claimed, before the date of priority; or before the date of filing of an application for a short-term patent for the invention or, if priority was claimed, before the date of priority.[123]

The provisions above are important to patent protection in outer space. Scientific staff normally station in the ISS for some period of time. Before formal application for the Patent protection is submitted, the invention could have been used in the ISS or known by other staff stationed in the ISS. In this situation, it is important to make sure that the present rules will not cause problems in interpreting the term of "novelty". Relevant rules could be formulated to clarify the issue as to whether such application in the ISS or the fact of the invention being widely known by staff stationed in the ISS constitutes an obstruction for future patent applications.

If not, to what extent will the above situation be exempted from normal rules? With no clear rules in place, we may rely on the strict confidentiality rules in the ISS Crew Code of Conduct, which was adopted by the Partners on February 4, 2000.[124] According to this Code, each Cooperating Agency, or the data owner or provider shall give instruction to their astronauts for the marking of data generated onboard the ISS and consequently trigger the application of the protective measures;[125] any disclosure by the crewmembers without prior written approval will be considered as violation of the confidential requirement; the crewmembers are required to mark and protect as long as the confidential requirement remain in place; such requirement may last until after the return phase and when the mission is finished.[126] Based on the above strict rules, we can see that the novelty requirement will not be easily compromised by acts of any disclosure without prior approval.

The Patent Ordinance requires that to qualify for a patent an invention must involve an inventive step.[127] This element decides on whether the invention or product arising out of outer space is sufficiently inventive to be patentable. That is, the invention or product is not obvious to a person skilled in the art or not within the ordinary skills of a competent artisan at the time the invention was made. The requirement of non-obviousness or inventiveness, forming one of the important bases for patent application, is particularly relevant for space

[122] Patent Ordinance (Cap. 514), s. 94 (1).

[123] Patent Ordinance (Cap. 514), s. 94 (2).

[124] The Code of Conduct for the International Space Station Crew was approved on September 15, 2000 in Washington DC by the Multilateral Coordination Board, the highest level coordination body established through the ISS Agreements (the 1998 ISS IGA and the 4 Memorandums of Understanding between NASA and each of the four other ISS Cooperating Space Agencies, *i.e.* the Russian Space Agency, the European Space Agency, the Canadian Space Agency and the Government of Japan acting on behalf of various Japanese government agencies). ESA Council Information Document: The ISS Crew Code of Conduct, ESA/C (2000)14, February 29, 2000. This document contains a set of standards to govern the conduct of ISS crew members.

[125] Andre Farand, Head of new initiatives, ESA legal department, Astronauts' Behavior onboard the International Space Station: Regulatory Framework, available at <http://portal.unesco.org/shs/en/file_download.php/785db0eec4e0cdfc43e1923624154cccFarand.pdf> (last visited May 11, 2006).

[126] The ISS Crew Code of Conduct, Section V.

products (for example, products of pharmaceutical and biotechnical industries) or inventions. Outer space provides a zero-gravity and ultra-vacuum environment not available on Earth. For example, it may produce a level of purity in certain materials not achievable in normal conditions. The purity level may be sufficient to justify the inventiveness requirement in a patent application.

If not, the process of production or invention in the unique environment itself could possibly provide another justification for inventiveness. It has been suggested that the process reactions in outer space are not the same and that the resulting product is patentable.[128] When a novel product is difficult to describe in words, or its structure is insufficiently understood, but the process for producing the novel product is known, a product-by-process claim could be made to protect the process. By emphasizing and patenting the process, protection will automatically extend to the product of such process. However, it is important to note that "even though product-by-process claims are limited by and defined by the process, determination of patentability is based on the product itself" and if "the product in the product-by-process claim is the same as or obvious from a product of the prior art, the claim is unpatentable even though the prior product was made by a different process."[129] A recent decision from the U.S. Court of Appeals for the Federal Circuit (CAFC) again states, "Regardless of how broadly or narrowly one construes a product-by-process claim, it is clear that such claims are always to a product, not a process."[130] The above observation is especially meaningful to the potential product-by-process claim for products arising out of scientific experiments in outer space. By identifying at least one novel feature of the product, relevant parties may submit product-by-process claim upon returning to the Earth and successfully obtain patent protection.

2.3. USE, TRANSFER AND OWNERSHIP OF PATENTS

Once the patent satisfies the requirement, we still need to consider who can be the owner of the patent. Formerly, only States are financially viable for space projects and the ownership of the patent is undisputable. If an invention is made in the framework of any employment contract, such invention should belong to the employer. This is the normal practice around the world. The US has made it more specific to the application of space activities in its 1958 National Aeronautics and Space Act: no matter whether an invention is made in the framework of any work or contract with National Aeronautics and Space Administration (NASA) by an employee or not, such invention shall be the exclusive property of the United States and patented by NASA.[131]

---

[127] Patent Ordinance (Cap. 514), s. 96.

[128] Sa'id Mosteshar (ed.), Research and Invention in Outer Space: Liability and Intellectual Property Rights 193 (Martinus Nijhoff Publishers: Dordrecht, 1995).

[129] The Manual of Patent Examining Procedure of the U.S. Patent and Trademark Office, s. 2113, quoting *In Re Thorpe*, 777 F.2d 695, 698, 227 USPQ 964, 966 (Fed.Cir. 1985).

[130] *SmithKline Beecham Corp. v. Apotex Corp.*, Fed. Cir., No. 04-1522, decided February 24, 2006.

[131] Section 305 (a) 1-2 of the 1958 National Aeronautics and Space Act, P.L. 85-569, as amended.

2.3.1. Present Regimes Concerning Ownership of Patents

With private entities increasingly active in space activities, a proper framework to identify the ownership of a certain patent becomes more and more important. Based on the 1958 regime, a patent is property of the US if any private entities enter into a contract with NASA. This will no doubt discourage private parties from participating in space activities, which is detrimental to the process of commercialization in outer space. While no governments so far have made explicit and specific policies and rules in this aspect, the US has taken the initiative to formulate a structure for the creation, use, transfer and ownership and protection of patent with relation to the ISS as an ISS intellectual property reference guide.[132] While private parties can be encouraged to invest in space activities, such an arrangement will also facilitate and promote the use of Government-developed space technology.[133] Thus, the arrangement is beneficial to both private sectors and the Government.

NASA makes allocation of the ISS resources available to a commercial user through two forms of agreements: Space Act Agreement and Cooperative Research and Development Agreement (CRADA). The two forms are quite similar, but the first form is more flexible, thus, the second form is not routinely used by NASA.[134] The form of Space Act Agreement is especially meaningful for the commercialization of outer space. Previously, under the 1958 National Aeronautics and Space Act (Space Act), NASA may enter into and perform contracts, leases, cooperative agreements, or other transactions as may be necessary to conduct its work;[135] the owner of the inventions arising out of the above contracts or agreements shall be the United States government.[136] The form of Space Act agreement does not fall under any specific category defined in the above Space Act, but is considered as other transactions.[137] Under this categorization, the Space Act Agreement aims to procure property or services for the direct benefit of NASA with little or no involvement of NASA. Accordingly, NASA can tailor the allocation of intellectual property rights according to the nature of the particular agreement and contributions of the parties.[138]

With this new arrangement, NASA can further elaborate on the detailed ways of allocation. Space Act Agreements are further divided into non-reimbursable and reimbursable agreements based on whether NASA received payment for the goods or services it provides. No matter which type of agreement it belongs to, title to inventions will remain with the respective investing parties. In view of the fact that NASA is reimbursed under reimbursable agreements, NASA will grant an exclusive, royalty-free, irrevocable license to the other party.[139] No exchange of patents is required under non-reimbursable agreements, but NASA

---

[132] Intellectual Property and the International Space Station: Creation, Use, Transfer, and Ownership and Protection, prepared by the Office of the General Counsel, National Aeronautics and Space Administration, September 1999, available at <http://www.hq.nasa.gov/ogc/iss/index.html> (last visited April 29, 2006).

[133] Jocelyn H. Shoemaker, The Patent in Space Act: Jedi Mind Trick or Real Protection for American Inventors on the International Space Station, 6 *Journal of Intellectual Property* 395 (1999).

[134] For a brief outline of some of the significant differences between CRADAs and Space Act Agreements, see *id.*

[135] Space Act, section 203 (c) 5.

[136] *Id.* Section 305 (a).

[137] 42 U.S.C. section 2473 (c) (5) and (6).

[138] Part II: Relationship of Intellectual Property Provisions in the ISS Agreements to NASA's Agreement Authority and Policies, in Intellectual Property and the International Space Station: Creation, Use, Transfer, Ownership and Protection, available at <http://www.hq.nasa.gov/ogc/iss/main.html> (last visited May 3, 2006).

[139] Space Act Agreement, Annex I sample clause 1.2.e.e. II-III.

may consider granting to the participant an exclusive or partially exclusive commercial license.[140]

European Space Agency (ESA), as one of the most important international organizations on space activities, does not have specific regulations on the above issue. Relevant rules and guidelines can only be found in the General Provisions on Intellectual Property Right: the General Clauses and Conditions for ESA Contracts (General Provision)[141] and the Resolution on the Rules concerning Information, Data and Intellectual Property (ESA Resolution) adopted by the ESA Council on December 19th, 2001[142]. Both documents adopt similar position as defined by NASA despite the elaboration being much simpler. Under the General Provision, "the contractor shall be the owner of any invention made in the course of or resulting from the work undertaken for the purpose of the contract and shall be entitled to protect such invention by patent or other form of industrial property right in accordance with the applicable laws."[143] Similarly, the ESA Resolution takes it as the general principle that the ownership of information, data and intellectual property developed under a contract with ESA will remain with the contract whoever has developed them.[144]

2.3.2. Joint Invention

Joint invention is another issue we cannot ignore, especially considering the special environment of the activities. For joint inventions on earth, there is so far no clear answer to the application of rights and obligations. Usually, in agreements related to joint invention on earth, the resolution of the issue depends on the definition of joint invention and any provisios relating to invention where the owner is only one of the cooperating parties.[145]

Scientific experiments in outer space normally require the involvement and collaboration of the inventive endeavors of two or more parties. Many other members can also be involved in the process; for example, for experiments in the ISS, the crew or astronauts could be assigned to perform some experiments. Thus, the first issue arises as to who can be defined as an inventor. Inventors should be those making contribution to the inventive idea and to the final result.[146] Normally, crew members or astronauts merely follow instructions in performing experiments and thus, cannot be considered as inventor(s). But it is of course possible that a crew member or astronaut conceives of a patentable invention while working on the experiment. In this situation, inventorship can be confirmed based on the above standard of contribution to the inventive idea and the final result. This situation is, however, quite rare; no crew member or astronaut has become an inventor so far.[147]

---

[140] Space Act Agreement, Annex I sample clause 1.2.d.d.

[141] ESA/C/290, rev. 5.

[142] ESA/C/CLV?Res.4 (Final).

[143] General Provision, Clause 37.

[144] ESA Resolution, Chapter II: Rules concerning Information, Data and Intellectual Property, section I.

[145] O. Vorobieva, Intellectual Property Rights with Respect to Inventions Created in Space, in Sa'id Mosteshar (ed.), *Research and Invention in Outer Space: Liability and Intellectual Property Rights* 181-187 (Martinus Nijhoff Publishers: Dordrecht, 1995).

[146] Office of Technology Licensing, University of Florida, Invention and Inventorship to Potential Investors, available at <http://www.rgp.ufl.edu/otl/inventorship.html> (last visited May 10, 2006).

[147] Marguerite B. Broadwell, ISS Commercial Development Manager, National Aeronautics and Space Administration, Intellectual Property and the Economic Development of the International Space Station, Presentation on the Space Technology and Applications International Forum (STAIF-2000), Albuquerque, NM, February 2000. Broadwell further elaborated on the means to minimize or even eliminate the possibility of any crew member or astronaut becoming an inventor: fully scripting the experiment or packaging the experiment as a self-contained unit.

The second issue relates to the rights of each co-inventor. In the US, each co-inventor named on a patent application owns that patent. In the absence of any agreement, each co-inventor owns 100 per cent of the patent, regardless of the share of contribution of each inventor.[148] NASA offers general principles on joint inventions arising out of Space Act Agreements: NASA and the other party will identify and report the invention to each other and cooperate in obtaining patent protection; the two sides will consult with possible support and advice from the US Government, and agree on the title of ownership, protection and license conditions.[149] While we cannot find the term "joint invention" in the ESA document, we do find the general principles concerning partnership activities in the ESA Resolution: the partnership agreements are negotiated on an *ad hoc* basis.[150] Thus, the issue of joint invention will be resolved through mutual negotiations; if there is no possibility of negotiation or negotiation fails, then, the existing general patent practice shall be followed.

2.3.3. Patent Regime in Hong Kong

Outer Space Ordinance (Cap. 523) is the only law in Hong Kong which specifically deals with outer space activities. However, this Ordinance is a mere restatement of existing principles of public space law; it does not touch on protection of intellectual property rights, for which we must turn to the Patent Ordinance. It provides detailed rules on patent protection in all circumstances. As discussed above, the substantial requirements for patent protection in Hong Kong follow the international practice.

Normally, the right to a patent shall belong to the inventor or his successor in title.[151] However, in the situation of employment, the right to a patent is determined in accordance with the law of the country, territory or area in which the employee is wholly or mainly employed or where the employer has his place of business to which the employee is attached.[152]

Under the section of "right to employees' inventions" of the Hong Kong Patent Ordinance, if a person is employed to carry out scientific experiments in outer space, an invention made by the employee is, as between him and his employer, taken to belong to his employer if it is made in the course of the normal duties of the employee or in the course of duties falling outside his normal duties, but specifically assigned to him, and the circumstances in either case were such that an invention might reasonably be expected to result from the carrying out of his duties; or if the invention was made in the course of the duties of the employee and, at the time of making the invention, because of the nature of his duties and the particular responsibilities arising out from the nature of his duties he had a special obligation to further the interests of the employer's undertaking.[153]

Concerning joint invention, Patent Ordinance obviously adopts party autonomy in the first place: where a patent is granted to 2 or more persons each of them is, subject to any agreement to the contrary, entitled to an equal undivided share in the patent.[154] Thus, when more than two parties are involved in the invention, each party is entitled to take any action in

---

[148] Stephaniel Paul, Joint Ownership of Patents: A to Z, available at <http://wwe.legalzoom.com/articles/article_content/article14005.html> (last visited May 3, 2006).

[149] Space Act Agreement 3.5.10.2.

[150] ESA Resolution, Chapter II: Rules Concerning Information, Data and Intellectual Property, section 4.

[151] Patent Ordinance (Cap 514), s. 100 (1).

[152] *Id.*, s. 100 (2).

[153] *Id.*, s. 57 (1).

[154] *Id.*, s. 54 (1).

respect of the invention concerned, for his own benefit and without the consent of or the need to account to the other or others.[155] The Patent Ordinance makes further rules in other situations. But basically, the co-owners are able to reach an agreement to deal with their rights towards to the invention. Only when there is no such agreement will the parties follow the rules. The rules in the Patent Ordinance basically mirror the general international practice and rules on joint inventions.

2.4. The IGA Provision Concerning Intellectual Property

The IGA is an international treaty establishing "a long term international co-operative framework on the basis of genuine partnership, for the detailed design, development, operation, and utilization of a permanently inhabited civil Space Station for peaceful purposes, in accordance with international law."[156] This document, providing the basic legal structure, covers almost every aspect in the operation procedure of the ISS in general. Intellectual property is one of the most important aspects to be defined in the document in this sense. One of the main objectives is to avoid the infringement of intellectual property rights owned by another partner and their entities. Article 21 of the IGA specifically deals with intellectual property protection. Concerning the term "intellectual property", this IGA adopts a general definition by reference to the broad framework set up by the World Intellectual Property Organization (WIPO)[157].

As discussed above, scientists and relevant staff involved in the scientific experiments with the location in the ISS can define their rights and obligations through contractual agreements with relevant parties. But The IGA touches on other important aspects. First of all, it clearly provides a territorial approach based on the ownership/registry of elements for the issue of jurisdiction: an invention taking place in or on a Space Station flight element shall be deemed to have occurred in the territory of the Partner State of that element's registry.[158] Therefore, if the invention was performed in the Japanese laboratory, the patent must be filed initially in Japan.[159] Such a conclusion results from the application of the principles of jurisdiction and control of the state of registry over the individual flight element.[160] This provision is similar to the flag-law principle in high sea. It is also in line with the principles in the Outer Space Treaty that a State, whose registry of an object was launched and carried into outer space, shall retain a jurisdiction and control over space object.[161]

---

[155] *Id.*, s. 54 (2).

[156] IGA 1998, Article 1.

[157] Convention Establishing the World Intellectual Property Association, July 14, 1967, Art. 2, para. Viii, 21 U.S.T. 1770, 828 U.N.T.S. 3. According to this Convention, intellectual property rights relate to literary, artistic and scientific works; performances of performing artists, phonograms and broadcasts; inventions in all fields of human endeavor; scientific discoveries; industrial designs; trademarks, service marks, and commercial names and designations; protection against unfair competition; and all other rights resulting from intellectual activity in the industrial, scientific, literary or artistic fields.

[158] IGA 1998, Article 21 (2).

[159] Broadwell, *supra* note 141.

[160] Leo B. Malagar & Marlo Apalisok Magdoza-Malagar, International law of Outer Space and the Protection of Intellectual Property Rights, 17 Boston University International Law Journal 363-364 (Fall 1999).

[161] Outer Space Treaty, Article 8.

However, the above assumption does not impact the ownership of the invention, nor does it preclude the right to file a patent application in multiple States.[162] The IGA further provides that, "in respect of an invention made in or on any Space Station flight element by a person who is not its national or resident, a Partner State shall not apply its laws concerning secrecy of inventions so as to prevent the filing of a patent application in any other Partner State that provides for the protection of the secrecy of patent applications contacting information that is classified or other protected for national security purposes."[163] Accordingly, the territorial provision in the IGA simply supports the place where the invention takes place.

The territorial approach in the IGA is especially meaningful in dealing with the issue of utilizing a patent in outer space, but it does not clearly speak out under which law patent utilization or infringement activities are governed. Under normal situation, once the utilization of a patent occurs in a US space element, then it will be treated in the same way as any other such activities within the US territory. That means, any patent utilization or infringement activities will be solely governed by the national law of the Partner State of that space element's registry. This understanding is also in line with the normal national rules on intellectual property protection whose application extends to anywhere within its jurisdiction. However, it can be argued that the activities will be governed by the law of the State which grants the patent. This argument can be deduced from relevant provisions in the IGA. According to Article 21 (4), if the infringement occurs in or on an ESA-registered element, it is not possible to recover in more than one European Partner State for the same infringement of the same intellectual property; in the event multiple actions are brought for the infringement of the same right in different European Partner States, a court may grant a temporary stay of proceeding in order to wait for the outcome of an earlier-filed action. Furthermore, satisfaction for recovery of damages in one of the above actions shall prevent further recovery in any pending or future action based on the same act of infringement.[164]

2.5. A Special Space Patent Regime

With States drastically relaxing their monopoly over space exploration and activities, private entities are increasingly interested in space investment and research.[165] However, they have been hesitant in view of the current ambiguous property rights regime created by several concepts in outer space, in particular the term of common heritage of mankind (CHM). Space lawyers have started the work on property rights in outer space, aiming to create incentives

---

162 International Space Station Legal Framework, available at <http://www.esa.int/esaHS/ESAH700VMOC_iss_0.html> (last visited on March 29, 2006).

163 IGA 1998, Article 21 (3).

164 IGA 1998, Article 21 (4) provides, "where a person or entity owns intellectual property which is protected in more than one European Partner State, that person or entity may not recover in more than one such State for the same act of infringement of the same rights in such intellectual property which occurs in or on an ESA-registered element. Where the same act of infringement in or on an ESA-registered element gives rise to actions by different intellectual property owners by virtue of more than one European Partner State's deeming the activity to have occurred in its territory, a court may grant a temporary stay of proceeding in a later-filed action pending the outcome of an earlier-filed action. Where more than one action is brought, satisfaction of a judgment rendered for damages in any of the actions shall bar further recovery of damages in any pending or future action for infringement based upon the same act of infringement."

165 Dan L. Burk, Protection of Trade Secrets in Outer Space Activity: A Study in Federal Pre-emption, 23 *Seton Hall Law Review* 563 (1993).

for private entities to invest in outer space. The same situation applies to intellectual property protection in outer space.

As discussed above, the three requirements of patentability need to be further elaborated to accommodate the special outer space environment. While the IGA provides guidelines for intellectual property protection at international level, national laws have a final say in detailed application process. Patent protection in the outer space environment is not well coordinated against the international background. Conflicts can arise when two patents from two nations cover essentially the same invention out of scientific experiments in outer space. Considering the exorbitant expenses involved in space activities, the lacking of a coordinated patent regime specially designed for the environment of outer space will in the end let many potential interested private entities down and drive them away from this field. Accordingly, it is important to consider creating a special international legal regime for patents arising out of space activities.[166]

There are currently two important treaties that deal with patent application: the Paris Convention and the Patent Cooperation Treaty. Now the question is whether we should have a separate treaty to define the new type of patent. The author takes the view that it is not necessary to add to the patent field a new treaty. All patents are the same in essence. As discussed above, the difference lies in the evaluation stage: how to apply the existing requirements. The purpose of creating a regime for this type of patents basically serves to facilitate the patent application process and easy reference, while keeping in mind the fact that outer space is a special environment to carry out scientific experiments. Accordingly, the present coordination work needs to focus on the procedural aspects. The author proposes to set up a new category named 'space patent' under the framework of the Patent Cooperation Treaty. A special patent office (say, Space Patent Office) could be established for the purpose of the space patent application.[167]

2.5.1. Space Patents

The first question is what kind of invention can be registered as 'space patent'. Or we may say what subject matter will be dealt with by the 'space patent office'. No doubt, space patent office shall deal with patents related to space activities. Five categories of inventions have been identified to be related to space activities: (a) inventions made on earth for space applications; (b) inventions made on earth for terrestrial applications as a result of space activities (including telecommunications); (c) inventions made in outer space for terrestrial applications; (d) inventions made in outer space for spatial applications; (e) inventions patented on earth for spatial applications used in outer space.[168] One scholar has been able to re-categorize space patents into two: space-activity inventions resulting from job done on earth (including categories (a), (b) and (e)); space-related inventions made in outer space

---

[166] Similar views have been expressed by Chukeat Noichim, The Protection of Intellectual Property Rights in Outer Space of the EU and Thailand, available at <http://www.thailawforum.com/articles/ipspacenoichim.html> (last visited May 15, 2006).

[167] Similar suggestion has been made by Bryan E. Erickson & Gary C. Fisher, Mars Society Steering Committee, Mars Foundation, Treasurer & Design Team, Space Patents: Intellectual Property in Outer Space, presentation at the 8th Mars Society Convention, August 12, 2005, available at <http://www.marshome.org/files2/SPACE-PATENTS-MS2005.ppt> (last visited May 11, 2006).

[168] European Space Agency, Intellectual Property Rights and Space Activities in Europe, ESA Publication Division: the Netherlands, 4-5 (1997).

(including categories (c) and (d)).[169] The author would single out category (e) for discussion due to its special legal status as mentioned below.

2.5.2. Space Patent Cooperation

Space-activity inventions resulting from work done on earth do not distinguish much from other inventions on earth. The only difference is the original purpose of the activities. Thus, the existing patent regime does not need significant changes for those inventions, but we do need to note that considerations on public policy and national security will play an important role in the application process due to its sensitivity toward national interests. The problems exist with the other two types of space patents, which will be discussed below.

2.5.2.1. Extension of Patent Protection in Outer Space

As mentioned above, intellectual property law is territorial in nature. No protection will be provided outside national boundaries, and of course not to the non-sovereignty area of outer space. Then, the problem arises as to whether inventions patented on earth enjoy protection when applied in outer space (referring to categories (c), (d) and (e)). The IGA resolved the issue in a restricted sense: for purposes of intellectual property law, national jurisdiction shall extend to a specific part or a flight component of the ISS itself.

However, outer space is much broader; so how about the protection of intellectual property in other parts of outer space? Little national legislation has touched on this point. International agreements on patent protection (namely, the Paris Convention, [170] the Patent Cooperation Treaty[171] and the WTO Agreement on the Trade-related Intellectual Property Rights (TRIPs)) have also been very ambiguous, lacking ostensible wording on the issue. The only possibility for patent protection in outer space is to extract some words or provisions in the international agreements and give them a broad explanation. For example, we may interpret the term "vessel" in the Paris Convention[172] to include a space object or rely on the simple statement in the TRIPs that patents shall be available and patent rights enjoyable without discrimination as to the place of invention[173]. But all these efforts are marginal and do not form a strong legal basis for patent protection in outer space.

The actual legal vacuum and uncertainty of the legal status on patent protection in outer space is a major concern for potential private entities. It is vital to clarify the issue by noting that relevant national laws will be extended to outer space and that inventions patented on earth will be protected while using in outer space. While the States can make explicit national rules on the issue of extension, it would be more efficient and effective to make such rules in an international agreement like the present one (the IGA).

A further unresolved question concerns the applicable law. By referring to the Outer Space Treaty, jurisdiction and control over a specific space object lies on the State of registry.[174] The act of registration has accordingly resolved the issue of jurisdiction. With regard to patent protection in outer space, we can similarly rely on the connecting factor of

[169] R. Oosterlinck, Intellectual Property and Space Activities, *The Proceedings of the 26th Colloquium on the Law of Outer Space*, IISL, October 10-15, 1983.

[170] Paris Convention for the Protection of Industrial Property, March 20, 1883, as last revised at Stockholm on July 14, 1967, 21 U.S.T. 1583, 828 U.N.T.S. 305.

[171] Done at June 19, 1970, 28 U.S.T. 7813, T.I.A.S. No. 8733.

[172] Paris Convention, Article 5 ter.

[173] TRIPs, Article 27.

[174] Outer Space Treaty, Article 8.

the State patenting the invention. The national law of the State which has patented an invention will continue to apply to the use or infringement of the patent in outer space.

2.5.2.2. Cooperation on Priority of Claims

Following the same model in the Patent Cooperation Treaty, a centralized 'international application' procedure will be set up for the granting of various space patents at the national or regional level. A declaration may be attached in the application claiming the priority of one or more earlier applications filed in or for any State. This will be done through a single operation which calls for the designation of targeted States. As discussed above, a space patent office will be established to examine applications and issue space patents. An 'international search' system will also be created to facilitate the application examination process. The rules in the existing Patent Cooperation Treaty on the priority of claims will continue to apply.[175] However, we need to reconsider the issue of the priority period concerning space patents in categories (c) and (d).

Two main patent systems exist currently: first-to-invent and first-to-file.[176] Under the two systems, the awarding of patent will be based on the two different factors: the activity of developing an invention and the act of filing an application. During the WTO Uruguay Round negotiations, TRIPs was reached, trying to unify the intellectual property regime, particularly with respect to patents. One of the most significant achievements was the adoption of the "first to file" system.[177] That means, whoever submits documents earlier will be patented and this must be done before anyone else has access to the information before the filing date.[178] The act of filing becomes a vital point. However, as mentioned above, scientific staff will normally station in the ISS for several months. The act of filing will start only after their return to the earth and showing of the product or invention. The priority period of six months may not be sufficient for the purpose of protection in this situation. It is thus necessary to consider a longer priority period for space patent in categories (c) and (d).

2.5. Conclusion

Space commercialization and privatization is an irreversible trend. Private entities are increasingly interested in space activities in view of the potential profits. With the initiation of private space exploration over the coming years, wide-ranging issues need to be addressed in a legal and regulatory framework. The legal vacuum in relation to those space activities needs to be filled up.

The present legal regime for outer space does not provide clear guidelines on property rights. The situation is also true for the protection of intellectual property rights. It has become clear that inventions will arise out of space experiments and that patent protection is especially vital in space activities. From the first sight, the territorial nature of Patent law and the non-territorial nature of space law are difficult to reconcile. However, we should note that

---

175 Patent Cooperation Treaty, Article 8.

176 Alejandro Piera, Intellectual Property in Space Activities: An Analysis of the United States Patent Regime, 29 *Air & Space Law*, No. 1, 50-51 (February 2004).

177 Patent Perspectives, available at <http://www.ladas.com/patents/patpers.html> (last visited on April 29, 2006).

178 Margaret A. Boulware, Jeffrey A. Pyle & Frank C. Turner, An Overview of Intellectual Property Rights Abroad, 16 *Houston Journal of International Law* 12 (1994).

intellectual property has attracted a significant amount of interest on an international scale and international conventions have been adopted ensuring minimum rights and providing certain measures for enforcement of those rights by the Contracting Members.[179] Intellectual property protection is increasingly going beyond national border and requires cooperation from various States. Accordingly, barriers between these two areas of law are not insurmountable.

This present section has analyzed the application of the existing patent conception to space activities and necessary accommodations need to be made for protection of space patents. The NASA and the ESA, as the two main bodies regulating space activities, have taken the efforts to regulate the use, transfer and ownership of intellectual property rights. These experiences are useful to Hong Kong. As mentioned above, Hong Kong does not have special legislation on the issue; while Hong Kong is endeavoring to be the hi-tech hub, outer space will be one important area for Hong Kong to set foot on in the near future. This is especially true in view of the rapid development of space technology in mainland China. Thus, Hong Kong has the realistic basis to get involved in space projects, not only in technological area, but also in legal field.

National legislation is one way to realize patent protection, however, space activities requires more on international cooperation. A complete and internationalized patent protection regime for outer space activities is helpful to boost private investment in the technologies that will provide us with ever greater capabilities to explore and settle outer space. The author proposes to set up a special regime for space patent protection within the current regime created by the Patent Cooperation Treaty. Further conceptual clarification is made to the extended application of patent protection on earth to outer space. Such an international framework will in the end promote the development of space activities and respond primarily to the need of intellectual property protection by the States and private entities.

[179] A.M. Balsano, ESA Legal Affairs, Paris, Intellectual Property Rights and Space Activities, available at <http://esapub.esrin.esa.it/ecsl/ecsl15/ecsl15ba.htm> (last visited May 11, 2006).

Chapter 3

DEVELOPMENT OF SPACE REGISTRATION AND LIABILITY REGIME

1. APPLICATION OF REGISTRATION CONVENTION

1.1. Introduction

One important step in the work of the Legal Sub-Committee of the Committee on the Peaceful Use of Outer Space (COPUOS) was successfully finalized in 1975. The UN General Assembly adopted the Convention on Registration of Objects Launched into Outer Space (Registration Convention),[180] which contains detailed rules on the registration of space objects launched into outer space.[181] The establishment of the registration requirement basically serves two functions as identified by Professor Diederiks-Verschoor: "(1) a well-ordered, complete and informative register would minimize the likelihood and even the suspicion of weapons of mass destruction being furtively put into orbit; (2) it is not possible to identify a spacecraft that has caused damage without an international system of registration."[182]

The Registration Convention, consisting of 12 Articles, supplements Article VIII of the Treaty on Principles Governing the Activities of States in the Exploration and Use of Outer Space, Including the Moon and Other Celestial Bodies (the Outer Space Treaty).[183] The Convention provides administrative arrangements for States to register all objects, either launched from their territory, or whose launch they have procured and report the existence of this registry and contents to the Secretary General of the United Nations.[184] The Registry was established to create a central depository of all objects launched into space to facilitate the enforcement of other space treaties.[185] Accordingly, as an important international document,

---

[180] Opened for signature on 14 January 1975, 28 U.S.T. 695, 1023 U.N.T.S. 15 (entered into force 15 September 1975).

[181] See Preamble of the Registration Convention.

[182] I.H.Ph. Diederiks-Verschoor, *An Introduction to Space Law*, 47 (Kluwer, 2nd ed., 1999).

[183] Outer Space Treaty, Trb. 1967, No. 31, Annex to GA Res. 2222(XXI) of 19 December 1966. Article VIII provides that a State on whose registry an object launched into outer space is carried shall retain jurisdiction and control over such object and over any personnel thereof, while in outer space or on a celestial body.

[184] Registration Convention, Article II and III.

[185] See Preamble of the Registration Convention.

the Convention is not merely an attempt to resolve questions of public international law, rather it is an international effort to produce an international codification of administrative legal doctrine.

Since the Convention has existed for more than 30 years without many problems, its applicability is assured. According to Article X of the Convention, the question of the review of the Convention is included in the provisional agenda of the United National General Assembly in order to consider the necessity of revision.[186] In 1986, ten years after the implementation of the Convention, the Assembly decided that there was no such need.[187]

Nevertheless, with more and more space activities taking place on a daily basis, along with the trend of commercialization, severe challenges have been set on the continuing application of the Convention. Particular concerns arise because of the privatization of space activities. It is now time to carry out a serious review of the Convention taking into account the development of space activities. Furthermore, as identified by some scholars, the Convention entails several drawbacks.[188] As stated in Article X of the Convention, at the request of one third of the States Parties to the Convention and with the concurrence of the majority of the States Parties, a conference of the States Parties shall be convened to review the Convention at any time after the Convention has been in force for five years.[189]

This section will take on this challenging task and identify several areas for possible revision. Part 2 discusses the application of three terms in the Registration Convention and possible improvements in defining the three terms. Part 3 assesses the regulatory regime created by the Registration Convention and makes recommendations for reform. Part 4 concludes that revision is necessitated by new developments in commercial space activities and changing attitudes among the space practitioners.

1.2. Clarification of Certain Conceptions

Similar to the Convention on International Liability for Damage Caused by Space Objects (Liability Convention)[190], the Registration Convention starts by defining several important terms: "launching State", "space object" and "State of registry". Clearly, these terms require explanations that are more thorough and thus are areas of the Convention that are now regarded as unsatisfactory.

---

[186] Registration Convention, Article X provides, "Ten years after the entry into force of this Convention, the question of the review of the Convention shall be included in the provisional agenda of the United Nations General Assembly in order to consider, in the light of past application of the Convention, whether it requires revision. However, at any time after the Convention has been in force for five years, at the request of one third of the States Parties to the Convention and with the concurrence of the majority of the States Parties, a conference of the States Parties shall be convened to review this Convention. Such review shall take into account in particular any relevant technological developments, including those relating to the identification of space objects."

[187] Michel Bourely, Is it Necessary to Re-Negotiate the Convention on Registration?, *Proceedings 30th Colloquium on the Law of Outer Space* 231 (Bangalore, 1988).

[188] See for example, Nandasiri Jasentuliyana (ed.), *Maintaining Outer Space for Peaceful Uses*, Proceedings of a Symposium held at the Hague, 111-120 (March 1984); Armel Kerrest, *Commercial Use of Space: Remarks on Some Legal Issues,* Proceedings of 2004 Space Law Conference, Beijing, 205 (April 2004); Diederiks-Verschoor, *supra* note 3, 47-50 ; Peter van Fenema, The Registration Convention, *Proceedings of the United Nations Workshop on Capacity Building in Space Law* 33 (2002).

[189] Registration Convention, Article X.

[190] March 29, 1972, 24 U.S.T. 2389, 961 U.N.T.S. 187.

1.2.1. Launching State

The definition of "launching State" is a difficult issue. A launching state, as defined in the Registration Convention, includes four categories: (a) a state that launches a space object; (b) a state that procures the launch of a space object; (c) a state from whose territory a space object is launched; (d) a state from whose facility a space object is launched.[191] According to many scholars, it is one of the major impediments to the development of commercial space activities.[192] An appropriate definition of "launching State" is vital to the determination of State liability for national activities under the Outer Space Treaty and the Liability Convention.[193]

Problems arising out of the definition may include a proper understanding of a procuring State; the application of Article VIII of the Space Treaty; the determination of a launching State in case of transfer of ownership and the relationship between a private entity and a State. The current definition is criticized for failing to answer the new issues arising out of commercialization and privatization of space activities. While commercialization is an inevitable trend in outer space, we must urgently clarify the concept of "launching State".

One working group of the Legal Subcommittee of the UNCOPUOS presented its deliberations in 2002, offering the first result of intergovernmental discussions on this issue.[194] The working group, with the mandate of dealing with the wide topic of the status and application of the five United Nations Treaties on Outer Space, continued its work on the review of the launching State issue in light of the most recent experiences, State practice and doctrine on the basis of the general understanding that the existing space treaties do not require amendment.[195]

1.2.1.1. Transfer of Ownership (Non-Launching State)

The practice of transferring the ownership of satellites is not particularly significant. References can be made to the transferring of AsiaSat 1 from the United Kingdom register to the Chinese register during the sovereignty transfer of Hong Kong to China.[196] In this case, there should be no problem since China, as the place for the original launching, is a launching State.[197]

However, problems will arise when a satellite is sold to a State that is not an original launching State, as defined by the Registration Convention. The new State, while not a

---

[191] Article I of the Registration Convention provides that the term "launching State" means (i) a State which launches or procures the launching of a space object; (ii) a State from whose territory or facility a space object is launched.

[192] See for example, Karl-Heinz Bockstiegel, The Term "Launching State" in International Space law, *Proceedings 36th Colloquium on the Law of Outer Space* 80-83 (Israel, 1994).

[193] *Ibid.*

[194] For the recent UNCOPUOS work on the concept of "launching State", see Kai-Uwe Schrogl & C. Davies, A New Look at the "Launching State": The Results of the UNCOPUOS Legal Subcommittee Working Group "Review of the Concept of the 'Launching State" 2000-2002, *Proceedings 44th Colloquium on the Law of Outer Space* 286-301 (Huston, 2002).

[195] See *United Nations Treaties on Outer Space: Actions at the National Level*, United Nations/Republic of Korea Workshop on Space Law, 137-139 (March 2004).

[196] Another recent example was the acquisition of Optus by SingTel in 2001. See Mark Westfield, SingTel was Sold on an Optus Pup, *The Australian,* (2002), <http://www.sfdonline.org/Link%20Pages/Link%20Folders/02Pf/aus220102.html>, (last visited 19 November 2004). Other examples include the purchase of satellites by NewSkies Satellites, a Dutch company and the registration of the privatized Inmarsat Limited, now a British company, see U.N.Doc. A/AC.105/806 (22 August 2003) and U.N.Doc. ST/SG/Ser.E/417 (25 September 2002).

launching State, will not bear any liability according to the Liability Convention, which states that only launching States will bear liability. This is obviously unfair. In general, the space object is under the new State's jurisdiction and control, but this new State will not bear any liability under the Liability Convention for damages caused by the space object simply because it is not an original launching State. Those original launching States are liable for damages that they cannot foresee and prevent. It is possible that relevant States will conclude bilateral/multilateral agreements requiring "the new State" to indemnify the original launching State(s) for any damages caused after the transfer. However, when referring to the Liability Convention, fault liability for damages caused in outer space is based on the fault of the launching States collectively; a State sustaining damage may seek compensation from any original launching States.[198]

The above agreements, while offering indirect solution, make the issue complicated; the new State needs to locate each and every original State, negotiate and reach agreements.[199] Such a solution increases the plurality of control that will be detrimental to the efficacy of the Convention. To resolve this problem, the meaning of "launching State" could be extended so that it does not refer exclusively to an original launching State. Without prejudice to the right of a State sustaining damage, "launching State", for the purpose of registration, may further refer to the State having "jurisdiction and control". This extensive explanation actually reflects the US proposal to the UNCOPUOS in that: the US register every space object according to the nationality of the company; and the US only register space objects of American companies.[200] Further determination of other possible launching States can be identified in the term "State of registry", which will be discussed later.

1.2.1.2. Involvement of Private Entities

Private entities, including international organizations and multinational corporations, are becoming increasingly involved in the launching activities. As far as an international organization is concerned, this will be easy since the organization represents all the States concerned. Such organizations can declare their acceptance of the rights and obligations provided in the Convention. If no declaration is made, constituent documents may need to be checked to try to find out their legal personality in certain circumstances.

In fact, even if the organization has the capacity to act as a virtual State of registry, it will never have the capacity to exercise true jurisdiction, since that is a typical and very fundamental prerogative of a sovereign State.[201] Accordingly, under the circumstance described above, legal ownership of the organizations does not automatically lead to "jurisdiction and control". It is the individual member States, not the organizations *per se*, that exercise jurisdiction and control over the space objects.

When other private parties are involved, the situation becomes more complicated. States are not necessarily aware of the detailed operations. Thus, is it still reasonable to subject a

---

197 UN Doc. ST/SG/SER.E/333 of 3 April 1988; UN Doc. ST/SG/SER.E/334 of 3 April 1998.

198 Liability Convention, Article V.

199 The satellite builder, the launch service provider and the satellite operator in a typical "delivery in orbit" arrangement may each come from different countries. See Review of the Concept of the "Launching State"-Report of the Secretariat, UN Doc. A/AC. 105/768 of 21 January 2002, para. 48.

200 Armel Kerrest, Commercial Use of Space, including Launching, *Proceedings of Space Law Conference 2004: Asia: a Regional Force in Space*, 205-206 (2004).

201 Frans G. von der Dunk, The Illogical Link: Launching, Liability and Leasing, *Proceedings 35th Colloquium on the Law of Outer Space* 351 (Graz, 1993).

State, instead of the private entity directly involved in the operation, to possible liability? In a private launching activity, where States cannot control the operations, is it still appropriate to restrict liability only to States?

It seems that retaining the existing system, which provided that launching States should be responsible for all space objects, commercial or government, launched into space, is reasonable.[202] They are liable because of the national registration system for the private entities. A corporation needs to be registered in a State, which will examine the legality of the entity and issue approval for its future operations. The activities of corporations are subject to the State's supervision. As far as the issue of flags of convenience is concerned, the State, by relaxing the registration and supervision of the corporations, should take the risk of possible liability.

Therefore, to prevent unnecessary liability, the State should strengthen its registration system and issue an appropriate permit. As provided by some national legislation, States should always maintain a register of space objects, no matter if they are launched or procured by the Government or private entities.[203] One potential approach as recommended by the working group of the UNCOPUOS is to implement national laws to authorize and provide continuing supervision of the activities of their nationals in outer space.[204] Accordingly, States should act in good faith[205] when passing national laws on the issues of authorization, supervision and licensing of private enterprises to operate launch services and to ensure the availability of a just compensation to avoid international obligations becoming a dead letter.[206] The same should also apply to non-governmental organizations so that the State of registration of the organization should also be the State that is responsible.

1.2.1.3. Understanding of "Procurement"

Quite a lot of discussions have taken place on the issue of "a State procuring the launching". It is obvious from the wording of the Convention that a distinction was made between the "act of launch" and the "procurement of a launch". It is also evident from this term that a procuring State is acting on behalf of outside entities that actively initiate the launch of a space object. It has been suggested that a State has to be somehow actively involved by requesting, or at least promoting the launching of a particular space object in order to consider it as having "procured" the launching.[207] The sole action of providing a space object *per se* will not satisfy "procurement"; the procurement requires active and substantial participation in launching activities.[208] Accordingly, in an increasingly interrelated

---

202 D.L. Willson, An Army View of Neutrality in Space: Legal Options for Space Negation, 50 *Air Force Law Review* 191 (2001).

203 See for example, Hong Kong Outer Space Ordinance (Cap. 523), Section 9 provides that the Chief Executive shall maintain a register of space objects.

204 Conclusion of the Working Group on agenda item 9, entitled "Review of the concept of the 'launching State'" as contained in the Report of the Legal Subcommittee on its Forty-first session, held in Vienna from 2 to 12 April 2002, UN Doc. A/AC. 105/787 of 19 April 2002, Annex IV, Appendix, section 10.

205 National legal regime should offer detailed rules implementing the obligations provided in relevant international treaties.

206 Maureen Williams, Perceptions on the Definition of a "Launching State" and Space Debris Risks, *Proceedings 44th Colloquium on the Law of Outer Space* 285 (Houston, 2002).

207 Karl-Heinz Bockstiegel, The Terms 'Appropriate State' and 'Launching State' in the Space Treaties—Indicators of State Responsibility and Liability for State and Private Space Activities, *Proceedings 34th Colloquium on the Law of Outer Space* 15 (1992).

208 Edward Frankle & Jason Steptoe, Legal Considerations Affecting Commercial Space Launches from International Territory, *Proceedings of the Workshop on "Legal Framework for Commercial Launch and*

scientific and technological society, where a finished product is often the result of many components manufactured globally, there is a substantial need to know what is to be identified as a procurement and the circumstances upon which legal liability may be assessed.[209]

Considering the sheer number of States which might be involved in the launching, from the production of space objects to the final registration, it has been further suggested that an "active and substantial participation" in the launch be present in order for a State to be considered as one of the launching States.[210] Doubtlessly, the term "procurement" should entail the elements identified by the statement above for "launching State": a procuring State is itself a launching State. Accordingly, "procurement" also requires actual control over the launch or the payload in orbit.[211]

1.2.1.4. Application of Article VIII of Space Treaty

By acknowledging the difficulty in defining the "launching State", it has been suggested that non-launching States can make use of Article VIII of the Outer Space Treaty.[212] This suggestion, while trying to accommodate the needs of bringing non-launching States to the liability regime, is in contradiction with the general legal practice.

Article VIII of Space Treaty provides, "A State Party to the Treaty on whose registry an object launched into outer space is carried shall retain jurisdiction and control over such object, and over any personnel thereof, while in outer space or on a celestial body." It has been widely recognized that Registration Convention is a further elaboration of Article VIII of the Space Treaty and the purpose of the Registration Convention is to clarify and consolidate this Article.[213] In this way, the Registration Convention is a specific regulation, and the Space Treaty (considered as constitution for outer space) is general law. According to the principle of jurisprudence, once there is conflict between general law and specific law, specific law prevails. Only when the subject matter is outside the scope of specific law, will the general law be considered.[214]

The emergence of non-launching States results from the practice of transferring the ownership of space objects, which did not exist during the drafting of the Registration Convention. The Convention specifically identified the scope of launching States, but has now obviously fallen behind the present practice. The task for the time being is to make

Associated Activities", Bremen, January 2000 (Project 2001), at 67; Peter Nesgos, International and Domestic Law Applicable to Commercial Launch Vehicle Transportation, *Proceedings 27th Colloquium on the Law of Outer Space* 102 (1984).

209 Carl Q. Christol, Nuclear Power Sources (NPS) for Space Objects: A New Challenge for International Law, *Proceedings 35th Colloquium on the Law of Outer Space* 250 (1993).

210 Armel Kerrest, Remarks on the Notion of Launching State, *Proceedings 41st Colloquium on the Law of Outer Space* 310 (1999).

211 William B. Wirin, Practical Implications of Launching State—Appropriate State Definition, *Proceedings 37th Colloquium on the Law of Outer Space* 113 (1994).

212 Ricky J. Lee, Commentary Paper on Discussion Paper Titled "Commercial Use of Space, Including Launching", *Proceedings of Space Law Conference 2004: Asia: a Regional Force in Space*, 230-231 (2004).

213 Fred Kosmo, The Commercialization of Space: A Regulatory Scheme that Promotes Commercial Ventures and International Responsibility, 61 *Southern California Law Review* 1069 (May 1988).

214 See further *Amoco Int'l Fin. Corp. v. Iran*, 15 Iran-US Claims Tribunal Rep. 189, para. 112 (1987): "As a *lex specialis* in the relations between the two countries, the Treaty supersedes the *lex generalis*, namely customary international law....However, ...the rules of customary law may be useful in order to fill in possible lacunae of the law of the Treaty, to ascertain the meaning of undefined terms in its text or, more generally, to aid interpretation and implementation of its provisions."

modifications to the present Convention, without returning to the Space Treaty, which consists only of principles for further clarification. It is easy for the Space Treaty, with general principles to act as panacea; however, this will forestall the development of space law. Loopholes always exist in laws no matter how well they have been elaborated. The point is to improve the existing rules to enhance the effectiveness of this mechanism.

1.2.2. Space Object

It has been pointed out that the definition of "space object" is neither clear nor satisfactory.[215] For instance, do the space objects entailed in the Convention include those launched in outer space? There is no consensus on whether a spacecraft or satellite constructed or launched in outer space falls within the definition of "space object".[216] It is evident that the location of the launching activities does not change the nature of the space object. Territorial connection only has relevance when defining launching States from whose territory space objects are launched. This can happen in the high seas, the Antarctic, as well as in outer space where no State can claim sovereignty. The identification of such objects can be more difficult than those launched from a territory, but registration can be a solution.

Further, the Convention provides that States must notify the UN Secretary General of objects that are no longer in space;[217] however, the status of space debris is not identified.[218] Will the original launching States continue to be liable for damages caused by space debris from the original space object? If this space debris can be identified, then the issue is easily resolved. Once a space object ceases operation, the original launching States should take some measures to prevent future damage.[219] In case damage does occur, these States should continue to be liable. Furthermore, the original launching States should have more knowledge and the necessary technology to alleviate the damage. Conceivably ongoing liability should make the original States more cautious while initiating an original launch.

However, what happens when the space object cannot be identified? Of course, it is difficult to determine the claims and measure the damage.[220] It appears that the drafters of the Convention failed to foresee this situation, believing that registry of objects will facilitate claims by identifying the origins of space objects.[221] It is important to address this problem and possibly provide in the Convention some guidelines for claims when the object causing

[215] Diederiks-Verschoor, *supra* note 3, at 47; Stephen Gorove, Definitional Issues Pertaining to "Space Object", *Proceedings 37th Colloquium on the Law of Outer Space* 88 (1994); Bin Cheng, "Space Objects", "Astronauts" and Related Expressions, *Proceedings 34th Colloquium on the Law of Outer Space* 17 (1991).

[216] Vladimir Kopal, Some Remarks on Issues Relating to Legal Definitions of "Space Object", "Space Debris" and "Astronaut", in *American Institute of Aeronautics and Astronautics*, Inc. 1 (1994); Karl-Heinz Bockstiegel, The Terms "Appropriate State" and "Launching State" in the Space Treaties: Indications of State Responsibility and Liability for State and Private Space Activities, *Proceedings 35th Colloquium on the Law of Outer Space* 15 (1992).

[217] Article IV (3) of the Registration Convention provides that each State of registry shall notify the Secretary-General of the United Nations....of space objects concerning ...which have been but no longer are in Earth orbit. See further Glenn H. Reynolds & R.P. Merges, *Outer Space: Problems of Law and Policy* 195 (1989).

[218] C.D. Williams, Space: The Cluttered Frontier, 60 *Journal of Air Law & Commerce* 1148 (1995).

[219] The UNCOPUOS is the primary inter-governmental organization dedicated to resolving issues involving space debris. A number of programs have been proposed to remove existing space debris. For example, inactive payloads may be deorbited with the help of a space tether. See further R.C. Bird, Procedural Challenges to Environmental Regulation of Space Debris, 40 *American Business Law Journal* 644 (Spring 2003).

[220] P.T. Limperis, Orbital Debris and the Space-faring Nations: International Law Methods for Prevention and Reduction of Debris, and Liability Regimes for Damage Caused by Debris, 15 *Arizona Journal of International and Comparative Law* 338 (Winter 1998).

[221] Williams, *supra* note 39, at 1163.

the damages cannot be identified.[222] This issue will be elaborated later along with the information needed as part of the registration.

Another issue is what if a space object consists of component parts individually registered by different States? How do we identify the object as a whole? There are no obligatory guidelines available yet. The resolution of the problem relies on cooperation among the States. The launching States should agree beforehand the State of registry that registers the complete structure as a new space object in accordance with the Convention.[223] One good example is the construction of the International Space Station (ISS): each Partner registers the ISS elements it provides as space objects and retains jurisdiction and control over the elements it registers. This arrangement allows each Partner to treat the elements carried on its registry as an extension of its territory for jurisdictional purposes and ensures that its national laws can apply to elements and personnel it provides.[224] This arrangement shall be further discussed in the following part on cooperation among launching States.

1.2.3. State of Registry

This term can only be found in the Registration Convention. No other space treaties have made use of this term. For example, in the Liability Convention, the launching State(s), not the State of registry, is liable for damage. Many scholars have concluded that State of registry is the launching State or one of the launching States.[225] Therefore is the sole purpose of using the term "State of registry" simply to require that one State must register the space object? From the absence of the term in other treaties, we might conclude that the term does not help in regulating the status of space objects or the consequences of operating them. For this purpose, it is thus not necessary to identify nationality with the relevant registration, although in practice it happens that the State of registry automatically confers its nationality on a space object.[226]

Nevertheless, this understanding can cause some problems. Does it mean then that the State of registry is the one which has full control and jurisdiction over the space object? This might be true when the practice of selling space objects is uncommon. The launching States may agree upon the State of registry, which can exercise its jurisdiction and control over the object. Accordingly, an agreement will settle the issue of registry. However, the transfer of ownership of space objects to a State not being a "launching State" has become a reality, which means that a transfer of the power of control will take place. This brings about the ridiculous situation where the buyer, while not a launching State, is neither allowed to be the State of registry, nor takes on any liability under the Liability Convention.

While it is possible that launching States may claim compensation from the buyer after making reparations to a third party, surely it would be better to extend the State of registry to

---

[222] L.R. Roberts, Orbital Debris: Another Pollution Problem for the International Legal Community, 11 *Florida Journal of International Law* 622 (1997).

[223] A. Gorbiel, Large Space Structures: The Need for a Special Treaty Regulation, *Proceedings 26th Colloquium on the Law of Outer Space* 247-250 (Lausanne, 1984).

[224] Andre Farand, Legal Environment for Exploitation of the International Space Station, Presentation to the International Symposium at Strasbourg, France (26-28 May 1999), in G. Haskell & M. Rycroft (eds.), *International Space Station: The Next Market Place* 141 (2000).

[225] See for example, Bin Cheng, Space Objects and their Various Connecting Factors, in G.L. Lafferranderie & D. Crowther (eds.), *Outlook on Space Law over the Next 30 Years* 205 (1997); William B. Wirin, Practical Implications of Launching State—Appropriate State Definitions, *Proceedings 37th Colloquium on the Law of Outer Space* 109-113 (1994); Schrogl & Davies, *supra* note 15, 286-301.

[226] Cheng, ibi*d,* at 205.

a State with full jurisdiction and control. This will bring the Convention in line with the new development. In the case of a non-original launching State, one solution that could be suggested is that the "State of registry" further refers to a State maintaining its jurisdiction and control over the said space object. Several elements can assist in determining "jurisdiction and control": direct commercial benefits from operation of the space object, the transfer agreement and the restriction of re-transfer.

1.3. Ambiguities in the Existing Registration System

The Convention provides the first step in formalizing the registration system. Proposals for revision were submitted as early as 1984, but no measures have actually been taken. It is necessary to reiterate some identified shortcomings and offer further comments on the existing registration system.

1.3.1. Provision of Information

Article IV provides the requirements for registration identifying five items.[227] This provision is challenged by the use of nuclear power sources (NPS). The risks inherent in using NPS caused a debate amongst States. A Resolution was adopted concerning the safe use of NPS (the NPS Principles) in 1992 - the Principles Relevant to the Use of Nuclear Power in Outer Space. This Resolution provides that any State launching a space object with NPS on board should in a timely fashion inform States concerned in case of malfunctioning of the space object with a risk of re-entry of radioactive materials to the Earth. Furthermore, the updated information should also be transmitted to the Secretary-General of the UN.[228] As understood from a UNCOPUOS document, [229] the Registration Convention does not obligate any State to furnish information on the presence of NPS on board space objects, although such information could be voluntarily given.[230] Accordingly, one might think that the NPS Principles bring additional rules to the Registration Convention, which, being of only recommendatory character, may not be considered to amend the legally binding treaty.[231]

It is thus necessary to consider whether the information concerning the use of NPS should be provided during the registration, as this question also applies to the information concerning the presence of arms systems on board space objects and the purpose and functioning of space objects. For example, the Convention provides that the "general function" of the space object needs to be disclosed. However, the term "general function" is subject to various interpretations, allowing for the protection of the identity of military satellites, which perform an entirely legitimate function under the law.[232] Furthermore, while giving answers as to what

---

[227] The five items are name of launching State or States; an appropriate designator of the space object or its registration number; date and territory or location of launch; basic orbital parameters, including nodal period, inclination, apogee, perigee; and general function of the space object.

[228] Principles Relevant to the Use of Nuclear Power Sources in Outer Space, Principle 5.

[229] See U.N.Doc. A/AC.105/430, 26 April 1989, at 17.

[230] See for example, JoAnn C. Clayton, Nuclear Power Sources for Outer Space: Political, Technical and Legal Considerations, *Proceedings 31st Colloquium on the Law of Outer Space* 287 (1989).

[231] M. Hoskova, The Notification Principle in the 1992 NPS Resolution, *Proceedings 35th Colloquium on the Law of Outer Space* 308-309 (Graz, 1993).

[232] For example, protection of the "national technical means" (including space reconnaissance capabilities) under the Anti-Ballistic Missile (ABM) Treaty between the US and Russia is indispensable for an effective verification structure. For the ABM Treaty to survive in its present form, the two parties must protect the

objects are in outer space, the Convention fails to provide information on where the space objects can be found.[233]

As identified earlier, the main problem emanating from the requirements of provision of information lies in the unwillingness of States to disclose relevant information concerning its military purposes. Since no better way has been found so far, we should give it the benefit of the doubt. Nevertheless, the provision in the Convention should further reiterate the principle of peaceful use of outer space and be used as a safety valve in case of serious violations. Some might argue that the inclusion of additional requirements is not practicable in reality, but this inclusion can serve as a potential preventive force that can constantly remind the potential launching States of the obligation to peaceful means.

Another matter raised is the timing of the information. The term "as soon as practically possible" is used in the Convention.[234] This is a rather subjective criterion - launching States may and do interpret the term as weeks or months following the launch. Scholars have rightly criticized the ambiguity of the term.[235] A proposal has been put forward to impose a limit of two hours within which a report of a launch of a NPS would have to be made to the UN Secretary-General and a limit of 24 hours for reporting other satellite launches.[236] This proposal might be too strict and therefore, flexibility should be allowed for legitimate reasons. Some other proposals have been less restrictive, requiring the change of the term to "the UN Secretary-General shall be informed promptly".[237] Thus, it is necessary to take into account all those proposals and set an appropriate schedule for determining the timing of the information.

1.3.2. Enforcement Mechanism

Becoming a party means that the State needs to comply with the rules of the Convention, otherwise some measures might be imposed in case of violation.[238] It is without doubt that the Convention, as an important international treaty, obliges member States to fulfill the commitments contained in the document. This is the same with the Registration Convention as well as with all other space law Conventions.

However, the fact remains that space law treaties are generally weak in enforcement mechanisms. The present space treaties were drafted during the cold-war period when the two superpowers were the two main actors in space activities. The political tension had a direct impact on the law-making process, which became more difficult when it came to the issue of enforcement. At the time, in view of the urgent need of written documents guiding space activities, the States were rather glad to have finalized the space treaties in their present form.[239]

---

secrecy of their space reconnaissance assets. See further R.A. Ramey, Armed Conflict on the Frontier: The Law of War in Space, 48 *Air Force Law Review* 93 (2000).

[233] R. Moenter, The International Space Station: Legal Framework and Current Status, 64 *Journal of Air Law and Commerce* 1044 (Fall 1999).

[234] Article IV (1) provides, "Each State of registry shall furnish to the Secretary-General of the United Nations, as soon as practicable, the following information…."

[235] Jasentuliyana, *supra* note 9, 117-120.

[236] Edward R. Finch, Jr., Heavenly Junk II: Recent Developments in Space Debris, 8 *Air & Space law* 9 (1994).

[237] Jasentuliyana, *supra* note 9, 111-120.

[238] In international law, measures include reparation, compensation, reprisal, retortion.

[239] Lafferranderie, *supra* note 46, xvii.

This weak enforcement mechanism differs from the current treaties relating to the protection of intellectual property rights. Thanks to the WTO Agreement on Trade-Related Aspects of Intellectual Property Rights (TRIPs), strong enforcement and dispute settlement mechanisms are in place, which provide strong support to the enforcement of intellectual property rights.[240] One may even consider space treaties as "quasi-soft law". The term "quasi-soft law" differs from "soft law" in that the latter cannot be considered as "full-fledged" rules of international law. The space law treaties are indeed rules of international law. While not soft-law in the real sense, the lack of an enforcement mechanism can depreciate the value and effectiveness of the Conventions. "Grey areas" exist in their enforcement and compulsory nature, just as in "soft law" where there exists a considerable "grey area" between the white space of law and the black territory of non-law.[241] Accordingly, the performance of the obligations in the space law treaties rests based on good faith or voluntary compliance.

Consequently, some provisions might be added to describe in detail how enforcement should be handled, including the rules for provisional measures, injunctions, damages and other penalties. An appropriate body, perhaps UNCOPUOS or the UN Secretary-General, should have the right, under certain conditions, to order the obligatory registration of certain objects and certain information (for example, in launching a space object with NPS on board).

1.3.3. Customary Law

It is very important to see whether the provisions in the Convention constitute customary law. This is relevant to the question of the application of the Convention to non-State parties, since to date there are only around 50 State parties to the Convention. It is noted that early in 1961 the UN General Assembly had requested launching States to furnish information promptly to UNCOPUOS for the purpose of registration. However, only after the enactment of the Registration Convention in 1975, did the registration and provision of relevant information become a legal obligation.

To be regarded as customary law, two elements should be satisfied: practice and acceptance of such practice as law. While it is no longer true that customary law may be established only after decades of uniform practice by States, international law still requires that the passage of some time. The notion of "instant customary law" has been rejected in the 1986 *Nicaragua* case by the reasoning that "the mere fact States declare their recognition of certain rules is not sufficient for the Court to consider these as being part of customary international law…Bound as it is by Article 38 of the Statute…the Court must satisfy itself that the existence of the rule in the *opinio juris* of States is confirmed by practice."[242] Furthermore, such practice is accepted as law by the relevant States.

This point has also been well elaborated in another International Court of Justice (ICJ) case. In *North Sea Continental Shelf* case, the Court stated, "with respect to the other elements usually regarded as necessary before a conventional rule can be considered to have become a general rule of international law, it might be that, even without the passage of any considerable period of time, a very widespread and representative participation in the

---

[240] A.H. Qureshi, *International Economic Law* 284-286 (Sweet & Maxwell, 1999).

[241] For discussion of soft law, see further G.J.H. van Hoof, *Rethinking the Sources of International Law*, 187-188 (1983).

[242] Military and Paramilitary Activities (*Nicaragua v. US*), 1986 I.C.J. Report 4, 97.

convention might suffice of itself, provided it concluded that of States whose interests were specially affected."[243]

It is doubtful that the provisions in the Registration Convention constitute customary law. Far fewer States are parties to the Convention, compared with the Outer Space Treaty, which has around 100 parties. More importantly, even among the signatories, some are unwilling to furnish information which is deemed sensitive, and some might provide information at a time totally at their own discretion. Often States delay registering or do not register completely. Accordingly, the practice has been rather divergent concerning registration.

This is contrary to the implication of customary law. As Lauterpacht comments,

> "...assuming here that we are confronted with the creation of new international law by custom, what matters is not so much the number of States participating in its creation and the length of the period within which that change takes place, as the relative importance, in any particular sphere, of States inaugurating the change."[244]

To the extent customary law exists for space law at all, it binds all States whether their consent be express or implied by silence in the face of emerging legal norms.[245] Consensus has developed that customary law applicable to space activities includes essential principles of the Outer Space Treaty which have been accepted by all States active in outer space by practice and with *opinio juris* after ratification, and where no evidence of dissenting practice on the part of non-ratifying States is available.[246] Unfortunately, this is not the case for the practice identified by the Registration Convention.

1.3.4. Cooperation among Launching States

Cooperation among launching States during the launching stage is vital to a successful launch. As provided in the Convention, in case of joint launching, agreement between the signatories is required as to which of them is to be deemed the "State of registry".[247] Such cooperation should certainly continue at a later stage. As provided in the Convention, the launching States will jointly determine the State of registry and will be jointly and severally liable for any damage caused. Thus, coordination among the States is crucial in sorting out these issues. The cooperation among the States involved in the International Space Station (ISS) Project is a very good example of this.

The Intergovernmental Agreement (IGA) was reached in 1988. It was later substituted in 1998 to take account of the participation of Russia.[248] The IGA offers a long-term international cooperative framework for detailed design, development, operation, and

---

[243] North Sea Continental Shelf Cases (*Germany v. Denmark; Germany v. the Netherlands*), 1969 I.C.J. Report 4, 42.

[244] H. Lauterpacht, Sovereignty Over Submarine Areas, *British Yearbook of International Law* 376, 394 (1950).

[245] This is a reiteration of the Article 38 of the Statute of the International Court of Justice with regard to International custom. See further Peter Malanczuk, *Akehurst's Modern Introduction to International Law*, 44 (Routledge, 7th edition, 1997).

[246] Peter Malanczuk, Space Law as a Branch of International Law, 1994 *Netherlands Yearbook of International Law* 147 (1995). The principles include the freedom of exploration and use of outer space by all States, and the prohibition on national appropriation of outer space.

[247] Registration Convention, Article VI. This point has been well elaborated by Judge Lachs. See further Manfred Lachs, *The Law of Outer Space, An Experience in Contemporary Law Making* 70 (Sijthoff Leiden 1972).

[248] History of the ISS Project (1999), <http://iss.sfo.jaxa.jp/iss/history/index_e.html>, (last visited 31 March 2005).

utilization of a permanently manned civil Space Station for peaceful purpose.[249] Article 5 of the IGA deals with the issue of registration, jurisdiction and control.[250] The agreement also establishes a distinct liability regime among the States, which should resolve future disputes. Accordingly, it might be advisable that all launching States reach an agreement before carrying out launching activities setting down detailed arrangements for registration and liability.

It has been reported that the US, China and most other major nations with satellites in space have failed to register all of them.[251] Legally speaking, interests arising out of registered space objects, under protection through the act of registration, can have priority over any other interests from unregistered objects.[252] As far as the identification of possible liabilities is concerned, there will still be difficulties with unregistered objects. This is why an agreement will be important for the future of unregistered objects. By referring to the agreement, the unregistered object can be identified and liabilities arising out of the object can be coordinated among the launching States, even though no one is the State of registry. Furthermore, agreements on the national insurance and safety requirements can effectively resolve the issues of compensation at a later stage.

1.4. Conclusion

The Registration Convention is an important development in the history of space law. It mandates that each party register and maintain a registry of its launched space objects. In addition to keeping a registry, a State must provide to the UN Secretary-General information proving the establishment of a registry.[253] The enactment of the Convention has helped clarify troubling issues concerning the identification of space objects and has contributed to the application and development of international law governing peaceful use of outer space.

However, as widely advocated by space lawyers, more mandatory and extensive requirements are needed to improve the Convention.[254] Substantial academic debates have covered various issues, including the application of several terms and specification of registration requirements. New developments in space activities and changing attitudes

[249] Agreement among the government of Canada, governments of Member States of the European Space Agency, the government of Japan, the government of the Russian Federation, and the government of the United States of America concerning Cooperation on the Civil International Space Station, 29 January 1998, in K.F. Nagel, Das neue Regierun sab kommenuber die Internationale Raum Station, 47 *Zeit Schrift fur Luft-und Weltraumrecht (ZLW)* 149-163 (1998).

[250] This provision provides that: (1). In accordance with Article II of the Registration Convention, each Partner shall register as space objects the flight elements listed in the Annex which it provides, the European Partner having delegated this responsibility to ESA, acting in its name and on its behalf. (2). Pursuant to Article VII of the Outer Space Treaty and Article II of the Registration Convention, each Partner shall retain jurisdiction and control over the elements it registers in accordance with paragraph 1 above and personnel in or on the Space Station who are its nationals. The exercise of such jurisdiction and control shall be subject to any relevant provisions of this Agreement, the MOUs, and implementing arrangements, including procedural mechanisms established therein.

[251] Large Nations Fail to Register Satellites, 17 August 2001, <http://archives.cnn.com/2001/TECH/space/08/17/space.satellites.reut>, (last visited 27 October 2004).

[252] See further Paul B. Larsen & Jurgen A. Heilbock, UNIDROIT Project on Security Interests: How the Project Affects Space Objects, 64 *Journal of Air Law and Commerce* 727 (Summer 1999).

[253] Registration Convention, Art. II and IV.

[254] See for example, Diederiks-Verschoor, *supra* note 3, 48-49.

among the space practitioners necessitate revision.[255] It is on this forever-shifting carpet that the ongoing research must dance for the Convention is more than necessary right now. The Registration Convention, concretizing Article VIII of the Outer Space Treaty, has obviously lagged behind with the rapid development of space commercialization and privatization, which was wholly unimaginable 30 years ago.

Formal discussion has been initiated in the UN forum concerning the application of space treaties.[256] A working group of the UNCOPUOS chaired by Schrogl conducted its deliberations on the concept of "launching State" from 2000 to 2002.[257] On 10 December 2004, the UN General Assembly adopted a resolution concerning the application of the concept of "launching State". One of the recommendations was that States consider enacting and implementing national laws authorizing and providing for supervision of non-governmental space activities under their jurisdiction.[258] Hopefully, the above discussion of loopholes and possible areas for improvement will lay the foundation for future work taken by UNCOPUOS.

2. Development of Space Liability Regime

2.1. Introduction

The international liability regime governing space activities came into being with the enactment of the Convention on International Liability for Damages Caused by Space Objects (Liability Convention).[259] This regime is a clear example of the interaction of international policy, international relations and economy. As humans become more active in space, disputes will arise and claims concerning damage caused in outer space will need to be settled. The Liability Convention undertakes the task of defining liability in case of damage caused by space objects. It took almost 10 years to complete the Convention given the great complexity of the issue.

The Convention contains 28 articles and supplements the provisions of the 1967 Outer Space Treaty. The Convention is broad in scope, trying to include all types of possible damage that might occur in outer space in one document. It provides for the possibility of collisions and malfunctioning and their consequences, including the identification of certain kinds of harm for which damages might be recovered.

As an important international legal document, the Convention is not solely an attempt to resolve principles of public international law; rather it is an international effort to produce an international codification of private law doctrines.[260] Although the drafters of the Convention attempted to establish internationally accepted principles of liability, it does little more than

---

255 See Lubos Perek, The 1976 Registration Convention, 47 *ZLW* 351-360 (1998).

256 See for example, Ken Hodgkins, International Cooperation in the Peaceful Uses of Outer Space, Remarks on Agenda 75 in the Fourth Committee of the United Nations General Assembly, (2002), <http://www.state.gov/g/oes/rls/rm/2002/14362.htm>, (last visitied 5 April 2005).

257 Schrogl, *supra* note 15, at 286.

258 General Assembly Adopts Resolution on the Concept of the "Launching State", *Space Law Update*, UNCOPUOS, Vol. 2, Issue 1 (March 2005).

259 Opened for signature on March 29, 1972, 24 U.S.T. 2389, 961 U.N.T.S. 187.

260 G. Zhukov & Y. Kolosov, *International Space Law* 101 (1984).

set forth goals for a space law adjudicator.[261] This result is understandable considering the diverse political interests held by the US, the former Soviet Union, India and the European nations during the negotiations.

Scholars have commented on the Convention in depth concerning its application in space operations. Though admittedly the Convention has some drawbacks, it did help define liability in case of damages. The more than 30 years of its peaceful existence clearly demonstrates its applicability. Nevertheless, with more and more space activities taking place on a daily basis, along with the trend towards commercialization, the Convention faces severe challenges to its continued application. Particular concerns have been raised with the ongoing construction of the International Space Station (ISS) and launch activities. While founding documents of these activities can provide specific exceptions to the Convention, this will largely compromise its integrity. It is indeed time to carry out a serious review of the Convention and make revisions to take account of the development of space activities.

This section will present the changes and developments in space activities which lay a solid basis for accommodating the demand for a serious review of the Convention and its possible revision. Several areas for possible revision will be further identified. A short conclusion shall be made concerning the application of the revised Convention.

2.2. New Developments in Space Activities

Since the first man-made space object entered outer space on October 4, 1957, the exploration of outer space has been on the immediate agenda of human beings. This can be evidenced by the large budget allocated annually by space-faring States. Setting foot on the Moon, the wide use of satellites, etc. have been among the most significant developments in space activities. The rapid development of technology, together with ample resources in outer space, provides as a strong incentive for more challenging space activities. Space activities are becoming more complicated than at the time when the Liability Convention was drafted.

2.2.1. Commercialization and Privatization of Space Activities

Space activities require sufficient financial support. Until the 1980s only States could afford the required budget. Meanwhile, the benefits from space activities could not be instantly realized. In contrast, private entities with difficulties in financing relevant space programs, had little interest in a business with no instant or short-term profits. Nevertheless, technological development changed the whole situation.

The rapid development of space technology has to a large extent shortened the interval between space operations and the realization of profits. Moreover, private entities have also developed in structural terms. Various multinational corporations, large corporations and non-governmental organizations have come into being with solid financial capability and potential. While the exploration and use of outer space is carried out in the common interest of all mankind, [262] the ambiguity in the wording concerning property rights in relevant

[261] M.S. Firestone, Problems in the Resolution of Disputes Concerning Damage Caused in Outer Space, 59 *Tulane Law Review* 764 (January 1985).

[262] Article 1, the 1967 Outer Space Treaty.

treaties[263] does not prevent the involvement of private entities: they firmly believe that space activities will bring profits to them in the end.

More and more private entities are getting involved in space activities. The need to privatize, commercialize, and promote space activities by private entities has been addressed by scholars.[264] Nevertheless, their participation causes a problem for the Liability Convention: is it still appropriate, under the current system, for the State to be directly liable for private space activities? According to Article VI of the Liability Convention, only a launching State that qualifies the requirement of the Convention shall be responsible for damage. Private entities are not a qualified subject of the Convention. This was reasonable during the drafting of the Convention when few private entities were involved. However, this is not the case now.

One significant example is the active engagement of private entities in launch activities. This successful business brings companies substantial profits. But if damage occurs during or after launch, the launching entities are not held liable, rather it is the launching State, as defined in Article I of the Convention. Under such a legal framework, a State should be held responsible for the activities of private entities registered in its territory that procures a launch in a different State, irrespective of the host State's knowledge or involvement in the launch.[265] With more and more private entities getting involved in space activities, it is neither feasible, nor fair, for relevant States to be responsible in all cases.

Furthermore, the Convention does not take into account of individual liability of private satellite operators when the space object has been transferred, whether by sale, lease, or secured financing, to private operators in countries that are not launching states.[266] It is totally unfair to still hold the original state liable in such cases.

Consequently, a regime whereby private entities accept liability in certain situations should be developed as commercialization and privatization move forward.[267] It is necessary for private entities which participate in and benefit from commercial space activities to accept international liability, at least for damage to third parties resulting from their private launching activities.[268]

Another problem with the Convention can be the apportionment of liability.[269] The Convention specifies three types of States as "launching State". In case of international co-operation, more than one State can be liable, including the State where the private entities are

---

263 See generally K.M. Zullo, The Need to Clarify the Status of Property Rights in International Space Law, 90 *Georgetown Law Journal* 2413-2444 (July, 2002).

264 See H.A. Wassenbergh, A Launch and A Space Transportation Law, Separate from Outer Space Law?, 21 *Air & Space Law* 28 (1996); K.H. Bockstiegel, *Commercial Use of Space Stations—The Legal Framework of Transatlantic Cooperation* 217-222 (1986).

265 R.J. Lee, Reconciling International Space Law with the Commercial Realities of the Twenty-First Century, 4 *Singapore Journal of International & Comparative Law* 230-231 (2000).

266 P.B. Larsen, Future Protocol on Security Interests in Space Assets, 67 *Journal of Air Law & Commerce* 1091-1092 (Fall, 2002).

267 R. Moenter, The International Space Station: Legal Framework and Current Status, 64 *Journal of Air Law & Commerce* 1051-1052 (Fall, 1999).

268 H.A. Wassenbergh, The Law of Commercial Space Activities, in G. Lafferanderie & D. Crowther (eds,), *Outlook on Space Law over the next 30 Years* 179-182 (1997); H.A. Wassenbergh, International Space Law: A Turn of the Tide, 22 *Air & Space Law* 334 (1997).

269 L.L. Manzione, Multinational Investment in the Space Station: An Outer Space Model for International Cooperation?, 18 *American University International Law Review* 519-520 (2002).

established. One scholar has even made a list of 15 possible States that may be responsible.[270] Another situation involves satellite launches from floating platforms on the High Seas, rather than the territory of any specific State. One example quoted was the launch on March 27, 1999 by the Consortium Sea Launch, using a platform located on the Equator in order to make the launch cost-effective and competitive.[271] In this situation, liability apportionment will pose a difficult problem.[272] No appropriate resolution can be expected from the present Convention. It is thus necessary to add clauses on this issue in the Convention. We might refer liability apportionment to different levels of States concerned, thus avoiding the evasion of liability.

2.2.2. The International Space Station (ISS) and Cross-Exemption of Liability

The ISS is considered the largest international scientific cooperative program in the history of space exploration. Sixteen States are involved in the Program. After lengthy negotiations the program partners were able to reach the Intergovernmental Agreement (IGA) in 1988. However, with the involvement of Russia in 1990s, renegotiations concerning the IGA 1988's terms gave rise to the IGA 1998.

To encourage cooperation and participation in the exploration, exploitation, and use of outer space, the IGA established a broad cross-waiver of liability by the Partner States and related entities involved. The scope of Article XVI is broad enough to cover all protected space operations, which include all activities or actions related to the Space Station operation, unless caused by willful misconduct, and claims made by natural persons for injury or death, claims between a Partner State and its own related entity or entities and intellectual property claims.[273]

To prevent uncertainty, Article XVI clarifies that the cross-waiver of liability also applies to the Liability Convention, provided that the damage is directly related to protected space operations.[274] In contrast to the Liability Convention, the IGA defines the term "damage"[275] and separates the definition of the launch vehicle into two parts--the "vehicle" and its "payload".[276] The cross-waiver of liability is not applicable to claims made by a natural person, the state, survivors or subrogees for bodily injury, other impairment of health, or death unless the claim has been subrogated to the Partner State.[277]

---

[270] I. Awford, Legal Liability Arriving from Commercial Activities in Outer Space, in S. Mosteshar (ed.), *Research and Invention in Outer Space, Liability and Property Rights*, 95-110 (1995); K.H. Bockstiegel, The Term "Appropriate State" in International Space Law, in *Proceedings 37th Colloquium on the Law of Outer Space* 77-79 (Jerusalem, 1994); K.H. Bockstiegel, Launching State in International Space Law, *Proceedings 37th Colloquium on the Law of Outer Space* 80-83 (Jerusalem, 1994); B. Cheng, Article VI of the 1967 Space Treaty Revisited: "International Responsibility", "National Activity" and "The Appropriate State", 26 *Journal of Space Law* 7-32 (1998).

[271] See further I.H.Ph. Diederiks-Verschoor, *An Introduction to Space Law* 38-39 (Kluwer, 2nd ed., 1999).

[272] A. Kerrest, Launching Spacecraft form the Sea and Outer Space Treaty: the Sea Launch Project, 23 *Air and Space Law* 16-21 (1998).

[273] See further IGA, Article XVI.

[274] C.M. Petras, "Space Force Alpha": Military Use of the International Space Station and the Concept of "Peaceful Purposes", 53 *Air Force Law Review* 165-166 (2002).

[275] According to IGA, Article XVI, para. 2 (c), damage refers to bodily injury to, or other impairment of health of, or death of, any person; damage to, loss of, or loss of use of any property; loss of revenue or profits; or other direct, indirect or consequential damage.

[276] IGA Article XVI, para. 2 (d) defines the term "launch vehicle" as an object (any part thereof) intended for launch, launched from Earth, or returning to Earth which carries payloads or persons, or both; the term "payload" means all property to be flown or used on or in a launch vehicle or the Space Station.

[277] See IGA 1998, Article XVI, para. 2 (a).

In case other nations besides the Partner States are offered the opportunity to send astronauts to and conduct experiments on the Space Station, the exemption of liability will also apply to these nations.[278]

The IGA further provides that the Partners shall consult promptly on any potential liability and on the defense of such claim in the event of a claim arising out of the liability. Regarding the provision of launch and return services, the Partners concerned may conclude separate agreements regarding the apportionment of any potential joint and several liability arising out of the Liability Convention.[279]

As far as cross-waiver of liability is concerned, we can make further reference to the Launch Services Agreement (LSA) between a launch company and the provider of the space object to be launched. The original NASA Launch Services Agreement provided that, because the parties were engaged in the common goal of the meaningful exploration, exploitation and use of outer space, the parties would further this goal by agreeing to a no-fault, no-subrogation, inter-party waiver of liability.[280] The inter-party waiver was extended to other customers involved in the space operation and to the contractors and sub-contractors at every level of participation.[281]

The provisions above diverge from the general rules in Liability Convention: nations are held strictly liable for any damage caused on Earth or to aircraft in flight by space objects they have launched;[282] nations are held to be a fault-based liability standard for damage caused in space[283]. However, the existence of these provisions is not fortuitous. The high risks entailed in space operations require close cooperation among Partner States. Cross-exemption of liability can be a good way to soothe tension and maintain a good relationship.

The growing complexity of space operations will further intensify the need for closer cooperation among states. More and more states tend to work together to carry out a specific space project. The cross-exemption of liability in the IGA and the LSA sets a good example for space operations. It has become common in commercial space operations for the parties to agree to assume the consequences of losses however caused, whether attributable to the acts of another party or not, and to agree not to make a claim against any responsible party in the space operations. With more space practice in place, we need to reconsider the rules in the Liability Convention: whether it is necessary to include this exemption in the Convention and if so, in what way.

What is more, while concluding a separate agreement on liability apportionment in the IGA provides a flexible approach;[284] it also carries the risk that the Partners may not be able to reach a satisfactory agreement. Failure to do so could have adverse effect on further cooperation.[285] Accordingly, it is advisable to look further into this issue and find appropriate means or guidelines for such agreements.

---

[278] See IGA 1998, Article XVI.

[279] See IGA 1998, Article XVII.

[280] The LSA is the contract between NASA and the launch company. NASA created the first LSA in 1986.

[281] P.D. Nesgos, The Challenges Facing the Private Practitioner: Liability and Insurance Issues in Commercial Space Transportation, 4 *Georgetown University Law Review* 24 (Winter 1989).

[282] The Liability Convention, Article II.

[283] The Liability Convention, Article III.

[284] M.C. Devlin & W.G. Schmidt, Legal Issues Continue to Surround the International Space Station, 8 *USAFA Journal of Legal Studies* 248 (1997/1998).

2.3. Defects Inherent in the Convention

Heated discussions have taken place since the enactment of the Convention. Because of the political situation (Cold War) during the drafting period, scholars tend to be satisfied with the achievements made. Nevertheless, the situation has totally changed in the new era. It is now time to have a second look at the Convention. One obvious defect that has been pointed out is the absence of a meaningful provision for general problems that may arise when injuries are sustained in the environment of space or on a celestial body.[286] To make the Convention a real Liability Convention in Outer Space, it is necessary to include this point. One way forward would be the extensive explanation of "space object", which is discussed in the following.

2.3.1. Space Objects

To claim liability, the claimant must establish that the damage is caused by a space object. The Convention simply provides that "space object" includes component parts of a space object as well as its launch vehicle and parts thereof.[287] Natural objects such as meteorites are excluded.[288] This definition is obviously not sufficient with the construction of the ISS. As provided in the IGA, this definition is improved by clarifying the individual components of the ISS provided by the Partners as "space objects".[289] Scholars have argued the feasibility of this extensive definition.[290] Some suggested that the minimal requirement of a space object was that it should be an object designed for movement in outer space.[291] This minimum requirement is not the end of the story. What about space debris? What is the status of the property contained within or attached to a space object or component parts facilitating the objectives of the launch? It is also irrational to set apart a specific instrument from a stated space object. Accordingly, the vagueness in this term is detrimental to the application of the Convention. It is important to look into this definition and offer a clear scope for space objects.

2.3.2. "Fault" and "Gross Negligence"

The Convention provides two bases of liability: absolute liability and fault-based liability.[292] However, no definition is provided for "fault", [293] nor does the Convention refer to a duty of care in outer space, the breach of which would constitute fault.[294] Generally speaking, we can assert "fault" only when the act violates duty of care or standard of conduct. While requiring proof of fault, the Convention does not provide clear obligation to act or to abstain. Thus, proof of fault is difficult to implement in practice.

---

285 A.D. Watson & W.G. Schmidt, Legal Issues Surrounding the International Space Station, 7 *USAFA Journal of Legal Studies* 172 (1996/1997).

286 H. Reis, Some Reflections on the Liability Convention for Outer Space, 6 *Journal of Space Law* 127 (1978).

287 The Liability Convention, Article I (d).

288 S. Gorove, *Studies in Space Law: Its Challenges and Prospects* 105 (1977); H.A. Baker, *Space Debris: Legal and Policy Implications* 62 (1989).

289 IGA 1998, Article 5, para. 1.

290 See for example Lee, *supra* note 86, at 212-213.

291 N. Jasentuliyana & R. Lee, *Manual on Space Law* 317 (1981).

292 B.A. Hurwitz, *The Legality of Space Militarization* 40 (1986).

293 DeSaussure & P. Haanappel, A Unified, Multinational Approach to the Application of Tort and Contract Principles to Outer Space, in *Proceedings of 21st Colloquium on the Law of Outer Space* 138 (1978).

294 Firestone, *supra* note 82, at 761.

Likewise, the lacking of a definition of "gross negligence" can also cause problems in further application: what is the standard of care? Can *force majeure* and acts of a third party be valid defenses against liability? And so on. Moreover, no provision was made for imputing negligent conduct to others or for the attribution of a principal's vicarious liability for an agent or employee.[295] No substantive rules were formulated in the Convention to guide the application concerning damage arising out of fault or negligence. Such loopholes will cause serious problems in light of the rapidly increasing amount of space operations in which damage may be sustained.

2.3.3. Damages

The Convention provides for the availability of damages; however, no further clarification is provided concerning direct and indirect damages. Obviously, direct damage should be compensated; however, indirect damage constitutes a gray area for the Convention. No statutory or jurisprudential guidance exists to help decide exact recoverable damages in the context of space tort. Moreover, the Convention offers flexible guidance on the standard of compensation: in accordance with international law and the principles of justice and equity to restore the damaged party to the condition which would have existed if the damage had not occurred.[296] Such guidance is difficult to follow in reality since some basic areas still remain blank: how should one compute the quantum of damages in individual cases? Which national law should be applied to determine recoverable damages? In this respect, the Warsaw Convention for the Unification of Certain Rules Relating to International Carriage by Air[297] could offer a good example for resolving this problem: providing the maximum compensation in different situations.[298] The provision of a maximum would also make it easier to solve insurance problems.[299]

Another point to note is the criterion for determining damage that does not become apparent until long after the event. A time limit should be introduced for this purpose.[300]

2.3.4. Exception to the Principles of Total Compensation

Article VII of the Convention provides one exception: the Convention shall not apply to damage caused by a space object of a launching State to (a) nationals of the launching State; (b) foreign nationals, during such time as they are participating in the operation of that space object from the time of its launching or at any stage thereafter until its descent, or during such time as they are in the immediate vicinity of a planned launching State.[301] This exception is obviously subject to debate, since these two categories of persons are actually the ones running the highest risks.[302] According to this exception, individuals on a Space Station

---

[295] C.Q. Christol, International Liability for Damage Caused by Space Objects, 74 *American Journal of International Law*368 (April, 1980).

[296] The Liability Convention, Article XII. See T.S. Twibell, Space Law: Legal Restraints on Commercialization and Development of Outer Space, *65 University of Missouri at Kansas City Law Review* 596 (Spring, 1997).

[297] ICAO Doc. 7838, 9201 (1929).

[298] See for example, C.E. Fumarola, Stratospheric Recovery: Recent and Forthcoming Changes in International Air Disaster Law and Its Effect on Air Terrorism Recovery, 36 *Suffolk University Law Review* 835-836 (2003).

[299] I.H.Ph. de Rode-Verschoor, Observations on Comparing the responsibility for Damage Caused by Space Craft and that Caused by Nuclear Installations and Nuclear-Powered Ships, Proceedings 4th Colloquium 329 (Washington, 1961).

[300] Diederiks-Verschoor, *supra* note 92, at 41.

[301] The Liability Convention, Article VII.

[302] H.L. van Traa-Engelman, *Commercial Utilization of Outer Space—Legal Aspects* 35 (1989).

cannot resort to the Convention even when they suffer damage resulting from intentional or negligent wrongdoing.

Based on this exception, several other situations are consequently excluded from this Convention, *e.g.*, pollution control requirements because of the development of power complexes; security of space stations, including obtaining temporary jurisdiction and control over visiting objects and personnel coming within a defined "security zone"; intellectual property protection for products emanating from material processing and other new inventions.[303] It is obvious that these situations will occur more frequently with the development of new space operations. Accordingly, it is necessary to examine the feasibility of this exception.

2.4. Conclusion

The Liability Convention was a great achievement in establishing internationally accepted principles of liability in space in the 1970s, considering the complicated political environment of the time. It offers a good base for claiming damages. However, with the development of space operations and the change in the political environment, it is time to look seriously at the Convention again and evaluate its application.

It is obvious to all that, while compelling a just and equitable decision, the Convention does not provide any procedural or substantive guidelines to achieve the said decision. It leaves too much discretion to the decision-makers. The emergence of new space operations, demanding consistent rules in place, further weakens the Convention's applicability. Consequently, a serious review of the Convention is now needed. With some revision the Convention would offer clear guidelines for decision-makers to decide cases in a rational way best suited to the development of space operations.

---

[303] See G.C. Sgrosso, International Legal Aspects of Commercialization of Private Enterprise Space Activities, *Proceedings 30th Colloquium* 251-262 (Brighton, 1987).

Chapter 4

SATELLITE LAUNCHING SERVICES AND SPACE TOURISM

1. SATELLITE LAUNCHING SERVICES

1.1. Introduction

The successful launch of Sputnik I by the former Soviet Union around 50 years ago signaled the start of the space race. Space launching, forming the basis for other activities in outer space, has achieved great success since then. The development of space technology has greatly improved the reliability and frequency of launching activities. As reported, a total of 56 launches to Earth orbit were attempted in 2005, as compared to 55 in 2004, 62 in 2003, 63 in 2002, and 60 in 2001.[304]

Launch services, once the exclusive domain of the US and the Soviet Union, is now an important industry, with competitors from the US, Europe, China, Russia, Ukraine, Japan and India. While satellite companies are increasingly ready to contract with those non-Western launch services based in the nations claimed by the US to be non-market economies, the US is able to exert great control over the launch services market due to the fact that most satellites are manufactured by US companies or include US components. The US reached bilateral trade agreements with China, Russia and Ukraine concerning launch services to ensure that those countries did not offer unfair competition because of their non-market economies.

While there are no such bilateral agreements among the Western nations setting launch quotas, it is questionable whether or not such a practice is reasonable or discriminatory. It can be further questioned whether the above arrangement is viable or can contribute to further space technology development in the present globalized world. This section looks at this issue. Part two examines the existing bilateral trading regime for launch services and discusses the problems entailed in such an arrangement. Part three proposes a plurilateral regime under the auspices of the World Trade Organization (WTO) and studies the feasibility of liberalizing launch services. Part four concludes that launch services would be the second

304 Marco Caceres, Near-Term Outlook for Satellite Launches, *Aerospace America*, April 2005, available at <http://www.rsicopyright.com/ics/prc_main/prs_request.html> (last visited April 13, 2005).

area in space activities to be liberalized under the WTO regime, following the example of telecommunications services.

1.2. Bilateral Regime for Launch Services

China launched its first satellite, the DFH-1, with a Long-March 1 rocket as far back as 24 April 1970.[305] Since 1985, China's Long March rocket series has been made available for international commercial launch services and the first foreign-made satellite was successfully launched in 1990.[306] Twenty-three launches have been completed since then with a commercial primary payload as marketed by the China Great Wall Industry Corporation.[307] The latest commercial launch was carried out in April 2005, after a six-year freeze, when the AsiaSat-6 satellite was launched atop a Long March 3-B carrier rocket from a launch center at Xichang in the southwestern province of Sichuan.[308] All these launches were carried out under the bilateral trade regime.

In 1989, noting that China was close to its first commercial launch, the US negotiated a six-year agreement with China restricting the number of Chinese commercial space launches. Witnessing China's success in attracting more prospective business following its sixth foreign-satellite launch, the US renegotiated with China in October 1994, allowing China to launch nine commercial satellites into Geostationary Earth Orbit (GEO).[309] The two parties then signed a bilateral space launch agreement replacing the 1989-1994 one. China made major gains compared to the previous agreement. However, the two agreements basically serve the same function: establishing pricing levels and launch quotas. Under the new agreement, China is required to price its launches within 15 percent of what Western countries charge. The issue of launch quotas constitutes the major part of the new agreement. According to the new agreement, the launch quota was set to be 15 geostationary satellites through 2001; if the average annual number of commercial launches were 20 or more over the next three years, the quota could rise to 17; however, the quota could not exceed 20.[310] No express limit was provided on Low Earth Orbit (LEO) launches, but the US could review Chinese LEO launches on a constellation-by-constellation basis.[311] This agreement expired on December 31, 2001 and no new agreement has since been negotiated.

---

[305] Alexander Witze, Here Comes the Space Competition, *The Dallas Morning News*, September 7, 2003, available at <http://www.globalsecurity.org/org/news/2003/030907-space01.htm> (last visited May 31, 2005).

[306] China to Export First Chinese Satellite, Xinhua General News Service, Xinhua News Agency, April 12, 2005; China to Launch Another Satellite for Hong Kong Firm: Space Firm, Xinhua General news Service, Xinhua News Agency, Beijing, April 13, 2005.

[307] Stephen Clark, China Launches First Commercial Spacecraft in Six Years, *Spaceflight Now*, April 13, 2005, available at <http://www.space.com/missionlaunches/sfn_longmarch_apstar6_050413.html> (last visited May 25, 2005).

[308] China Launches New Commercial Communications Satellite, Beijing, Agency France Press, April 12, 2005

[309] Franceska O. Schroeder, Developments in Agreements on International Trade in Commercial Launch Services, ECSL News No. 16, May 1996, available at <http://esapub.esrin.esa.it/ecsl/ecsl16/schr16.htm> (last visited May 24, 2005).

[310] J. Barry Patterson, China's Space Program and Its Implications for the United States, A Research Report Submitted to the Faculty in Fulfillment of the Curriculum Requirement, Air War College, Air University, Maxwell Air Force Base, Alabama, April 19, 1995.

[311] Satellite Launches in the PRC-Loral, The Robinson Rojas Archive: China's Intelligence on US Nuclear Arsenal, available at <http://www.rrojasdatabank.org> (last visited June 14, 2005).

The US reached similar bilateral agreements with Russia and Ukraine. The agreement with Russia was signed in 1993, with an amendment in 1996 which allowed Russia to lift eight commercial payloads to GEO through December 31, 2000, so long as no more than two launches occurred in any 12-month period.[312] The US-Ukraine agreement was concluded in 1996, to expire in 2001, but this agreement was terminated in 2000 in recognition of Ukraine's steadfast commitment to international non-proliferation norms.[313]

While trying to establish a level playing field for all the parties, the US did not reach such agreements with other launching countries. In essence, the US failed to control the business practice of Arianespace, which is the US' biggest competitor in launch services. The US government contends that such agreements with non-market economies or economies in transition are necessary to ensure the stability of the highly competitive international commercial launch services market, which has been dominated by the US and European providers.[314] Two main concerns were identified as underlying such agreements, namely, safeguards on technology transfers[315] and engaging in fair trade[316]. The section will examine whether these two concerns continue to justify the bilateral trade regime.

1.2.1. Safeguards on Technology Transfer

The US has on various occasions expressed concern over technology transfer which might threaten its national security.[317] It is very doubtful whether this concern constitutes the main obstacle to open the launch services market. First of all, launch services and technology transfer, though there is some inter-relationship, are, in essence, two different issues. Debate exists over the national interest: weighing the benefits of trade and commercial competitiveness *versus* the risks to national security. We should de-link these two different matters and bring them into discussion in two different forums. Secondly, a series of strict control and security measures can be taken to prevent possible technology transfers. Actually, China and the US signed a Memorandum of Agreement on Satellite Technology Safeguards, which provides, among other measures, for:

> "...(a) Round-the-clock surveillance by American security personnel between the satellite's arrival in China and its launch into space; (b) Presence of American government officials at all satellite/launch vehicle technical coordination meetings; and (c) Prior approval of US government of all data and information provided to the Chinese side by American satellite manufacturers."[318]

---

[312] Agreement between the Government of the United States of America and the Government of the Russian Federation Regarding International Trade in Commercial Space Launch Services, 2 September 1993, State Dept. No. 93-117; Agreement between the United States and Russia Amending the Agreement of 2 September 1993, regarding International Trade in commercial Launch Services, 30 January 1996, State Dept. No. 96-37.

[313] Agreement Between the Government of the United States of America and the Government of Ukraine regarding Internatioanl Trade in Commercial Launch Services, 21 February 1996, State Dept. No. 96-51.

[314] Schroeder, *supra* note 6.

[315] See Memorandum of Agreement on Satellite Technology Safeguards, 17 December 1988, US-PRC, State department 89-114.

[316] See Memorandum of Agreement Regarding International Trade in Commercial Launch Services, 26 January 1989, US-PRC, State department 89-116.

[317] Richard D. Fisher, Jr., Commercial Space Cooperation Should not Harm National Security, No. 1198, The Heritage Foundation, June 26, 1998, available at <http://www.heritage.org> (last visited June 17, 2005).

[318] Normal Space Commercial Cooperation Between China and US Must Not be Jeopardized, January 7, 1999, available at <http://www.fas.org/news/china/1999/990107-prc-lv.htm> (last visited June 17, 2005).

First, an export license issued by the US government must be obtained for each and every launch service. Second, the strict measures as stated above should be able to relieve the concerns of the US. Third, the Chinese side has been able to develop its space technology on its own. One of the main principles for China's space industry as identified by the State Council is the principle of independence, self-reliance and self-renovation: China shall rely on its own strength to tackle key problems and make breakthroughs in space technology.[319] Some observers have correctly pointed out that launching satellites for customers from other nations has not provided breakthroughs and that China had deployed Intercontinental Ballistic Missiles (ICBMs) since 1980, before launching the first US satellite.[320] Also, some have pointed out that China already has access to European satellite technology and that the restrictions above prove to be bad business.[321] Last but not the least, the non-proliferation guidelines of the Missile Technology Control Regime (MTCR)[322] can be well maintained by the fact that China, Russia and other possible nations agree to join the regime and undertake treaty obligations.

In essence, the concern of technology transfer has been used as an excuse by the US to refuse to open the launch services market. Actually, all the agreements reached between the US and other nations do not forbid those nations from launch services under the main purpose of restricting launches. This is most obvious to all: the concerns raised simply serve to maintain the monopoly in the market.

1.2.2. Fair Trade

Pricing restrictions were provided in the US-China Agreement: prices had to be on a par with those offered by Western launch service providers; [323] if more than 15 percent less than the price for a comparable Western launch were offered, China had to consult with the US. The US-Russia Agreement provided for such consultation when Russia offered 7.5 percent less than the price of a comparable Western launch.

The terms "on a par" and "comparable" are ambiguous, since no one could agree on what they really mean: what is included in the total price? How to compare the total cost? Thus, the pricing restriction provisions could not be easily enforced. Competition is sharp in the launch market, which is now flooded with carrier rockets. The price is constantly decreasing. For example, US$ 70 million was formerly required for a launch by the Proton, which is believed to be the most reliable heavy rocket in the world; now the price is estimated to be only US$ 40 million, little more than the cost of the rocket itself.[324] It is very difficult to decide on a comparable price agreeable to all the parties.

Furthermore, price is not the major reason for the choice of a launch services provider. A study in 2001 indicated that reliability, instead of price, is the most important factor in the

---

319 China's Space Industry Flying High, November 23, 2000, Xinhua News Agency, available at <http://www.chinagate.com.cn> (last visited March 21, 2005).

320 A Joint Hearing of the Committees on International Relations and National Security, U.S. House of Representatives, U.S. Policy Regarding Satellite Exports to China, Testimony by Shirley A. Kan, June 17, 1998.

321 Michael Cabbage, China Finds Launches Lucrative, Taiwan Security Research, December 10, 2001, available at <http://www.orlandosentinel.com> (last visited March 21, 2005).

322 Henry Sokolski, U.S. Satellites to China, 27 *International Defense Review*, 21 (April 1994).

323 Andrew Lawler, U.S. to Confront China on Launch Sales, *Space News*, No. 26, Vol. 1, at 29, 9-15 July 1990.

324 The Time is Coming for Commercial Space Exploration, RIA Novosti, April 12, 2005.

minds of most commercial launch clients.[325] China, while having a relatively competitive price, has been thwarted by a well-publicized launch failure in 1996 which killed a civilian on the ground.[326] The failure had made obtaining insurance nearly impossible.[327] This fact further confirms that consideration of reliability is of utmost importance to space clients: the attractiveness of a launch service provider is measured in terms of the likelihood that the satellite will achieve orbit on time, not necessarily at the lowest contract price.[328] While evaluating all the elements leading to fair trade in space launch services, we should take all the factors into account: reliability, insurance, launch capacity; and scheduling.[329]

As reported, third world countries spending in the launch industry was estimated at US$ 1.4 billion per year and at US $155 million per launching.[330] This rapid development has been strongly argued to result from the success of Chinese "Long March" rocket and the relatively low cost.[331] We can imagine what the situation would be for developing countries if the launching price were set at a forbiddingly high level.

On the other hand, launch prices should be based on actual expenses entailed in the launch services; unreasonably low prices established with the purpose of grabbling market share no doubt constitute dumping.[332] China has been criticized for governmental subsidies for launch services leading to dumping. However, this is not the case for China. Subsidization exists in all the nations providing launch services. For example, the US itself supported two important providers--Boeing and Lockheed Martin--by providing substantial funds through the Department of Defence (DOD) for assured access to space.[333] Title IX was added to the fiscal year 2003 DOD appropriations act, creating a loan guarantee program for companies developing commercial, reusable, in-orbit space transportation systems.[334] The European Space Agency (ESA), though not legally constrained from using other launch vehicles, does give preference to its own provider, Ariane; it proposed in 2002 to make a guaranteed purchase of three Arianes annually at a reported cost of 650 million euros per year.[335] From all these examples, we can see that the accusation of government subsidies is not reasonable nor convincing.

As constantly stated by the Chinese side, China has a cheap labor market, low-cost Chinese-made materials for manufacturing launchers, and comparatively low operation fees.

---

[325] Linda A. Williams, Launch Vehicles Price Elasticity of Demand, Space Technology and Application International Forum, February 13, 2001, Futron Corporation, available at <http://www.futron.com/pdf/STFELST.PDF> (last visited May 25, 2005).

[326] Foreign Launch Vehicles, US Centennial of Flight Commission, available at <http://www.centennialofflight.gov/essay/SPACEFLIGHT/foreign_launch_vehicl...> (last visited May 31, 2005).

[327] Janet Guyon, Satellite Venture Seeks Shortcut to Space: Global Partners to Fire Rockets from Sea Along Equator, *The Wall Street Journal*, March 20, 1996.

[328] SS/Loral Inks Multimillion Dollar Launch Deal with Arianespace, Satellite News, May 6, 1996.

[329] Satellite Owners Get Big Price Break from New Launch Suppliers, *Space Business News*, January 8, 1997.

[330] David Frost & James Sullivan, World Satellite Communications Equipment Market: VSAT and Mobile Applications Unleash Satellite Communications, New York: Frost & Sullivan Market Intelligence, 1993.

[331] Jonathan N. Goodrich, Jerry Haar & Manuel A. Mindreau, Third World Activities in Space Commercialization: A Note, April 1996, available at <http://www.docentes.up.edu.pe/Mmindreau/docs/Space%20Commercialization.PDF> (last visited June 14, 2005).

[332] Marcia Smith, 93062: Space Launch Vehicle: Government Requirements and Commercial Competition, Congressional Research Service Issue Brief for Congress, July 2, 1998.

[333] Ricky J. Lee, Legal and Policy Aspects of Launch Services Provided by Governmental and Private Providers, paper presented at the International Space Law Conference, Bangalore, India, June 26-29, 2005.

[334] P.L. 107-248.

[335] Marcia S. Smith, Space Launch Vehicles: Government Activities, Commercial Competition, and Satellite Exports, Issue Brief for Congress, February 3, 2003, Order Code IB93062.

The relatively low launch services fee will be further lowered by the possible establishment of a fourth launch center in Hainan, the southernmost province of China, [336] because Earth-synchronous satellites that are launched from a center closer to the equator enjoy a longer shelf life and reduce the cost of launching, compared with those launched from a site in higher latitudes.[337] Moreover, compared with the US launch services, China is a newcomer, so there is a need to offer a favorable price for the introduction of a new product. This also applies to other new and/or potential service providers, or these providers will not be able to survive in the market.[338]

1.3. A Plurilateral Regime for Launch Services

Space technology has developed rather rapidly in the modern world, causing a boom in the commercial launch market. However, the average launch number of 60 per year during the period 2001-2003 proves to be the lowest number since the early 1960s; the launch number in 2005 was even lower than 60. Accordingly, it has been claimed that the launch industry has taken a turn in the wrong direction.[339] Another boom is expected to come in the next one to two years in view of the fact that the service life of most satellites will end in 2007-2008.[340] How to get well prepared for the coming boom needs to be urgently dealt with. With the considerations underlying the bilateral trade regime unjustified, it is now time to explore an appropriate regime for launch services.

Since launch services are an important type of trade in services, the market for such services should be a place for normal, well-regulated commerce and trade between nations, an arena where nations compete fairly with each other solely based on their material, financial, technical and overall industrial resources. On the basis of such consideration, the WTO appears to be the best choice to regulate the launch services. The WTO was established with the ultimate goal of trade liberalization. This organization has established a specific set of rules for liberalizing trade in services: General Agreement on Trade in Services (GATS). Trade in basic telecommunications services, once believed to be a sensitive area for national security, was brought within the purview of the WTO. This is the first successful story of bringing a sensitive area of space activities into this multilateral framework.

Actually, the entire satellite industry, from manufacturers to operators, has been under intense competition. In view of a downturn of new payloads in recent years, launch services providers have been competing to maintain the market shares they currently have with as much realistic growth as possible.[341] What they should do now is to provide quality services to attract customers, not to monopolize the market and exclude other providers from the market. This is what the WTO intends to procure for international trade.

---

[336] China's Fourth Satellite Launching Center Likely to be Built in Southernmost Province, Xinhua News Agency, Xinhua General News Service, March 11, 2005.

[337] NPC Deputies Push for New Satellite Launch Center, People's Daily Online, available at <http://english.people.com.cn/200303/06/print20030306_112787.html> (last visited May 31, 2005).

[338] Yanping Chen, China's Space Commercialization Effort, 9 *Space Policy*, No. 1, at 45 (February 1993).

[339] Marco Caceres, Launch Market Takes a Wrong Turn, Industry Insights, at 12, *Aerospace America*, American Institute of Aeronautics and Astronautics, Inc., February 2005, available at <http://www.rsicopyright.com/ics/prc_main/prs_request.html> (last visited April 13, 2005).

[340] Russia Out to Retain Quarter of Space Market-Koptev, ITAR-TASS News Agency, November 1, 2004.

[341] Julie Blondeau, Launchers: Competing for Customer Satisfaction, 20 *Via Satellite*, No. 3, March 1, 2005.

While continuing to manufacture rockets and satellites for States, the space industry has started setting up facilities for private companies to produce satellites for private clients. As a general trend, privatization is an ongoing process. Launch services, following the example of telecommunications services, could be the second category of space activities to be regulated by the WTO rules. However, governments will remain major parties in the transactions. Accordingly, it would not be viable to liberalize launch services within the GATS framework, since government procurement is expressly excluded from the application of the provision of this Agreement.[342] Seeking to eliminate adverse effects on launch services resulting from governmental support in the development of space activities while recognizing that such governmental support, of itself, would not be deemed a distortion of trade, we may nevertheless consider the use of a plurilateral regime under the WTO. Trade liberalization in launch services can be achieved through trade rules mutually agreed among relevant parties, not necessarily free from substantial government support.[343] A plurilateral trade agreement can be reached through negotiations among interested Members in the WTO forum, providing for possible accession of other WTO members.

Making referring to the Plurilateral Agreement on Trade in Civil Aircraft, several issues could be covered in such an agreement:

- *technical barriers*: basically the measures safeguarding technology transfer could be provided in this section, trying to relieve some signatories' concerns.[344]
- *government-directed procurement*: customers should be free to select services providers on the basis of commercial and technological factors; the signatories should not exert any unreasonable pressure on customers and oblige them to procure from any particular provider; the signatories should not create any discrimination against providers from any other signatories.[345]
- *trade restrictions*: the signatories should not apply quantitative restrictions to prevent export of satellites; however, export licensing requirements may be continued.[346]
- *government support*: pricing of launch services should be based on a reasonable expectation of recovery of all costs, taking into account the special factors in this area, in particular the existing practice of government support, international economic interests, and the desire of services providers of all signatories to participate in the expansion of the world launch services market.[347]

For better administration, a Committee on Trade in Launch services should be established consisting of representatives of all signatories. The Committee should meet as necessary, affording the signatories the opportunity to consult on any matters arising out of the operation

[342] GATS, Art. XIII:1 provides that "Article II (MFN Treatment), XVI (Market Access) and XVII (national treatment) shall not apply to laws, regulations, or requirements governing the procurement by governmental agencies of services purchased for governmental purposes and not with a view to commercial resale or with a view to use in the supply of services for commercial sale." See Jon C. Garcia, Heaven or Hell: The Future of the United States Launch Services Industry, 7 Harvard Journal of Law & Technology 364 (1994); See also Ricky J. Lee, *supra* note 30.

[343] James L. Reed, The Commercial Space Launch Market and Bilateral Trade Agreements in Space Launch Services, 13 *American University International Law Review* 175 (1997).

[344] Agreement on Trade in Civil Aircraft, Art. 3.

[345] *Id.*, Art. 4.

[346] *Id.*, Art. 5.

of the agreement and trying to reach a mutually acceptable solution.[348] Should a signatory consider that its trade interests in launch services have been or are likely to be adversely affected by any action of another signatory, it could request the Committee to review the matter, the latter being able to issue such rulings or recommendations as might be appropriate.[349] The signatories should undertake negotiations in due course with a view to broadening and improving the agreement on the basis of mutual reciprocity.[350] For dispute settlement, we may refer to the existing WTO dispute settlement mechanism, which has been well received by the WTO Members due to its binding effect. This mechanism should similarly apply to disputes in launch services, through which the strict enforcement of the agreement can be ensured.

1.4. Conclusion

China posited its ambitious plan to enter the space competition in 2003: successful launch of manned satellite that year; launch of a satellite to the moon within three years and launch of a space station to establish a permanent outpost on the moon within 15 years.[351] Some may wonder whether China's achievement is the beginning of the end of the US's dominance in space.[352] As observed by William Martel, Professor of National Security Affairs and the Chair of Space Technology and Policy at the Naval War College in Newport, Rhode Island, China has now entered the ranks of the "first tier" states: "[I]n terms of prestige and technological ability, China is now of the primary players in space. This, by itself, has significant implications for the US and its position of unquestioned strategic superiority in space."[353]

China and the US will be sure to engage in some form of a space race, which has significant military and technological implications for both sides. However, China has made clear to the public its position towards space activities. In various documents, China has avowedly claimed its persistence towards peaceful use of and international co-operation in outer space.[354] Previous experience is a strong support for this in that China is striving to realize the goal stated in the Outer Space Treaty: exploration for the benefit of mankind. Furthermore, the concerns, while related to a specific space activity to a certain extent, can be dealt with in other agreements. We should de-link the two different issues: space commercialization and national security or politics.

Two facts are sufficient to support the above position: the launch services market will become more and more competitive, no matter whether the US likes it or not; and the US

[347] *Id.*, Art. 6.
[348] *Id.*, Art. 8.1.
[349] *Id.*, Art. 8.7.
[350] *Id.*, Art. 8.3.
[351] Chinese Launch could Signal New Space Race: Nation's First Taionaut Blasts Off Early Wednesday, available at <http://edition.cnn.com/2003/TECH/space/10/14/space/race/index.html> (last visited May 25, 2005).
[352] *Id.*
[353] Leonard David, What Next for China? Friendly Competition or New Cold War?, October 17, 2003, available at <http://www.space.com/missionlaunches/china_future_031017.html> (last visited April 11, 2005).
[354] White Paper: China's Space Activities, November 2000, Beijing, available at <http://www.comefromchina.com> (last visited March 21, 2005).

cannot isolate itself from other nations in this globalized world. Thus, what we should pursue for the time being is to find out the best forum and means to open the market.

Commercialization, an irreversible trend in modern society, also applies to space activities. Launch services is one of the most capital-intensive and politically visible categories of space commercialization.[355] The WTO provides the solid groundwork for trade liberalization. Liberalizing space launch services in a plurilateral regime instead of a bilateral one is now increasingly recognized as a feasible way to further improve the viability of space activities.[356] We should start preparing for talks and negotiations among the interested parties within the framework of the WTO and push for the early establishment of a plurilateral regime for launch services.

2. The Issue of Nuclear Power Sources in Space Launching Activities

2.1. Introduction

Nuclear power sources (NPS) have been used since 1961 for the purpose of generating energy for space objects[357] and have, since then, been recognized as particularly suited or essential to some space operations. The use of NPS in outer space aims to provide electric power for spacecraft sub-systems such as altitude control, communications and command, as well as for the operations of various equipments on board. Two types of NPS are presently in outer space, namely isotopic source and nuclear reactor.[358]

In the mid 1960s American government and industry looked to a cheaper and reliable alternative to chemical rocket engines. Other than Russian nuclear achievements in space at that time, no other entity had succeeded in demonstrating the raw power of crafted nuclear rocket propulsion, except Project Rover in the US.

However, the risks inherent in using NPS caused much concern.[359] The risk and the disastrous consequence were well demonstrated by the incident in 1978 when the Russian nuclear-powered satellite Cosmos 954 crashed on Canada.[360] Discussions started since then on an international technical framework for the regulation of NPS in outer space.[361] Years of deliberation have finally led to the adoption of the United Nations (UN) Resolution on the

---

[355] Goodrich, *supra* note 28.

[356] See for example, Peter van Fenema, *The International Trade in Launching services: The Effect of U.S. Laws, Politics and Practices on Its Development*, 372 (1999).

[357] The first nuclear satellite was Transit 4A, a navigational satellite launched on June 29, 1961. It was a time when space and nuclear power were seen by some as coupled.

[358] See further D. Tan, Towards a New Regime for the Protection of Outer Space as the "Province of All Mankind", 25 *Yale Journal of International Law*149 (Winter 2000).

[359] See generally R.I.R. Abeyratne, The Use of Nuclear Power Sources in Outer Space and Its Effect on Environmental Protection, 25 *Journal of Space Law* 17 (1997).

[360] The satellite was designed for ocean reconnaissance and was powered by a nuclear reactor working on uranium enriched with isotope of uranium-235. For discussion, see further B. Schwartz & M.L. Berlin, After the Fall: An Analysis of Canadian Legal Claims for Damage Caused by Cosmos 954, 27 *McGill Law Journal* 6767 (1982); A.F. Cohen, Cosmos 954 and the International Law of Satellite Accidents, 10 *Yale Journal of International Law* 80 (1984).

[361] M. Benko & K. Schrogl (eds.), *International Space Law in the Making: Current Issues in the UN Committee on the Peaceful Uses of Outer Space* 19-21 (1993).

safe use of NPS in 1992, [362] listing 11 principles for the safe application and assessment of NPS. While acknowledging the fact that national activities involve the use of NPS in outer space, it recognizes that certain restrictions are necessary to ensure the safe use of NPS. The Resolution aims to promote the protection of persons and 'the biosphere' against radiological hazards.[363]

According to Principle 11, these Principles shall be opened for revision no later than two years after their adoption. To date, however, revisions have not been made. After more than ten years' existence, it is time to take a serious look at the principles again considering the rapid development of modern technology and the drastic change of the political atmosphere.

The present section takes up the position in discussing the possible modification to the Resolution. Part two gives an overview of the Resolution and describes the necessity of modifying the current principles. Part three concentrates on the substantial areas for improvements and modification, which is followed by Part four, discussing the improvement on the formality of the Principles. A short conclusion in Part five portrays a prospect for the Principles in the new century.

2.2. Brief Review of the 1992 NPS Principles

The 1992 Principles apply to NPS in outer space devoted to generation of electric power on board space objects for non-propulsive purposes. It considers only the use of nuclear fuel as it relates to NPS.[364] Principle 1 sets a broad framework for NPS: international treaties and customs shall be valid in the regulation of NPS. The present resolution is a further statement of these rules in the specific activity. Principle 2 defines the terms to be applied in this resolution. This shall help clarify the ambiguity concerning "launching State" and "State launching".

Principle 3 offers guidelines and criteria for safe use. It is the heart of the Resolution.[365] The use of NPS is strictly limited to space missions which cannot be operated by non-nuclear energy sources. Such use shall, further, be conducted in a reasonable way. The obligation of safety assessment is provided in Principle 4 in accordance with the criteria for safe use contained in Principle 3. Rules of the notification of re-entry for consultation and requests for additional information between states are respectively provided in Principle 5 and 6. The issues concerning assistance to States, responsibility, liability and compensation, and dispute settlement are set forth in the next four Principles.[366]

The Principles provide the basic document guiding the use of NPS in limited situations. The necessity of the Principles is obvious: the high risks entailed in the use of NPS. This also justifies the limited use of NPS: not for propulsion purposes. The provisions satisfy the needs in the early 1990s with the existence of strong arms control advocates and

[362] Principles Relevant to the Use of Nuclear Sources in Outer Space, UN G.A. Resolution A/Res/47/68 (December 14, 1992); GAOR, 47th Session, Supp. No. 20, UN Doc. A/47/20 (1992).

[363] Section 1.1 of Principle 3.

[364] R. Dusek, Lost in Space?: The Legal Feasibility of Nuclear Waste Disposal in Outer Space, 22 *William and Mary Environmental Law and Policy Review* 213 (Fall 1997).

[365] R.A. Ramey, Armed Conflict on the Final Frontier: The Law of War in Space, 48 *Air Force Law Review* 116 (2000).

[366] For further description of the Principles, see I.H.Ph. Diederiks-Verschoor, *An Introduction to Space Law*, 108-109 (Kluwer, 2nd Edition, 1999).

environmentalists.[367] However, with the development of space technology and the enthusiasm for further exploration of outer space, the use of NPS again becomes the topic for heated discussion. The National Aeronautics and Space Administration (NASA) is now moving to revive its scheme to build nuclear-propelled rockets[368] and expand its use of atomic power to generate electricity on space probes and planetary rovers.[369] The program, called Nuclear Systems Initiative, is trying to develop safe and reliable nuclear power and propulsion systems.[370] NASA announced its intention to revisit the issue of NPS in space early in 2002, shortly after the September 11th event.[371] This announcement has, on the one hand, advocated the use of NPS beyond non-propulsion purposes; on the other hand, it closely referred to the war against terrorism. The situation nowadays is no longer like that in 1994 or even later (two years or longer after the adoption of the Principles), and the technical advancement and the reality has urged revision of the Principles and further accommodations.

2.3. Improvement on Substantial Aspects of the 1992 Principles

Heated discussions had been in place before the adoption of the Principles. Various scholars recognized the necessity of rules guiding the legitimate use of NPS. After years of deliberation, the Principles were successfully adopted. However, comments and evaluations continued to be presented on the merits and demerits of the Principles. In general, the Principles offer a platform for space activities involving the use of NPS. This set of Principles can be viewed as a great leap forward in history. Considering the sensitive nature of NPS, it is appropriate to have a set of Principles in the first place: something is better than nothing. Nevertheless, it has been obvious to all, even at the time of adoption, that further revision is necessary. For various reasons, the speculated revision has not, so far, been made. However, the necessity of revision is now at the forefront when the US put forward the plan of using NPS for propulsion purposes and other applications. Confronting the new challenge, it is accordingly the right time to study the principles and make possible improvements.

2.3.1. Applicable Scope

The Principles have a clear applicable scope. As stated above, NPS shall be only allowed for non-propulsive purposes. According to the analysis of some scholars, the Principles do not refer to the use of NPS on celestial bodies including the Moon.[372] However, the reality is that NPS has been used[373] and can be further used for space operations, not only in outer space but

[367] In an attempt to square this circle, the Federation of American Scientists and Soviet colleagues in 1988 proposed a ban on the operation of nuclear reactors in earth orbit that would nevertheless permit their use for space exploration.

[368] P. Pae, NASA Seeks $1 Billion for Nuclear Propulsion Plan, *Los Angeles Times*, February 7, 2002, at 112.

[369] The Return of Space Nuclear Reactors, Secrecy News from the FAS Project on Government Secrecy, Volume 2002, Issue No. 11, January 31, 2002, available at <http://cndyorks.gn/apc.org>.

[370] NASA Administrator Honorable Sean OKeefe, NASA biography of OKeefe, available at <http://www.nasa.gov/bios/okeefe.html>.

[371] K. Grossman, Plutonium in Space (Again!), Global Network Against Weapons and Nuclear Power in Space, Covert Action Quarterly, No. 73, Summer 2002, available at <http://www.globenet.free-online.co.uk/articles/morenukesinspace.htm>.

[372] N. Jasentuliyana, An Assessment of the United Nations Principles on the Use of Nuclear Power Sources in Outer Space, *Proceedings 36th Colloquium on the Law of Outer Space* 316 (Graz, 1993).

[373] The US has launched some two-dozen spacecraft utilizing plutonium-powered electrical generators.

also at the stage before and after the space objects enter outer space; not only as electric power but also as propulsion power. Several NASA notables have mentioned publicly that nuclear power in space transportation deserves a closer look. The comments indicate that if public relation efforts can gain acceptance for the possibility, future interplanetary missions may include nuclear-power options.[374] The former "taboo" of not using NPS for propulsion purposes has been under severe challenge.

The efforts from the US's side serve as the powerful motivating force. The justification presented is, no doubt, strong enough to stand against those sticking to the restrictive use of NPS. The European Space Agency (ESA), as a support for the restrictive use of NPS, is devoted to developing safer ways of propelling rockets and energizing space probes and planetary landers, which include solar electric propulsion and the use of "solar sails" and other solar technologies that stress the generation of electricity with new high-efficiency solar cells.[375] Nevertheless, such a position shall not prescribe the fact of using NPS for wider space operations. Outer planet exploration using advanced radioisotope electric propulsion has been evaluated by teams at the NASA Glenn Research Center in Cleveland, Ohio, as well as The Johns Hopkins University Applied Physics Laboratory in Laurel, Maryland.[376]

Some might quote the 1963 Treaty Banning Nuclear Weapons in the Atmosphere, in Outer Space and under Water (Limited Test Ban Treaty)[377] as proof against the use of nuclear fission as a means of space propulsion by referring to the provision that outlaws any nuclear weapon test explosion or any other nuclear explosion.[378] However, according to the provision, it directly refers to the prohibition of NPS application by means of explosion, the treaty does not prohibit the use by means other than explosion. Moreover, this treaty, basically, deals with nuclear weapons, not nuclear use for normal space activities.

While witnessing the actual development, we should acknowledge that theoretical debates on the feasibility of NPS's extensive use are meaningless or at least diverging our regulatory direction. We have only two possible outcomes: either that space will be colonized illegally or the current laws are to be changed.[379] Politically speaking, the right attitude should be to formulate an appropriate legal framework for their legitimate and safe application, offering a guideline for possible use of NPS in space operations (including heat, power or propulsion) in interplanetary traveling, in celestial bodies, in earth orbit, beyond earth orbit or even for launching spacecraft from the surface of the earth. This is a pragmatic means to realize order in the use of NPS, which also represents the extension of positivism in the field of space law. The availability of a legal framework for extensive use of NPS shall put a safety valve and provide preventive measures against future illegal use of NPS in all other cases.

Considering the ongoing discussions and technical development, it is time to justify the possible areas for extension. The application of NPS for propulsion purposes is one promising area. Nuclear propulsion can take many forms ranging from low thrust nuclear electric propulsion to higher thrust nuclear thermal propulsion and electrical or thermal "pulsed nuclear" propulsion. Supporting arguments include the sufficient energy for space operation

---

[374] G. Clark, Will Nuclear Power Put Humans on Mars?, available at <http://www.space.com>.

[375] New Solar Cells with Record Efficiency, ESA Press Information Note No. 0794, April 29, 1994.

[376] L. David, NASA to Seek Nuclear-Powered Spaceflight Alternatives, February 1, 2002, available at <http://cndyorks.gn.apc.org>.

[377] Done on August 5, 1963, 14 U.S.T. 1313, 480 U.N.T. 43 (entered into force on October 10, 1963).

[378] G.H. Reynolds & R.P. Mergers, *Outer Space: Problems of Law and Policy* 61 (2nd ed., 1997).

[379] S. de Cordoba, Changing Basic Space Laws: Popularity, Pragmatism and Historical Lessons, *Proceedings 36th Colloquium on the Law of Outer Space* 330 (1993).

which can, largely, shorten the necessary time for space operations. Actually, astronauts are among the most enthusiastic boosters of such a nuclear-powered mission.[380] The restrictive use of NPS will add to the cost and the length of the missions, which will levy a burden on the pressure and anxiety of astronauts. Nuclear propulsion can be more efficient than any other traditional chemical propulsion, it has twice the propellant mileage of chemical propulsion. The mere use of enriched uranium will increase the efficiency of space operations. Several other advantages have also been quoted: creating artificial gravity and the reuse potential of the nuclear thermal rocket.[381] Some space missions, although they can be operated by non-nuclear energy sources, will not be able to enjoy the advantages of NPS. Confident assertion came from the Center for Space Science and Exploration, Los Alamos Laboratory, that the future of nuclear activities in space will revolve around Nuclear Electrical Propulsion (NEP), at least in the immediate future, involving light payloads on long duration missions.[382]

However, it is yet to be seen whether it is advisable to extend the use of NPS in the earth orbit or near earth regions. It has been strongly argued that the nuclear powered rockets should not be used to get off the ground but only outside the Earth orbit. The nuclear system can be controlled to function only when desired and the distances involved would be far from any earthly influence in any event. Nevertheless, we cannot preclude this possibility with technological improvement. Thus, it is also necessary to bring this possible development into the legal framework: providing clear statement on whether its application within earth orbit is legal or not; if confirmed as legal, then higher standards should be provided.

Scholars have also been arguing whether the Principles apply to the use of NPS systems on planetary surfaces.[383] The Resolution itself does not contain clear guidance. It is, thus, necessary to clarify this ambiguity. To take the style of the Outer Space Treaty, outer space shall include the moon and other celestial bodies. The adoption of this conception shall ensure the consistency of the terms among international space law documents.

The extensive application of NPS shall no doubt add to the danger inherent in the NPS posed to the humans, animals, plants and natural environments on the earth. Actually the cons over extensive use of NPS have been largely based on the above concerns. Thus, the vital point to substantiate the use of NPS is to provide a convincing mechanism to ensure the safety or lessen the risks entailed from legal and technical angles. Generally speaking, Principles 3 and 4 are appropriate in defining the safe use and assessment from a technical point of view; however, for the purpose of further extension, it is necessary to check the wordings and include the possible extension. This extension and revision shall include the higher level of safety standards, reconsideration of appropriate orbit position, etc. The duty to inform the use of NPS, duty to warn, international consultation, etc. have been defined in other Principles but it is also necessary to review to keep up with new developments. Furthermore, when reviewing the Principles, we need to refer to the Outer Space Treaty.[384]

---

380 A fast mission using nuclear thermal rockets could get astronauts to Mars in as little as 4 months.
381 For the discussion of the advantages, see further Clark, *supra* note 71.
382 B. Behrhorst, Nuclear Rocket Power in Space: Generational Legacy, available at <http://www.nuclearspace.com>.
383 See for example, M.S. Smith, Legal Aspects of Using Nuclear Reactors on the Moon, *Proceedings 35th Colloquium on the Law of Outer Space* 312 (1992).
384 For example, Article XI of Space Treaty provides the commitment in providing the information to promote international co-operation in the peaceful exploration and use of outer space.

2.3.2. The "Reasonableness" Test in Principle 3

With possible application of NPS closer to humans, high standards and preventive measures shall be adopted to procure against high risks. This shall have most relevance with the reasonableness test defined in Principle 3. With the availability and feasibility of solar energy well testified, a clear understanding of the term shall be needed. Failing the reasonableness test, relevant States causing the damage should bear higher level of liability accordingly.

The term "reasonableness" basically provides the idea of defining the applicable scope for NPS. The "chapeau" of Principle 3 provides that the use of NPS shall be restricted to space missions which cannot be operated by non-nuclear energy sources in a reasonable way. This chapeau has tried to rule out the use of NPS in other situations, however, the term "in a reasonable way" softens the assertion, which shall be subject to an appropriate interpretation. Without defining "reasonable", the Resolution attempts to limit use of NPS while acknowledging that NPS is appropriate for some space operations. Nevertheless, the flexible use of the term has aroused much criticism after the adoption of the Resolution. It is now time to revisit this term.

While offering the chapeau, Principle 3 goes a step further by defining the situations when nuclear reactors and radioisotope generators can be operated. The principle further provides that the reliability of systems important for safety shall be ensured, *inter alia*, by redundancy, physical separation, functional isolation and adequate independence of their components.[385] It also lists several situations when nuclear reactors may be operated: on interplanetary missions; in sufficiently high orbits and in low-Earth orbits if they are stored in sufficiently high orbits after the operational part of their mission.[386] According to the Resolution, "sufficiently high orbits" are those in which the orbital lifetime is long enough to allow for a sufficient decay of the fission products to approximate the activity of the actinides. Such orbits must be such that the risks to existing and future outer space missions and of collision with other space objects are kept to a minimum.[387]

However, the indeterminacy has been further exacerbated by the use of the terms such as "sufficient", "long enough" and "minimum". While this resolution provides the basic mechanism for securing the safe use of NPS, the crux is how to provide a safety valve for the application, not to preclude the use of NPS. We should take note of two relevant issues: applicable scope and the procurement of safe use within the applicable scope. The definition of "reasonableness" shall be directly related to the two issues above. The status confronting the new development should, thus, be the extension of NPS to broader space operations and the provision of a higher level of safety procurement from the technical part.

While the issue of extending applicable scope has been discussed earlier, we should now examine the formulation of appropriate standards for safety procurement. This proves to be a difficult topic, having been evidenced by the tedious deliberations during the drafting of the Principle. The constant technological development has a high possibility of making newly formulated technical standards outdated very quickly. It is almost impossible to stabilize such rules in a legal document. As stated by Cocca, the inclusion of technical regulation in legal guidelines seems to be a resignation of law in the benefit of technology which could not solve

[385] Section 1.4 of Principle 3.
[386] Section 2.1 of Principle 3.
[387] Section 2.2 of Principle 3.

its own difficulties and therefore decides to put law under its subordination.[388] One possible way out could, thus, be to differentiate technical issues from legal guidelines: while developing a treaty with broad and general guidance, the UN can leave the establishment of standards and recommended practices for States to an international technical body.[389] The International Atomic Energy Agency (IAEA) and the International Commission on Radiological Protection (ICRP) can be appropriate bodies to undertake technical tasks.[390] Whilst providing legal guidelines, the Principle can make express reference to the recommendations of these two organizations. This can resolve the heated debates concerning the adoption of technical standards in a legal document.

2.3.3. The Issue of Environmental Protection

Environmental protection or sustainable development has been an important issue considering the possible dangers posed to the earth. The issue of space debris has been deeply studied by various space law bodies.[391] We should note the Limited Test Ban Treaty, [392] one important consideration of which has been environmental protection: the prevention of global nuclear contamination, to put an end to the contamination of man's environment by radioactive substances.[393] It can even be viewed primarily as an environmental agreement rather than a military one.[394] NASA conceded the serious dangers of a Cassini accident in its Final Environmental Impact Statement for the Cassini Mission, the most recent nuclear space probe mission in 1997.[395] It is proposed that those space activities which might harm the local and global environment are carried out in a manner that limits such effects to the largest possible extent.[396] However, the discussions did not direct to NPS in space operations. This fact does not underestimate the highly dangerous nature of the pollution resulting from the use of NPS.

While providing the safety guidance for the use of NPS, the resolution can be argued to have implicitly included the idea of environmental protection. Nevertheless, such an implied idea will not impose much strength on the actual performance. It is necessary to insert this principle into the main body of the resolution, among those include the disposition of nuclear

[388] A.A. Cocca, Are the Principles on the Use of Nuclear Power Sources in Outer Space a Progress in Space Law?, *Proceedings 36th Colloquium on the Law of Outer Space* 258 (1993).

[389] N. Jasentuliyana, A Survey of Space Law as Developed by the United Nations, in N. Jasentuliyana (ed.), *Perspectives in International Law* 349 (Kluwer, 1995).

[390] A.D. Terekhov, Review and Revision of the Principles Relevant to the Use of Nuclear Power Sources in Outer Space, *Proceedings 36th Colloquium on the Law of Outer Space* 340 (1993); see also Y. Lodico, Developing Legal Principles for the Safe Use of Nuclear Power Sources in Outer Space, *Proceedings 34th Colloquium on the Law of Outer Space* 134 (1991); E. Galloway, United Nations Consideration of Nuclear Power for Satellites, *Proceedings 22nd Colloquium on the Law of Outer Space* 135 (1979).

[391] J.M. Seymour, Containing the Cosmic Crisis: A Proposal for Curbing the Perils of Space Debris, 10 *Georgetown International Environmental Law Review* 907 (Spring 1998).

[392] Treaty Banning Nuclear Weapon Tests in the Atmosphere, in Outer Space and under Water, August 5, 1963, 14 U.S.T. 1313.

[393] Jankowitsch, Legal Aspects of Military Space Activities, in N. Jasentuliyana (ed.), *Space Law: Development and Scope* 143 (1992).

[394] Reynolds & Merges, *supra* note 75, at 54.

[395] Final Environmental Impact Statement for the Cassini Mission, National Aeronautics and Space Administration, Solar System Exploration Division, Office of Space Science, June 1995, at 476. As stated, if an inadvertent reentry occurred and Cassini fell back into the Earths atmosphere, it would break up (it had no heat shield) and 5 billion of the world population could receive 99 percent or more of the radiation exposure.

[396] See further Vienna Declaration on Space and Human Development, Adopted by UNISPACE III, as it concludes two-week session, Third United Nations Conference on the Exploration and Peaceful Uses of Outer Space, UNISPACE III SPACE/V/9, Final Meeting (AM & PM) and Round-Up, July 30, 1999;.

wastes. This shall promote the compliance by Members without further arguments. Thus, international cooperation could be directed at addressing this issue.

By inserting environmental protection in the Preamble, we can have a stronger stand and a more justifiable commitment to support several measures in the main text, which include avoiding heavily populated parts of the earth, safety measures, etc. As for stating responsibility and liability arising out of the use of NPS, reference can be made to the existing Principles 8 and 9.[397] This is very important since we note that in resolutions relating to environmental questions, state responsibility and liability are not referred to even in international agreements or conventions. A trend to omit these questions can be observed.[398] Considering the magnificent work having been done on space debris, it is also necessary to refer to this achievement as far as the issue of environmental protection is concerned. Anyhow, the conventions, resolutions and treaties, as long as they are related to space regulation, should be integrated and work effectively to supplement each other. Only in this way can space operations be carried out for the common interests of all mankind.

2.3.4. The Issue of War under the Guise of Research

While the high risks entailed in NPS applications were the main concerns for supporters of restrictive use of NPS, another topic can not be disregarded. This became even more important after September 11th with the severe challenge of terrorism. Besides the five original nuclear powers, several other states have claimed or been asserted to hold or have the ability to produce nuclear weapons. Nuclear power is no longer controlled by limited states, and the spreading of nuclear power adds to the concerns over the legitimate use of NPS.

NASA's announcement, to a certain extent, has relevance to the war against terrorism. How the Bush Blueprint on budget deficits and the war against terrorism will affect NASA is still under stressful study. However, states or relevant bodies may carry out space missions under the guise of research. The so-called "peaceful" use of NPS in space can be merely a cover to develop power systems to be used for space-based weapons. Once developed under the guise of space exploration, nuclear reactors could be used to drive dangerous space-based laser weapons. Such concerns are justified, however, as such a guise is difficult to identify. It is, thus, claimed that: the military's future testing and deployment of nuclear rocketry is necessary; security only works when people responsible for defence have access to advanced nuclear propulsion in space to perform the tasks.[399] Nevertheless, those concerns cannot hold back the earnest idea of using NPS for broader space missions.

Peaceful use of outer space has been widely advocated and enacted in several international documents. The Outer Space Treaty provides that States Parties undertake not to place in orbit around the earth any objects carrying nuclear weapons…, install such weapons on celestial bodies, or station such weapons in outer space in any other manner.[400] The

---

[397] See generally A. Bianchi, Environmental Harm Resulting from the Use of Nuclear Power Sources in Outer Space: Some Remarks on State Responsibility and Liability, in F. Francioni & T. Scovazzi (eds.), *International Responsibility for Environmental Harm*, 231-272 (Graham & Trotman, 1991).

[398] M. Benko, G. Gruber & K. Schrogl, The UN Committee on the Peaceful Uses of Outer Space: Adoption of Principles Relevant to the Use of Nuclear Power Sources in Outer Space, *Proceedings 36th Colloquium on the Law of Outer Space* 238 (1993).

[399] See further Behrhorst, *supra* note 79.

[400] Article IV of Space Treaty (1967).

International Space Station (ISS) Agreement[401] also provides the application for peaceful purposes.[402] However, the sensitive nature of NPS justifies the reiteration of this issue in the preamble of the Principles. The reiteration should, at least from the legal side, firmly rule out the possibility of war in outer space using NPS. Such a reiteration, while well accommodating concerns about war, shall provide a solid basis for claiming international liability in the possible use of NPS in outer space against terrorism.

2.3.5. Notification, Consultation and Miscellaneous

Naturally there are many other areas requiring improvements. Firstly, several terms need to be clarified, including "launching State" and "Procuring State".[403] Secondly, due to the high risks to humans and the environment, it is necessary to notify and hold consultations with relevant parties well before, during and after the formal launching activities. Principles 5 and 6 have provided a basic structure for notification and consultation. With further extension to broader space operations, notification and consultation appears even more essential. Various scholars have specified that Principle 5 is in conflict with the IAEA Convention on Early Notification of a Nuclear Accident, [404] it is necessary to elaborate this issue at this stage. One way out could be to make specific reference to this Convention, ensuring Principle 5 and the Convention are complementary in nature.[405]

Thirdly, to the extent space operations using NPS could harmfully interfere with other states, international consultations must be performed before proceeding with any such activity or experiment. This is also in accordance with the Outer Space Treaty.[406] Such an "obligatory" consultation could also provide a possible disincentive to carrying out space activities with military purposes.

2.4. The 1992 Principles: Resolution vs. Treaty

The General Assembly adopted the Principles as a Resolution in 1992. Considering the pros and cons during the negotiations, it was sensible to adopt such a resolution to fix the guidelines and criteria for safe use as a first step. It is obvious from the nature of the UN General Assembly and a Resolution that the Principles are addressed not only to the State Parties to the Outer Space Treaty but also to all the states.[407] The universal nature can, to a

---

[401] Agreement Among the Government of Canada, Government of Member States of the European Space Agency, The Government of Japan, The Government of the Russian Federation, and The Government of the United States of America Concerning Cooperation on the Civil International Space Station, January 29, 1998, in S. Gorove (ed.), *United States Space Law: National & International Regulation (IV)*, 98-1 (1998).

[402] Article 1(1) of the Agreement requires that uses of the ISS be reserved for peaceful purposes.

[403] C.Q. Christol, Nuclear Power Sources (NPS) for Space Objects: A New Challenge for International Law, *Proceedings 36th Colloquium on the Law of Outer Space* 248-251 (1993); see also E. Molodtsova, Nuclear Accidents on Space Objects with Nuclear Power Sources: Applicable International Law, Proceedings 34th Colloquium on the Law of Outer Space 142-144 (1991).

[404] See for example, M. Hoskova, The Notification Principle in the 1992 NPS Resolution, *Proceedings 36th Colloquium on the Law of Outer Space* (Graz, 1993), at 304-311; A.D. Terekhov, The 1986 IAEA Conventions on Nuclear Accidents and the Consideration of the Use of Nuclear Power Sources in Outer Space in the Legal Subcommittee of COPUOS, *Proceedings 30th Colloquium on the Law of Outer Space* 403 (1987).

[405] Jasentuliyana, *supra* note 69, at 318.

[406] See further Article IX of Space Treaty.

[407] See A.D. Terekhov, International Responsibility for Using Nuclear Power Sources in Outer Space-Reflections on the text adopted by COPUOS, *Proceedings 34th Colloquium on the Law of Outer Space* 147-149 (1991).

certain extent, strengthen the claim of the Principles as part of customary international law, which shall further give insight into the politically acceptable treatments of space.[408] However, the Resolution *per se* is not a formal legal instrument.[409] In view of the existing Conventions on space law, this resolution can, at most, be regarded as a supplement to the provisions of the Conventions with regard to the use of NPS by a set of recommendations.[410] The non-binding nature[411] has aroused some problems in further implementation, even though members generally highly respect the resolution. The resolution only codifies the international perspective on the hazards presented by NPS in space. Members have no obligation to strictly comply with the resolution. Once disputes arise, members can argue either way supporting their own position. The indeterminacy of the status of the Principles has, thus, allowed the implementation largely at the discretion of the members.

Indeed, many scholars have acknowledged that several Principles in the resolution represent customary international law. More specifically, this assertion refers to rules concerning notification and use of NPS in outer space that are of a fundamentally norm-creating character and could be regarded as forming the basis of a general character of law.[412] The international practice has further evidenced this view. Ample examples showed that international society conforms to the Principles defined in the resolution: sufficient notice, responsibility and liability, etc. Russia reported to the UN Secretary General of its anticipated launch of the Mars 96 satellite powered by plutonium-238;[413] the US notified the UN of its launch of the Cassini space probe, containing about 35 kg of plutonium-238 dioxide.[414]

To the extent customary law exists for space law at all, it binds all States whether their consent be express or implied by silence in the face of emerging legal norms.[415] However, what little customary law for space there is has been derived from the activity of very few states. This is exactly the truth in the use of NPS, only five states publicly claim to hold nuclear power and the rate of use has been comparatively low. Furthermore, with the increasing role of treaties both in international law in general and space law in particular, customary law is of far less importance and its significance for outer space activities has, in many aspects, not been secured.[416] Except for the principles widely regarded as part of customary international law, the status of other principles is not settled. This drawback can largely weaken the effect of the resolution on state practice.

After more than ten years of existence, it is the right time to consider concluding a treaty with regard to this issue. This is in accordance with the objective of the UN to the progressive

408 M.A. Gray, The International Crime of Ecocide, 26 *California Western International Law Journal* 247 (1996).

409 S. Tai & T. Bissett, 2000 Manfred Lachs Space Law Moot Court Competition: Winning Briefs: Respondent Brief, 13 *Georgetown International Environmental Law Review* 328-329 (Fall 2000).

410 V. Kopal, The Use of Nuclear Power Sources in Outer Space: A New Set of United Nations Principles?, *Proceedings 34th Colloquium on the Law of Outer Space* 128 (1991).

411 M.B. Gerrard, Asteroids and Comets: U.S. and International Law and the Lowest Probability, Highest Consequence Risk, 6 *New York University Environmental Law Journal* 44 (1997).

412 See *North Sea Continental Cases*, 1969 ICJ 3, at 71.

413 A.D. Terekhov, U.N.G.A. Resolutions and Outer Space Law, *Proceedings of the 40th Colloquium on the Law of Outer Space* 101 (1998).

414 Is Cassini Risky? Look to Facts, Not Emotion, 147 *Aviation Week & Space Technology*, No. 13, September 29, 1997, at 66.

415 This is a reiteration of the Article 38 of the Statute of the International Court of Justice with regard to International custom. See further P. Malanczuk, *Akehurst's Modern Introduction to International Law*, 44 (Routledge, 7th edition, 1997).

416 P. Malanczuk, Space Law as a Branch of International Law, 1994 *Netherlands Yearbook of International law* 147 (1995).

development and codification of international law. The binding nature of a treaty can provide a strong impetus to the legal use of NPS, even more meaningful to the legitimate use of NPS in the proposed extensive arena. Such a binding treaty can also help provide a mechanism for the international society in agreeing to the extended use of NPS and mitigating the anxiety.

2.5. Conclusion

The 1992 Principles provide a good framework for the use of NPS. Over the previous years, the international society has strictly complied with the Principles, creating an orderly regime for the use of NPS in outer space. Nevertheless, with rapid development of space technology, states have claimed that the use of NPS for other possible purpose is well justified. This trend is well led by the US in its NASA program, the ongoing review of the existing structure will, no doubt, exert a heavy influence on the existing legal framework established by this resolution. Acknowledging the advantages of using NPS in broader space operations, the technicians and space activists are leading the trend toward wider use of NPS. The theoretical debate on the appropriateness of such a wider use should, no doubt, give way to the pragmatic approach in formulating a proper legal framework in coping with the incoming severe challenge. The improvement of the legal framework shall include not only the substantive part but also the formality of such a document. The initiative taken by NASA can be the right incident that touches off the revision of the resolution, provide an impetus to the realization of a formal treaty in this field and push the development of a space treaty after a blank period of space law legislation. A large portion of the cost can be saved or devoted to more promising projects if the result of the revision is known as early as possible. It is expected that the improved Principles shall well accommodate the renewed call for the application of NPS in broader space activities and the well-being of modern society as a whole.

3. Space Tourism and Formulation of Space Rules

"Just tell me the general idea you have in mind-the idea Sven and my daughter keep so mysteriously to themselves. What is this thing that's so revolutionary and so daring? Fantastic and at the same time logical? I'm quoting, of course, my daughter." He looked steadily at Lee. His eyes brightened as if an inner light had been turned on. Lee glanced at the architect and the girl. He found response in their faces. "I need your assistance in building a hotel in outer space," he said artlessly.[417]

3.1. Introduction

A story like the above must be the truly classic scene for space futurists. Outer space exhibits an unlimited source for the imaginative science fiction writers. Earlier in the mid-19th

[417] Kurt Siodmak, *Skyport* (Mass, 1959). See further Space Tourism in Science Fiction, available at <http://www.spacefuture.com/tourism/sciencefiction.shtml> (last visited October 11, 2004).

century a number of science fiction stories have been written showing the rich imagination from renowned authors.[418] Space tourism was among the most popular topics for those writers. But no one has taken this idea so seriously at that time as in the late 20th century.

The successful launch of first satellite-Sputnik I in 1957[419] and Gagarin's first manned space flight in 1961[420] marked a breakthrough in space history. The rapid development of space technology brings the dream of conquering outer space to a reality. State monopoly has been the typical characteristic of space activities since the launch of Sputnik I. The space treaties formulated by the United Nations (UN) also acknowledged this fact, which has been well justified by the large amount of investment and the long period of time needed to realize the benefits. However, private parties have increasingly shown interests in space activities, posing strong challenges to the former regime.

Space tourism, considered not an area of priority for commercialization, has never been so heatedly discussed until the historic arrival of two "unexpected" tourists-American Dennis Tito and the twenty-eight year-old South African multimillionaire Mark Shuttleworth-at the International Space Station (ISS) in April 2001[421] and April 2002[422] respectively. The ISS partners officially cleared the way for space tourism with the approval of the two visits.[423] However, these private visits were very costly except for some tycoons. As reported, Tito and Shuttleworth flew to the ISS for an amount of US$ 20 million each[424]. This amount is impossible to most people.

However, market research has clearly demonstrated that many people have strong interest in space travel if it were more affordable. These wishes can be met with the development of reusable launch vehicle (RLV) technology, which could reduce space launch costs from $ 10, 000 per pound to $ 1, 000 per pound.[425] Just as Bachula stated, "reliable, affordable access to space is a fundamental prerequisite if we are to realize the full potential of the outer space frontier."[426]

The development of space tourism no doubt calls for a legal regime, which can better regulate the market and offer clear guidance and expected outcomes. It has been widely

---

[418] Jules Verne, a French writer, authored several science fiction stories and the most famous amongst was entitled "De La Terre `a la Lune" in 1865.

[419] Sputnik I was launched from the Baiknur Cosmodrome in Southern Kazakstan on October 4, 1957. See Craig Covault, Policy and Technology Shape Manned Space Ops, *Aviation Week & Space Technology*, January 8, 2001, at 44.

[420] The First Cosmonaut in the World is in Space, April 1, 1998, available at <http://news.bbc.co.uk/1/hi/special_report/1998/03/98/gagarin/72182.stm> (last visited March 30, 2005).

[421] Anna Badkhen, US Tourist Arrives at Space Station: Tito is Greeted by Russians after Weekend Flight, *Boston Globe*, May 1, 2001, at C4.

[422] First African in Space, available at <http://www.africaninspace.com/home/mission/logs/1/index.shtml> (last visited March 30, 2005).

[423] Decision Paper on Russian Aviation and Space Agency (Rosaviakosmos) Request for MCB Approval of Exemption to Fly Mr. Dennis Tito Aboard the April 2001 Soyuz 2 Taxi Flight to the International Space Station, April 24, 2001, available at <http://ftp.hq.nasa.gov/pub/pao/reports/2001/tito<uscore>decision.pdf> (last visited March 19, 2003).

[424] Peter Baker, U.S., Russia Agree to Allow "Space Tourists", *Washington Post*, August 10, 2001, at A 20; see also African Space Tourist Ends $ 20 Million Odyssey, May 5, 2002, available at <http://edition.cnn.com/2002/TECH/space/05/04/sfrica.tourist> (last visited March 30, 2005).

[425] Roscoe M. Moore, Risk Analysis and the Regulation of Reusable Launch Vehicles, 64 *Journal of Air Law & Commerce* 245, 251 (1998).

[426] Statement of Gary R. Bachula, Acting Undersecretary for Technology, US Department of Commerce, US Commercial Space Launch Industry: Hearing before the Subcommittee on Science, Technology and Space of the Senate Committee on Commerce, Science, and Transportation, 105th Congress (1998).

argued that the existing international space treaties are inadequate for space commercialization. The development of a clear and predictable legal regime before space tourism becomes affordable for the masses is essential It is noted that the Russian Space Agency had intended to send two civilians into outer space every calendar year until the February 1, 2003 Space Shuttle Columbia disaster.[427]

Space tourism is also an interesting topic in China. It has been reported that the first Chinese space tour is expected as early as in 2006, though it did not come out as expected.[428] Similar reports are expected from other nations in the coming period.

With the strong demand for space tourism a strong legal regime is essential, no matter whether the RLVs can be successfully developed in the near future or not. As long as the space travel technology is mature, there are always business opportunities for space tourism. The present section discusses the potential for a commercial space tourism industry and advocates a legal regime. Part two offers a comparison of space and air travel and the rules applicable to each traveling means. This part further proposes an appropriate liability regime for space travel, trying to borrow the experience from air transportation. Part three examines the appropriate level of state interference through licensing measures. Part four specifically discusses the status of space tourists, as differed from astronauts. Part five concludes that current space law inadequately addresses space tourism and that the inadequacies justify an urgent need to develop an appropriate legal regime for the development of space tourism.

3.2. Space Travel and Air Transportation: Different Applicable Law

The Wright Brothers' successful flight at Kitty Kawk in 1903 opened a new era in transportation history. The international society was quick to respond to develop a legal regime regulating commercial air transportation. The Warsaw Convention was formulated in 1929 to develop a forward-looking international aviation regime. The regime proved to be vital to the development of the air transportation industry by balancing cost prohibitive insurance premiums and liability measures protecting the struggling airline industry.

Space travel stands exactly at the same crossroad as air transportation in the early 1920s. The potential liability for accidents is a major obstacle. The legal vacuum in this respect deters the commercializing process of space travel. Insurance is not the way out since the cost prohibitive insurance premiums for space travel will be passed on to the tourists and the ticket price will go far beyond a reasonable level as to kill the whole space industry. Accordingly, the formulation of an appropriate liability regime for space travel appears all the more important.

Air transportation and space travel share a number of similarities, leading to the discussion of extending the air transportation regime to space travel. The discussion again goes back the classic question on the boundary of outer space and air space, and thus the application of air law and space law.

Outer space begins where territorial air space ends. There is currently no clear internationally recognized boundary of outer space [429]and consequently not a proper

[427] STS-107: Columbia Disaster, February 1, 2003, available at <http://www.space.com/columbiatragedy> (last visited March 30, 2005).

[428] First Chinese to have Space Travel, available at <http://news.creaders.net/headline/newsPool/30A220050.html> (last visited November 1, 2004).

definition despite the separate bodies of international law governing air space and outer space.[430] Striking criteria distinguishing air space and outer space for applicable law include purpose and function, technical configuration and capabilities, and the medium where the operation predominantly takes place.[431] Space travel, as denoted by its concept, has clearly classified itself as activities in outer space; furthermore, activities in sufficient distance from the earth have no problem in justifying the application of space law for space travel.

The air transportation regime, characterized by state sovereignty over air space, substantially differs from the space travel regime where no state can claim sovereignty over outer space. This fundamental difference justifies the necessity of developing a distinct legal regime for space travel. Nevertheless, we should not neglect the fact that air transportation and space travel, though in different geographical locations, are basically transportation in essence. While the vehicles used for space tourism are rocket-powered and designed to enter outer space, they take off and land like airplane.[432] Taking space vehicles to outer space will be like taking an airplane for the travelers, although the destinations are different. Space travel, while still in its infancy, is similar to the air transportation industry in its early stage. The question posed to the air transportation industry comes to space travel now: how to alleviate the liability so that the regime can effectively promote the rapid development and commercialization of the industry. In this regard, we can certainly borrow the successful legal experience of air transportation to facilitate the formulation of an appropriate regime for space travel.

3.2.1. Commercial Liability Regime

By referring to the liability issue in outer space, one may immediately think of the Outer Space Treaty and the 1972 Liability Convention. Article VII of the Outer Space Treaty provides that states are internationally liable for any damage caused by their objects or personnel while in space. The Liability Convention, further elaborating on Article VII of the Outer Space Treaty, envisions two situations when the launching state(s) are liable: damage caused by its space object on the surface of the earth or to aircraft in flight; damage being caused elsewhere than on the surface of the earth to a space object of one launching state or to persons or property on board such a space object by a space object of another launching state. Strict liability applies to the first situation[433] while negligence liability to the latter[434].

---

[429] Report of the Legal Subcommittee on its 41st Session held in Vienna from April 2-12, 2002, United Nations Committee on the Peaceful Uses of Outer Space, UN Doc. A/AC.105/787, at 10 (2002).

[430] I.H.Ph. Diederiks-Verschoor, *An Introduction to Space Law* 5 (2nd ed., Kluwer, 1999).

[431] Michael Wollersheim, Considerations towards the Legal Framework of Space Tourism, 2nd International Symposium on Space Tourism, Bremen, April 21-23, 1999, available at <http://www.spacefuture.com/archive/considerations_towards_the_legal_framework_of_space_tourism.shtml > (last visited April 25, 2005).

[432] Recent Development: Commercialization of Space Commercial Space Launch Amendments Act of 2004, 17 *Harvard Journal of Law & Technology* 626 (Spring 2004).

[433] The Liability Convention, Article II provides, "A launching state shall be absolutely liable to pay compensation for damage caused by its space object on the surface of the earth or to aircraft in flight."

[434] The Liability Convention, Article III provides, "In the event of damage being caused elsewhere than on the surface of the earth to a space object of one launching state or to persons or property on board such a space object by a space object of another launching state, the latter shall be liable only if the damage is due to its fault or the fault of persons for whom it is responsible."

In view of its international nature, this Convention does not apply to two types of people, including the nationals of the launching state.[435] Furthermore, only a state may present a claim for compensation.[436] Accordingly, the Convention fails to specifically outline civilian liability in space.[437]

The ISS IGA, while incorporating the Liability Convention, has further included a provision concerning the mutual exemption of liability on board the ISS for the purpose of better cooperation among the partners. This provision applies to any claims brought by a Partner State for damage, against another Partner State, a related entity of another Partner State, and/or the employees of any of the above entities.[438] Obviously, space passengers cannot rely on this provision for any claims. The public nature of the IGA does not fit well in the present commercial regime. Liability arising out of the disputes in space tourism should be resolved according to the general international law. Thus, the space object shall be regarded as an extension of the jurisdiction of the launching state, whose law prevails.

The current liability system thereby excludes space tourism and only extends to efforts by states or international non-governmental organizations sending equipment and astronauts into space for the purpose of exploration and scientific research[439].[440]

Liability to passengers is the main concern in space tourism, which is totally missing in the relevant conventions. In the air transportation legal system, domestic and international transportation are differentiated, which shall not exist in space travel. National passengers of a launching state, like that in international air transportation, should be allowed to claim compensation for damages suffered; accordingly, a uniform regime should be introduced covering all the passengers, goods and related natural and legal persons directly.

In international air transportation, the Warsaw Convention[441] sets a good example in helping to establish a uniform international system, which has further enabled insurance companies to provide coverage in a new field of international transportation with confidence.[442] A negligence standard, instead of strict liability, was adopted and maximum damages to a passenger were originally set at $ 10, 000.[443] However, the limitation of liability in the Convention is now considered unnecessary in view of the improving reliability of

---

435 The Liability Convention, Article VII provides, "The provisions of this Convention shall not apply to damage caused by a space object of a launching state to : (a) nationals of that launching state; (b) foreign nationals during such time as they are participating in the operation of that space object from the time of its launching or at any stage thereafter until its descent, or during such time as they are in the immediate vicinity of a planned launching or recovery area as the result of an invitation by that launching state."

436 The Liability Convention, Article VIII (1) provides, "A state which suffers damage, or whose natural or juridical persons suffer damage, may present to a launching state a claim for compensation for such damage."

437 Nandasiri Jasentuliyana, *International Space Law and the United Nations* 390 (1999).

438 Article16, para. 3 (a), the 1998 IGA.

439 Richard Berkley, Space Law Versus Space Utilization: The Inhibition of Private Industry in Outer Space, 15 *Wisconsin International Law Journal* 422 (1997); Joseph A. Bosco, International Law regarding Outer Space-An Overview, 55 *Journal of Air Law & Commerce* 614-620 (1990)

440 Ezra J. Reinstein, Owning Outer Space, 20 *Northwestern Journal of International Law & Business* 71 (1999).

441 Convention for the Unification of Certain Rules Relating to International Carriage by Air, opened for signature October 12, 1929, 49 Stat. 3000, 137 U.N.T.S. 11.

442 Patrick Collins, The Regulatory Agenda for the Era of Passenger Space Transportation, Proceedings of 20th ISTS, Paper No. 96-f-13, available at <http://www.spacefuture.com/archive/the_regulatory_reform_agenda_for_the_era_of_passenger_space_transportation.shtml> (last visited April 28, 2005).

443 James E. Dunstan, Is Launching a Rocket Still an Ultra-Hazardous Activity? Toward a Negligence Theory for Launch Activities, 9 *Space Manufacturing the High Frontier: Accession, Development & Utilization* 226, 229 (1993).

aviation; the 1999 Montreal Convention shows the sign for relaxing the above limitation.[444] Nevertheless, this Convention proves to provide the protection and freedom necessary for the air transportation industry. The industry was able to flourish and has now become the safest means of transportation.[445] The Warsaw Convention has been under revision, trying to balance the interests of the industry and other parties (including passengers and third parties). The maximum amount of damages has been changed according to social environment. However, the negligence standard remains the ground stone of the Convention.[446]

The success of the international aviation system indicates that a negligence standard should be initially introduced for space travel. The maximum damages payable to passengers should be formulated. Limiting the carrier's liability will not necessarily deter potential space tourists since they can buy additional insurance, as the case in aviation. An appropriate amount shall be determined based on several factors, including the ultimate goal of pushing the development of space travel, the financial situation of the space travel industry, and the general background of space passengers. The duration of liability should similarly be the period during which the accident takes place on board the space object or in the course of any of the operations of embarking or disembarking.[447]

Legislation providing the above propositions is indispensable for space tourism. The uncertainty concerning the liability issue can make potential investors afraid that any unknown future regulation may kill the business they are investing in. We may simply modify the Warsaw Convention for space tourism, but of course, we can formulate a new document written along similar lines.[448] By referring to the proposed document, space tourists, governments, commercial operators and insurance companies would all know in advance of possible liabilities and make sensible decisions. Thus, the international society will benefit from the transparency and legitimacy brought by such an international document.

3.2.2. Space Insurance

Space insurance has been available for a couple of years, especially in the field of satellite launching activities. Further development of space activities has called for more active involvement of private parties. However, a complete set of rules are still to be formulated to realize private financing for space program. In view of the high risks in space activities, the availability of insurance has been a critical element for private parties. Insurance provides relief for a whole range of liability risks currently associated with space activities, including space tourism.

---

444 See for example Montreal Convention, Article 17. The carrier is always liable to a maximum amount of 100, 000 SDR; for damages exceeding this amount, the carrier is liable without limitation unless he proves that the damage was not the result of his negligence or wrongful act (nor of his servants or agents), or such damage was solely due to the negligence or wrongful act of a third party. From this provision, it is obvious that a strict liability applies to the carrier.

445 Between 1959 and 2002, there were 1, 337 accidents worldwide out of a total of 412 million departures. However, approximately 40, 000 people died in automobile accidents and 1096 in railway accidents each year. See U.S. department of Transportation, A Comparison of Risk, Accidental Deaths-United States-1994-1998, at <http://hazmat.dot.gov/riskcompare.htm> (last visited November 4, 2004).

446 The Guatemala Protocol in 1971 provides that the fault liability at present attaching to the carrier will be changed into a risk liability. However few states have ratified this Protocol to date.

447 See Article 17 of the Warsaw Convention.

448 Anders Lindskold, Space Tourism and Its Effects on Space Commercialization, Master of Space Studies Program 1998/99, available at <http://www.spacefuture.com/pr/archive/space_tourism_and_its_effects_on_space_commercialization.shtml> (last visited April 29, 2005).

Space insurance may be divided into two categories: insurance of space objects and liability insurance. Of course other categories of insurance which are related to space activities also exist, such as product liability insurance. As mentioned above, insurance of space objects have been in existence. Three types of insurance can be further differentiated: pre-launching insurance; launch failure and initial operation insurance; and insurance of the satellite itself.[449] The first satellite insurance contract providing for pre-launching insurance services was concluded in 1965 for Intelsat's "Early Bird".[450] The US Commercial Space Launch Act (CSA) requires entities that launch space vehicles to purchase $ 500 million in third-party liability insurance.[451] It is thus nothing anew. The legal basis and principle of insurance remain to be largely applicable.

However, the CSA further provides that the US government will cover excess damages up to $ 1.5 billion and that the launch entities are liable for any damage beyond the $ 2 billion.[452] Understandably, considering the high risks involved in launching activities, insurance companies are not willing to take possibly high damages. As provided in the CSA, an insurance provider may list specific exclusions to the insured's liability insurance policy.[453] To a certain extent, the US government acts as an excess insurance carrier, providing a layer on top of the required insurance. On the other hand, insurance policies for commercial launch activities have not been standardized and need to be negotiated on a case-by-case basis.[454] To a certain extent, insurance companies' confidence concerning the scale of risks involved in launching depends much on agreed standards of acceptable risk.[455]

The CSA insurance requirements do not mention space tourists.[456] Insurance for the carrier's liability for the tourists is thus something new to be added to the insurance industry with the development of space tourism. The existence of liability insurance cooperates with the commercial liability regime for space tourism. However, insurance companies might be again unwilling to undertake too much risk. As one scholar has identified, "[I]f tourism is to become a vital part of the commercial space equation, limits on liability for the owners and operators of space facilities and vehicles will be a necessity."[457] Limits exist for liability arising out of death, personal injury or loss or damage to property; limits can also be set for each and every space flight. Several factors are relevant to the fixed limits, including the length of flight, module and model of space objects; experience of astronauts; air condition during the flight.

One the one hand, it is important to introduce insurance to the space tourism industry. At the present stage, this young industry requires support from various corners. The insurance industry is indispensable to space carriers, given the high market value of spacecraft and the

---

449 I.H.Ph. Diederiks-Verschoor, *An Introduction to Space Law* 117 (2nd Ed., Kluwer, 1999).
450 *Id.*, at 117.
451 49 U.S.C. 70, 112 (2003).
452 *Id.*
453 14 C.F.R. 440.13(a)(5).
454 Peter D. Nesgos, The Challenges Facing the Private Practitioner: Liability and Insurance Issues in Commercial Space Transportation, 4 Journal of Law & Technology 25-26 (Winter 1989).
455 Statement of Patricia A. Mahoney, Chair, Satellite Industry Association, Extension of Space Launch Indemnification: Hearing before the Subcommittee on Space and Aeronautics of the House Committee on Science, 106th Cong. (1999).
456 See generally 49 U.S.C. 70, 112 (2003).
457 Patrick Collins, The Regulatory Reform Agenda for the Era of Passenger Space Transportation, Proceedings of 20th ISTS, Paper No. 96-f-13 (1993), available at <http://www.spacefuture.com/archive/the_regulatory_reform_agenda_for_the_era_of_passenger_space_transportation.shtml> (last visited April 28, 2005).

great financial risks. On the other hand, it is critical to set an appropriate rate so that the insurance industry is willing to enter this potentially profitable market. Again, we can borrow successful experience from aviation. The evolution of space technology has a close relationship with the insurance industry. We are fortunate to see that the insurance industry has been mature enough to accept the risks in space industry since 1965.

The development of space tourism has introduced a new challenging market for the insurance industry. This will probably cause a temporary increase in premiums. But in the long run, with the progress of space technology and safety improvement, insurance premiums will be reduced.

3.2.3. Criminal Jurisdiction Regime

The criminal jurisdiction issue has so far been considered as not highly relevant to outer space activities. Currently no international treaty exists for crimes committed on private space vehicles.[458] This situation is understandable when space activities are still largely monopolized by the state. The people on board the space object are normally astronauts trained for a special mission. The commander on board the space object has the authority to enforce order and discipline during the whole flight phase.

The ISS Agreement provides the authority of a commander on board the ISS to maintain order. However, it is notable that the ISS Agreement contains a provision on criminal jurisdiction. This is necessary in view of the long-term character of the ISS and the international and multicultural character of the astronauts on board the ISS. Besides the execution of criminal jurisdiction over its nationals, article 22 further provides the jurisdiction over nationals of another Partner State whose conduct in orbit "(a) affects the life or safety of a national of another Partner State or (b) occurs in or on or causes damage to the flight element of another Partner State". It is thus obvious that the criminal jurisdiction is based on customary principles of nationality and the protective principle. That means, the criminal law of the victim's country will normally apply.

However, the development of space tourism brings new trouble. Space tourists are less prepared and controlled than astronauts, increasing the risk of criminal activities. Furthermore, the situation when a non-member country tourist becomes the target of a criminal offence, which is often the case in space tourism, will bring trouble to the above arrangement among the members. Will a non-member country's law be applied here? The arrangement in the ISS Agreement becomes insufficient to deal with similar new problems.

In this aspect, we can refer to the similar situation in air transportation. The Tokyo Convention imposes a series of obligations upon the Contracting States that are geared towards stamping out hijacking. According to this Convention, apart from national criminal jurisdiction, each state shall take measures as may be necessary to establish its jurisdiction over the offense and any act of violence against a passenger or crew when (a) the offense is committed on board an aircraft registered in that state....[459] The above provision is claimed to establish the "semi-universal jurisdiction principle". All states have the criminal jurisdiction over any acts causing danger to the aviation industry, which has important impact on the safe operation of the industry and the confidence from the passengers.

---

[458] R. Thomas Rankin, Space Tourism: Fanny Packs, Ugly T-Shirts, and the Law in Outer Space, 36 *Suffolk University Law Review* 716 (2003).

[459] Tokyo convention, Article 4 (3).

Space travel also needs to build confidence from potential passengers, preventing the infant industry from fatal criminal activities. The "semi-universal jurisdiction principle" in the air transportation is also meaningful to space travel. Interested parties should convene to discuss the draft of a similar treaty cracking down criminal acts against space safety.

3.3. Registration and Licensing Regime

As mentioned above, large scale space tourism depends on the development of reusable launch vehicles (RLVs). No doubt, RLVs are space objects as identified in the Registration Convention. According to this Convention, each party is required to register and maintain a registry of its launched space objects;[460] in addition, the party must provide the UN Secretary-General information proving the establishment of a registry.[461] This requirement is reasonable for purposes like identification of space objects and determining liability. However, when space tourism develops and the launching of RLVs becomes more and more frequent, the requirement of registration appears infeasible and unnecessary. However, national registry is sufficient for the above purposes. Thus, two types of registration are suggested: that the current registration regime continues to exist; however, once space objects like RLVs are used specifically for commercial space travel, only national registry be required.

To guarantee the safety of space travel and enforcement of the international obligation of peaceful use of outer space, the state should establish a licensing regime which can provide sufficient supervisory function over space tourism. An appropriate licensing regime, as the safety valve for security in space travel is the obligation of the relevant state in guaranteeing the legitimate operation of those licensees.

The US has established a rather complete legal framework in the licensing regime. The CSA of 1998 laid the regulatory groundwork for RLV licensing. According to the CSA, prospective applicants are required to participate in pre-application consultations with the office of the Associate Administrator for Commercial Space Transportation (FAA-AST);[462] following pre-application consultations, applicants must obtain policy approval, safety approval, payload and payload reentry approval, and environmental approval.[463] The requirements have been argued to be too complicated, which will ultimately prevent private companies from getting off the ground.[464]

The 2004 Space Launch Act Amendment, [465] with the aim of regulatory reform and improved interaction with RLV developers, has further ensured its purpose to promote the development of the emerging commercial human space flight industry.[466] It represents the trend of deregulation in the field to avoid "the potential danger of industry-killing over-

460 Registration Convention, Article 2.
461 Registration Convention, Article 2 and 4.
462 14 C.F.R. 431.31.
463 14 C.F.R. 413.5, 415 (2001).
464 Charity Trelease Ryabinkin, Let there be Flight: It's Time to Reform the Regulation of Commercial Space Travel, 69 *Journal of Air Law and Commerce* 129 (Winter 2004).
465 H.R. 3752, 108th Cong. (2004).
466 House Floor Debate on Commercial Space Launch Act of 2004, House of Representatives, November 19, 2004, available at <http://www.spaceref.com/news/viewsr.html?pid=14565> (last visited December 1, 2004).

regulation".[467] For example, the time period needed for relevant bodies to take actions has been clearly defined, thereby preventing unduly interference from relevant bodies.[468] Considering the high risks entailed and unwavering emphasis on safety, the complex licensing process is retained. However, it has been acknowledged that a more streamlined system of requirements is needed to facilitate the licensing process.[469]

The US example clearly shows the vital role of a licensing regime in commercial space activities and represents the first significant step towards nurturing and supporting commercial efforts in space tourism. In view of the complicated but indispensable licensing process, the FAA/AST has taken realistic measures to work directly with RLV developers, helping them better understand the process and reflecting their concerns in future space flight policy. This will help streamline the licensing requirements.

3.4. The Status of Space Tourists (Space Hotel Rules)

The emergence of space tourists who go to outer space for leisure pose challenges to the existing space legal regime. The astronauts as defined in the 1968 Rescue Agreement outlines procedures for astronaut rescues if the astronauts in an accident, distress, emergency or an unintended landing are on the high seas or in any other place not under the jurisdiction of any nation.[470] According to the Agreement, nations are obliged to perform rescue duties for the personnel of a spacecraft in the event of accident, distress or emergency landing.[471] It is to be noted that "personnel of a spacecraft", instead of "astronaut", is used in the text of the Agreement. Obviously, the term "personnel of a spacecraft" does not necessarily limit to only astronauts.

Literally, tourists are not astronauts or the personnel of a spacecraft. If they are the same as mission specialists, like space engineers or scientists, there will not be much dispute concerning the application of Rescue Agreement.[472] For example, the first space tourist Tito spent six days on board as both a tourist and as an assistant to the crew, helping with a variety of tasks to include the transfer of supplies and scientific experiments.[473]

However, this is only an exceptional case. Space tourists generally do not play a direct role for the benefit and in the interests of all countries. Their main objective is not to

---

467 H.R. 3752, 108th Congress, 2nd Session, Report No. 108-429, available at <http://www.theorator.com/bills108/hr3752.html> (last visited December 1, 2004).

468 For example, Art. 3(c)(7) provides that the Secretary of Transportation shall issue the experimental permit required by human space vehicle operators no later than ninety days after receipt of an application and that the Secretary of Transportation would be obliged to inform the applicant of any issues arising during the review of an application and actions to be taken to resolve them, within the first sixty days after the receipt of the application.

469 Ryabinlin, *supra* note 155, at 137.

470 Rescue Agreement, Article 1-4.

471 Rescue Agreement, Article 1. David Tan, Towards a New Regime for the Protection of Outer Space as the "Province of All Mankind", 25 *Yale Journal of International Law* 158 (2000); Ty S. Twibell, Space Law: Legal Constraints on Commercialization and Development of Outer Space, 65 *UMKC Law Review* 595 (1997).

472 Yasuaki Hashimoto, The Space Plane and International Space Law, available at <http://www.spacefuture.com/pr/archive/the_space_plane_and_international...> (last visited October 11, 2004).

473 Jim Banke, Space Tourist Pays His Full Fare, available at <http://www.msnbc.com/news/509288.asp> (last visited January 2, 2001).

contribute to the public interest, but just for their personal pleasure. In no sense do they qualify as "envoys of mankind in outer space" [474]. Accordingly, obstacles exist in applying the Rescue Agreement to space tourists.

Nevertheless, just as identified in the preface, the Rescue Agreement is prompted by sentiments of humanity. This consideration similarly applies to the rescue of tourists. Thus, ways need to be sorted out to deal with the issue of rescuing tourists in the event of accident, distress or emergency landing. Two ways can be easily identified: formulation of a new agreement with similar provisions of the Rescue Agreement, or extending the existing agreement to the application of space tourists. Considering similar measures underlying the rescue of astronauts and tourists, may logically lead to the second option.

In this respect, the 2004 Commercial Space Launch Amendments Act and the ISS Agreement offer useful experience. The two documents take different approaches. The 2004 Act clearly defines two different types of people involved in space flight. It provides definitions for the terms "crew" and "space flight participants" and amends existing commercial launch legislation to include these terms alongside the inanimate payloads currently covered.[475] According to this Act, "crew" means "any employee of a licensee or transferee, or of a contractor or subcontractor of a licensee or transferee, who performs activities in the course of that employment directly relating to the launch, reentry, or other operation of or in a launch vehicle or reentry vehicle that carries human being".[476] "Space flight participant" means "an individual, who is not crew, carried within a launch vehicle or reentry vehicle".[477] So it is quite obvious space tourists are considered as space flight participants. This is a direct way to differentiate "crew" from "space tourists". However, this approach does not effectively resolve the issue of protection for space tourists as defined in the Rescue Convention.

The ISS Agreement, same as the Rescue Agreement, defines the term "crew" as qualified personnel.[478] But this Agreement further provides the activities of all individuals involved in outer space activities under the heading "Protected Space Operations".[479] This extensive provision validly resolves the above dilemma: the ISS Agreement covers all individuals, no matter if he/she is piloting a spacecraft, conducting experiments or merely a passenger for fun. By covering anyone whoever is piloting a space object, conducting experiments or merely traveling for fun, this approach is instructive to extend application of the Rescue Agreement to space tourists.[480]

While receiving necessary protections, space tourists, as passengers of a spacecraft, should also comply with rules for good order during the journey. Basically their rights and obligations fall within the competence of the State exercising jurisdiction and control, namely, the State of registry of the RLV. The commander, providing for the safety and well-being of all persons on board, shall have sole authority throughout the flight; tourists, irrespective of their nationality, are subject to the directions of the commander.

---

[474] Outer Space Treaty, Article 5.
[475] Recent Development, *supra* note 129, at 627.
[476] H.R. 3752, 108th Congress (2004), Article 3 (b) (2).
[477] H.R. 3752, 108th Congress (2004), Article 3 (b) (9).
[478] ISS IGA, Article 11 (1).
[479] ISS IGA, Article 16 (2)(f).
[480] Lara L. Manzione, Multinational Investment in the Space Station: An Outer Space Model for International Cooperation?, *18 American University International Law Review* 521 (2002).

3.5. Conclusion

Space tourism has received great interest from various sides. Some scholars believe that space tourism may be one of the first space industries to emerge and that it will pave the way for everything else.[481] Encouraged by the success of the first two space tourists, space tourism companies, having been set up in recent years and are actively promoting the program and soliciting support from the governments. As reported, Hong Kong Space Travel Agency has signed a cooperative agreement in early 2005 with American Space Exploration Company; more than 20 Chinese tourists will be sent to the US for training.[482] The reports released so far have sent a clear sign to the public that space tourism has come to a new era.

Drastically different from other means of transportation, such as shipping and aviation, which are governed by a comprehensive framework of national and international commercial law, space activities are supported by inter-governmental treaties negotiated during the cold-war period. While commercial space tourism is coming to reality, the legal regime is still lagging far behind. In view of the many commonalities shared by aviation and space travel, the present section takes the example of aviation and elaborates on the formulation of a legal regime for space tourism. Actually it is gradually being accepted that the most appropriate regulatory framework for space tourism is to treat it as an extension of aviation.[483] A proper and attractive legal regime will in the end help assure the future of safe and responsible commercial space tourism.

[481] Albert A. Harrison, *Spacefaring: The Human Dimension* 12 (2001).

[482] The First Chinese Tourist Expected to Explore in Space Next Year, February 28, 2005, available at <http://tour.huash.com/gb/tour/2005-02/28/content_1668183.htm> (last visited March 8, 2005).

[483] Patrick Collins & Koichi Yonemoto, Legal and Regulatory Issues for Passenger Space Travel, *Proceedings 49th Colloquium on the Law of Outer Space*, available at <http://www.spacefuture.com/pr/archive/legal_and_regulatory_issues_for_passenger_space_travel.shtml> (last visited October 11, 2004).

Chapter 5

LIBERALIZATION OF TELECOMMUNICATIONS SERVICES

1. WTO REGIME FOR TELECOMMUNICATIONS SERVICES

1.1. Introduction

Since time immemorial, one of man's greatest desires has been to communicate with others. To achieve this goal, his intelligent mind invented different ways of communication. The fervent desire to communicate accelerated the invention of different systems for this purpose and in the end, resulted in the emergence of telecommunication,[484] which has revolutionized communications and has an enormous educational as well as entertainment potential.[485] Indeed, during the development of modem society, few inventions, if any, have transformed our economic, social, political and cultural lives in a more dramatic fashion than satellite technology.[486]

Formerly, the sector of telecommunications has been regarded as vital to national economic development and security, which excluded foreign services.[487] Due to its technical and economic features, monopoly in this sector has been taken for granted. However, in the new era, things are changing.

Economic development was endowed with priority status in national agendas. Bearing this in mind, no States can be truly isolated from international society. How to achieve the maximum economic advantage through international trade is even more urgent for developing States. Globalization has proven successful in achieving this objective. From the 1940s onwards, liberalization of goods was on track and ostensible results have been obtained through several negotiations under the auspices of the GATT. The successful experience

---

484 See further N. M. Matte, Aerospace Law: Telecommunications Satellites, *Recueil des Cours*, No.I, at 129 (1980); see also generally ITU, *From Semaphore to Satellite* (1965); J. O. Pastore, *The Story of Communications: From Beacon to Telstar* (1964).

485 M. N. Shaw, *International Law*, 386 (4th ed., 1997); see also e.g. the use by India of US satellite to beam educational television programs to thousands of isolated settlements that would otherwise not have been reached, *Digest of US Practice in International Law (DUSPIL)*, 427-428 (1976).

486 I.H.Ph. Diederiks-Verschoor, *An Introduction to Space Law*, 51 (1993).

487 See further T. G. Berg, Trade in Services: Toward a "Development Round" of GATT Negotiations Benefiting Both Developing and Industrialized States, 28 *Harvard International Law Journal*, No.1, at 19 (1987).

inspired the problem of whether the rule of GATT can also be applied to services. However, it was yet too soon to see the benefits of liberalization of services. Not until 1986, when the Uruguay round of negotiations started, did such an issue reach the ambit of general notice.[488]

This is partly due to the significant portion in national revenue. Since then, services became a larger force in the world economy and liberalization in services has been intensively dealt with. After seven and half years of negotiations, the Uruguay Round of GATT was finally completed on 15 April 1994 with 111 of the 125 participating States signing the final document.[489] The Final Act contains the results of intense negotiations by fifteen negotiating groups and includes the General Agreement on Trade in Services (GATS), which also includes telecommunications services in a special annex.[490]

From then on, telecommunications liberalization is well underway around the world. It seemed unimaginable to bring competition to the telecommunications industry even thirty years ago. States' attitudes towards telecommunications have thus changed drastically. The regulatory opening up to competition stems from two main factors.

Firstly, the early deregulation undertaken in industrialized countries such as the United States and Japan has given a new international dimension to the sector, which was traditionally rooted in domestic markets. Due to deregulation, American and Japanese telecommunication operators have been able to impose themselves at the forefront of the international scene, and to penetrate foreign markets - whenever possible - using the dominant positions secured in their own domestic markets as market leverage.[491]

Secondly, technological development has further stimulated the integration of the telecommunications sector. By accelerating the speed and efficiency of transmitting information worldwide, modem telecommunications technology is significantly affecting the realm of international services transactions, both by allowing for new or improved services which enter directly into international trade and by enhancing the tradability of traditional services.[492] New opportunities also arose in accordance with the new technological conditions and the range of both supply and demand has been increased. In particular, developments in microelectronics, digital technology and the increased sophistication of software, associated with new transmission techniques (optical fiber and satellite) have significantly modified the technology available for telecommunications networks. These developments have contributed in particular to the increased capacities of telecommunications systems and the extended range of services provided. Furthermore, they have affected the way these services and products are used, by stimulating and widening the needs of both private and professional users.

In accordance with the factors above, the general role of telecommunications services for the economy is increasing and accordingly, globalization in the telecommunications services seems inevitable in the new era. Nevertheless, many States are concerned about the possibly grave consequences of liberalization, especially developing countries. It proved impossible to reach fundamental commitment during the Uruguay Round. However, it did liberalize some

---

[488] Ministerial Declaration on Uruguay Round, 33d. supp. B.I.S.D., 19ff (1987).

[489] P. Malanczuk & H. de Vlaam, International Trade in Telecommunications Services and the Results of the Uruguay Round of GATT, 3 *Telecommunications and Space Journal,* 269 (1996).

[490] 20 December 1991, GATT Doc. MTN. TNC/W/FA, Annex II.

[491] See further B. Lasserre, The Role of Regulation in Telecommunications: From Opening up to Competition to the Regulation of Competition, 1 *Telecommunications and Space Journal,* 18 (1994).

[492] Secretariat note, MTN. GNS/W/52, 19 May 1989.

of the area which is not so sensitive and did reach consensus on further negotiation on basic telecommunications. The Uruguay Round of negotiations is rather a momentous opportunity for showing the way to further liberalization in telecommunication rather than setting out detailed commitments for Member States. Further negotiations in the sector were guided by the Negotiation Group on Basic Telecommunications (NGBT), which was later substituted by the Group on Basic Telecommunications (GBT).[493]

It was exciting that on February 15, 1997, free trade in telecommunications received a major boost. Some sixty-nine countries taking part in the GBT reached an agreement on basic telecommunications services. A complete round of negotiations on the liberalization of telecommunications services within the WTO was hereby completed. As a consequence, on January 1, 1998, the international telecom environment would shift from a framework which is based on bilateral relations to one which is multilateral in nature, and from closed to open markets.[494] This section shall first examine the considerations for including telecommunications services into the WTO negotiations and the different stages in the negotiations of the telecommunications services; obligations and commitments undertaken by Member States shall be discussed in depth; an evaluation of the present framework of telecommunications will be made and light shed on further liberalization in this promising area.

1.2. A Brief Review of the WTO Telecommunications Negotiations

The Uruguay Round of negotiations started in 1986 intended to launch the most ambitious multilateral negotiation in history. It was originally planned for trade in goods. However, according to suggestions from Member States, services were included in the GATT/WTO framework. Even then, there were few discussions centered on telecommunications services. In the first few years, discussions centered on the outlines of a general agreement on services. Sectoral discussions on telecommunications began in 1989.[495]

As said, telecommunications services play a central role in the globalization of economic enterprises and constitute the connecting belt of the world economy. Meanwhile, technological development has further advanced the advent of the 'information society', in which information becomes tradable invisible goods. Various international organizations have been set up to make full use of telecommunications. However, the existence of national monopolies in the telecommunications has been an obstacle to full economic use. In the past few years, several States have taken steps to liberalize part of telecommunications and achieved manifest benefits, which further allured other States to follow. It becomes apparent that the mechanism of the International Telecommunication Union is not appropriate for

---

[493] The GBT was created by a Decision of 30 April 1996 of the WTO Council on Trade in Services (WTO/S/L/19), and it replaced the NGBT which had been created pursuant to the Decision on Negotiations on Basic Telecommunications, attached to the Final Act of the Uruguay Round Negotiations.

[494] As a matter of fact, it entered into force on February 5, 1998. The Member States were unable to reach a consensus on going forward with entry into force as originally scheduled because 20 participants had not yet deposited their acceptance pending the completion of domestic ratification processes.

[495] M.C.E.J. Bronckers & P. Larouche, Telecommunications Services and the World Trade Organization, 31 *Journal of World Trade*, No.3, at 7 (1997). For a contemporaneous study favoring sectoral examinations, *see* M. van Empel, The Visible Hand in Invisible Trade, 16 *Economic Issues of European Integration*, No.2, 23-43 (1990).

carrying out the liberalization.[496] The successful experience of GATT negotiations in liberalization of trade in goods provides the right example.

Furthermore, the establishment of WTO has further improved and perfected the normal function of the organization. Many techniques of negotiations seem to serve the telecommunications negotiations. More and more States realized the importance of the telecommunications services and the benefits to negotiate under the auspices of WTO; therefore, telecommunications negotiations were formally included in the WTO agenda.

While negotiation under WTO is one thing, there is no problem of applying the general principles and obligations of GATS to the telecommunications services; it is still another matter for Member States to offer and undertake specific commitments. Since the United States was the most advanced country in terms of telecommunications, [497] it came as no surprise that its views and perspectives were in the dominant position at the first stage, which set up the basic structure of negotiation. The fundamental influence of the United States was the distinction between basic and value-added services.[498]

Negotiations on value-added services were relatively easier since most States have, from the inception of telecommunications, opened certain parts to competition; more importantly, it provides the basic means of other services. It is unthinkable to pursue liberalization in other services without access and use of public telecommunications transport networks and services. Thus, it came easily to the conclusion in the Annex on Telecommunications, which specifically deals with value-added services. Most specific commitments offered at this stage were largely in this category.

However, difficulties arose with respect to basic telecommunications services. On the one hand, most States were still uncertain about the possible results and concerned about its sensitivity to national economy and security. Moreover, trade officials from developing countries recognized that basic telecommunications services were far less advanced than those of industrial countries, and consequently opening markets to foreign services could retard the growth of indigenous capabilities, result in unwanted reliance on foreign service providers as well as exacerbate balance-of-payments problems. On the other hand, the United States was ambitious to obtain as many offers as possible to enter foreign markets; it was reluctant to unilaterally make commitments without corresponding offers from other States. In the end, no agreement was reached on basic telecommunications when the final GATS texts were adopted. Nevertheless, a Decision on Negotiations on Basic Telecommunications was taken at the end of the Uruguay Round.

Accordingly, a NGBT was created to guide further negotiations on basic telecommunications. Discussions started in May 1994 and were to be concluded no later than

---

496 ITU was originally set up for the technical issues, like allocation of spectrum. It is not the right place to talk about economic liberalization, while GATT/WTO is a forum to discuss liberalization in trade, which naturally includes the liberalization in trade in services.

497 As with most trade negotiations, the United States had the most to gain or lose. Since large trade deficits in goods occurred, it wished to get better situations in national budgets through liberalization in services, especially in telecommunications services, in which the United States occupies the first position. Without the US leadership and pressure, negotiations would never have started or would quickly have bogged down, as shown in the latter negotiations on basic telecommunications.

498 The borderline of this distinction, which is absent in the European Union, is rather vague and subject to controversies, however, it did help to conclude the Annex on Telecommunications and the Decision on Negotiations on Basic Telecommunications.

April 30, 1996.[499] As the deadline approached, it became apparent that no final deal was in sight. The obstacle was apparently created by the US insistence on two deal breaking issues: first, certain aspects of satellite telecommunications services; and second, the traffic distortions resulting when communications occur between liberalized and non-liberalized markets.[500] However, a group of countries prepared a brief Reference Paper in the run-up to the April 1996 deadline, which was adopted by most States as additional commitments concerning regulatory principles to be applied to the telecommunications services.

In order to avoid a premature end, members of the NGBT agreed to extend the negotiating deadline to February 15, 1997 with all offers on the table being 'frozen'.[501] The talks resumed in July 1996 and formal negotiations on January 15, 1997, during which the Member States could further review their own policy and consider new offers.[502] A new body (GBT) took the place of NGBT to be responsible for implementing the further extension of negotiations. At the end, thirty-two of the thirty-four offers tabled in April 1996 were revised and twenty-one new offers were submitted, bringing the total number of schedules of commitments to fifty-five (counting as one the offer of the European Community and its Member States). Nine governments had submitted lists of exceptions to the Most-favored-nation Treatment (MFN).[503] On February 15, 1997, an agreement was reached and the fifty-five schedules were attached to a brief document, set to be the Fourth Protocol to the GATS.[504] The Protocol was open to ratification and the formal entry into force of the commitments took place on February 5, 1998. Till then, the whole round of telecommunications services negotiations came to an end.

With the new agreements, competition in the provision of basic telecommunications services has been enhanced significantly, leading to simultaneous decreases in service rates and growth in revenues.[505] It was exalted as one big success in telecommunications services. However, the agreement, just as announced, is only the beginning of the battle to bring competition to the telecommunications industry. Many obstacles must be overcome before competition becomes a practical reality.[506] Nevertheless, it provides a very nice basis for further negotiations.

---

[499] Participation in the NGBT was voluntary and by end of April 1996, 53 WTO Member governments had decided to participate fully in the Group. Another 24 governments (including some in the process of accession to the WTO) requested to participate with observer status.

[500] S. Lessard, International Trade in Telecommunications Services: Towards Open Markets, 23 *Annals of Air and Space Law*, 406 (1997).

[501] The effect of both the Decision on Negotiations on Basic Telecommunications and the Annex on Negotiations on Basic Telecommunications were extended in substance to February 15, 1997 by the Decision on Commitments in Basic Telecommunications of April 30, 1996. The concessions already made by the Member States should not be withdrawn. *See* further WTO/S/L/19.

[502] One consideration is that during that period, liberalization of the telecommunications services was underway among the Member States of the European Union. .

[503] See further Paragraph 6 of the Report of the Group on Basic Telecommunications, WTO/S/GBT/4, February15, 1997.

[504] See further Fourth Protocol to the General Agreement on Trade in Services, WTO/S/L/20, April 30, 1996.

[505] See further P. L. Spector, Business Transactions, Disputes and Regulation: The World Trade Organization Agreement on Telecommunications, 32 *The International Lawyer,* No.2, at 217 (1998).

[506] See further G. C. Hufbauer & E. Wada (eds.), *Unfinished Business: Telecommunications after the Uruguay Round,* 3-4 (1997).

1.3. Economic Aspects of Telecommunications Services

1.3.1. Definitions

As usual, it was difficult to agree upon the definition of telecommunications, which has often been discussed among the delegates to the Uruguay Round. This absence of consensus reflects the dissension between developing countries and developed countries, but also one has to remember that GATT does not contain a definition of 'goods'.[507] What the experts could do is resort to the pragmatic method. The definition in relevant documents was set out mostly from a technical angle.

The International Telecommunication Union Convention defines telecommunications as: 'Any transmission, emission or reception of signs, signals, writing, images and sounds or intelligence of any nature by wire, radio, optical or other electromagnetic systems'.[508] We may also trace to the European legislation, which provides an identical definition.[509] However, the Annex on Telecommunications provides that telecommunications means 'the transmission and reception of signals by any electromagnetic means'.[510] Compared with the above definition, it is even more ambiguous. This definition largely explains the current difficulties in the negotiations of telecommunications services.[511]

Trade in telecommunications can include any sale of telecommunications equipment or services that crosses national borders. However, the import and export of telecommunications equipment conforms well to our traditional understanding of trade as buying and selling, which is not covered by GATS. What we shall deal with in this section is trade in telecommunications services. This is a more difficult concept to grasp. At the moment, telecommunications services trade is a main feature of the European Union's single telecommunications market program, a prominent section of the North-American Free Trade Agreement, and the subject of a number of bilateral agreements.[512] In practice, trade in telecommunications services includes cross border transactions, such as telephone calls or electronic mail sent from one country to another; it also covers foreign investment, such as the purchase of telephone companies by foreign investors or joint ventures between local and foreign partners to establish new telecommunication service companies.[513] It is generally agreed that trade in telecommunications services includes all four forms of sales.[514]

---

507 See further A. Mencik von Zebinsky, The Agreement on Trade in Services: Its Implications for Air Transport, 18 *Annals of Air and Space Law*, 360 (1993); see also R. van den Hoven van Genderen & A.C.M. Nugter & J.M. Smits, Recent Developments in Telecommunications Law, 1987 *Netherlands International Law Review*, 220.

508 See Annex 2 of the ITU Convention.

509 See International Telecommunications Convention 1982, Annex 2, No. 2015, Tractatenblad, No. 164 (1983).

510 See Article 3(a) of the Annex on Telecommunications to GATS; the Results of the Uruguay Round of Multilateral Trade Negotiations: The Legal Texts, by World Trade Organization, at 360.

511 For further discussion on the definition of telecommunications, please see R. van den Hoven van Genderen & A.C.M. Nugter & I.M. Smits, Recent Development in Telecommunications Law, *Netherlands International Law Review*, 220 (1987).

512 *Trade in Telecommunications: Towards a New World of Telecommunications Development*, Keynote Address by Dr. P. Tarjanne, Secretary-General, International Telecommunication Union, Tenth Anniversary and Eleventh Annual Conference and Trade Exhibition, Caribbean Association of National Telecommunications Organizations (CANTO), 5 June 1995, Nassau, the Bahamas.

513 See further presentation by Dr. P. Tarjanne, *The WTO Basic Telecommunications Agreement: An ITU Viewpoint*, ITU Negotiating International Trade Issues, Geneva, WTO, November 28, 1997.

514 In the GATS agreement on Basic Telecommunications, four modes of delivery are identified: cross-border supply, commercial presence, consumption abroad and movement of staff.

According to the United States, telecommunications services are divided into two categories: basic and value-added telecommunications. At the outset of the negotiations, participants agreed to set aside national differences as to how basic telecommunications might be defined domestically and to negotiate on all telecommunications services, both public and private, to involve end-to-end transmission of customer supplied information. They also agreed that basic telecommunications services provided over network infrastructure as well as those provided through resale would both fall within the scope of commitments. They further agreed that value-added services mean telecommunications for which suppliers add value to the customer's information by enhancing its form or content or by providing for its storage and retrieval.

1.3.2. Barriers to Trade in Telecommunications Services

Until recently, opportunities for telecommunications services have been more limited than for equipment. Of the four delivery modes, cross-border provision is by far the most important. The second most important way is through foreign investment to establish a commercial presence. However, as mentioned above, comparatively little international telecommunications traffic is traded across borders. Two main reasons may be identified: high prices for users and restricted market access for service providers. Firstly, consumers have to pay at least three times more for each minute of international telecommunications traffic than they do for domestic telecommunications traffic, even though the costs of services provision may be quite similar; Secondly, until the start of 1998, only a handful of countries permitted competitive provision of international telecommunications services.

It is important to note that trade in services faces rather different problems than trade in goods.[515] As a rule, trade in telecommunications services does not encounter difficulties at national borders in the form of traffic or other customs barriers, as is primarily the case with trade in goods, apart from the problem of the so-called non-tariff barriers resulting from internal measures as a substitute for customs barriers to foreign goods.[516]

Historically, opportunities for the telecommunications services sector have been limited by the fact that most countries owned monopoly carriers. They are very often the subjects of government and market regulations. These regulations may implement various barriers to trade in telecommunications services and this raises several issues which were discussed in the negotiations.[517] One main issue is the accounting rate.[518] However, the barriers caused as such may come more from national regulations structuring particular service sectors, [519] from

---

[515] See further Ch. Bail, Conceptual Problems and Possible Elements of a Multilateral Framework for International Trade in Services, in Sacerdoti (ed.), *Liberalization of Services and Intellectual Property* in *the Uruguay Round of GATT,* 46-47 (1990).

[516] See further A. Sapir, The Agreement on Trade in Services: From 1994 to the Year 2000, *33 JWT,* No. 1, at 52-53 (1999). Although regulation of service activities may be imposed for purely domestic purposes, it almost always creates a powerful trade barrier. Trade in services is only affected by this and other non-tariff barriers; tariffs are totally absent.

[517] As to the issues dealt with in the negotiations, see Bronckers, *supra* note 12, at 10-14.

[518] With respect to accounting rate as a barrier to trade in telecommunications services, see M. Scanlan, Why is the International Accounting Rate System in Terminal Decline, and What Might be the Consequences? 20 *Telecommunications Policy,* 739 (1996); see also D. Walker, *International Accounting Rates - A Perspective,* 20 *Telecommunications Policy*, 239 (1996).

[519] See further E. Petersmann, International Competition Rules for the GATT-MTO World Trade and Legal System, 27 *JWT,* No.6, at 36 (1993). Conflicting national regulations can entail market access barriers (such as non-tariff barriers), market distortions (such as subsidies), and harmful international externalities (such as export cartels).

lack of sufficient transparency of rules, regulations and standards, from technical barriers, from the protection of nationals from foreign competition, from the reservation to monopolies or excessive providers of sectors considered to be of essential national, social, or public importance, or from restrictions on the right of establishment or the free movement of persons where a presence in the importing country is essential to the trans-border provision of services.

It would be outside the scope of this section to go further into the problem of barriers to trade in telecommunications services. However, it should be noted that it is the existence of those barriers that certain countries were willing and actively pushing for the inclusion of telecommunications services within the forum of WTO negotiations. This situation changed with the inclusion of the WTO Basic Telecommunications Agreement. Member States are obliged to undertake certain obligations to open their markets and provide non-discriminatory treatment, the barriers are obviously against the general principles and obligations of the GATS. Thus, we have reason to believe that this is a healthy way of making telecommunications services a more profitable and promising area.

1.3.3. An Economic Perspective from Statistics

The telecommunications sector is one of the major components of the world's economy. With the successful conclusion of WTO negotiations in 1997, globalization of telecommunications was imminent. The results of the negotiation extended the coverage of the GATS to virtually all of the US$ 600 billion telecommunications services sector. Furthermore, telecommunications networks are a major facilitator of trade in other goods and services. As trade economists understand, telecommunications are vital to the development of services trade because it is a rapid, reliable, relatively inexpensive, distance-insensitive mode of delivery for most services sectors. For instance, the value of financial services traded over the SWIFT (Society for Worldwide Interbank Financial Telecommunication) international telecommunications network exceeds USD 1 trillion each day.[520] However, when it comes to basic telecommunications, the traded volume is still rather low. This was also reflected in the process of negotiations. Many developing countries were apprehensive about opening up their markets because of the fear that firms from a few industrial countries may dominate their national markets.

Nevertheless, freer trade in telecommunications promises to deliver at least three economic gains: new and improved products and services, lower prices and additional investment. Probably the clearest evidence comes from the market segment where competition is currently the most keen: international telephone services. For developed economies, competition has raised the growth rate of traffic per subscriber from 5.6 percent to 9.3 per cent per year since 1990. However, for emerging markets over the same period competitive markets grew their international traffic per subscriber by 11.7 per cent per year compared with just 5.2 per cent per year in monopoly markets.[521] Thus, we can see, the potential benefits shall be magnificent for each State, even better for the emerging markets.

---

[520] See Secretary-General's Report to the Second World Telecommunication Policy Forum, Geneva, March 16-18, 1998, paragraph 9.

[521] See further World Telecommunication Development Report 1996/97, ITU, February 1997.

1.3.4. Liberalization versus Monopoly[522]

Why liberalize? It is the primary question to be answered before proceeding to the next part. Traditional argument for a natural monopoly is that a given pattern of demand can be met at least with cost if supplied by only one firm. However, from economic theory, monopoly may mean inefficiency: monopolized prices are higher than costs, so consumers would have to pay more for extra units than it costs to produce them. That is, there are unexploited gains from trade. This decision-making procedure is also the same for service providers. In production decisions, the provider faces a trade-off between obtaining production from the market or from within the firm. Given the costs of transacting, monitoring, and so forth, the provider can decide on an optimal arrangement of contracts and resource allocations. By lowering prices through liberalization, extra transactions take place and extra gains from trade are achieved. The convergence of prices and costs reduces domestic producer surplus and (assuming relatively elastic demand) increases the volume of outgoing traffic. At a given accounting rate, more outgoing traffic increases the terminating carrier's revenue in absolute terms and its share of the total revenue accruing to both carriers. To be sure, domestic welfare in the liberalized originating market may well rise because the gains domestic consumer benefits from lower prices outweigh the shrinkage of producer surplus gathered by the domestic carriers. Thus, economic efficiency is derived with all gains from trade fully exploited.

Furthermore, liberalization can offer the chance to redistribute economic resources as mentioned above. There are a number of different forms of redistribution that may be of interest to public policy, any of which may have impact on telecommunications. For example, vertical redistribution from richer to poorer may motivate concerns about telecommunications tariffs to disadvantaged groups; horizontal distribution may give rise to policies which aim to prevent discrimination within a particular class of customers.

Like other network industries, telecommunications may exhibit economies of density, which shall occur where costs to serve are significantly affected by the spatial density of consumers. In an industry with economies of density, liberalization will tend to lead to quite marked spatial variations in the prices of otherwise similar services: 'geographical matters'. The net effect of liberalization is that international telecommunications services trade, which traditionally reflected accidents of geography and the impact of regulation, will be increasingly determined by underlying comparative advantage - most notably by the ability of service providers to generate innovative, cost-effective services.[523] Thus, we could now discern that liberalization can well serve the theory of economy and the best use of limited resources in the world.

---

522 Most of this part is a tentative conclusion through my recent studies on telecommunications offered by G. Yarrow: *The Economics of Telecommunications Regulation.* No articles have yet been found to cover this area.

523 See further H. Ergas, International Trade in Telecommunication Services: An Economic Perspective, in G. C. Hufbauer & E. Wada (eds.), *Unfinished Business: Telecommunications after the Uruguay Round,* 95 and 105 (1997).

1.4. The Framework of the GATS for Trade in Telecommunications Services

1.4.1. An Overview of the Framework of GATS

The results of the telecommunications negotiations, including the period during the Uruguay Round and later period under the auspices of NGBT and GBT, constituted a complete framework for trade in telecommunications services at the present stage. It is therefore useful first of all to sketch briefly this framework in order to gain an overall impression of the meaning of the discussion.

The General Agreement is an introduction to the telecommunications services. It is applied to all services defined in the Articles. The general principles and obligations and the specific commitments are applicable to each sector. All the national commitments were made under the guidance of the Agreement. However, there are few provisions in the Agreement which can be directly applicable to concrete situations. Most provisions shall be applied through commitments offered by each State.

The telecommunications services sector, of course, is also under the guidance of the Agreement. During the Uruguay Round, one Annex was concluded concerning value-added services. At this stage, most commitments made were also limited to this category. After the Uruguay Round, new negotiations began and obtained significant achievements in the basic telecommunications. In the first period, although no definite results came out, one Reference Paper was agreed upon; later, momentous success was reached by the adoption of the Fourth Protocol.

To understand the results of the negotiations on telecommunications services, it is necessary to take the above agreed documents into account. These documents will be discussed in more detail in the following discussion, from which we shall be able to discern how trade in telecommunications services in the present stage shall be carried out in accordance with the achievements so far reached. Firstly, we shall briefly discuss the general principles and obligations which shall be born in mind throughout the negotiations and later implementation. Since most principles and obligations can become operational only after specific commitments are made by Member States, accordingly, commitments undertaken on value-added and basic telecommunications services shall be discussed in greater detail.

1.4.2. The General Agreement on Trade in Services (GATS)

The GATS negotiators arrived at a model that was based on GATT, but in ways quite different to reflect in part the intangible and non-storable nature of services. The General Agreement formally consists of 29 Articles. The Articles lay out the scope of the Agreement and the general obligations and disciplines to be observed. They also define the specific commitments to be inscribed in schedules and how to go about negotiating them. In the GATS, the only major obligation that a country assumes with respect to trade in all services is MFN. Other commitments to foreign services or service suppliers as national treatment and market access, apply only to sectors and modes of supply in which countries have made specific commitments.[524] Finally, there are provisions for dispute settlement and the establishment of the Council for Trade in Services. It is clear from the provision that the Agreement applies to telecommunications services.

---

[524] J. du Pré Gauntt, *The Internet and International Trade Policy*, http://ksgwww.harvard.edu/iip/iicompol/Papers/Gauntt.html

1.4.2.1. General Obligations and Disciplines

The Agreement sets down 15 obligations and disciplines.[525] Two of the most important general obligations of the Agreement are the MFN treatment, and the transparency obligation. Actually, the Articles on general obligations and principles vary in character. Some apply only to the sectors or sub-sectors for which commitments have been taken in schedules, and still others define the exceptions to the Agreement which are permitted under specified circumstances. Certain general obligations of the Agreement are of particular relevance to telecommunications, such as Article VI on domestic regulation; Article VIII on monopolies and exclusive service providers and Article IX on restrictive business practice.

1.4.2.1.1. MFN Treatment

The MFN principle, one of the characteristics of multilaterality, is the most effective engine to further liberalization. Favor one, favor all. MFN means treating one's trading partners equally. Concessions, in terms of trade barrier reduction, made within a multilateral framework will apply to all trading partners who have subscribed to it.[526]

Under GATS, if a country allows foreign competition in a sector, equal opportunities in that sector should be given to service providers from other WTO Members. The principle constitutes one of the basic legal rules designed to prevent economic discrimination between States and presupposes equality of States in their commercial and economic dealings.[527] This applies even if the country has made no specific commitments to provide foreign companies access to its markets under the WTO. MFN treatment prohibits Members from discriminating among themselves, or in fact from treating other Members less favorably than any other country, Member or not. It is the cornerstone of multilateralism, without it the WTO would be little more than an overseer of special bilateral and regional trade deals.

However, although MFN is a general obligation, the GATS contains an Annex allowing countries to invoke exemptions to MFN. The coverage of MFN for each Member is therefore determined by a so-called negative list.[528] According to the Annex, exceptions granted are subject to conditions with respect to their termination and shall be reviewed no more than 5 years after the entry into force of the Agreement and should, in principle, not exceed the period of 10 years. Applications for exemption shall provide the information listed in the attachment to the Annex.[529] The exceptions are also confirmed in Article II paragraph 2[530]

---

[525] Or to be more accurate, there are 15 general obligations and disciplines plus three corollary principles: MFN; transparency; disclosure of confidential information; increasing participation of developing countries; economic integration agreements and a corollary on labor market integration; domestic regulation; mutual recognition of standards or criteria for the authorization, certification, and licensing of service suppliers; monopolies and exclusive service providers; business practices; emergency safeguard measures; payments and transfers; restrictions to safeguard the balance of payments; government procurement; general exceptions; national security exceptions; and subsidies.

[526] W. von Dewitz, The Legal and Economic Problems of Making GATT Rules Applicable to Telecommunications Services, in E. Mestmacker (ed.), *The Law and Economics of Transborder Telecommunications*, , 329 (1987).

[527] *E.* Aghatise, Services and the Development Process: Legal Aspects of Changing Economic Determinants, 24 *JWT*, No.5, at 109 (1990).

[528] See further B. Hoekman & M. Kostecki, *The Political Economy of the World Trading System*, 131 (1995).

[529] See further the Annex on Article II Exemptions, which was divided into four parts: scope, review, termination and lists of Article II exemptions.

[530] It states: "a Member may maintain a measure inconsistent with paragraph 1 provided that such a measure is listed in, and meets the conditions of, the Annex on Article II Exemptions".

and further illustrated in paragraph 3.[531] Furthermore, we can deduce exceptions from Article XIII on the government procurement exceptions,[532] and other relevant provisions.[533]

MFN treatment under GATS is definitely 'unconditional' in its wording and in legal terms. However, during negotiations, there was a tendency towards conditional application and interpretation of the clause. The overuse of Article II exemptions as a negotiation leverage, would indeed undermine the functioning and credibility of the unconditional MFN treatment. A balance needs to be struck between individual national concerns and the limitation or prevention of abusive uses of such exemptions. In order to secure such a balance, it has been suggested that the listing of an Article II exemption be temporary, exceptional and unambiguous in accordance with the relevant provisions of the GATS.[534]

1.4.2.1.2. Transparency

The principle of transparency requires governments to make public their laws, rules and regulations affecting trade in telecommunications services, so that service suppliers know the rules under which they can do business. It is a key element in promoting the stability and predictability of the trading system. Governments must set up inquiry points within their bureaucracies. Foreign companies and governments can use these inquiry points to obtain information about regulations in any service sector. They should notify the WTO of any changes in regulations that apply to the service that come under specific commitments. Transparency is obviously a vital requirement for effective opening of services markets. Greater transparency could reduce uncertainty in international transactions.[535] However, nothing in the Agreement shall require any Member to provide confidential information, the disclosure of which would impede law enforcement, or otherwise be contrary to public interest, or which would prejudice legitimate commercial interests of particular enterprises, public or private.[536]

It seems that the general transparency obligation of the GATS will have considerable effect on the practice of telecommunications regulators of the WTO Member States in spreading information about their laws, rules, regulations. The Telecommunications Annex states that in applying the transparency provision of the GATS, Members shall ensure that information about conditions of access and use be made publicly available; these would include tariffs, technical specifications, standards adoption procedures and institutions, terminal equipment attachment rules, and notification, licensing, or registration procedures, if

---

[531] Actually, this provides another exception to the MFN as GATT does, which enables any party to confer or accord advantages to adjacent countries. It is important to note that the exemption of paragraph 2 applied for after the entry into force of the Agreement, according to the Annex, shall be dealt with under this paragraph.

[532] According to Article XIII, the MFN treatment shall not apply to laws, regulations or requirements governing the procurement by governmental agencies of services purchased for governmental purposes. This wording has rightly echoed the scope of GATS, which excludes application to services supplied in the exercise of governmental functions.

[533] For example, General Exceptions, as customary practice in international trade, are provided in Article XIV for Members to exempt from GATS obligations; similar exceptions can also be found in Security Exceptions.

[534] See further Y. Wang. Most-Favored-Nation Treatment under the General Agreement on Trade in Services - And Its Application in Financial Services, 30 *JWT*, No.1, at 106-107 (1996).

[535] See further P. Nicolaides, Economic Aspects of Services: Implications for a GATT Agreement, 23 *JWT*, No.1, at 131 (1989).

[536] Telecommunications and the GATS, Regional Telecommunication Development Conference for the Arab States (AR-RTDC-96), Beirut (Lebanon), Document 45-E, Telecommunication Development Bureau, November 5, 1996.

required.[537] Regulators in countries where regulatory rules are already published need not drastically alter their behaviour. By contrast, very few countries ordinarily publish or have no such requirement. Consequently, conforming to the transparency obligation will require significant or even radical modification of their existing regulatory regimes.[538]

1.4.2.1.3. Domestic Regulation

Article VI on domestic regulation sets out some rules of fair play for regulations not directly addressed by commitments in the schedules. Since domestic regulations are the most significant means of exercising influence or control over trade in services, the agreement provides that government should regulate services reasonably, objectively and impartially. When a government makes administrative decisions that affect a service, it should also provide impartial means for reviewing the decision (for example a tribunal).[539]

For telecommunications services, this would include areas such as licensing schemes, universal service obligations, frequency allocation, numbering, and ONP (open network provision) type regulation.[540] It requires that Members make up rules to ensure that qualification requirements, technical standards, and licensing procedures are based on objective and transparent criteria; are no more burdensome than is necessary to ensure the quality of the telecommunications services; and do not constitute restrictions on telecommunications services (thereby possibly circumventing a specific commitment).

1.4.2.1.4. Monopolies and Exclusive Services Providers

The inclusion of telecommunications services in the Agreement reflected fundamental economic and technological changes in telecommunications, one change being an increasing national need to treat telecommunications as a "normal industry", and not to regard it as a "special" industry or "natural monopoly" requiring governmental ownership or other treatment different from those generally afforded to other sectors. [541]

The obligation requires reasonable and non-discriminatory access to the telecommunications services. Each Member shall ensure that any monopoly services provider in its territory does not, in the supply of monopoly services, act in a manner inconsistent with that Member's obligations. Where a Member's monopoly provider competes, either directly or through an affiliated company, in the supply of a service outside the scope of its monopoly, the Member shall ensure that such a provider does not abuse its monopoly position in a manner inconsistent with such commitments.[542] While this language will apply to monopolies in telecommunications services, its general nature and lack of enumerated offences and

---

[537] Potential Impact on the US Economy and Industries of the GATT Uruguay Round Agreements, Investigation No. 332-353 June 1994, Publication No. 2970, Volume I, United States International Trade Commission, page IX-22.

[538] See further Executive Summary of Trade Agreement on Telecommunications, http://www.itu.int/pforum.

[539] See Article VI of the GATS, *supra* note 27, at 333-334

[540] For further discussion, see Empel, *supra* note 12, at 35-37.

[541] See further The Changing Role of Government in an Era of Telecom Deregulation, Trade Agreements on Telecommunications: Regulatory Implications, Report of the Fifth Regulatory Colloquium held at the ITU Headquarters, December 6-8, 1995.

[542] See further Article VIII of the GATS. This part of the provision is particularly important. This presumably means that a telecommunications operator in this situation would not be permitted to abuse its monopoly of the local network in order to compete unfairly with a foreign entrant in the competitive value-added long distance or international business, for example, by denying its competitor local interconnection or leased lines, overcharging for these services, or providing them at low levels of quality.

remedies will in all probability result in better protection against monopoly charges.[543] In one word, there should be a "level playing field" whereby government-sanctioned monopoly or exclusive providers of telecommunications services do not use their market position to harm interests of service suppliers participating in activities where competition has been introduced.[544]

1.4.2.1.5. Restrictive Business Practices

This obligation is closely connected with Article VIII. It recognizes that certain business practices may restrain competition and thereby restrict trade in services. The GATS does not embody any specific commitments by its Members on the elimination of such practices. Instead, it provides that each Member shall, at the request of another Member, enter into consultations with a view to eliminating such practices.[545] It is even more urgent for telecommunications services since it relates to the kinds of anticompetitive behavior in a national market that could be carried out by private companies, irrespective of their size, to restrain the success of newcomers. In highly competitive markets, this obligation continues to be important to ensure that national telecommunications operators do not act in a manner calculated to unfairly disadvantage foreign participants in the national market.

1.4.2.2. Specific Commitments

The General Agreement provides for Members to make, via national schedules, commitments on telecommunications services. The essential provisions on Specific Commitments are the Market Access provision, the National Treatment clause and the Additional Commitments. These are the provisions envisaged by the GATS to provide for the reduction of barriers to trade in services, without which the prohibition of discrimination provided in the General Obligations would not make sense.[546] The specific commitments on market access and national treatment are the core of the GATS, and the impact of the Agreement depends to a large extent on the commitments made by Members.[547] Specific Commitments apply only to the service sectors listed in each Member's schedule. Those contain each Member's commitments on market access, national treatment, and possible additional commitments. In the schedules, Members may grant full market access and national treatment or they may enter any limitations, conditions, and qualifications that they maintain on those two provisions. The schedules may also indicate the time frame for implementing a Member's commitments. Whether full or limited access is granted, signatories may not take measures that reduce the level of access inscribed in their schedules.[548]

---

543 McCarthy Tétrault, Canada's national Law Firm, Intellectual Property-Telecommunications, http://www.mccarthy.ca/mt-itel.html

544 See G. Russell Pipe, *Trade of Telecommunications Services: Implications of a GATT Uruguay Round Agreement for ITU and Member States*, May 1993, ITU documents Database.

545 See further Article IX of the GATS.

546 See further Zebinsky, *supra* note 24, at 376.

547 A. Mattoo, National Treatment in the GATS, Corner-stone or Pandora's Box? 31 *JWT*, No.1, 109 (1997).

548 See further *Structure of the General Agreement on Trade in Services (GATS) and How It Pertains to Telecommunications,* Outline for Discussion of 5th Colloquium Report.

1.4.2.2.1. Market Access

Under this provision, each Member shall accord services and service suppliers of any other Member treatment no less favorable than that provided for under the terms, limitations and conditions agreed and specified in its schedule. A Member is assumed to have granted total market access if it has not negotiated the right to impose such limitations and conditions. In sectors where market access commitments are undertaken, measures which a Party shall not adopt or maintain are limitations on the number of service providers, the total value of service transactions, the total number of service operations or total quantity of service, the total number of natural persons that may be employed in a particular service sector and lastly, measures which restrict specific types of legal entity or limit participation of foreign capital.[549]

During the Uruguay Round negotiations, the countries providing market access for telecommunications services account for 99 per cent of all revenues from telecom services worldwide.[550] The lists of market access commitments were negotiated as multilateral packages, although bilateral bargaining sessions were needed to develop the packages. The commitments therefore, contain the negotiated and guaranteed conditions for conducting trade in telecommunications services. If a recorded condition is to be changed for the worse, then the Member has to give at least three months' notice and it has to negotiate compensation with affected Members. But commitments can be improved at any time. When a Member undertakes a commitment, it must indicate for each mode of supply with limitations, if any, it maintains.

1.4.2.2.2. National Treatment

For liberalization of telecommunications services, national treatment is a very important rule. A Member may accord services and service providers of any other Member by according either formally identical treatment or formally different treatment to what it accords to its own services and service providers if it does not modify the conditions of competition in favor of its own service providers.[551] It means that once a foreign company has been allowed to supply a service in one Member, there should be no *de jure* or *de facto* discrimination between the foreign and local companies, the criterion being equality of opportunity in competition. It constitutes the other major legal principle of the GATT/WTO framework and is an extension of the MFN treatment.

Under GATS, a Member only has to apply this principle when it has made a specific commitment to provide foreigners access to its services market. It does not have to apply national treatment in sectors where it has made no commitments.[552] As national treatment is made obligatory only for sectors that each Member promises, a Member does not voluntarily liberalize, but instead watches other Members' moves. However, limitations and other conditions imposed on this principle have to be registered in the schedule of specific commitments.[553]

---

549 See further Article XVII of the GATS.

550 Statement of Ambassador C. Barshefsky: *Basic Telecom Negotiations,* February 15, 1997.

551 See further Article XVII of the GATS.

552 Unlike MFN treatment, which is in principle an obligation necessarily undertaken by each Member, this principle does not apply comprehensively.

553 This contrasts with the way applied in trade for goods. In the latter case, once a product has crossed a border and been cleared by custom, it has to be given national treatment even if the importing country has not made any commitment under the WTO to bind the tariff rate.

Telecommunications liberalization originally comes from a market-based policy founded on a belief that increased competition in the domestic market brings about telecommunications innovation and cost decreases. Thus, new entrants should be welcomed to bring in new competition. However, during the Uruguay Round negotiations, the position of reciprocity took the prevalence.[554] The main regulatory constraint for the telecommunications market is argued to be market access, not discriminatory treatment after permission to operate. If this is the case, market access may have more significance than national treatment for the telecommunications sector.[555]

1.4.2.2.3. Additional Commitments

Members may negotiate additional commitments with respect to measures affecting trade in services which are not recorded in their schedule, including those regarding qualifications, standards or licensing matters.[556] Entries in this category are not obligatory but it may decide in a given sector to make additional commitments relating to measures other than those listed under market access and national treatment. It is used to indicate positive undertakings, not the listing of additional limitations or restrictions.

1.4.3. Commitments for Value-added Telecommunications

During the Uruguay Round negotiations, a total of 56 commitments were submitted, most of which were limited to the value-added telecommunications services. However, the services covered accounted for only a minor proportion of the overall telecommunications markets, which for the time being is still largely accounted for by public voice telephony. The major countries in the international telecommunications market did not make any notable limitations to their commitments on value-added services.[557] In addition, negotiations after the Uruguay Round have further added commitments on value-added services.[558]

The most significant achievement at this stage was the Annex on Telecommunications, which was attached to the GATS. The Annex applies to measures by a Member that affect access to and use of public telecommunications transport networks and services (PTTNS) for the supply of any services included in its schedule of commitments. If, for example, a Member undertakes a commitment to allow entry into its telecommunications services, suppliers of such services shall be given access to and use of PTTNS on reasonable and nondiscriminatory terms. It does not apply to measures affecting the cable or broadcast distribution of radio or television programming. In the era of convergence of multimedia services, such a limitation on the scope and field of application of the Annex on telecommunications can only be viewed as astonishing.[559]

The definitions of the terms "telecommunications" and "public telecommunications transport service and networks" generally conform to those recognized by

[554] See further T. Takigawa, The Impact of the WTO Telecommunications Agreement on US and Japanese Telecommunications Regulations, 32 *JWT*, No.6, at 43 (1998).

[555] See *supra* note 61.

[556] See further Article XVIII of the GATS.

[557] See further Empel, *supra* note 12, at 18-19.

[558] Although negotiations after the Uruguay Round were concentrated on basic telecommunications, ten governments did schedule some commitments on value-added telecommunications services (e.g. e-mail, on-line data processing or data base retrieval).

[559] See *supra* note 55.

telecommunications services providers and the ITU. Intracorporate communications have been defined to be consistent with other GATT trade instruments.[560]

There are two basic principles in this Annex. First, the principle of transparency. This obligation restates and refines the general obligation of transparency set out in the General Agreement. Members undertake to ensure that relevant information on conditions affecting access to and use of basic PTTNS is publicly available, including: tariffs and other terms and conditions of services, specifications of technical interfaces, registration or licensing requirements.[561]

Second, the principle of access to and use of PTTNS, which sets forth a number of obligations on telecommunications service providers. First of all, access to and use of PTTNS, including private leasing circuits, must be granted on reasonable and non-discriminatory terms. Several obligations are specified: to permit customers to purchase or lease attachment equipment of their own choice; to interconnect private leased or owned circuits with public networks; and to use operating protocols of the services suppliers' or customer's choice. PTTNS may be used for the movement of information within and across borders, including for intracorporate communications of such service suppliers and for access to information contained in databases or otherwise stored in machine-readable form in the territory of any Member. However, a Member is entitled to take measures to ensure the security and confidentiality of messages, or to safeguard the public services responsibilities, to protect the technical integrity of the networks and services or to ensure that no services are provided outside the scope of a Member's Schedule. Furthermore, developing countries can claim an exception in order to strengthen their domestic telecommunications infrastructure or their participation in international negotiations on telecommunications.[562]

There is wide recognition of the importance of global technical standards for compatibility and inter-operability of PTTNS, requiring cooperation among relevant international bodies.

1.4.4. Commitments for Basic Telecommunications

No significant results on basic telecommunications could be achieved in the conclusion of the Uruguay Round due to its sensitivity. Accordingly, one Annex on Negotiations on Basic Telecommunications was adopted and a new organ was set up to be responsible for further negotiations. After another three years' negotiations, 69 countries, which account for about 95 per cent of the world's telecommunications traffic, signed the WTO Telecom Pact. This pact was the first multilateral agreement geared toward global liberalization of the telecommunications industry.[563] During this stage, negotiations concentrated on specific commitments undertaken by each Member on basic telecommunications. The February 1997 deadline for the negotiations on basic telecommunications resulted in the tabling of 55 offers, a substantial improvement over earlier offers from both the technical and substantive aspects. A decision was made to adopt commitments in basic telecommunications as the Fourth Protocol.[564]

---

[560] See further Article 3 of the Annex on Telecommunications.

[561] See further Article 4 of the Annex on Telecommunications.

[562] See further Article 5, paragraph (b) through (g) of the Annex on Telecommunications.

[563] Bronckers, *supra* note 12, at 3.

[564] See further Decision on Commitments in Basic Telecommunications, adopted by the Council for Trade in Services, S/L/19, 30 April 1996, (95-1746).

1.4.4.1. Specific Commitments

Fifty-five schedules of specific commitments were attached to the Fourth Protocol, accounting for sixty-nine countries, a substantial improvement over the April 1996 results when only thirty-four offers were submitted. Participants in the negotiations annexed their commitments to a one-page Protocol to the General Agreement and thus became an integral part of the existing GATS schedules of specific commitments on services.

Forty-nine schedules committed to liberalize the provision of voice telephony to some extent. International voice services were liberalized in forty-five schedules (fifty-nine governments); local services in forty-four schedules (fifty-eight governments); and domestic long distance services in forty-one schedules (fifty-five governments). These commitments permitted competition in the supply of public voice services, either immediate or phased-in, in at least one market segment, except for one, which committed to voice only over closed user groups in all market segments.[565] A large number of commitments (twenty-six governments) were phased-in beyond 5 February 1998. Resale of public voice telephone services was included in thirty schedules which permitted or planned to introduce a degree of competition in public voice services.

One characteristic of the commitments is that a wide range of services was covered. Besides voice telephone services, fifty-one schedules (sixty-five governments) include commitments on data transmission services; forty-eight (sixty-two governments) on cellular/mobile telephone services; forty-two (fifty-six governments) on leased circuits services (the supply of transmission capacity); forty-eight (sixty-two governments) on other types of mobile services (personal communication services, mobile data, paging, etc.). For satellite-related communications, thirty-nine schedules (fifty-three governments) committed on some or all types of mobile satellite services or transport capacity and thirty-eight (fifty-two governments) on fixed-satellite services or transport capacity.[566]

1.4.4.2. Additional Commitments

The most remarkable feature of the Fourth Protocol is undoubtedly that sixty-five of the seventy-two Members which have submitted schedules on basic telecommunications included additional commitments on regulatory disciplines, which was the biggest conceptual and policy breakthrough in the process. The consensus on these disciplines shows that liberalization does not mean that no governmental regulations exist at all. As elaborated in the Reference Paper, domestic regulations are still very important after liberalization. However, it needs to be limited. The economic theory of optimal intervention teaches that, whenever market imperfections call for a government intervention, the government should choose that policy instrument which corrects the market distortion directly at its source without causing costly by-product distortion.

These disciplines are derived from a brief Reference Paper, which lays out six key principles for the redesign of national regulatory rules and institutions to ensure compatibility

[565] Some scholars suggest two countries, which includes Switzerland. However, Switzerland has undertaken to upgrade its commitments when it passes a new telecommunications law, as it did later on.

[566] The number of schedules is different from that specified by M. C. E. J. Bronckers & P. Larouche in their article *Telecommunications Services and the World Trade Organization.* The reason is that after February 1997, two of the sixty-nine participants (Switzerland and Pakistan) have submitted improved basic telecom schedules and three WTO Members who have not participated in the negotiations (Barbados, Cyprus and Surinam) have submitted commitments.

with trade disciplines. They are in line with the regulatory reforms presently taking place in a large number of countries. They touch upon the important areas of regulations that have to be settled in the process of creating competition in national markets. It is not sufficient in a national market to simply declare that competition is allowed; it is necessary to provide an appropriate framework for establishing a competitive market. Potential foreign competitors must also be provided with opportunities and ways to enter the new markets.[567] Thus, the Reference Paper can be considered the first multilateral effort developing agreed regulatory principles and structures to facilitate competition in telecommunications markets.

1.4.4.2.1. Competitive Safeguards

Virtually all existing international trade agreements or arrangements contain safeguard provisions. The issue of safeguards is playing a prominent role - safeguards against anti-competitive behavior by market participants are necessary parts of national regulatory regimes for telecommunications. Governments are required to ensure that major suppliers do not engage in or continue anti-competitive practice.[568]

It is clear from the provision that only a "major supplier" is covered, not all the suppliers. According to the Reference Paper, a supplier who has fulfilled the following three conditions shall be qualified as a major supplier: (1) he has the ability to materially affect the terms of participation (having regard to price and supply); (2) he can affect in the relevant market for basic telecommunications services; and (3) his ability to affect comes from the control over essential facilities[569] or the use of its position in the market.

This definition deviates from the normal understanding of monopoly suppliers. The potential effects of the supplier are not dependent on quantity, but the so-called 'quality'. It covers far more suppliers than monopoly suppliers. The supplier who has a large share of the market does not necessarily, although in most situations it probably does, belong to this category. The basic standard is the substantial effect on price and supply, implying that temporary effects cannot be qualified here. The supplier shall have a strong dominant position in the market which can exist for a relatively long period. Furthermore, the major supplier does not need to be active in person on the relevant markets. It could exert power on the upstream, downstream or neighboring markets to the telecommunications services based on its present position or former influence. Thus, from the definition, we should not be constrained by the superficial activity of a supplier, but look into the potential or extant position or influence of the supplier on the relevant market.

As stated, the "major supplier" is the target of the government's regulation to prevent anti-competition practice. However, it remains within the limits of government to take measures it deems appropriate. Voluminous of materials have dealt with different types of anti-competitive practices. The Reference Paper lists three types, which is certainly not a complete list.

---

[567] See further W. H. Melody (ed.), *Telecom Reform: Principles, Policies and Regulatory Practices*, 418 (1997).

[568] See further Article 1.1. of the Reference Paper.

[569] 'Essential facilities' were defined in the Reference Paper. They are facilities of a public telecommunications transport network or service with the following two characters: firstly, they are exclusively or predominantly provided by a single or limited number of suppliers; secondly, they cannot feasibly be economically or technically substituted in order to provide a service. From the definition, we can see that the local supplier(s) shall have priority in owning or accessing to essential facilities which serve as basis of the services. This situation can not be changed in a short period of time, even though the Reference Paper is carried out. The realistic way is to limit the activity zone of dominant suppliers.

The first practice is cross-subsidization. This consists in the use of profits derived from one area of operations to finance another area. Normally, this is not forbidden in international trade. However, when the operations in the profit-making area are conducted pursuant to exclusive or special rights or when the major supplier in question holds a dominant position in the profit-making area, then it becomes an anti-competition practice.[570] In order to allow for monitoring under the applicable rules of possible anti-competitive cross-subsidies between, on the one hand, areas for which providers of telecommunications services or telecommunications infrastructures enjoy special or exclusive rights and, on the other, their business as telecommunications providers, Member States of the European Union were directed to take the appropriate measures to achieve transparency as regards the use of resources from such protected activities to enter into the liberalized telecommunications market.[571]

The second practice is using information gathered from competitors with trade-restricting results. This practice has been widely accepted as anti-competitive. The third practice is failure to make available, on a timely basis, the technical information about their facilities and operations needed by competitors to enter the market. That means a major supplier is obliged to disclose technical and commercial information to potential suppliers.

1.4.4.2.2. Interconnection

Efficient interconnection is crucial to the effective implementation of virtually all public policies opening competitive telecommunications markets. Interconnection has been an issue of considerable controversy since the earliest days of telephony.[572] It is the cornerstone of competition. Actually, it is closely connected with anti-competitive practice discussed above and may be viewed as the most important competition safeguard. The mandatory interconnection rules for dominant service suppliers are an indispensable requirement for effective infrastructure-based competition.[573] However, the complexity qualifies its being dealt with separately.

Interconnection is clearly defined in the Reference Paper.[574] It sets out the obligation to provide market entrants with interconnection at any technically feasible point in the network. This obligation, to some extent, corresponds to the Annex on Telecommunications. However, we cannot equalize interconnection with access as shown in the additional commitments of the European Union under the Fourth Protocol.[575] According to the Reference Paper, interconnection is to be provided at non-discriminatory terms, conditions, and rates, and should be of a quality no less favorable than what the provider gives its own services.

---

[570] See further Empel, *supra* note 12, at 27.

[571] See further Commission Directive (96/19/EC) of 13 March 1996 Amending Directive 90/388/EEC with regards to the Implementation of Full Competition in Telecommunications Markets, OJ L74/13, March 22, 1996, in J. Angel & I. Walden, *Telecommunications Law Handbook*, 627 (1997). It further provides that Member States should at least require such undertakings once they achieve a significant turnover in the relevant telecommunications service and/or infrastructure provision market, to keep separate financial records, distinguishing between *inter alia*, costs and revenues associated with the provision of services under their special and exclusive rights and those provided under competitive conditions.

[572] Melody, *supra* note 84, at 53.

[573] *Green Paper on Liberalization of Telecommunications Infrastructure and Cable Television Networks*, Comments of the United States of America, March 14, 1995.

[574] See further Article 2.1 of the Reference Paper.

Moreover, interconnection rates are to be cost-oriented, transparent, and, where economically feasible, unbundled.[576]

The principle of transparency is included in order for potential suppliers to obtain interconnection agreements or a reference interconnection offer. Moreover, a dispute mechanism administered by an independent body is required to handle disputes over interconnection terms, conditions and rates. This is supplemental to the provisions on dispute settlement of the GATS. A supplier may have recourse to an independent domestic body, which must resolve such disputes within a reasonable period and if no satisfactory results ensue, then the State it depends may seek help from the WTO dispute settlement procedure.

1.4.4.2.3. Universal Service

Universal service is, for many reasons, a vitally important goal of telecommunications policy. It is generally motivated by distributional considerations, but the precise considerations vary. For example, it could be imposed in such a way as to ensure that similar demands at different locations are supplied at similar prices; or to ensure that the poor can "afford" a telecoms service; or to ensure that groups with special needs (e.g., the disabled) are provided with appropriate services at an affordable cost.

Under such considerations, the Member States may maintain universal service obligations administered in a transparent, non-discriminatory, and competitively neutral manner that is no more burdensome than required to meet the policy objectives.[577] However, such public policy should be guided by the need to make such obligations subsidiary to the promotion of competition. Apportioning the universal service burden must not distort competition and must be done in the context of the rate rebalancing that competition necessitates.[578] As to the type of the obligation, the State has the option to define within the limits set above.

1.4.4.2.4. Public Availability of Licensing Criteria

The reference Paper recognizes the legality of the practice of license. There are three possible types of license which may be granted: a license granted to all persons (general), to persons of a particular class (class) or to a particular person (individual). Licensing policy is exactly what the title suggests--it is merely a policy and is not really to be found in the legislation.[579]

However, when licenses are needed, information and decision-making procedures should be transparent. It is an obligation to make publicly known the licensing criteria, time periods required to decide on a license application, and terms and conditions of individual licenses. Furthermore, reasons shall be given when licenses are denied.[580] The Member States have the right to decide on the situations when a license is needed and the way to make publicly known. However, the national regulator, together with the Member's trade negotiator, must carefully consider the degree and extent to which it wishes to reserve its regulatory discretion

---

[575] In the commitment, the European Union made a distinction between the right of suppliers of non-public services or networks to connect with public networks and services and the right of suppliers of public telecommunications networks and services to interconnect with one another.

[576] See further Article 2.2 of the Reference Paper.

[577] See further Article 3 of the Reference Paper.

[578] See further *supra* note 90.

[579] See further C. D. Long, *Telecommunications Law and Practice*, at 41 and 51(2nd ed., 1995).

[580] Article 4 of the Reference Paper.

in a wide variety of different circumstance. As to limiting licenses to a specific number of providers for a fixed service, if such reservations of regulatory discretion are considered to be desirable, they need to be included as "Limitations" in a Member's Schedule.[581]

1.4.4.2.5. Independent Regulators

Under the liberalized environment, market forces would be relied upon to regulate service providers. The regulatory body would then be able to concentrate on preventing providers from abusing their market position. Competition safeguards, if adopted, will only be effective if the responsible regulatory authorities are sincerely committed to their enforcement. Enforcement of such rules must be fair and even-handed.

The regulatory body is to be separated from service providers, particularly dominant providers, and not accountable to them. One of the main benefits of independent regulation is the transparency it brings to regulatory decision-making. Regulators undertake very important tasks in telecommunications services. For example, the dissemination of information by the regulator is a key element in assuring transparency and in turn promoting the regulatory process and its objective.[582] Regulators shall be vital in guaranteeing the competitiveness of the telecommunications services. It is essential for them to be impartial in decision making. Separating from suppliers is one way to guarantee their independence and build trust from actual suppliers. There are still other ways necessary to put regulators in an impartial position and these are left to the Members to decide.

From the above analysis, we can see that the Reference Paper works to make domestic telecommunications regulations become market-oriented. The discretionary power of the regulatory body is thus largely curtailed. It would be free to concentrate on preventing incumbent providers from abusing their market position. The independence of the regulatory body shall to a large degree help to change the previous situation when public interests have played a key role in sustaining discretionary power of the regulatory body. The task of establishing rules to safeguard competition can be best accomplished by adopting rules of general applicability to all service providers, which is exactly the job of the regulatory body.

1.4.4.2.6. Allocation and Use of Scarce Resources

Frequencies, numbers and rights of way are to be allocated and used in an objective, timely, transparent and non-discriminatory manner, with exception to the national security interests in the secrecy of certain frequency spectrum allocation.[583] Decisions on frequency spectrum issues constitute one of the key responsibilities of national regulators. These decisions are often expressed in terms of granting licenses by deciding on the applicable technical criteria and then, for suppliers of radio communications services, selecting the winner or winners from contending applicants, who may include domestic and foreign

---

[581] See further *supra* note 52. Normally, telecommunications regulators reach considered judgments on many elements involved in issuing licenses based on a weighing of the relevant financial, technical and policy considerations. But when related commitments are made within the WTO framework, these domestic telecommunications regulatory and technical considerations must be based on objective criteria and be no more burdensome on the licensee than is necessary to attain the regulator's legitimate policy goals (GATS Article VI).

[582] *See* further Melody, *supra* note 84, at 313.

[583] Article 6 of the Reference Paper.

suppliers.[584] Therefore, this principle is interconnected with other principles in the Reference Paper. The ultimate goal is to create a competitive atmosphere.

1.4.5. Dispute Settlement

One of the motivations for including services in the WTO framework is the innovative dispute settlement mechanism. This mechanism is known as the WTO's most individual contribution to the stability of the global economy.[585] Indeed, the questionable enforceability of the present ITU rules has raised many doubts. At root, the ITU coordination process depends on the good will of participating administrations. Sanctions for violation are uncertain and rarely applied.[586] Without enforcement, the rule-based system would be worthless.

The Understanding on Rules and Procedures Governing the Settlement of Disputes which incorporates the streamlined dispute settlement mechanism emerged from the Uruguay Round negotiations and is a key text. It is clear from the very beginning that this Understanding shall cover from traditional goods to new areas such as services.[587] This Understanding was further elaborated in the General Agreement according to the specific character of services.[588] We shall discuss the general dispute settlement mechanism first and then focus on the special procedures provided for telecommunications services.

The dispute settlement mechanism begins with bilateral consultations. The Members in dispute shall have the chance to talk to each other directly to see if their differences can be settled by themselves. The General Director of the WTO can also be asked to mediate or try to help in any other way. This stage can take up a period of a maximum of sixty days. This is normal practice for the WTO Members to start proceeding and in most cases it does operate; however, according to the wording of relevant provisions of the GATS, it is not an obligatory procedure. If one Member is considered to have failed its obligations or specific commitments, other injured Members shall directly have recourse to the Understanding on Dispute Settlement. On the other hand, even after the appointment of the panel, the disputing Members can continue the consultation trying to reach an agreement. Thus, the priority is to settle disputes through consultations if possible.

If the consultation fails, the complaining State can request to set up a panel by the Dispute Settlement Body (DSB) with clear terms of reference and an agreed composition.[589] The panel shall hold hearings with the complaining State, the responding State and those that

---

[584] See further *supra* note 58.

[585] See further R. Ruggiero's statement, *Settling Dispute: The WTO's most Individual Contribution*, April 17, 1997. For general discussion on dispute settlement mechanism of the WTO, see L. Wang, Some Observations on the Dispute Settlement System in the World Trade Organization, 29 *JWT*, No.2 (1995); G. Horlick, Dispute Resolution Mechanism: Will the United States Play by the Rules?, 29 *JWT*, No.2 (1995); E. Vermulst & B. Driessen, An Overview of the WTO Dispute Settlement System and Its Relationship with the Uruguay Round Agreements: Nice on Paper but too Much Stress for the System? 29 *JWT*, No.2 (1995); P. T.B. Kohona, Dispute Resolution under the World Trade Organization: An Overview, 28 *JWT*, No.2 (1994); N. Komuro, The WTO Dispute Settlement Mechanism: Coverage and Procedures of the WTO Understanding, 29 *JWT*, No.4 (1995).

[586] See further G C. Staple, The New World Satellite Order: A Report from Geneva, 80 *AJIL*, 708 (1986).

[587] See further Article 1 of Annex 2 to WTO: Understanding on Rules and Procedures Governing the Settlement of Dispute.

[588] See further Article XXII, XXIII of GATS.

[589] Panels are like *ad hoc* tribunals as claimed by Marco C.E.J. Bronckers & P. Larouche at 41, *supra* note 12. However, unlike in a normal tribunal, the panelists are usually chosen in consultation with the countries in dispute. Only if the two sides cannot agree does the General Director of the WTO appoint them.

have announced an interest in the dispute over a period not exceeding six months. A final report is submitted to the two sides and the DSB shall decide on the report within sixty days. Nevertheless, either side can appeal a panel's report based on points of law such as legal interpretation. The appeal review shall not last more than sixty days, with an absolute maximum of ninety days. The losing party must follow the panel report or the appeal report within a reasonable period of time, or it has to enter into negotiations with the winning side in order to determine mutually-acceptable compensation pending full implementation. If all these fail, the DSB shall authorize retaliatory measures against the infringing party.

The GATS provides one special procedure for disputes relating to the avoidance of double taxation. According to Article 22(3) of the GATS, the Council for Trade in Services shall refer the matter to arbitration if seized by parties. However, this situation is rather rare in the telecommunications services.

The special procedure which needs to be mentioned here is the interconnection dispute settlement mechanism in the Reference Paper. As mentioned above, this procedure can be regarded as domestic remedies available to service suppliers. To my understanding, this is an extra remedy for service suppliers who are affected by interconnection regulations. The principle of exhaustion of domestic remedies does not apply here. These suppliers may choose to solve the dispute at the DSB or domestic level in the first instance.

Domestic remedy offers a better solution to the interconnection disputes in telecommunications services. Telecommunications market evolves rather quickly, which is different from other services. This special procedure contains time-periods that are often considerably shorter than those contained in the WTO Understanding. No matter how efficient and fast the WTO dispute settlement mechanism might be, it is difficult for them to make a decision which can keep up with the pace of telecommunications development. Comparatively, the domestic remedies can be more efficient and the final decisions will be based on the actual situation in national telecommunications market. In this sense, it would be advisable to provide rules in relevant documents extending domestic remedies to other aspects of telecommunications services.

1.4.6. Institutional Arrangement

NGBT and GBT were the main organs supervising the negotiations on basic telecommunications; however, they were only temporary in nature, with certain functions in a certain period of time. When the Members reach final deal, they automatically terminate their missions. As far as trade in telecommunications services is concerned, there are two key bodies in the WTO institutional arrangement (other than the Secretariat),

First, the Council for Trade in Services. It works under the guidance of the General Council and oversees the functioning of the GATS. It carries out the functions assigned by the GATS and the General Council. Considering the diversity of services, a subsidiary body (Committee) in charge of telecommunications services was also established.[590] The Council is charged with the duty to establish disciplines to ensure that national regulations are objective, transparent, and not unduly burdensome nor restrictive of cross-border competition in a manner inconsistent with the GATS principles. The Council procures the competitiveness in the telecommunications services in the first place. The Committee on Telecommunications is

[590] See further Article IV of the Marrakesh Agreement Establishing the World Trade Organization.

not under the guidance of the General Council but operates within the general framework and informs the Council of its activities.[591]

Second, the Dispute Settlement Body (DSB). It was established to administer the rules and procedures set out in the GATS, including the consultation and dispute settlement provisions.[592] The DSB has its own chairman and procedure to carry out its responsibilities under Annex 2. However, the General Council shall be able to convene as appropriate to discharge the responsibilities of the DSB.[593]

1.5. Evaluation and Tentative Conclusions

The advent of telecommunications has been significant: it both demands and facilitates international cooperation and agreement. It is recognized that the improvement of telecommunications is an essential condition for the harmonious development of economic activities and a competitive market for both service providers and users.[594]

The pace of restructuring the telecommunications sector has increased dramatically in recent years. During the past decade, the developing countries have experienced rapid change in the demand for telecommunications services and in the institutions and technologies necessary to deliver these services.[595] Further progress in science and technology has been made possible by the implementation of legal regulations through agreements, standards and recommendations.[596]Liberalization of telecommunications services can only be achieved through this way. As a result of the conclusion of the basic telecommunications agreement and the GATS, the telecommunications world has changed fundamentally for the first time.

Never before had people thought of liberalizing the telecommunications market under the multilateral framework. Until a few years ago the provision of basic telecommunications services was seen as a natural monopoly, in which it made no sense to envisage the introduction of competition, let alone foreign competition.[597] Many scholars have spoken highly of the achievements thus obtained; however, some are calm enough to say the opposite. It is true that the results obtained were still far from perfect, nevertheless, it is only a start of the whole liberalization process which has for the time being established a solid foundation for further negotiations. We need to be more objective and enthusiastic to carry out the agreements and at the same time, aiming for aspiring improvements. Undoubtedly, the measures being considered to open up basic telecommunications markets to international trade could have far-reaching consequences at all levels in many countries. Considering the telecommunications sector as a whole, it is clear that the effects of the results of the Uruguay

---

591 See further *supra* note 45, at 38.

592 See further Article 2 of the Annex 2 to the Marrakesh Agreement.

593 *Supra* note 102. This implies that the General Council can turn itself, as needed, into a body to adjudicate trade disputes.

594 See further Commission Directive (90/388/EEC) of 28 June 1990 on Competition in the Markets for Telecommunications Services, OJL 192/10, 24 July 1990, in J. Angel & I. Walden, *Telecommunications Law Handbook*, 589 (1997).

595 See further The Framework for the Future, International Telecommunication Union.

596 See further M. Lachs, Views from the Bench: Thoughts on Science, Technology and World Law, 86 *AJIL*, 687-688 (1992).

597 *Trade in Telecommunication Services*, address delivered by R. Ruggiero, Director-General of the WTO, to the ITU 2nd World Telecommunication Policy Forum, Geneva. March 16, 1998.

Round on the liberalization of international trade in telecommunications services are the most appropriate starting points.

1.5.1. General Observations

It is true that liberalization shall happen simultaneously even outside the WTO framework; however, the WTO provides the most appropriate forum to liberalize the telecommunications services. Actually, by making commitments to open their market, governments are merely acknowledging what is already happening. In particular, it is necessary to reflect on the changing role of governments, from being direct players in telecommunications to policy makers and regulators. With liberalization, the governments' direct operational influence may be greatly diminished, and there will be more work for governments to do under a competitive market environment than was the case under monopoly service provision. The reason is that existing market players as well as potential new entrants will be looking for clear guidance on what sort of regime will be established for issues such as interconnection, numbering, universal service obligations and traffic policy.[598]

Liberalization is an irreversible trend; however, being included into the WTO framework shall quicken the whole process and push the process a step further. Under the auspices of the WTO, the Members were able to reach the first multilateral trade agreement in telecommunications services, which has, first of all, confirmed the trend towards opening telecommunications market around the world. Sixty-nine countries that accounted for more than 90 per cent of the global market made commitments in February 1997 confirming the status of liberalization of their telecommunications services. They were aware that the commitments made could not be withdrawn or modified easily and could only be extended in scope in future rounds of negotiations. The organs set up to implement and supervise the operations of the Agreements have further guaranteed the extensive compliance of the Members. Moreover, the net effect of these surveillance and consultation mechanisms serves to create a measure of convergence in the pace and content of national liberalization programs.[599]

The dual function of the telecommunications services was widely recognized. On the one hand, it is an important service sector *per se*; on the other hand, it is also an important facilitary service. The Members realized the role of telecommunications services as a mode of delivery for other services. It is safe to say that telecommunications are a production factor for almost all economic activities. Through its multiplier effect, it enhances activities in the entire economy and becomes increasingly essential for the international competitiveness of national industries.[600] Those planning to diversify their economies, with emphasis on services, recognize the importance for new entrants in these sectors to have easy access to cheap and reliable telecommunications--an objective which can be facilitated under more liberal conditions of delivery of telecommunications services.[601]

---

[598] This concern has been deeply dealt with in the Reference Paper, from which the Member States undertook additional commitments in regulatory regime. *See* further WTO Reference Paper on Basic Telecommunications, which covers six domestic areas.

[599] See further Hufbauer, *supra* note 23, at 47.

[600] J. Karlsson, *Dynamics of Economic Telecom Growth, Transnational Data and Communications Report*, July/August, 1993, at 23-24.

[601] See further P. Tarjanne, Trade in Telecommunications Services: The WTO Agreement and the Role of the ITU, *The World Business Agenda for Electronic Commerce*, published by ISC.

A more significant achievement is the adoption of the Reference Paper by almost all the Members. It touches on the sensitive part of regulatory principles at national level and accordingly, the traditional principle of State sovereignty. We have witnessed that the entire history of telecommunications services has been the inherent right of States to regulate their national system as they see fit. However, with the additional commitments, they are obliged to take other factors into account. This is a big stride away from the traditional arena.

It is evident that the ultimate object of the WTO "game" is to bring complete competition to the telecommunications services. Careful study of the agreements can show that competition law can be traced in each and every provision. The Members undertake wide-range obligations to fight against anti-competitive practice. This has further strengthened the belief that liberalization in telecommunications services is well underway. However, we will still need to wait and see the fruit of the arrangements.

Whilst admiring the success of the negotiations, we shall keep sober-minded about the insufficiency which needs further improvements in the next round of negotiations. Firstly, some important telecommunications services are still excluded from the agreement. For example, the transmission of audiovisual material could become a loophole as telecommunications and broadcasting converge through digital technologies. Secondly, many Members made exception to the Agreement, especially to Article II of the GATS. For example, the United States retaliated against the perceived shortcoming of the Canadian commitments by filing an Article II Exception on foreign ownership of US-based companies active in certain satellite services.[602] Thirdly, as discussed above, the dispute settlement mechanism may not keep up with the rapid development of telecommunications. The situation changes rather frequently, nice as the procedure might be, it might become meaningless with the passage of time. Therefore, a more simplified and efficient procedure must be found to fit the needs. Actually, the case in interconnection might be one way. With the implementation of the highly valued Reference Paper, the vagueness of the wording shall cause a lot of practical problems. It is possible that the national governments shall take measures to damnify its function. Further clarification is needed to improve its validity.

1.5.2. Implication for Developing Countries

Increased attention is being paid to the special needs of developing countries, in particular to the possibility of achieving maximum benefits from their participation. The developing countries' concerns were highly evaluated during negotiations, and special provisions were set out to accommodate the needs of developing countries.[603]

Most developing countries are not so technologically advanced as the developed countries. In addition to domestic employment considerations, many developing countries claimed that the US was far ahead of other parts of the world in the telecommunications sector. They were rather afraid that once the market were open, their national market would suffer and accordingly refusal to open their market serves to prevent developed countries to

---

[602] The United States' limitations on market access include no issuance of radio licenses to operators with more than 20 per cent direct foreign ownership. It submitted an MFN Exemption List on telecommunications services involving the one-way satellite transmission of DBS television services and digital audio services.

[603] The most important provision is Article IV of the GATS, which set the general principle of increasing participation of developing countries.

dominate their own "infant" service sector.[604] For decades, the pursuit of universal service seemed in direct conflict with competition.

However, the truth is that governments have practically lost the power to dictate service providers at the international level. As a result, almost all markets are now open to some degree of competition. At the present stage, internalization of telecommunications services is at the very core of economic globalization. The pace of restructuring the telecommunications sector has increased dramatically in recent years and will continue well into the next decade. For developing countries, the growing globalization of services presents both opportunities and challenges. From the statistic part, contrary to what they have been afraid of, developing countries will gain from multilateral agreements. There are opportunities for developing new exports and attracting more services-related foreign investment. Developing countries are likely to benefit from embracing the WTO principles of market opening and allowing foreign investment as a way to keep up investment needed to bring their networks to a level allowing them to compete internationally and attract investment in other economic activities to speed their development.[605] Whilst worrying about what possible disadvantages may occur, developing countries are continuing with liberalization *per se*, especially Brazil and Indonesia which have a comparatively obvious advantage in this field. Actually, the most improvements in the Uruguay Round negotiations came from developing countries and a significant portion of the expected 100 to 200 per cent growth over the next few years in worldwide telecommunications services revenues was expected to come from developing countries.

Furthermore, as telecommunications services industries rely increasingly on information technology, technological progress will allow countries to leapfrog stages of development in building their info-infrastructures. Actually, the services revolution places a premium on the development of a competitive telecommunications system. Most developing countries are hard pressed to meet the demand for even basic telecommunications services by themselves, and investment in networks for value-added services is considered an unaffordable luxury. However, technology now allows a country to develop a dual structure for telecommunications services: a country can invest in low-cost, dedicated networks for business needs in parallel with expanding the basic infrastructure, [606] while other able countries fill in the gap.

Nevertheless, based on the current domestic situation, developing countries face challenges in the new era. Formerly, telecommunications services were monopolized. With the commitments to open their markets and compete with international suppliers, they urgently need to design a relatively operationable domestic regulatory policy, which can fight against anti-competitive practice and more important, procure domestic benefits; experts in telecommunications shall be needed to help structuring national regulations. All in all, the key word here is "transition".[607] In the same way as the WTO agreements take several years to complete, we can expect the transition in developing countries will also take some time. The adoption of a liberal trade and investment in telecommunications services is essential for

---

[604] See further S. F. Benz, Trade Liberalization and the Global Service Economy, 19 *JWT*, No.2, at 99 (1985).

[605] *Supra* note 60.

[606] C. A. Primo Braga, *The Impact of Internationalization of Services on Developing Countries, USIS-Economic Perspectives*, April 1996.

[607] Opening address by Dr. P. Tarjanne in ITU 2nd World Telecommunication Policy Forum: *Trade in Telecommunication Services*, Geneva, March 16, 1998.

countries to maximize the benefits to be derived from internationalization of services and to move towards the information age. This is particularly true for developing countries.

1.5.3. The Role of the ITU

The success of the Uruguay Round negotiations, together with the establishment of the WTO, is a significant step towards liberalization and globalization. It was suggested that the above development in the field of telecommunications services would diminish the role of the ITU. However, this is not the truth. In essence, the WTO is a trade organization. Telecommunications services are not only subject to trade regulation, but also to technical regulation. When dealing with commercialization of telecommunications, it is impossible to avoid touching on the technical aspects. The WTO shall not be competent in this area. It is vital to recognize the complementary role of the ITU as regards trade agreements on telecommunications services.

The ITU has an important role to play in the liberalization process, which is being undertaken under the auspices of the WTO. There are several ways the ITU can help do this. As the Telecommunications Annex to the GATS recognizes, global standards are essential to the efficient, nondiscriminatory operation of global markets. The WTO is not a specialized telecommunication body. It does not have the technical expertise of the sector, which is the domain of the ITU.[608] The ITU could provide qualified experts to assist the WTO in making detailed trade policies and regulations. The development of global markets will also be facilitated, particularly in the area of satellite services, if there are global allocations of spectrum to particular services. The whole question of how countries manage spectrum and other scarce communications resources is a very important element of trade liberalization and the prevention of discrimination between domestic and foreign suppliers, which the ITU is up to.[609]

More importantly, when it comes to the dispute settlement, the ITU might function as advisor or even members of panels to help clarify technical aspects involved in the disputes. Moreover, the ITU has been dealing with the issue of telecommunications for a long time. Its practice of extensive private sector participation might serve as a model to the WTO activities. The two organizations should be more closely integrated in dealing with the issue of telecommunications services.

1.5.4. Towards a Multilateral Trade Framework

The old paradigm of monopolies confined within national frontiers is out; a new model of cross-border competition is in.[610] with the negotiations of the GATS, policies affecting telecommunications services are firmly on the multilateral trade-policy agenda. The progressive opening up of world markets for telecommunications services through the dismantling of barriers and the introduction of competition is vital. By now, it has become trite to insist on the changes affecting the telecommunications sector, in what has appropriately been termed a revolution. Today's space companies are no longer just subcontractors to the government. Competition is a keyword in today's space corporation.

---

[608] *Supra* note 118.

[609] See further Dr. P. Tarjanne, *The Role of Telecommunications in Globalization and Regional Integration*, ITU, Keynote Address, Fourth International Seminar on New Technologies and Telecommunications Services, SEMINT 97, Foz do Iguaçu, Paraná, Brazil, October 7, 1997.

[610] 'Cheap Talk', *Financial Times*, February 17, 1997, at 20.

The new environment includes competition from all comers, including backyard ventures and aggressive small firms.[611]

However, only time will tell how effective the GATS will be in terms of liberalizing world trade in telecommunications. No doubt after the conclusion of the agreements, a new paradigm is emerging for international trade in telecommunications - a new pattern based on global competition. It recognizes that trade in telecommunications services now takes place in a multilateral environment in which the majority of trade relationships include multiple intermediaries between buyer and seller.[612]

By moving towards a policy of liberalization, the Members at the same time become much more aware of the costs and benefits of their actions. The transition to a multilateral framework will bring benefits in terms of more wide choices and lower prices of services to customers; to the suppliers, they will be able to have access to new markets and accordingly, new profits. Over and above, the benefits of the multilateral system are sure to outtrump the costs in the long run. The GATS framework should be positively welcomed. There is widespread hope that the new framework shall help to establish a new architecture for global telecommunications policy that facilitates increasingly deep liberalization in the years to come. Only then will benefits of the new emerging framework serve to the benefits of international society.

2. Further Liberalization of Telecommunications Services

2.1. Introduction

Telecommunications services were previously subject to tight national regulatory control. This concept changed when approaching the end of the 20th century. Telecommunications, as tradable services, underwent significant liberalization with the introduction of 1997 WTO Agreement on Basic Telecommunications. [613] Growing recognition by governments that competitiveness is increasingly dependent on innovative and cost-effective telecommunications services has led to telecommunications deregulation and liberalization of the international trade environment.[614] The United States (US) has been a leader in this aspect and various laws have been put in place to liberalize the telecommunications sector.[615] The

611 See further J. Fuller & K. Lacobie, Economics of Strategic Planning, in J. S. Greenberg & H. R. Hertzfeld (eds.), *Space Economics*, 360 (1992).

612 Executive summary of World Telecommunication Development Report 1996/97: Trade in Telecommunications, ITD, February 1997.

613 See further Fourth Protocol to the General Agreement on Trade in Services, WTO/S/L/20, April 30, 1996. For general discussion of the achievements and definitions of relevant concepts in the present discussion, see Y. Zhao, The Commercial Use of Telecommunications under the Framework of GATS, 24 *Air & Space Law*, No.6, 304-328 (1999).

614 Communication from Canada: Initial Negotiating Proposal on Telecommunications Services, WTO, S/CSS/W/53, 14 March 2001 (01-1410), Council for Trade in Services, Special Session.

615 See for example, Telecommunications Act of 1996, Pub. L. No. 104-104, 110 Stat. 56 (codified in scattered sections of 47 U.S.C. 151-170). See also K.L. Haennicke, The Raging Telecommunications War: The Offensive Steps the World Trade Organization Should Take, 9 *Tulsa Journal of Comparative & International Law* 180-181 (Fall 2001).

European Union (EU) took the same attitude and is well underway towards total liberalization.[616]

The implementation of the 1997 WTO Agreement helped intensify this trend. The policies have increased liberalization, privatization and competition. While this is the first step to liberalize telecommunications in an international context, the achievements obtained therefrom have been extolled as remarkable.[617] For example, less than five years into the implementation of the WTO Agreement, the average international accounting rates have been significantly lowered: rates on the US-UK are as low as 10 cents (US) per minute.[618] In liberalizing the telecommunications industry, Thailand permits domestic and foreign private business to apply for licenses to operate telecommunications services, which substantially diversify the services available in Thailand and lower the prices for services.[619]

Nevertheless, this first attempt also raised expectations, and much remains to be accomplished. Since the conclusion of the Agreement, rapid development in technology has produced new challenges to telecommunications.

Lots of changes have taken place since the conclusion of the 1997 WTO Agreement.[620] Confronting the competitive situation in the telecommunications market, three international satellite organizations (INTELSAT, INMARSAT, EUTELSAT) have been privatized.[621] Other historic events include the collapse of the dot.coms[622] and failures of major telecom corporations, such as Qwest, Global Crossing and Worldcom, and bankruptcies of all the mobile satellite communication providers (Iridium, Globalstar, ICO, Orbcomm, etc.). The current state of the industry is characterized by widespread economic slowdown, overcapacity, market and regulatory failures, excess debt and corporate fraud.[623] To a certain extent, the current turmoil in the communications industry results from immature markets. The policy of self-regulation functions well in a mature market. In light of all the changes above, scholars have extensively evaluated the impact of the Agreement and pointed out possible areas for further improvements.

The failure of a new round of negotiations has not forestalled various demands for the further liberalization of telecommunications. Member States of the WTO have submitted

---

[616] Beginning in 1990, the European Commission and the Council launched a decade-long program to introduce service sector competition into the telecommunications market in Europe. See for example, Liberalization of International Telecommunications, at <http://www.bt.com> (last visited April 4, 2002); see also M.A. Lamb, Legislative Development: Directive 99/64/EC Amending Directive 90/388/EEC on Telecommunications Networks and Cable TV Networks Owned by a Single Operator: Telecommunications and TV Networks, 6 *Columbia Journal of European Law* 142-143 (Winter 2000); E.J. Dommering, Article 90 of the EEC Treaty and the Telecommunications, Broadcasting and Postal Sectors, in Stuyck & Vossestein (eds.), *State Entrepreneurship, National Monopolies and European Community Law* 53 (1993); H. Papaconstantinou, *Free Trade and Competition in EEC Law, Policy and Practice* 27 (1988).

[617] C. Blouin, The WTO Agreement on Basic Telecommunications: A Reevaluation, 24 *Telecommunications Policy* 135 (2000).

[618] *World Trade Organization Basic Telecommunications Agreement*, available at <http://www.fcc.gov> (last visited October 28, 2003).

[619] *The Forthcoming Liberalization of the Thai Telecommunications Market: Present and Future Trendds*, available at <http://www.tilleandgibbins.com> (last visited October 28, 2003).

[620] See for example, C. DeFrancia, Local Competition and Telecommunications Convergence: Gauging the Need for New Legislation, 17 *Journal of Law & Politics* 739 (Fall 2001).

[621] See further International Organizations, available at <http://www.hunsat.hu/angol/emuholdak.html> (last visited July 31, 2003).

[622] See for example, As Dot.Coms Collapse, Sloan Applicants Speed up Study Plans, available at <http://mitsloan.mit.edu/news/release/2001/2003.html> (last visited July 31, 2003).

[623] UNI World Telecom Press Conference, London & Washington DC, October 9, 2002, Telecom Meltdown Fact Sheet, available at <http://www.union-network.org/telecom> (last visited June 27, 2003).

proposals and liberalization in telecommunications has been generally accepted by international society as a whole. Thus, while taking into account of the existing WTO Agreement, it is more than urgent to research into the possible areas for liberalization of telecommunications.

This section will be divided into several parts. Part two will deal with the issue of conceptual confusion. While basic and value-added telecommunications were delineated in former negotiations, further work should be done to classify the new telecommunications services. This Part will try to make clear the difference of relevant concepts. Based on this structure, Part three will elaborate on possible commitments that could be offered in the near future. While regulatory issues occupy an important position in procuring competition, Part four will intensively discuss further improvements in Reference Paper (RP). Conclusion will be offered in Part five.

2.2. Delineation of Telecommunications Services

Telecommunications services were defined as tradable and brought to the framework of WTO in Uruguay Round of negotiations. However, this conception should be further strengthened. The character of "tradability" constitutes the basis for including telecommunications in the arena of WTO. The complication involved in different types of telecommunications services caused much trouble to the smooth negotiations at that time.[624] Later the conceptions of basic and value-added telecommunications services were introduced, which largely solved the awkward situation.

Fifteen categories of telecommunications services were defined in the negotiations, which were further differentiated as basic and value-added services.[625] Basic services include all telecommunications services, both public and private that involve end-to-end transmission of customer supplier information; value-added services are telecommunications for which suppliers add value to the customer's information by enhancing its form or content or by providing for its storage and retrieval.[626] It is to be noted there are different understandings on this differentiation in different national background.[627] But the present differentiation is now well accepted within the framework of WTO.[628] What may result in the meantime is the application of existing sector-specific regulation, depending on whether particular converging services are deemed to be captured by definitions that were designed for the

---

624 A fundamental contribution, and subsequent influence of the US was the distinction between basic and value-added services. However, this distinction was absent in the legislation of some European Union Members States and some other Members of the WTO.

625 See further WTO, S/C/W/120. The first eight categories of services were agreed to be examples of basic services, which include voice telephone services, packet-switched data transmission services, circuit-switched data transmission services, telex services, telegraph services, facsimile services, private leased circuit services. Value-added services include electronic mail, on-line information and database retrieval, electronic data interchange, enhanced facsimile services, code and protocol conversion, on-line information and/or data processing.

626 See <http://www.wto.org> (last visited July 31, 2003).

627 This can arise out of the flexibility of the model schedule adopted for basic telecommunications, which authorizes distinction between local/long distance/international, wire or radio-based, public or non-public, resale or facilities-based services, satellite/non-satellite, mobile/fixed services.

628 Decision on Commitments in Basic Telecommunications, April 26, 1996, para. 1.

telecommunications sector alone.[629] Thus, the present task is to clarify the sub-categories for commitments concerning the different distinctions under different categories.

This division is further connected with the issue of regulation. After the Uruguay Round of negotiations, during which commitments were largely made concerning value-added services, further negotiations were held concerning basic services. Reference Paper (RP) was reached to provide guidance on domestic regulation. It is generally acknowledged that appropriate regulation should be drafted, or in place regarding basic services, but the policy of self-regulation should be adopted for value-added services.[630]

With the development of modern technology, new services are available.[631] However, since the WTO Agreement was reached in 1997, new services arising thereafter are totally left out. Moreover, technological convergence brings together fiber optics, digital compression and packet switching, all having their most profound effect on communications at the network level.[632] While convergence encourages functional integration, it typically produces a plurality of distribution technologies and consumer devices.[633] It is thus now important to bring these services to the WTO, especially the application of information networks whose quality, capacity and cost meet the needs of the users. Moving from the core to the periphery of the Internet, the past years have seen a battle over so-called "open access" rules for high-speed Internet access providers, typically cable modem providers.[634] In this respect, the barriers of access to the Internet, such as the requirement of connectivity with local telecom companies, should be eliminated. Furthermore, it is expected that other new services will continue to arise later on, and mechanism should thus be provided to offer periodical review for timely inclusion of new services in the WTO Agreement. The phenomenon of the increasing overlap between new and existing services could produce differential regulation for similar services[635] also justified the necessity of periodical review.[636]

The following new services should be listed and explained: Internet delivery services; online distribution services; computer and related services; online advertising services; express delivery services; and certain financial services.[637] For the purpose of classification,

---

[629] W.J. Drake & E.M. Noam, Assessing the WTO Agreement on Basic Telecommunications, in G.C. Hufbauer & E. Wada (Eds.), *Unfinished Business: Telecommunications after the Uruguay Round* 53 (Washington, D.C.: Institute for International Economics, 1997).

[630] P.L. Spector, Business Transactions, Disputes and Regulation: The World Trade Organization Agreement on Telecommunications, 32 *The International Lawyer*, No. 2, 217 (1998); A.J. Campbell, Self-Regulation and the Media, 51 *Federal Communications Law Journal* 715-716 (1999).

[631] R. Frieden, Adjusting the Horizontal and Vertical in Telecommunications Regulation: A Comparison of the Traditional and a New Layered Approach, 55 *Federal Communications Law Journal* 211-212 (March 2003).

[632] D.J. Collis *et al.*, Winners and Losers: Industry Structure in the Converging World of Telecommunications, Computing and Entertainment, in D.B. Yoffie (ed.), *Competing in the Age of Digital Convergence* 160 (Boston: Harvard Business School Press, 1997).

[633] D. Ellis *et al.*, *New Media Networks: Selling Broadband Connections to Consumers* 1 (Toronto: Omnia Communications, 1999).

[634] See further J.B. Speta, A Common Carrier Approach to Internet Interconnection, 54 *Federal Communications Law Journal* 233-234 (March 2002).

[635] B. Clements, The Impact of Convergence on Regulatory Policy in Europe, 22 *Telecommunications Policy*, No. 3, 200 (1998).

[636] Changes in technology and market development make definitions difficult. Canadian Radio-television and Telecommunications Commission (CRTC), Report on New Media, Broadcasting Public Notice 1999-84/Telecom Public Notice 99-14, May 17, 1999.

[637] See further Communication from the United States: Market Access in Telecommunications and Complementary Services: the WTO's Role in Accelerating the Development of a Globally Networked Economy, WTO S/CSS/W/30, 18 December 2000 (00-5571), Council for Trade in Services, Special Session.

Internet delivery services, or more exactly, packet-switched data transmission services, should be considered as basic services so that the Reference Paper which has been agreed upon in 1997 can be applied. One WTO Member has proposed that all other new services could be categorized as value-added services.[638] With all these discrepancies, we need to examine the services stated above and try to identify the proper categories for each of them. This requires the inputs from technical experts.

2.3. Deepening Commitments in Telecommunications Services

The negotiations on telecommunications have produced fruitful results leading to successful liberalization in WTO Member States. Many scholars and politicians extolled this achievement as a great success against the traditional conception of monopoly in telecommunications services. Indeed, Member States made commitments under the framework of WTO, which is the first time in the history of telecommunications that sovereign States have agreed to submit to compulsory liberation of the sector.[639]

While the achievements should not be overlooked, it is indeed irrefutable that improvements could be made based on the existing commitments. The widely accepted perception that liberation will benefit the development of this sector should naturally lead to the conclusion that full commitments should be made.[640]

2.3.1. Market Access

Telecommunications liberalization originally comes from a market-based policy founded on a belief that increased competition in the domestic market brings about telecommunications innovation and cost decreases. Thus, new entrants should be welcomed to bring in new competition. However, during the Uruguay Round negotiations, this was not the case.[641] Market access was refused on several occasions.

Indeed, market access is a significant area for setting limitations, which are maintained generally by limiting the number of operators, limiting the type of legal entities, or setting a limit to the level of direct and indirect foreign ownership allowed.[642] Thus, the limitations are most often associated with commitments on commercial presence, more significantly, for basic services. Such limitations largely diminish the potential for real competition in the national market. This is because restrictions prevent foreign competitors from entering the market and displacing domestic companies that may be less efficient.[643] From the wording of the WTO documents, limitations on market access in telecommunications are justified only

---

638 Communication from Switzerland: GATS 2000: Telecommunications, WTO S/CSS/W/72, 4 May 2001 (01-2358), Council for Trade in Services, Special Session.

639 P. Malanczuk & H. de Vlaam, International Trade in Telecommunications Services and the Results of the Uruguay Round of GATT, 3 *Telecommunications and Space Journal* 269 (1996).

640 See for example, R.B. Self, Trade in Services: The Round is Underway, *The Metropolitan Corporate Counsel*, Mid-Atlantic Edition, at 6, May 2000.

641 T. Takigawa, The Impact of the WTO Telecommunications Agreement on US and Japanese Telecommunications Regulations, 32 *Journal of World Trade*, No. 6, 43 (1998).

642 GATS Article XVI, para. 2. For example, the US has one of the stringest limitations on foreign ownership—25%.

643 A. Gates, Convergence and Competition: Technological Change, Industry Concentration and Competition Policy in the Telecommunications Sector, *58 University of Toronto Faculty of Law Review* 113 (Spring, 2000); J.G. Sidak, *Foreign Investment in American Telecommunications* 5 (Chicago: University of Chicago Press, 1997).

on the basis of available resources.[644] Technical standards shall be offered to decide whether refusal of market access is qualified or not.[645] Any artificial limitations, like limitations based on cultural or industrial policy rationales, should be deemed against the principles of WTO and accordingly, be deleted.[646]

2.3.2. National Treatment

Limitations were registered regarding national treatment in terms of residence, of ownership of property or land, and in particular, limitations on nationality of certain categories of personnel. This is ostensibly contrary to the original idea of national treatment, which requires that no *de jure* or *de facto* discrimination should be made between foreign and local service providers.[647] As discussed in market access, limitations shall be based only on the availability of resources and no other limitations are justified. Only by sticking to this point, will the idea of equality of opportunity in competition be realized.

2.3.3. Most-Favored-Nation (MFN) Exemptions

The overuse of MFN exemptions would indeed undermine the functioning and credibility of unconditional MFN treatment. A balance needs to be struck between individual national concerns and the limitation or prevention of abusive uses of such exemptions. For further liberalization of telecommunications, Member States should at least consider the elimination of exemptions related to the following issues.

2.3.3.1. Satellite Services

Internet-based services are undergoing dramatic growth, similarly, satellite transport capacity will possibly become nearly important as land-based capacity within a short period of time.[648] Audio-visual services, such as broadcasting services, were not included during the negotiations, accordingly, satellite facilities used for Direct Broadcast Satellite (DBS) and Direct-to-Home (DTH) services were excluded from their commitments out of different considerations. For example, the US took the MFN exemption for the services as a leverage for the next round of negotiations.[649] The EU reserved its right to challenge this exemption as the MFN principle applies to services which are part of the audio-visual commitments undertaken by the US in 1994 as a result of the Uruguay Round.[650]

---

[644] The radio spectrum is a scarce resource whose administration is the responsibility of the competent national authorities, in accordance with the ITU Radio Regulations, allocations, allotments and assignments to different services.

[645] Communication from Australia: Negotiating Proposal for Telecommunication Services, WTO S/CSS/W/17, 5 December 2000 (00-5276), Council for Trade in Services, Special Session.

[646] D.W. Conklin, Foreign Ownership Restrictions, *in Adapting to New Realities: Canadian Telecommunications Policy Conference* 33 (London, Ont.: Richard Ivey School of Business, University of Western Ontario, 1998); S. Globerman & D.A. Hagen, Foreign Investment in Telecommunications: Assessing the Policy Environment, in D. Orr & T.A. Wilson (eds.), *The Electronic Village: Policy Issues of the Information Economy* 118 (Toronto: C.D. Howe Institute, 1999).

[647] GATS Article XVIII, para. 3.

[648] Telecommunication Services, background note by the Secretariat, WTO S/C/W/74, 8 December 1998 (98-4942), Council for Trade in Services.

[649] See further Global Competition in Telecommunications, Remarks of FCC Commissioner Susan Ness before the Women's Foreign Policy Group, Washington, January 23, 1997.

[650] See further Annex III to the July 2000 Communication to the 133 Committee on the Preparation of GATS 2000: Status of the Implementation of the WTO/GATS Commitments and Review of the Situation in Third Countries Telecommunications Markets, available at <http://europa.eu.int> (last visited July 31, 2003).

The satellite services sector of the telecommunications market is growing rapidly and continues to diversify its service offerings. It is expected that the new satellite systems will bring business and other consumers a wide variety of new broadband and mobile voice and data services and connect these users in countries around the globe.[651] The existence of this exemption will not only allow unfair discrimination, but also prevent the most efficient development of cross-border telecommunications. Thus, the issue is not whether the exemption should or can be lifted, but where and when to lift the exemption. A new round of WTO negotiations should provide the right forum for this initiative.

2.3.3.2. Accounting Rates

This is an issue closely related with liberalization. The vast majority of international telecommunications traffic is processed within a corresponding system, whereby the telecommunications operators of the originating country cooperate with those of the terminating country to complete the phone calls or other services. The operator of the originating country collects the fee and an "accounting rate" is agreed to among operators in different countries to compensate the latter. Generally a non-liberalized country has higher fees, which diverts the traffic to a liberalized country with lower fees. Thus, the balance of the two countries is upset as a consequence, operators of liberalized countries pay large compensation to non-liberalized countries. This in turn prevents these liberalized countries from further reducing fees.[652]

As a result, it is vital to note the charging arrangements. The charge should represent the true costs of the traffic. Fortunately, we have witnessed the progress made concerning accounting rates by the International Telecommunications Union (ITU).[653] Building on the achievements of the ITU, accompanied by the ensuing nondiscriminatory charging arrangements, this exemption could be optimistically expected to be lifted in a new round of negotiations.

2.3.3.3. Government Procurement

The MFN principle and specific commitments relating to market access and national treatment do not apply to government procurement. Nothing until now has touched on the non-discriminatory access by foreign operators to government bidding procedures for international services and other telecommunications services contracts. No timetable was set for the completion of the negotiations regarding this issue.[654] This policy probably has most influence on foreign operators since in most cases governments are the largest single consumers of telecommunications services. Efforts should be made to eliminate any non-tariff barriers, which inhibit full and open market access in telecommunications services, which includes particularly limitations on government procurement.

---

[651] International Bureau Issues Annual Report on Developments in International Telecommunications Markets to Senator Hollings, January 18, 2000, at <http://www.fcc.gov> (last visited July 31, 2003).

[652] See further M.C.E.J. Bronckers & P. Larouche, Telecommunications Services and the World Trade Organization, 31 *Journal of World Trade*, No. 3, 10-12 (1997).

[653] See further P. Tarjanne, Preparing for the Next Revolution in Telecommunications: Implementing the WTO Agreement, 23 *Telecommunications Policy* 54, 60 (1999).

[654] See Article XIII of the GATS.

2.3.4. Miscellaneous Commitments

Many States made commitments during the Uruguay round of negotiations, but they are to be implemented in a phase-in manner over long periods of time. This is not understandable in this sector, which is asked to provide very quickly to other sectors cheap, high-quality and fast-evolving services.[655] Witnessing the rapid development of telecommunications, it is time to urge the WTO Members to hasten the steps. The imbalance in commitments or incomplete competitive environment in the end will deter the implementation of the final economic gains. Furthermore, since 1997, new States have become the Members of WTO, it is also vital to urge them to conform to the regular rules in the playground.

Furthermore, the new round of negotiations on telecommunications services should be closely keeping the pace with the general WTO negotiations on issues like competition and subsidies. The agreement reached so far arguably signifies the emergence of a rudimentary international competition law governing telecommunications.[656] As fully competitive markets emerge, the provisions of competition law and subsidies should replace industry-specific regulation in many markets. It is to be expected that individual documents will be formulated in the Doha round of negotiations acknowledging the importance and universal nature of the topics mentioned above. Thus, further liberalization of telecommunications will need to reflect this trend.

2.4. Pro-Competitive Regulatory Environment for Telecommunications

More and more countries are opening most or all segments of their telecommunications sector to competition. Experience reveals, however, that successfully introducing effective competition in telecommunications usually requires more than simply eliminating barriers to entry in the various segments of the market.[657] Proper regulation also plays an important part in procuring effective competition to achieve ultimate liberalization. As discussed above, value-added services should be regulated as little as possible, while market forces should play a major role in regulation. The present discussion of regulatory environment deals only with basic services.

To be competitive, telecommunications regulations should be able to offer reasonably and competitively priced services, transparent and consistent licensing procedures, and pro-competitive and non-discriminatory policies.[658] One spectacular achievement in this aspect has been the conclusion of the Reference Paper (RP), which sets forth six guiding principles.[659] It is the first time that the issue of regulation will be discussed in a multilateral

---

[655] Communication from the European Communities and their Member States, GATS 2000: Telecommunications, WTO S/CSS/W/35, December 22, 2000 (00-5623), Council for Trade in Services Special Session.

[656] H.N. Janisch, International Influences on Communications Policy in Canada, in D. Orr & T.A. Wilson (eds.), *The Electronic Village: Policy Issues of Information Economy* 59 (Toronto: C.D. Howe Institute, 1999).

[657] M. Kerf & D. Geradin, Post-Liberalization Challenges in Telecommunications: Balancing Antitrust and Sector-Specific Regulation: Tentative Lessons from the Experiences of the United States, New Zealand, Chile, and Australia, 23 *Journal of World Competition*, No. 2, 27 (2000).

[658] See further A.P. Larson, Telecommunications: The Engine for Economic Development in the New Century, at <http://dosfan.lib.uic.edu> (last visited April 4, 2002).

[659] S.P. Montana, An Approach to the International Regulatory Issues of IP Telephony, 8 *Boston University Journal of Science and Technology Law* 699-700 (Summer 2002).

arena. As far as this point is concerned, it is a breakthrough against traditional idea (monopolized services).

However, the RP is annexed as an additional commitment for States. States are free to decide whether to adopt it or not, which has caused uncertainty, and arguably, has reduced the legal value of these principles.[660] After more than ten years of existence and experimental period, it is time to suggest including the RP as an integral part of the WTO Agreement. Meanwhile, the RP has been constantly criticized as being too general, subject to a wide degree of interpretation by national regulators. In its present form, the RP does not provide the sufficient criteria and underpinnings necessary to ensure truly effective competition and should therefore be strengthened.[661]

First of all, the provisions of the RP are meant to protect against anti-competitive activities. However, the important concept of "major supplier" contained therein is obscure and subject to various understandings.[662] Moreover, no concrete measures are provided to fight against anti-competitive activities. Member States remain free to adopt their own enforcement and antitrust actions. Out of national considerations and different policy choices, Member States unavoidably tend to adopt discriminatory measures. Thus, appropriate unified measures to prevent and fight against such activities should be listed as both countermeasures and remedies.

The issue of interconnection is a cornerstone, which opens competitive opportunities in telecommunications services. As the world's telecommunications infrastructure has grown, so has the drive for what is termed "interconnectivity", the linking of networks.[663] Three sub-issues define the efficiency of interconnection: the rates charged, the specific network(s) connected, [664] and relevant numbering. The RP only contains general guidelines requiring non-discriminatory terms, conditions and rates. But what terms and conditions are deemed non-discriminatory? Member States are quick to argue that their measures are in accordance with the provision, which might result in *de facto* discriminations. Fortunately, the Asia-Pacific Economic Cooperation (APEC) has undertaken significant work developing the APEC Principles of Interconnection, which aims to clarify the application of interconnection principles of the RP.[665] This document could provide the basis for further improvement of the RP.[666]

---

660 R. Frid, The Telecommunications Pact Under the GATS, 24 *Legal Issues of European Integration*, No. 2, 81 (1997).

661 Policy Paper: Future Negotiations on Telecommunications Services in the WTO, a Submission to the Department of Foreign Affairs and International Trade by the Canadian Council for International Business (CCIB), Ottawa, Ontario, June 18, 1999.

662 For further discussion, see M. Fredebeul-Krein & A. Freytag, The Case for a More Binding WTO Agreement on Regulatory Principles in Telecommunication Markets, 23 *Telecommunications Policy*, 628-629 (1999); see also H.N. Janisch, From Monopoly Towards Competition in Telecommunications: What Role for Competition Law?, 23 *Canadian Business Law Journal* 245 (1994); OECD, Directorate for Science, Technology and Industry, Working Party on Telecommunication and Information Services Policies, Cross-Ownership and Convergence: Policy Issues, Report DSTI/ICCP/TISP(98)3?FINAL, November 1998, at 26.

663 W. Jauk, The Application of EC Competition Rules to Telecommunications—Selected Aspects: The Case of Interconnection, 4 *International Journal of Communications Law and Policy* 100 (Winter 1999/2000).

664 Requirement for the interconnection of telecommunications networks may or may not be interpreted to apply to network infrastructure used for Internet broadcasting activities.

665 See further Annex C to the Cancun Declaration of APEC Telecommunications Ministers.

666 For further discussions on APEC's contribution to liberalization of telecommunications, see for example, WTO 2000 Preparatory Workshop on Basic Telecommunication Services, TELWG20/LSG/19, at <http://www.apectelwg.org> (last visited April 4, 2002).

The same holds true to the obligation of universal services. It is imperative both to capture the network externality[667] benefits that competitive markets cannot achieve and to implement important national economic and social policy objectives.[668] Nevertheless, no further detailed guidance is offered in the RP. One aspect to be singled out is the financial contribution burden, which should distort competition and must be done in the context of the rate balancing that competition necessitates.[669] This can be well exemplified by the US's Federal Communications Commission's (FCC's) longstanding practice of providing universal service support for telecommunications services for high cost rural and low income areas.[670] The FCC has identified several key principles underlying universal services in telecommunications: quality service at reasonable and affordable rates; access for rural and high-cost areas and for low-income users at comparable rates to other users; and equitable contribution to universal service by all telecommunications carriers.[671] The very basis of action in the telecommunications sector in the European Union (EU) was that the European Commission recognized the objective of universal service in the sector and strongly emphasized proportionality of measures to secure this goal. It generated the conviction that this goal could be secured by less restrictive means than retention of monopoly rights, e.g. by financial contributions or the creation of universal service funds.[672] Consequently, the obligation of universal services should not only be concerned with coverage, but also with satisfactory connectivity in terms of users' needs.[673]

Licensing provides the gateway for telecommunications services. This directly and closely relates to a specific commitment in the GATS: market access. While market access deals with more substantial and technical problems, the present obligation is set forth more or less from the administrative viewpoint of licensing. The RP acknowledges the legality of the practice of licensing. However, the RP does not define the situations for granting a license, nor provisions for the mutual recognition of licenses; it only contains an obligation to provide reasons in case of denying a license, but not in cases where a license would be granted with conditions which the applicant may have not desired. Concrete guidelines should thus be created to make the obligation subsidiary to the promotion of competition. For instance,

---

[667] A network externality exists for a service if users of the service benefit when more people use it. Network externalities are present in telecommunications since the value of a network increases, for each user, with the number of network subscribers. See further N. Economides, The Economics of Networks, 14 *International Journal of International Organization* 673 (1996).

[668] W.H. Melody, Telecom Reform: Progress and Prospects, 23 *Telecommunications Policy*, 16 (1999).

[669] See further W.H. Melody (ed.), *Telecom Reform: Principles, Policies and Regulatory Practices* 53 (1997).

[670] Section 254 of the 1996 Telecommunications Act. This section further instructed the FCC to extend universal service support to schools, libraries, and rural health care clinics. The FCC decided to fund a program in 1997 by collecting the funds from phone companies, who in turn collect it from their customers. Hence many argue that the program involves a tax. For further discussion, see Tauzin and Burns Re-Introduce Bills to Reform E-Rate, *Tech Law Journal*, available at <http://www.techlawjournal.com/educ/19990512.htm> (last visited April 4, 2002); see also J. Deprez, International Taxation: The Telecommunications Industry in the Information Age: A Case Study in Globalization, Deregulation, and Tax Competition, 23 *Loyola of Los Angeles International & Comparative Law Review* 537 (October 2001); S. Peng, Universal Telecommunications Service in China: Trade Liberalization, Subsidy, and Technology in the Making of Information Equality in the Broadband Era, 4 *University of Hawaii Asia-Pacific Law & Policy Journal* 2 (February 2003).

[671] FCC, Report and Order Released Pursuant to s. 254 of the Telecommunications Act (1996), May 1997.

[672] H. Burkert, Telecommunications Developments in the European Union: Principal Papers: The Post-Regulatory Landscape in International Telecommunications Law: A Unique European Approach?, 27 *Brooklyn Journal of International Law* 768 (2002).

[673] Communication from Colombia: Telecommunications Services, WTO S/CSS/W/119, November 27, 2001 (01-6058), Council for Trade in Services, Special Session.

according to Article 4 of the RP, Member States shall have the right to decide on the situations when to issue the license. This freedom offers the States the opportunity to formulate some potential anti-competitive measures. It would be helpful to define in a multilateral forum the licensing requirements in concrete terms, including the fees, reasonable period, etc. Moreover, further clarification of the obligation should take into account new technological developments. For example, digitization impacts on all license applications, which allows vastly more channels in existing frequency bands, so arrangements will be required to give program providers balanced, non-discriminatory access.[674]

One of the most important regulatory provisions has been the requirement of regulators to be independent from service providers and operators.[675] This appears all the more important in the liberalized environment as telecom investors begin to seek opportunities in countries with stable and independent regulatory environments.[676] The proper action of the regulators directly influences the actual implementation of the commitments made by the States. While Member States are not obliged to privatize their telecommunications industry, [677] this process is well underway in many States. Despite the fact that some States still maintain the ownership of the infrastructure, it is important to emphasize the independence of regulators from actual service providers. The independent regulators also play an important role in dispute settlement. As provided in the RP, service providers will have recourse to an independent body for resolving disputes regarding the terms, conditions and rates for interconnection.[678] But no indication is given as to what is meant by "resolving" the dispute: whether an agreement can be imposed on the parties or not. As a last resort, the WTO dispute resolution mechanism can be invoked. In this case, political support and resources from the States will be essential.[679] The national regulators should undertake responsibility in providing relevant support. Thus, it is essential to establish more clearly the obligations of the regulators.

Generally speaking, the regulators are responsible for the formulation of national policies in promoting the smooth development of telecommunications. Effective management of policy issues requires the regulators with adequate powers, transparent decision-making, and clear and stable policies.[680] One good example is the State Telecommunications Commission (STC) in the Republic of Bulgaria. Ten obligations are clearly defined in the Telecommunications Law.[681] Similar provisions can be adopted, offering clear guidance for the performance of the regulators.

---

674 H. Schadow, Essay: IV. Industries in the Process of Deregulation: 1. Telecommunications Price Control and Other Regulatory Issues, 23 *Fordham International Law Journal* 131 (2000).

675 J.H. Rohlfs & J.G. Sidak, Exporting Telecommunications Regulation: The United States-Japan Negotiations on Interconnection Pricing, 43 *Harvard International Law Journal* 355 (Summer 2002).

676 M.R. Sanchez & A.P. Hwa, Effective Regulators: A Response to the International Telecommunications Union's Case Study on Singapore, 4 *University of Hawaii Asia-Pacific Law & Policy Journal* 1 (February 2003).

677 The agreement itself does not directly lay out privatization requirements or distinguish between foreign investment and foreign government investment, leaving foreign governments to decide how, when and to what extent they must privatize their historic government-owned monopolies. See C. Huther & L. Friedlander, Success in the Global Marketplace?, *The National Law Journal*, B 12, October 30, 2000.

678 See further RP, para. 2.5.

679 R. Rosenthal, United States v. Mexico: The First Telecommunications Challenge Confronting the World Trade Organization, 10 *CommLaw: Conspectus* 335 (2002).

680 Y. Zhao, The ITU and National Regulatory Authorities in the Era of Liberalization, 18 *Space Policy* 294 (2002).

681 Article 22 of Telecommunications Law, Republic of Bulgaria, see Bulgaria Assessment: Annex D—Republic of Bulgaria, National Assembly, Telecommunications Law (published in State Gazette, Issue 93, 1998), available at <http://www.usaid.gov/info_technology/ied/reports/bulgaria/annexd.html> (last visited April 4, 2002).

2.5. Conclusion

As one of the world's largest markets, telecommunications are vital since they serve as both a backbone for other sectors and services, and as a service itself. Difficulties have arisen during the WTO negotiations regarding the disintegration of monopolies, market access and regulations as they pertain to telecommunications services.[682] Thus, when the agreements were reached in 1997, the negotiators felt relieved and believed the result of the negotiations to be a historic victory.[683] However, since then, objective analysis has been carried out, which has provided more sensible evaluations. With further implementation of the commitments, more problems appeared, which pushed demands for further commitments and clarifications. This is exactly the way that the General Agreement on Tariffs and Trade (GATT) has proceeded during the negotiations in different rounds. Consequently, the agreement reached so far constitutes more of a beginning than anything else.

While calling on further liberalization, many States have started this initiation unilaterally and voluntarily.[684] Though they failed to launch a new round of negotiations in 1999, [685] the process has never stopped.[686] It is good to find in the GATS rules that periodical review will be made to evaluate the development, which to a certain extent will make up for the failure of large-scale negotiations.[687] While different States, based on their own considerations, raise different areas for liberalization in the future, the present research attempts to provide an objective opinion on possible areas for further liberalization.

It is to be noted that the liberalization of the suggested areas could be difficult to achieve in a single round of negotiations, since various factors are involved in the WTO negotiations. Also since different States are at different stages of liberalization, more time is needed to accomplish total convergence.[688] Ensuring developing countries' confidence in the WTO system for telecommunications is of paramount importance in moving forward with the new round of negotiations.[689] Furthermore, with the continued development of the telecommunications markets and industry, together with the technical cooperation of the ITU, many limitations maintained until now are likely to become meaningless and disappear in future. Consequently, while acknowledging the difficulties in further negotiations, we can optimistically expect that liberalization will proceed in a stable, constant and homogeneous way and that a unified, healthy, competitive market will become reality.

---

682 M. Hill, The WTO and Telecommunications, at <http://www.washington.edu/wto/issues/telecom.htm> (last visited April 4, 2002).

683 P. Holmes, J. Kempton & F. McGowan, International Competition Policy and Telecommunications—Lessons from the EU and Prospects for the WTO, 20 *Telecommunications Policy* 756 (1996); see also P. Larouche, *Competition Law and Regulation in European Telecommunications* 157 (Oxford: Hart, 2000).

684 W.H. Melody, Shaping Liberalized Telecom Markets, 24 *Telecommunications Policy* 803 (2000).

685 M. Moore, The World Trade Organization, Globalization, and the Future of International Trade Essay: The WTO, Looking Ahead, 24 *Fordham International Law Journal* 6 (November/December 2000).

686 WTO Services Talks Press Ahead: Members Adopt Negotiating Guidelines at Special Session, WTO News, Press/217, April 2, 2001.

687 GATS Article VI, para. 2 provides that WTO Members are bound to institute review procedures before independent instances for administrative decisions affecting trade in services.

688 See for example, S. MacKnight, Weekly Review: Telecommunications and Deregulation, *Japan Economic Institute (JEI) Report*, No. 14, April 7, 2000.

689 Keidanren, Japan Federation of Economic Organizations, Expectations on the WTO Negotiations and Requests for Liberalizing Trade in Services, March 28, 2000, at <http://www.keidanren.or.jp> (last visited April 4, 2002).

3. THE RELATIONSHIP BETWEEN THE ITU AND NATIONAL REGULATORS

3.1.Introduction

In recent years a giant telecommunications boom has emerged. This development became even more spectacular with the conclusion of the World Trade Organization (WTO) agreement on Telecommunications in 1997. The emergence of many new telecommunications companies and the demand for light-handed regulations are just a few signs of the fast-growing need for people around the globe to communicate. The trend towards liberalization exerts a strong influence on the actions and attitudes adopted in different national States. Furthermore, the dramatic advances in communications and information technologies have been imposing severe strains on a governmental regulatory apparatus devised in the pioneer days of radio. They are raising policy issues with serious implications for national economic performance and social welfare.

National Regulatory Authorities (NRAs) are the main bodies enjoying regulatory powers in telecommunications services. To facilitate the smooth development of their own telecommunications, different States set up their own NRAs to undertake the task of regulation and implementation of relevant policy issues. In the monopoly era, NRAs had absolute power to adopt relevant policies and measures. However, when we entered the era of liberalization, this situation changed. While telecommunications are regarded as tradable services, the issue of regulation is set in the international arena. As one of the most important organizations in regulating telecommunications, the International Telecommunication Union (ITU) occupies an indispensable position.[690] Its relationships with NRAs are also important for the healthy development of the telecommunications market.

The present section sets out to discuss the relationships between the ITU and NRAs. The next part presents an introduction to the NRAs. Their general functions and their further obligations are discussed here. Part three offers an in-depth discussion of the relationships between the ITU and NRAs. Conclusions are drawn in the final part.

3.2. General Observation on NRAs

NRAs have been undertaking the important task of regulating and promoting the development of national telecommunications. They have various responsibilities in this field. In the days when telecommunications was almost always a public monopoly, NRAs had the comparatively simple job of making decisions according to their own policy choices. Nevertheless, regional and global cooperation were still needed at that time since telecommunications transcend national borders and individual activities have to be placed in a broader background.

---

690 See generally G.A. Codding, Jr., The International Telecommunications Union: 130 Years of Telecommunications Regulation, 23 *Denver Journal of International Law and Policy* 511 (Summer, 1995); A.A. Pisciotta & J.H. Barker, Current Issues in Electronic Data Interchange: Telecommunications Regulatory Implications for International EDI Transactions, 13 *Journal of International Law & Business* 95-96 (Spring/Summer, 1992).

This picture became much more complicated with the concept of liberalization was accepted. Liberalization means less interference from regulators. But NRAs cannot be totally dispensed with. Many aspects of the telecommunications industry, even as various segments become more competitive and less regulated, still have significant relationships with industry regulators and policy makers.[691] So what shall be the future role of NRAs? It is vital to define the limitations on NRAs exercising their power in this new era.

On the one hand, the erosion of sovereignty makes it all the more important for NRAs to work more closely together. The measures and the regulatory framework to take can have spillover effects outside national borders; when making decisions with far-reaching international effects, NRAs need to take account of the positions of other States and to react only after extensive bilateral or multilateral consultation. On the other hand, requiring States to open up their national markets means that NRAs could engage in competition with one other and experiment with various regulatory parameters.[692] Thus, it is also crucial to delineate the borderline between cooperation and competition among NRAs.

Generally, NRAs are responsible for the formulation of national policies in promoting the smooth development of telecommunications. Effective management of policy issues requires NRAs with adequate powers, transparent decision-making, and clear and stable policies.[693] More specifically, it is necessary to provide NRAs with significant essential powers, such as to set license conditions and/or to amend licenses, to set tariff limits, to determine interconnection agreements, to issue warnings, to close and to eliminate unlawful telecommunications activities.[694] A good example could be the State Telecommunications Commission (STC) in the Republic of Bulgaria. The STC is the state authority in Bulgaria undertaking the task of regulating and controlling the telecommunications, and the postal communications, in a manner defined by law.[695] As defined by its Telecommunications Law, the STC carries out the following activities:

1) convey a preliminary study of the necessity and technical feasibility of the issue of a license for the establishment of the telecommunications network and for provision of public telecommunications services, using radio frequency spectrum. A regulation of the Chairman of the Committee of Posts and Telecommunications (CPT) establishes the proceedings of the study;
2) prepare the documents and carry out the necessary activities relating to the granting of the licenses referred to in this law;
3) grant, amend, supplement, suspend, terminate and revoke licenses for telecommunications activities;

---

691 K.M.H. Wallman, The Role of Government in Telecommunications Standard-Setting, 8 *CommLaw Conspectus* 251 (Summer, 2000).

692 V. Mayer-Schonberger & M. Strasser, A Closer Look at Telecom Deregulation: The European Advantage, 12 *Harvard Journal of Law & Technology* 578 (Summer, 1999).

693 Chairman's Report of the First ITU Regulatory Colloquium and the Associated Briefing Report for a detailed description of the options for regulatory reform.

694 I.P. Chochliouros, *Market Regulations That can Accelerate the Introduction of Lower Cost and Higher Quality Telecommunication Services: The European Perspective*, at <http://www.sbpm.gwu.edu/igmr/chochliouros.htm>.

695 Article 22 of Telecommunications Law, Republic of Bulgaria, see Bulgaria Assessment: Annex D—Republic of Bulgaria, National Assembly, Telecommunications Law (published in State Gazette, Issue 93, 1998), at <http://www.usaid.gov/info_technology/ied/reports/bulgaria/annexd.html>.

4) grant, amend, supplement, suspend, terminate and revoke licenses for establishment of telecommunications networks and provision of telecommunications services, using radio frequency spectrum after approval by the Council of Minister (CoM);
5) grant, amend, supplement, suspend, terminate and revoke licenses for radio and television activities upon decision of the National Radio and Television Council (NRTVC);
6) grant, terminate and revoke the licenses under 5 above, which are using radio frequency spectrum, upon decision of the NRTVC and approval by CoM;
7) provides the necessary conditions for carrying out of telecommunications activities in case of maritime or air search and rescue, as well as safety information;
8) prepare the national numbering plan and allocate it among the operators in compliance with the adopted principles;
9) draft, co-ordinate and propose to the CPT the secondary legislation referred to in this law; and
10) inform the public and carry out public consultations and opinion polls on important telecommunications issues.[696]

Similar provisions can also be traced to Telecommunications Laws in other States.[697] From all those provisions, we can see that NRAs are generally endowed with important and detailed regulatory tasks concerning telecommunications services. Their importance is even more obvious in the new trend of liberalization.

Since the inclusion of telecommunications within the Uruguay Round of negotiations, NRAs have taken a vital position in defining its proper role in the bargaining; they are to procure the realization of the commitments offered. The measures to be taken in the future should not be contrary to their commitments.[698] This complication reached its climax when a Reference Paper (RP) was concluded in WTO negotiations, primarily concerning the sensitive issue of national regulation. It is the first time in the history that national regulations have been placed in the multilateral arena.

The RP provides basic guidance for the proper formulation and functions of NRAs. Although considered as additional commitments for Member States, the principles contained therein constitute a basic consensus among international society. An independent regulator is vital in the first place. The character of independence provides the basic procurement of further actions from NRAs. Five other principles offer detailed issues of regulation: safeguarding competition, interconnection, universal services, public availability of licensing criteria, allocation and use of scarce resources. Furthermore, NRAs, as provided, may act as a dispute resolution provider in interconnection disputes, which could be a challenge to the traditional function of NRAs.[699] From the wording, we can see that the RP provides only

---

[696] *Id.*, Article 27 of Telecommunications Law, Republic of Bulgaria.

[697] See for example, Act No. 474/1992 Coll. On the Central State Administration of the Czech Republic, at Section 3; Article 4 and 5 of the Law on Communications, Poland (1990). For general discussions on telecommunications laws in Europe, see further J. Scherer (ed.), Telecommunications Laws in Europe, (Kluwer, 3rd ed., 1995).

[698] See further Trade Agreements on Telecommunications: Regulatory Implications: The Changing Role of Government in an Era of Telecom Deregulation, Report of the Fifth Regulatory Colloquium held at the ITU Headquarters, December 6-8, 1995.

[699] In the European Union, NRAs were established in the Framework Open Network Provision Directive as the arbiter of disputes regarding refusals to supply leased lines, etc. See further W. Jauk, The Application of EC

general guidance rules, leaving detailed implementation to the discretion of NRAs. Accordingly, the regulation of telecommunications is not only an issue for each NRA, but one for the international society as a whole.

3.3. The Relationships between the ITU and NRAs

3.3.1. The ITU as an International Regulator

The ITU, one of the oldest international organizations and the only one in the specific area of telecommunications in the United Nations system, carries out the important activities of coordination, standardization and international regulation to enable telecommunications systems to operate seamlessly across borders, to generate larger markets for industry and to benefit users. From its inception, the ITU has been duty-bound to take this responsibility.

The functions of the ITU are defined as follows: to allocate bands of radio frequency spectrum and orbital positions in the geostationary satellite orbit to avoid harmful interference; to coordinate efforts to eliminate harmful interference between Member's radio stations; to facilitate world-wide standardization of telecommunications with satisfactory service quality; to foster international cooperation in delivery of technical assistance to developing countries; to coordinate efforts to harmonize the development of telecommunications facilities; to foster collaboration among Members with a view to establishing low rates and efficient services; to promote adoption of measures for ensuring safety of life through cooperation of telecommunications services; to undertake studies, make regulations, adopt resolutions, formulate recommendations and opinions, and collect and publish information concerning telecommunications matters; and to promote with international financial organizations the availability of lines of credit for development of telecommunications projects to isolated areas.[700] Thus, it is clear that the ITU provides an excellent forum for coordination and cooperation among Member States. NRAs in different States can be well coordinated and guided by the activities of the ITU. The ITU consists of several important organs, among which the following shall have most important impacts on NRAs.

The Plenipotentiary Conference is the supreme organ of the ITU, consisting of delegates from all the Member States; it is the law-making body empowered with both regulatory and constitutional authority.[701] Thus, this organ provides NRAs awith the chance of a periodic review of the general policy and other issues fundamental to the ITU. Administrative Conferences, another periodic conference organ of the ITU, legislate the substantive international law of the ITU--the Radio Regulations and the International Telecommunications Regulations (ITR)--which lay down the legal principles governing the provisions of international telecommunications services.[702] The Administrative Regulations, having the force of international treaties, are binding on all Members.[703] The third periodic

Competition Rules to Telecommunications--Selected Aspects: The Case of Interconnection, 4 *International Journal of Communications Law and Policy* 20-21 (Winter, 1999/2000).

700 Constitution of International Telecommunications Union, June 30, 1989, Chapter I, Article 1, para. 2.

701 R.L. White & H.M. White, *The Law and Regulation of International Space Communication* 67 (1988).

702 International Telecommunication Regulations, December 9, 1988, S. TREATY DOC. No. 13, 102d Cong., 1st Session (1991).

703 P. Tarjanne, The WTO Basic Telecommunications Agreement: An ITU Viewpoint, ITU Negotiating International Trade Issues, Geneva, WTO, November 28, 1997.

organ of the ITU is its Council, which serves the important task of providing continuity of administration and consider broad telecommunication policy issues in order to ensure that the Union's policies and strategy fully respond to the constantly changing telecommunications environment.[704]

Three vertical sectors are categorized; each sector includes a Bureau with staff, complimented by study groups and conferences.[705] The Standardization Sector is vital to the standardization activities of both wire and radiocommunication services. The World Telecommunication Standardization Conference can adopt recommendations related to standardization and devote time to policy issues, strategic planning, priority setting and work programs.[706] Its work programs are relevant to matters covered in the WTO, especially those involving technical standards, conditions for leased circuits, access to and use of public telecommunications networks and services, tariffs and definitions of terms.[707]

The Radiocommunication Sector is intended to achieve greater efficiency and transparency and to spur broader participation in radiocommunication activities. It ensures that at treaty level the Radio Regulations contain only those provisions necessary to respond to the needs of the international community; further, it meets the specific needs of Members by holding Radiocommunication Conferences, coordinating efforts to eliminate harmful interference of radio stations of different countries, making recommendations on technical radiocommunications matters through the radiocommunication assemblies and study groups, and developing rules of procedure for use in applying the Radio Regulations and the decisions of competent radiocommunication conferences.[708] The development of global markets can thus be facilitated with global allocation of spectrum to particular services.

Within the Radiocommunication Sector, there is a Radio Regulations Board (RRB), formerly as the International Frequency Registration Board (IFRB). It is a unique feature of the ITU and is central to the ITU's regulation of radiocommunication. The RRB, continuing the general tasks of the IFRB, functions like a court when it determines the legal status of members' radio stations; like a records office when it records members' radio stations in the Master International Frequency Register; a mediation and conciliation service when it assists members in resolving disputes involving harmful interference caused by their radio stations; an administrative or regulatory agency when it adopts interim standards and Radio Regulations; and like a technical assistance agency when it assists developing countries in selecting radio frequencies to meet their communications needs.[709] Thus, its work has a major influence on Member States. Although the RRB has no actual authority of enforcement, its decisions are respected by NRAs in most situations.[710] It is especially cherished by

---

[704] Draft for a Revised Constitution of the International Telecommunications Union, ITU Administrative Council Res. No. 1021 (1992), at Chapter 1, Article 10, para. 4 (2).

[705] Final Acts of the Additional Plenipotentiary Conference (ITU, Geneva), December 22, 1992.

[706] International Telecommunications Union, High Level Committee to Review the Structure and Functioning of the ITU, Tomorrow's ITU: The Challenges of Change (HLC Report), ITU Document 145-E, at 31 (1991).

[707] G.R. Pipe, *Trade of Telecommunications Services: Implications of a GATT Uruguay Round Agreement for ITU and Member States*, at <http://www.crocevia.org/videazimut/un/1.htm>.

[708] H.M. White, Jr. & R. Lauria, The Impact of New Communication Technologies on International Telecommunication Law and Policy: Cyberspace and the Restructuring of the International Telecommunication Union, 32 *California Western Law Review* 16 (Fall, 1995).

[709] A.L. Allison, Meeting the Challenges of Change: The Reform of the International Telecommunications Union, 45 *Federal Communications Law Journal* 514 (1993).

[710] H. Wong, The Paper "Satellite" Chase: The ITU Prepares for Its Final Exam in Resolution 18, 63 *Journal of Air Law and Commerce* 855-856 (May/June, 1998); S.A. Levy, Institutional Perspectives on the Allocation of

developing States for its technical assistance services and its reputation as an impartial and independent voice.[711]

The Development Sector continues the Union's development functions—ensuring that the ITU's catalytic role in stimulating telecommunication development is strengthened. It contains the World and Regional Telecommunication Development Conferences (WRTDC), Telecommunications Development Study Groups (TDSG), the Telecommunications Development Bureau (BDT) and a Telecommunication Development Advisory Board (TDAB).[712] The WRTDC serves the dual purpose of a forum for the discussion and consideration of topics, projects and programs relevant to telecommunications development bureau. Study groups have been set up researching questions of interest to developing countries. The BDT was created to facilitate and enhance telecommunications development by offering, organizing and coordinating technical cooperation and assistance activities.[713] Its work will culminate in World and Regional Development Conferences which will facilitate information exchanges among various States.[714] The TDAB will invite the participation of governments and other bodies in the formulation of relevant policies.

3.3.2. Traditional Functions of the ITU towards to NRAs

The ITU is essentially a technical and regulatory body. The three sectors within it have rightly taken up the task of coordinating telecommunications in each specific field. Technical regulation is indispensable to international telecommunications. As an organization, it depends on the efforts of its Member States. Thus, it can provide a good opportunity to bring together NRAs from throughout the world to discuss relevant issues, which could provide a direct way of resolving differences and misunderstandings between States. Such a function is well represented by the regional arrangement in Europe, where Ectra offers a forum for European NRAs to discuss and coordinate regulation.[715] The ITU has repeatedly proved that, despite the increasingly difficult nature of the task, it has been able to satisfy at least the majority of interests and produce worldwide agreements at relatively frequent intervals and with shorter conferences. As expressed in Article 1 of the ITU's Constitution, one of its missions is to harmonize the actions of Members.[716] In this way, various agreements on technical and legal points can be reached and will lay the ground for further clarification.

Meanwhile, the ITU is strengthened as the primary source of reliable, up-to-date information on regulatory issues. It can help enormously by gathering and sharing information. This could provide the basis for the ITU to provide expert consultancy, thereby making the best use of the wide expertise it has accumulated.

Space Orbital Resources: The ITU, Common User Satellite Systems and Beyond, 16 *Case Western Reserve Journal of International Law* 186 (1984).

[711] See G.A. Codding & A.M. Rutkowski, *The International Telecommunications Union in a Changing World* 135 (1982).

[712] HLC Report, *supra* note 223, 24-27.

[713] Constitution of the International Telecommunications Union, June 30, 1989, Chapter 1, Article 14, para 1.

[714] Bureau of International Communications and Information Policy, U.S. Department of State, Report of the Delegation of the United States to the Plenipotentiary Conference of the International Telecommunications Union, 4 (1989).

[715] See further F. Pombo, European Community Telecommunications Law and Investment Perspectives, 18 *Fordham International Law Journal* 578 (December, 1994).

[716] Constitution of the International Telecommunications Union, June 30, 1989, Chapter I, Article 1, para. 1.

3.3.3. The ITU and NRAs in the New Era of Liberalization

3.3.3.1. Introduction

With the rapid development of modern technology and the accelerating demands on its processes and resources, the ITU has expressed concerns over its ability to meet all the changes taking place.[717] Since the Tokyo Plenipotentiary Conference, the ITU has made significant changes of its own. One to be noted is the inclusion of representatives from private parties.[718] By offering opportunities for private parties to present their views at formal occasions, the ITU is able to gain an insight into the telecommunications industry and formulate objective opinions.[719] Business-driven decisions can encourage private parties proposing satellite systems to promote their own regulatory position at the ITU when the position of the State representing them is not working well.

Three principles were set forth for achieving the ITU's mission: cooperation between the ITU Member administrations in policy matters with a view to achieving the highest possible degree of harmonization of their actions; participation by non-administration organizations in the activities of the Union's Sectors; and information exchange among all ITU participants and with the wider community.[720] Bearing these principles in mind, the ITU should be able to promote a global vision of telecommunications by promoting open network-type approaches, such as policy coordination, and the building of common or complementary national legal frameworks.

Such developments can further make NRAs more confident of the feasibility of decisions by the ITU. The function of the ITU towards NRAs is rather general as shown above. However, the situation improved after the WTO Agreement on Telecommunications was reached. This marked a watershed for telecommunications: considering the technical origins of the ITU, some scholars cast doubts on its competence in regulatory issues, especially with the conclusion of the RP within the WTO framework.

Nevertheless, with a growing convergence between the goals of ITU and the WTO, the complementary role between both has now been widely recognized. While the WTO is able to reach agreements on regulatory issues, these agreements contain only general rules, which need further theoretical and technical clarifications. Their further implementation will largely depend on the technical definitions and practical guidance. The WTO lacks expertise as far as this is concerned; but, thanks to its previous accumulation and experience, the ITU rightly fills this gap. The two organizations thus complement each other and are increasing their cooperation. Their new cooperative relationship should include reciprocal commitments by NRAs to respect the multilateral dimension of the regulatory initiatives that will be taken. The outcomes of their cooperation will directly determine the relationship of the two organizations with other bodies. For the purpose of the present study, it is worth attempting to clarify the relationship between the ITU and NRAs in this new situation and for the future.

---

717 P. Tarjanne, Editorial, After 125 Years...Ready Again to Face the Challenge, 57 *Telecommunication Journal* 3 (1990).

718 See further K. Jayakar, Globalization and the Legitimacy of International Telecommunications Standard-Setting Organizations, 5 *Indiana Journal of Global Legal Studies* 718-721, 729 (Spring, 1998).

719 D.J. MacLean, A New Departure for the ITU: An Inside View of the Kyoto Plenipotentiary Conference, 19 *Telecommunications Policy* 179 (1995).

720 Final Acts of the Plenipotentiary Conference (ITU, Kyoto), October 14, 1994, Res. Com4/1: International Telecommunications Union Strategic Plan 1995-1999, Annex II, A, 5 & 6.

3.3.3.2. The ITU's New Functions

The ITU has traditionally provided a forum in which its membership can work together on achieving the goals set out in the Constitution and Convention. One of the goals is to promote the extension of the benefits of the new telecommunications technologies to all the world's inhabitants. It is therefore logical to expect that the ITU would play a major role in defining and adapting to the new environment. Besides the traditional functions described above, the ITU could further seek to strengthen its position as a forum and an information center in this new era. For example, by making use of the modern technology, the ITU can construct databases and websites to provide NRAs with easier access to each other's regulatory procedures, decisions and information and facilitate cooperative relationships between new and well-established NRAs.

Generally speaking, the ITU can serve as an international focal point for discussion of telecommunication policy and regulatory affairs. For this purpose, it provides the forum where NRAs from around the world can discuss key issues and obtain input from those to be regulated. Bringing together policy work, the Secretariat could create a center for regulatory expertise, which would serve as a proactive "knowledge center". It can further collect and collate best practice regulatory policies from different countries and act as a repository for benchmarking statistics in its area of expertise.[721] More detailed functions are described below.

The work undertaken by Study Groups of the Telecommunication Standardization Sector (ITU-T) considers various topics and develop Recommendations (and other documents) and report. The ITU-T is a permanent consultative committee that studies technical matters relating to telephony and other wired services. It prepares proposed revisions to the ITR and produces recommendations on technical subjects.[722] The work done so far has helped clarify the issues and provided useful data and analysis. The ultimate goal of these Recommendations is to promote worldwide *de facto* standards, to provide guidance and to guide coordination. Recommendations are thus useful to system designers and NRAs.

One thing to note is that such Recommendations are not obligatory for Member States;[723] however, in some countries they are considered mandatory requirements for policy making.[724] This phenomenon also proves true for recommendations from other Study Groups in the ITU.[725] Conceivably, the ITU could prepare its own, differing legal opinion, or attempt a definitive resolution of the legal issues through a recommendation or other regulatory

[721] ITU Reform Advisory Panel: Observations and Recommendations for Reform, at <http://www.itu.int/newsroom/reform/02-RapRecs.html>.

[722] See further Allison, *supra* note 226, 511-517.

[723] Letter from Ambassador Vonya McCann, United States Coordinator, International Communications and Information Policy, Department of State, to Reed E. Hundt, Chairman, FCC (March 22, 1995), at 1. Sometimes, ITU as claimed as powerless since it has no sanctions to enforce compliance and no mandate to develop operational services. See A.L. Lin, Comment, Telecommunications Competition in the European Union After France v. Commission--The Terminal Equipment Case, 9 *Connecticut Journal of International Law* 356 (1994); A.W. Branscomb, Overview: Global Governance of Global Networks, in A.W. Branscomb (ed.), *Toward a Law of Global Communications Networks* 5 (1986).

[724] The resolutions and recommendations, while not binding, are almost always complied with in practice. See S. Cahill, Give Me My Space: Implications for Permitting National Appropriation of the Geostationary Orbit, 19 *Wisconsin International Law Journal* 232 (Spring, 2001).

[725] For information on Study Groups, see for example, Objectives and General Information: ITU-R/Study Group Structure, at <http://www.ips.gov.au/asg3/itustruc.html>.

determination, [726] which can provide NRAs with a possible measure for consideration. Thus, the meaningfulness of the decisions can provide a basis for the ITU to continue its work and offer more viable guidance.

The ITU can further help avoid and resolve disputes among Member States. This activity will become more important as frequency conflicts arise between communication systems and communication frequencies that are the responsibility of more than one sovereign nation.[727] The decision-making function of the ITU reflects the modern, competitive environment in which the private party plays the leading role while the regulatory authorities act as arbitrator of the wider public interest. If doubtful of certain policy or measures, a State can submit them to the ITU for consideration and ask for an opinion. With so much expertise on various aspects of telecommunications, the ITU can take account of all relevant situations and give sensible advice. The opinions handed out by the ITU can provide important evidence for resolving disputes. Over the years the ITU has lent its "good offices" to addressing and attempting to resolve complex and contentious issues.[728]

The spectacular phenomenon of current times is that many monopolized regulatory regimes are being liberalized. States must now prepare their own NRAs. This may be difficult because in addition to passing the appropriate laws, States must establish regulatory procedures, obtain office space and equipment, and hire the regulators themselves.[729] The ITU is especially helpful in this respect. It can assist countries to set up effective regulatory regimes and systems, and to strengthen the capacity of the NRAs in the interests of stimulating telecommunications development.

A momentous record in the ITU's history was the establishment of the Telecommunications Development Bureau (BDT) in 1989 to increase the efforts being made towards development in the Third World. As Third World countries are rather behind in telecommunications, they will need independent advice on the best policy to pursue for each country's particular needs, the drafting of new laws and regulations and the setting up of an independent NRA.[730]

In light of this, the ITU can in the first place encourage a proactive response from NRAs to the opportunities presented by more open markets and new modes of operation and try to mitigate the adverse effects contained therein. With the responses, the ITU can continue its useful roles of publishing international technical standards and protocols, coordinating international spectrum allocations and registering geostationary satellite orbit slots;[731] the ITU Secretariat might prepare and distribute periodic reports, which can be of great benefit to NRAs in developing countries involved in interministerial preparations of government policy,

---

[726] K.R. Propp, The Eroding Structure of International Telecommunications Regulation: The Challenge of Call-Back Services, 37 *Harvard International Law Journal* 511 (Spring, 1996).

[727] C.R.M. Moore, III, Business-Driven Negotiations for Satellite System Coordination: Reforming the International Telecommunication Union to Increase Commercially Oriented Negotiations Over Scarce Frequency Spectrum, 65 *Journal of Air Law and Commerce* 52-53 (Winter, 1999).

[728] R. Frieden, Does a Hierarchical Internet Necessitate Multilateral Intervention?, 26 *North Carolina Journal of International Law & Commercial Regulation* 401 (Spring, 2001).

[729] M. Naftel, Countdown to 1998: Status of Telecommunications Competition in Europe and Comparison with the United States, 7 *Journal of Transnational Law & Policy* 2-3 (Fall, 1997).

[730] Second Draft of the Secretary-General's Report to the Second World Telecommunication Policy Forum on Trade in Telecommunications to be held in Geneva, March 16-18, 1998.

[731] W.S. Baer, Will the Global Information Infrastructure Need Transnational (or Any) Governance?, at <http://www.ksg.harvard.edu/iip/GIIconf/baerpap.html>.

bilateral relations, and consideration of these matters in international bodies.[732] The ITU could further help NRAs identify outside resources and help in obtaining training and human resource development to best meet the needs of countries undergoing the difficult adjustment process. In addition, the ITU can mobilize support from other parties to help those countries make the inevitable adjustment.[733]

Last but not least, the ITU should adopt the RP and look to its performance in its Member States. The introduction of a competitive atmosphere into the field of telecommunications is a rather new phenomenon, thus most countries are in urgent need of assistance. Even though the ITU lacks the enforcement authority, a regulatory regime can be developed at the ITU to encourage the flexibility and efficiency of business style negotiations. For this purpose, the ITU can play a role in providing impartial information and advice through its membership. It should also further enhance and coordinate existing technical assistance activities in this area, reinforcing local expertise on regulation through regional seminars, extended in-country missions, and education and training services. A key objective would be to make NRAs aware of the requirements. One situation to be noted is that not all Members of the ITU are Members of the WTO. Thus, it will be necessary for the ITU to introduce these developments into a wider arena.

3.3.3.3.The Importance of NRAs to the ITU

The ITU is helpful to NRAs in their national regulations. However, we cannot ignore the fact that the ITU is primarily composed of Member States. During conferences and meetings, it is the NRAs or other national delegates who represent the State and actually take part in the activities initiated by the ITU.[734] The information and materials submitted by NRAs and further discussions form the basis of relevant Recommendations and Regulations. Furthermore, under current practice, the use of the spectrum/orbit resource and implementation of the ITU's Regulations are based primarily on goodwill and cooperation between Member States, more specifically, NRAs.[735]

For example, the processes of coordinating a satellite system with the ITU and coordinating the acquisition of national licenses are two separate matters. A State can make its own decision about the ITU's offer of a particular type of satellite service, even though every other Member supported this service.[736] Private operators must first file for evaluation

---

[732] G.R. Pipe, Trade of Telecommunications Services: Implications of a GATT Uruguay Round Agreement for ITU and Member States, May 1993, at <http://www.itu.int>.

[733] Briefing Report By M. Tyler on Transforming Economic Relationships in International Telecommunications, Prepared for ITU Regulatory Colloquium No. 7, Geneva, December 3-5, 1997.

[734] ITU's primary binding element is consent of Member States. See W.P. Cassidy, Jr., Universal Service in a Competitive Telecommunications Environment: The Current State of Universal Service in the European Union and United States, 25 *North Carolina Journal of International Law & Commercial Regulation* 117 (Fall, 1999).

[735] J.M. Smith, Acceptance of Prior Consent as a Means of Regulating Direct Broadcast Satellites, 3 *Emory Journal of International Dispute Resolution* 108 (1988); see also M.A. Rothblatt, The Impact of International Satellite Communications Law upon Access to the Geostationary Orbit and the Electromagnetic Spectrum, 16 *Texas International Law Journal* 213 (1980); S.A. Hook, Allocation of the Radio Spectrum: Is the Sky the Limits?, 3 *Indiana International & Comparative Law Review* 332 (1993); B.E. Harris, The New Telecommunications Development: Bureau of the International Telecommunication Union, 7 *American University Journal of International Law & Policy* 85 (1991).

[736] See International Telecommunications Union, ITU's History, at <http://www.itu.int>. See also J.C. Thompson, Space for Rent: The International Telecommunications Union, Space Law, and Orbit/Spectrum Leasing, 62 *Journal of Air Law and Commerce* 286 (1996).

with the appropriate NRA before their application is forwarded to the ITU for coordination.[737] It is thus obvious that without firm support from NRAs, the ITU will lose ground. Accordingly, while emphasizing the importance of the ITU to the actions of NRAs, we should also stress the vital function of NRAs in furnishing detailed national conditions and taking an active role in the ITU's activities.

3.4. Conclusion

The development of telecommunications towards liberalization is irreversible. Fundamental change in the telecommunications structure is well underway. An appropriate regulatory framework is vital to the successful conclusion of this trend. While emphasizing the importance of the WTO in this process, we should not overlook the vital function of the ITU in realizing this goal. The ITU, complementary to the WTO, will need to take account of the WTO requirements when developing and applying technical and regulatory standards. It should also help intensify the sense of urgency among NRAs to understand the new environment, including the implication of the WTO commitments, and to reform their regulatory regimes to facilitate successful adaptation to an open market economy.[738]

Given the scene of competition, NRAs, as the actual bodies formulating and implementing national telecommunications policy, require stricter conditions. In this respect, the main concerns have been: independence of NRAs; their aptitude in respect of the technical feasibility, economic appropriateness and legal equity of their decisions; public and transparent procedures, and involvement of these subject to regulation in decision making.[739] In this situation, NRAs should intensify their cooperation with the ITU. The technical standards offered by the ITU in fulfilling the general principles, its abundant knowledge and information about procuring effective regulation will ultimately assist NRAs in realizing their national target of full liberalization in telecommunications services.

---

[737] H. Wong, Comment, 2001: A Space Legislation Odyssey--A Proposed Model For Reforming the Intergovernmental Satellite Organizations, 48 American University Law Review 558 (1998).

[738] Chairman's Report of the Seventh Regulatory Colloquium: Transforming Economic Relationships in International Telecommunications: The Changing Role of Government in an Era of Telecom Deregulation, ITU, December 3-5, 1997, Geneva.

[739] ITU ITU-D Study Groups, Questions 8/1: Establishment of an Independent Regulatory Body, Document 1/7-E, 3 August 1998.

Chapter 6

NATIONAL SPACE LEGISLATION

1. NECESSITY OF NATIONAL SPACE LEGISLATION

1.1. Introduction

Five space treaties drafted in the 1960s and 1970s provide important guidance to space activities; however, the year 1979 marked the end of international space legislation.[740] Since then, discussions have been carried out in various fora concerning the necessity and possibility of further international legislation. The United Nations Committee on the Peaceful Uses of Outer Space (UNCOPUOS), consisting of 67 nations, failed to adopt new rules due to the conflicting views expressed by different States.[741] While not favoring the adoption of new treaties, the UNCOPUOS encouraged ratification of the existing treaties and emphasized the importance of national space legislation.[742]

Against such a background, it is appropriate to examine the issue of national space legislation--its necessity, feasibility and means. To that end, the second part of this section will discuss the necessity, aims and objectives of national space legislation. By recognizing the importance of national legislation, the third part will examine basic principles and means to be followed in national space legislation. The section concludes that national space legislation is the main tool in regulating space activities in view of the inefficient mechanism of international space legislation.

---

[740] Agreement Governing the Activities of States on the Moon and Other Celestial Bodies, New York, done December 18, 1979, entered into force July 11, 1984; 1363 UNTS 3; ATS 1986 No. 14; 18 ILM 1434 (1979) (hereinafter "Moon Agreement).

[741] Proceedings of the United Nations/Republic of Korea Workshop on Space Law: United Nations Treaties on Outer Space: Actions at the National Level, Office for Outer Space Affairs, United Nations Office at Vienna, ST/SPACE/22, 137-139 (New York, 2004).

[742] UNCOPUOS organizes workshops in different regions annually to encourage the States to legislate national space laws. Such workshops have been held since 2002 in the Netherlands, Korea, Brazil and Nigeria.

1.2. Necessity of National Space Legislation

1.2.1. National Legislation vs. International Legislation

Countless articles and many books have thoroughly discussed the five international space treaties.[743] With the exception of the 1979 Moon Agreement, the other four treaties enjoy wide recognition. Some principles in the treaties are widely considered as international customary law: even if non-Parties to the treaty, States are obliged to comply with the obligations arising from its provisions.[744] Such principles include non-appropriation of and free access to outer space[745] and peaceful use of outer space.[746]

International space law plays an important role in regulating space activities. During the years when most nations did not have national space legislation, these treaties were the only source of written rules to rely upon. It is certain that these treaties will continue to be one of the most important sources of space law.

These treaties came into being in the first 25 years of space exploration. With the rapid development of space technology and the emergence of new space activities during the last 25 years, it would have been natural to expect additional rules and regulations to come into being. However, the reality is that no new treaties have been drafted or adopted since 1979. Does that mean that the existing treaties sufficiently resolve the problems arising out of new activities?

The answer is negative. One may refer to the discussions on the application of the term "launching state". Difficulties arise with the issue of registration and liability when a satellite is transferred to a non-launching state.[747] No firm decision has been made concerning the issue. In January 2005, the United Nations General Assembly (UNGA) adopted a Resolution recommending to States to consider enacting national laws providing for authorization and continuing supervision of the activities in outer space of non-governmental entities under their jurisdiction.[748] While as a main forum for the development of space law, the UNCOPUOS has faced difficulties in formulating new rules in view of the large number of Members increasingly involved in space activities and their uneven development. With no better means available, national space legislation seems a useful method in providing a regulatory framework for space activities at this time.

---

743 See for example, Ty S. Twibell, Space Law: Legal Restraints on Commercialization and Development of Outer Space, 65 *University of Missouri at Kansas City Law Review* 593-600 (Spring 1997).

744 Vladlen S. Vereshchetin & Gennady M. Danilenko, Custom as a Source of International Law of Outer Space, 13 *Journal of Space Law* 32 (1985).

745 Paul G. Dembling & Daniel M. Arons, The Evolution of Outer Space Treaty, 33 *Journal of Air Law & Commerce* 456 (1967).

746 Barry J. Hurewitz, Non-Proliferation and Free Access to Outer Space: The Dual-Use Conflict between the Outer Space Treaty and the Missile Technology Control Regime, 9 *High Technology Law Journal* 220 (1994).

747 For further discussion, see A/RES/59/115 (25 January 2005), at 2. Dr. Tennen argued that the legal framework, including the requirement for states to authorize and supervise national activities in space and the provisions regarding liability for damages, will ensure significant protection to private entities, and will safeguard the future of space commerce rather than hamper it. See IISL/ECSL Space Symposium 2004: "New Developments and the Legal Framework Covering the Exploitation of the Resources of the Moon".

748 *Id.*

1.2.2. Aims and Objectives of National Space Legislation

National space legislation provides legal certainty and transparency. A legal society is governed by laws, which set out basic parameters to govern the relevant activities. Potential actors can have the opportunity to evaluate their actions to be taken and assess expected results arising out of such actions. To improve legal certainty and transparency is common to all national legislation. However, with regards to national space legislation, further development in terms of more detailed objectives may be desirable.

1.2.2.1. Providing a Supervisory Framework for Space Activities

As recommended by the UNGA, national space legislation should provide a supervisory framework for space activities. This is the aim and objective of utmost importance for national space legislation. The five space law treaties were drafted in the cold-war period when a few States were engaged in space activities. This situation drastically changed with private parties increasingly becoming involved in space activities. The Outer Space Treaty provides for authorization, continuing supervision and the international responsibility for national activities in outer space, including those carried out by non-governmental entities.[749] However, different understandings exist for the term "national activities".[750] Would it be appropriate to hold a State responsible if the activity were carried out by a private entity without the knowledge of the State? If not, for what type of national activities shall a State be held responsible?

The Outer Space Treaty further provides that a State is internationally liable for damage to another State or its natural and juridical persons.[751] The liability of such a State, to satisfy the element of control and jurisdiction, is limited to four situations in the Liability Convention: a State which launches the space object, procures the launching of the space object, from whose territory the launching of the space object occurs, or from whose facilities the space object is launched.[752] Recent practice has cast doubts on the above limitation. In case the ownership of a space object is transferred to a non-original launching State, it would make no sense to hold the original launching State still liable and the transferee, with full control and jurisdiction of the space object, not liable.

While no consensus was reached on the above issues, it was agreed that private entities shall register with and be licensed by the States in the initial stage and that the States themselves shall be the first safety valve in regulating the activities of private entities through the license procedure.[753] States should formulate licensing rules when granting these private entities license to carry out space activities. Licensing an entity to carry out space activities implies that the licensing State shall continue to exercise supervision and make sure that such activities be carried out in accordance with its international obligations. Ignorance of private space activities shall, thus, not constitute a valid reason to absolve a State from responsibility and liability. Consequently, national space legislation shall serve as a supervisory framework

---

749 Outer Space Treaty, Article 6.

750 Frans G. von der Dunk, Heeding the Public-Private Paradigm: Overview of National Space Legislation around the World, *2004 Space Law Conference Paper Assemble*, Beijing, China April 25-27, 2004, China Institute of Space Law, at 22.

751 Outer Space Treaty, Article 7.

752 Liability Convention, Article 1(c).

753 United Nations/Republic of South Korea Workshop on Space Law, held in Daejon, November 3-6, 2003, available at <http://www.oosa.unvienna.org/index.html>.

for space activities and provide clear guidance on the issue of international responsibility and liability.[754]

1.2.2.2. Legal Obligation to Abide by International Treaty

According to international law, States party to a treaty are under a duty to implement the terms of that treaty within their national legal system.[755] The five space treaties constitute the most important legal source for those who intend to carry out space activities. As mentioned above, except for the Moon Agreement, the other four treaties have been accepted by many States. National legislation is one important means to implement international commitments. According to these international treaties, each State party shall be held responsible for certain national space activities conducted by its non-governmental entities. The space treaties do not provide detailed rules on their implementation. Consequently, each State party, no matter whether it automatically accepts international treaties as domestic law, shall need to enact clear and detailed national rules. In the case where there is a necessity to transform international treaties into domestic law, the State is implementing its international obligation through national legislation. In the case where international treaties are directly applicable, the State can expand and make more precise the ways to implement the treaties through national legislation.

1.2.2.3. Promotion of commercialization and Involvement of Private Entities

Private entities are increasingly interested in space activities in expectation of potential profits out of space use. Outer space is no longer a State-monopolized area. However, the space treaties were drafted when States were the only player in outer space. No consideration had been given to the commercial side of space activities. So far, no clear rules have been made relating to property rights; no agreements have been reached concerning the application of the term "Common Heritage of Mankind".[756] With all these legal issues pending, potential private investors will be hesitant, which will be detrimental to the healthy development of outer space resources.[757]

In view of the stagnant stage in international space legislation, national legislation shall be the only way to formulate rules in regulating new space activities. Compared with international legislation, national legislation is more flexible and more easily enacted. Given the rapid development of space technology and the irreversible trend of space commercialization, States should promptly act to fill in the current legal vacuum. A stable legal environment will procure economic returns and add confidence to potential space investors.

1.2.2.4. Optimization of the Utilization of Outer Space

Outer space is full of opportunities; however, lacking a clear legal framework prevents potential interested parties from taking advantage of the opportunity for economic and

---

754 Peter van Fenema, The Unidroit Space Protocol, the Concept of 'Launching State', Space Traffic Management and the Delimitation of Outer Space: The 41st Session of the UNCOPUOS Legal Subcommittee, Vienna, 2-12 April 2002, 28 *Air & Space Law* 277-279 (September 2002).

755 Statement by the Board of Directors of the International Institute of Space Law (IISL) on Claims to Property Rights Regarding the Moon and Other Celestial Bodies, IISL.

756 Charles C. Okolie, *International Law of Satellite Remote Sensing & Outer space* 42 (Kendall/Hunt, 1989).

757 Ezra J. Reinstein, Owning Outer Space, 20 *Journal of International Law & Business* 72-74 (Fall 1999).

technological gains. Since the International space legislative process is more complicated than national law-making for it requires consensus from various political, economic, military, and strategic interests, national legislation, comparatively simpler, could take initiative in making new rules for the use of outer space. Furthermore, national legislation could make rules liberal enough to realize the full benefits from the exploration of outer space.

Australia's Space Activities Act 1998 (Amendment 2002) (hereinafter "the Act") provides an excellent model. While recognizing that there is no internationally accepted or delimitation of the term "outer space", the Act replaced the term with the phrase "an area beyond the distance of 100 kilometers above mean sea level".[758] It does not matter much whether this above position on the border of outer space is acceptable to other nations; what matters is that States are starting to seriously deal with undefined matters at the national level. This process can serve as a testing bed for future international legislation. Accordingly, international legislation, though lagging behind, should not obstruct the utilization of outer space; national legislation provides an impetus for the utilization of outer space and international regulation comes into being.

1.3. Principles and Means of National Space Legislation

National space legislation has never been so important before. The rapid development of space activities and the difficulty in applying the existing space treaties has led to claims for national legislation. Sound development of space activities in the absence of appropriate international legislation largely depend on the national legal framework.

1.3.1. Principles for National Space Legislation

1.3.1.1. International Treaties and Existing National Space Legislation as a Basis and Guidelines

Without a doubt, international treaties, more specifically the existing space treaties, should serve as the starting point for national legislation. The principles and rules in those treaties offer useful guidelines. State parties undoubtedly have the obligation to implement those rules.[759] Rules which constitute part of customary international law also bind all States. Even rules which do not form part of customary law should help in securing the consistency of nationally enacted space rules. Particular attention should be paid to the existing national space legislations, especially those of the United States (US).

As defined by international treaties, each State should bear international responsibility and liability for national space activities. By transforming international treaties into national law, the State can show its commitments to the international standards concerning continued supervision of its space activities and secure appropriate indemnification in the case of personal death or injury, loss or damage to properties.

[758] United Nations General Assembly, Committee on the Peaceful Uses of Outer Space: National Legislation and Practice relating to Definition and Delimitation of Outer Space, Note by the Secretariat, Addemdum, March 20, 2006, A/AC.105/865/Add.1, para. 5.

[759] Antonio Cassese, *International Law*, , 217-218 (Oxford University Press, 2nd ed., 2005).

In brief, national space legislation should be able to reflect the principles inscribed in international treaties and concretize those principles in good faith. With respect to the issue of international responsibility and liability, the scope of national legislation should be expanded beyond simple transformation of international treaties.

1.3.1.2. Balancing International Obligations and National Interests

Development of space activities around the world is extremely imbalanced. For some time, outer space was monopolized by two superpowers. Such monopoly was broken when more and more States became space-faring nations.[760] But those nations differ in the scope of their activities. Different needs will require national legislation to be based on the actual national circumstance. National space legislation, while guided by the international space treaties, should differ based on national interests, the stage of social and economic development, national legal tradition and the nature of current and planned space activities by the State concerned.[761] Russia has developed its single omnibus law to further its economic and security interests in outer space. The purpose of its Law of the Russia Federation on Space Activity is to promote the well-being of the citizens of the Russian Federation, ensure its security and solve the global problems of mankind.[762]

National space legislation should serve the national needs. For example, in developing the national licensing regime for space activities, States shall consider factors such as the protection of public health and safety, property and the environment, including limited natural resources.[763]

1.3.1.3. Promotion of International Cooperation

International space legislation provides a basis for international cooperation on space activities. The special UN Resolution has been adopted concerning international space cooperation.[764] Bilateral or multilateral cooperation has been one of the most important characteristics of space exploration in recent years. The International Space Station is one excellent example. International space cooperation shall provide a means for States to complement each other; furthermore, it will be helpful to realize the aims of peaceful use of outer space and maximization of the benefits from the utilization of outer space.

Space cooperation appears all the more meaningful to developing countries when western countries prohibit the export of high-tech products. Space legislators of thus affected developing countries should be especially mindful of the importance of international space cooperation and try to formulate an efficient and feasible legal framework for space cooperation. Without a doubt, this principle should also apply to national space legislation in developed countries.

---

760 Glenn H. Reynolds & Robert P. Merges, *Outer Space: Problems of Law and Policy* 231 (Boulder: Westview press, 1989).

761 United Nations General Assembly, Committee on the Peaceful Uses of Outer Space: Report on the United Nations/International Institute of Air and Space Law Workshop on Capacity-Building in Space Law, The Hague, November 18-21, 2002, A/AC.105/802, para. 22.

762 Law of the Russian Federation on Space Activity, August 20, 1993, available at <http://www.jaxa.jp/jda/library/space-law/chapter_4/4-1-2-7/4-1-2-71_e.html>.

763 *Id.*, para. 24.

764 Declaration on International Cooperation on Exploring and Utilizing Outer Space for the Benefits and Interests of All Countries, Especially in Consideration of Developing Countries' Demands, adopted by the 51st United Nations General Assembly in 1996. UNGA Res. 51/122, of December 13, 1996.

Outer Space can never be lawfully monopolized by any State. Hence, space cooperation is beneficial to both developing and developed countries. For example, assistance in the rescue of astronauts as defined in the Rescue Convention clearly demonstrates that even States without space-faring ability can assist space activities.[765] National space legislation should not only define international cooperation in principle, but, more importantly, should provide a detailed structure to put space cooperation into practice.

1.3.1.4. Maintaining Flexibility and Constant Evolvement

Since the first artificial satellite launch in 1957, space activities have rapidly developed in variety. With further technological and economic development, we can expect more diverse activities together with new legal problems. In view of the novel space activities, States should develop new legislation to regulate new activities. On one hand, national legislation should specifically target the new activities and, on the other hand, the legislation should be flexible enough to accommodate new situations and problems that may arise in the future.

The balance between stability and flexibility is a new task for space legislators. However, this problem also exists in other high-tech areas. For example, the emergence of the Internet calls for rules to regulate online activities. Some scholars have argued that it is not sensible to formulate new laws just because of new technology.[766] Existing laws should continue to regulate new activities, subject to appropriate modification of certain provisions.

1.3.1.5. Gradual Process with Order of Priority

Legislating for space activities is a new task for most national legislators. A period of familiarization with outer space and space legal system is indispensable for those legislators to carry out their legislative task. Outer space has become an area of strategic importance to the States. National space legislators need to be wary of the potential implication of space legislation to national security and other significant national interests. The legislation should be carried out step by step.

For this purpose, the order of priority for the enactment of legislation is to be identified. As discussed above, given the rapid commercialization of outer space, national legislation on licensing should be given priority.[767] Other areas for early consideration include registration of space objects, state responsibility and liability (indemnification system), and financing system (including space insurance system).

1.3.2. Means

National space legislation is a complicated process. During the long march of this type of legislation, we need to take into account the following factors.

First, to better reflect and protect national interests, it is necessary to carefully examine such interests in the context of the draft legislation.

Second, commercialization of outer space is coupled with the process of privatization. Private entities are increasingly participating in the space exploration and will play an

---

765 Space-faring ability is not the condition for a State to become Contracting Party to the Rescue Agreement.

766 A.L. Shapiro, The Disappearance of Cyberspace and the Risk of Code, 8 *Seton Hall Constitutional Law Journal* 703 (1998).

767 P.P.C. Haanappel, *The Law and Policy of Air Space and Outer Space: A Comparative Approach* 10 (Kluwer Law International, 2003).

important role in future space commercialization.[768] This development has substantially changed the previous space arena. Therefore, key stakeholders in space activities should be encouraged to participate in national space legislative process. Opportunities should be provided for their participation. Consultation should precede space law-making. Presently, self-regulation has been advocated for high-tech areas.[769] We should not disregard its application in space legislation.

Third, customary law is an indispensable part of the laws regulating space activities.[770] One should not ignore its strong influence on space legislation. For example, countries with a remote sensing capability can influence the development of law by taking action to establish practice that could enhance and protect the right to access to data for all States not having such capabilities.[771] On one hand, customs enunciated in written documents can guide space activities; on the other hand, consistent space practice promotes and confirms the customs. In this way, legal vacuum concerning certain space activities can be somewhat mitigated.

Fourth, space legislation should follow normal procedures. We should, at this point, emphasize the existing experiences gained thus far and apply them in new space legislation. Legislation is also one way to publicize space law; other methods should also be used, including workshops, special courses, conferences and seminars to disseminate expertise in space law. In this manner, potential space legislators can be trained to have a better understanding of space law.

1.4. Conclusion

National space legislation has never been so important as at the present time. The understanding based on the concept of freedom of outer space and the belief that States are the sole actor in space activities have been so prevalent that led many to believe that international space legislation is the only effective means to regulate space activities.

With the nature and scope of space activities undergoing drastic changes, especially the process of commercialization of outer space, the existing international space law cannot adequately deal with all the new issues. The growing participation of private entities in space activities calls for national space regime to take the lead in providing a legal framework where at the present there is a legal vacuum. The world community has acknowledged the need and urgency for national space legislation; it is time to hear the reaction from the States. This section offers a guide to interested States space administrations.

When drafting national legislation for outer space affairs, the States, especially the developing countries, need to be wary of the strategic importance of balancing their international commitments and national interests. Such national space legislation should further promote the healthy development of space activities at both the international and national level.

---

[768] Mark J. Sundahl, Unidentified Orbital Debris: The Case for a Market-Share Liability Regime, 24 *Hastings International & Comparative Law Review* 125 (Fall 2000).

[769] J.I. Edelstein, Anonymity and International Law Enforcement in Cyberspace, 7 *Fordham Intellectual Property Media & Entertainment Law Journal* 284-286 (1996).

[770] I. H. Ph. Diederiks-Verschoor, *An Introduction to Space Law*, 10-12 (Kluwer Law International, 2nd ed., 1999).

[771] United Nations General Assembly, Committee on the Peaceful Uses of Outer Space: Report on the United Nations/Nigeria Workshop on Space Law on the theme "Meeting International Obligations and Addressing Domestic Needs", Abuja, November 21-24, 2005, A/AC.105/866, para. 33.

2. National Space Legislation in Mainland China

Although a major space-faring country, China has been slow in national space legislation. Its ambitious plan to reach out to the Moon and other, less ambitious, space projects underscore the urgent need for national space legislation. This section focuses on China as a useful illustration of how to go about creating national space legislation.

2.1. General Philosophy and Processes of Government Regulations

2.1.1. Law-making Processes

China's current legislation structure is a multi-leveled system. According to the Constitution and the Legislation Law of the People's Republic of China, national legislation is divided into three levels: (1) Laws enacted by the National People's Congress (NPC) and its Standing Committee, the body exercising the legislative power of the State;[772] (2) Administrative Regulations formulated by the State Council, the national administrative organ; (3) Departmental regulations formulated by the Ministries and Commissions of the State Council, the People's Bank of China, the State Audit Administration as well as other organs endowed with administrative functions directly under the State Council.

All the laws and regulations shall go through four stages: proposal of draft; deliberation of draft; adoption of draft and promulgation. The first level of laws requires a longer period of deliberation before approval. The procedures for other levels of laws are slightly simpler and faster.

The legislation procedures of the Standing Committee of the NPC are discussed here as an example to further elaborate the law-making processes. (1) Proposal of draft: the Council of the Chairmen of the NPC, the State Council, the Central Military Commission, the Supreme People's Court, the Supreme People's Procuratorate or a special committee of the NPC, ten or more of the members of the Standing Committee, ten or more of the members of the Standing Committee may submit a legislative bill to the Standing Committee for possible deliberation.[773] (2) Deliberation of draft: the draft of a legislative bill placed on the agenda of a meeting of the Standing Committee shall be delivered to the component members of the Standing Committee seven days before the meeting.[774] This bill shall be put to vote after deliberations at three meetings of the Standing Committee.[775] (3) Adoption of draft: the Law Committee of the NPC shall further revise the draft on the basis of the deliberated opinions of the members of the Standing Committee before preparing a draft for vote; then, the Council of Chairmen shall request the Standing Committee to put the draft to vote at a plenary meeting, and the draft shall be subject to adoption by a simple majority of the total membership of the Standing Committee.[776] (4) Promulgation: a law adopted by the Standing Committee shall be promulgated by Order of the President signed by the President of the People's Republic of China.[777]

[772] Legislation Law of the People's Republic of China (Order of the President No. 31), Article 7.
[773] Legislation Law, Article 24-25.
[774] Legislation Law, Article 26.
[775] Legislation Law, Article 27.
[776] Legislation Law, Article 40.
[777] Legislation Law, Article 41.

China launched its first satellite (DFH-1) by Long March vehicle in 1970 and became full member of the United Nations Committee on Peaceful Uses of Outer Space (UNCOPUOS) ten years later. China has always placed high emphasis on space activities and space regulation. Due to historical reasons, China has so far concentrated on technological development in outer space; development of and research in space law has been lagging far behind. However, China has, on various occasions, acknowledged the importance of space law in the development of space exploration and has taken efforts to improve in this area. The UNCOPUOS membership has accelerated China's pace in space legislation. The Chinese Government ratified the Outer Space Treaty in 1983 and the other three space treaties (except the Moon Agreement) in 1988.[778]

Efforts in develop national space legislation started around 1994; but most substantial work was carried out after 1998 when China reformed its administrative system for the industries. Currently, there are no national space laws in China. But several regulations have been passed concerning registration and launching of space objects: the Provisions and Procedures for the Registration of Space Objects on February 8, 2001; and the Interim Measures on the Administration of Permits for Civil Space Launch Projects on November 21, 2002.

2.1.2. Basic Principles of National Laws

National laws shall be made in compliance with the basic principles laid down in the constitution, principles of taking economic development as the central task, adhering to the socialist road and the people's democratic dictatorship, upholding leadership by the Communist Party of China, upholding Marxism-Leninism, Mao Zedong Thought and Deng Xiaoping theory and preserving in reform and in opening to the outside world.[779] Chapter 1 of the Constitution of the People's Republic of China defines 32 General Principles of Chinese national laws.

The other three articles of the Legislation Law further provide basic principles in law-making process: laws shall be made in accordance with the statutory limits of power and procedures, on the basis of the overall interests of the State and for the purpose of safeguarding the uniformity and dignity of the socialist legal system;[780] laws shall be made in order to embody the will of the people, enhance socialist democracy and guarantee that the people participate in legislative activities through various channels;[781] laws shall be made by proceeding from reality and scientifically and rationally prescribing the rights and duties of citizens, legal persons and other organizations, and the powers and responsibilities of State organs.[782]

China's space activities aim to explore outer space, and enhance understanding of the Earth and the cosmos; to utilize outer space for peaceful purposes, promote human civilization and social progress, and benefit the whole of mankind; to meet the demands of economic construction, scientific and technological development, national security and social

[778] China acceded to the Outer Space Treaty on December 30, 1983; the Rescue Agreement on December 14, 1988; the Liability Convention on December 12, 1988; the Registration Convention on December 12, 1988.

[779] Legislation Law, Article 3.

[780] Legislation Law, Article 4.

[781] Legislation Law, Article 5.

[782] Legislation Law, Article 6.

progress; and to raise the scientific quality of the Chinese people, protect China's national interests and rights, and build up the comprehensive national strength.[783]

The principles to be followed for the development of China's space industry, as identified in the White Paper on China's Space Activities in 2006, are as follows: maintaining and serving the country's overall development strategy, and meeting the needs of the state and reflecting its will; upholding independence and self-reliance policy, making innovations independently and realizing leapfrogging development; maintaining comprehensive, coordinated and sustainable development, and bringing into full play the functions of space science and technology in promoting and sustaining the country's science and technology sector, as well as economic and social development; adhering to the policy of opening up to the outside world, and actively engaging in international space exchanges and cooperation.[784] The above aims and principles apply generally to national space legislation in China.

It is also to be noted that international cooperation is elaborated in a separate part in the 2000 White Paper, implying that China attaches great importance to space cooperation in various levels.[785]

2.1.3. Organization of National Space Activities

China National Space Administration (CNSA) was established, as a government institution to develop and fulfill China's due international obligations, with the approval by the 8th National People's Congress of China. The 9th NPC assigned CNSA as an internal structure of the Commission of Science, Technology and Industry for National Defense (COSTIND). CNSA assumes the following main responsibilities: signing governmental agreements in the space area on behalf of organization, inter-governmental scientific and technical exchanges; and also being in charge of the enforcement of national space policies and managing the national space science, technology and industry.[786] Accordingly, the CNSA is the main administrative body in charge of national space industry and civil space activities; it is also the most important authority responsible for preparing space legislation, formulating policies for space industry and technology, making plans for space development and setting standards in these areas.[787]

There are four departments under the CNSA: Department of General Planning, Department of System Engineering, Department of Science, Technology and Quality Control, Department of Foreign Affairs. [788]

---

[783] The State Council Information Office, China's Space Activities in 2006 (White Paper), October 2006, Beijing, China.

[784] *Id.*

[785] *Id.* Guiding principles for international cooperation are: the aim of international space cooperation is to peacefully develop and use space resources for the benefit of all mankind; international space cooperation should be carried out on the basis of equality and mutual benefit, mutual complementarity and common development, and the generally accepted principles of international law; the priority aim of international space cooperation is to simultaneously increase the capability of space development of all countries, particularly the developing countries, and enable all countries to enjoy the benefits of space technology; necessary measures should be adopted to protect the space environment and space resources in the course of international space cooperation; the function of the United Nations Office of Outer Space Affairs (OOSA) should be consolidated and the outer space application programs of the United Nations should be backed up.

[786] China National Space Administration, <http://www.cnsa.gov.cn>.

[787] *Id.*

2.2. Licensing of Launch Services by Private Enterprises

The Interim Measures on the Administration of Permits for Civil Space Launch Projects, released by the COSTIND in 2002, established the licensing regime for all spacecraft launches within the territory of China, excluding launches for military purposes and the entry of such spacecrafts over which the natural persons, legal persons or other organization of China have had property or have property by means of on-orbit delivery into the outer space from outside of the territory of China.[789] The COSTIND is the authority responsible for examining, approving and supervising all civil space launch projects.[790]

The general project contractor should apply to the COSTIND with relevant documents nine months before the prearranged month for the launch of the project.[791] The COSTIND should organize the examination of the project within 30 days as of receipt of the application documents and notify in writing the applicant and the relevant departments of the decisions.[792] The permit should include the following: the name of the applicant and its legal representative, the registration address of the applicant's domicile, main contents of the project, the prearranged time for launch, validity period of the permit, the organ issuing the permit and the time of issuance.[793] An application for modification or cancellation should be filed 90 days before the expiry of the validity period of the permit. [794]

The permit holder must purchase the third party liability insurance and other relevant insurances for launching a space object.[795] For a project in the stage of a domestic executive launching site, the permit holder shall report the launching plan 6 months before the prearranged month for launch and file an application for approval to leave the factory with relevant materials before entering the stage of a launching site.[796]

The Interim Measures prescribed administrative penalties and criminal liabilities for acts such as concealing the truth, practicing fraud, damaging the interests of the State, undertaking projects without authorization, neglecting duties or abusing powers resulting in losses caused to the State.[797]

2.3. Intellectual Property and Transfer of Technology

2.3.1. Acquisition of Intellectual Property Rights

Intellectual property protection is vital for economic development, social progress, scientific and technological innovation and cultural prosperity. China has made great progress in IP protection over the past few years. A relatively complete system of laws and regulations has been established, including Patent Law, Trademark Law, Copyright Law. Patent rights

[788] *Id.*
[789] Interim Measures, Article 2.
[790] Interim Measures, Article 4.
[791] Interim Measures, Articles 5-6.
[792] Interim Measures, Article 7.
[793] Interim Measures, Article 10.
[794] Interim Measures, Articles 13-14.
[795] Interim Measures, Article 19.
[796] Interim Measures, Article 20.
[797] Interim Measures, Articles 24-26.

shall be most relevant for the present discussion. Thus, this section will focus on the patent protection regime in China.

Patent Law, originally promulgated in 1985, was revised in 2000. The revised Patent Law went into effect in July 2001. It provides that any invention or utility model for which a patent right may be granted must possess the characteristics of novelty, inventiveness and usefulness.[798] No patent right shall be granted for scientific discoveries; rules and methods for mental activities; methods for the diagnosis or treatment of diseases; animal and plant varieties; and substances obtained by means of nuclear fission.[799]

Relevant documents should be submitted for a patent application. Any applicant who claims the right of priority shall make a written declaration when the application is filed, and submit, within three months, a copy of the patent application documents that was first filed.[800] Where finding the application to be in conformity with the requirements of the Patent Law upon preliminary examination, the patent administrative department of the State Council shall publish the application promptly after the expiration of eighteen months from the date of filing.[801] Upon the applicant's request for an invention made at anytime within three years from the filing date of an application, the patent administration department of the State Council may carry out substantive examination of that application.[802] If, after completing the substantive examination of an invention patent application, the patent administration department of the State Council finds no reason for rejection, it shall make a decision for the grant of an invention patent right, issue an invention patent certificate, at the same time, register and publicly announce it; the invention patent right shall be effective from the date of public announcement.[803]

2.3.2. Mechanism of Exploiting IP Rights

After the grant of the patent right, no unit or individual may exploit the patent without the authorization of the patentee; the exploitation here include manufacturing, using, selling, agreeing to sell, importing the patented product or using the patented process for production or business purpose and using, selling, agreeing to sell or import the patented product which has been directly in accordance with the patented process.[804]

However, where a unit possesses the conditions for exploitation, requests the patentee of an invention or utility model to license the exploitation of the patent on reasonable terms and conditions, and cannot obtain the licence within a reasonably long period of time, the patent administrative department of the State Council may grant a compulsory licence for the exploitation of the said invention patent or utility model patent.[805]In cases of when an emergency state occurs in the country or extraordinary circumstances occur or for the purposes of public interests, the patent administrative department of the State Council may grant a compulsory licence.[806]

---

[798] Patent Law, Article 22(1).
[799] Patent Law, Article 25.
[800] Patent Law, Article 30.
[801] Patent Law, Article 34.
[802] Patent Law, Article 35.
[803] Patent Law, Article 39.
[804] Patent Law, Article 11.
[805] Patent Law, Article 48.
[806] Patent Law, Article 49.

A unit or an individual that has obtained a compulsory licence for exploitation does not have exclusive exploitation right and has no right to allow another person to exploit the patent.[807] The unit or the individual shall pay a reasonable fee to the patentee for the use of the patent, which amount shall be agreed upon consultation and when the parties cannot reach an agreement, the patent administrative department shall decide.[808]

2.3.3. National Legal Barriers to International Transfer of Space Technology

For a complete understanding of Chinese space legislation at the present stage, it is important to note some regulations relating to military space activities.[809] The Regulations on Control of the Military Products Export, first enacted in 1997 and revised in 2002, were introduced to strengthen unified management of military products export.[810] Several guaranties must be satisfied before allowing the export of military products: the product must be useful to the self-defense capability of the recipient country; not being harmful to the peace, security and stability of the relevant region of the world; not interfering in the recipient country's internal affairs.[811] As required by the above Regulation, the COSTIND and the People's Liberation Army (PLA) General Armament Department (GAD) further drafted the Military Products Export Control List in 2003, [812] which includes launch vehicles, missile weapon systems and military satellites.[813]

To further strengthen export control system and prevent the proliferation of missiles and other delivering systems that can be used to deliver weapons of mass destruction, [814] the State Council published the Regulations of the People's Republic of China on Export Control of Missiles and Missile-related Items and Technologies in 2002, together with the Missiles and Missile-related Items and Technologies Export Control List. According to the Regulations, rockets, unmanned air vehicles, missiles (ballistic and cruise missiles) and missile-related items and technologies are subject to export control.[815]

A licensing regime is established for the export of the above items and technologies. The exporter should apply to the competent foreign economic and trade department of the State Council with the export application form and relevant documents. The above department shall examine the application (possibly joined by other relevant departments of the State Council and of the Central Military Commission) and make a decision within 45 days after the receipt of the application.[816] The regulation also provides for possible administrative penalties and criminal liability for certain acts.[817]

---

[807] Patent Law, Article 53.

[808] Patent Law, Article 54.

[809] Space Law: China's Regulations, World Security Institute, China-US Dialogue on Space, available at <http://www.wsichina.org/subprogram.cfm?subprogramid=2&charid=1#00008> (last visited June 20, 2006).

[810] Regulations on Control of the Military Products Export, Article 1.

[811] Regulations on Control of the Military Products Export, Article 5.

[812] Regulations on Control of the Military Products Export, Article 2(2) provides that the military products export control list shall be formulated, adjusted, and promulgated by the state department in charge of military products export.

[813] The Military Products Export Control List.

[814] Regulations on Export Control of Missiles and Missile-related Items and Technologies, Art. 3.

[815] *Id.*, Art. 2.

[816] *Id.*, Art. 10.

[817] *Id.*, Art. 15-22.

2.4. Registration of Space Objects

The Provisions and Procedures for the Registration of Space Objects, published in 2001 by the Commission of Science, Technology and Industry for National Defense (COSTIND) and the Ministry of Foreign Affairs (MFA), is the first domestic administrative regulation adopted by China on space activities. The main purpose of this regulation is to fulfill China's commitments under the Registration Convention, while taking into account the practical situation in China.

All the space objects launched within the territory of China, or launched abroad but with China as a co-launching State, shall be registered with the COSTIND within 60 days after the space objects were launched into orbit. The COSTIND should maintain the National Registration Booklet. Modification to the registration shall be done within 60 days after the change of the relevant circumstances, such as changes of orbit, disintegration, end of operation, or re-entry into atmosphere. The COSTIND shall provide to the MFA relevant registration data within 60 days after domestic registration; the MFA will then register with the United Nations Secretary-General. With regard to the special case of Hong Kong and Macao, a special Sub-Registration Booklet shall be established with the registration procedure to be stipulated separately.[818]

2.5. Further Development

Space legislation is, at the moment, among the highest priorities on the CNSA's agenda. A special task force was set up under the CNSA to study the issue of national space legislation. It has been agreed that space legislation in China should move gradually. A comprehensive national law on outer space shall not be pursued at the present stage as the conditions for such a law are not ripe.

The administrative structure and code of conduct concerning space activities in China are still in the process of development; regulation of specific aspects of space activities shall be the priority of space legislation. Such specific regulations may touch on such issues as investment and financing, insurance and indemnification system, commercial operation and management, and international cooperation. Once the regulations prove to be efficient and practicable, a comprehensive law on outer space may be drafted and adopted. The ultimate goal for China is to have a national space law, complemented by a set of administrative laws/regulations and departmental rules.

Currently, China has draft legislation on space liability under discussion.[819] This draft legislation intends to implement the 1972 Liability Convention. The efforts above has sufficiently demonstrated Chinese Government's firm efforts in carrying out international obligations on space issues and commitment to achieving legal transparency in outer space.

---

[818] As identified by Xiaohong Liu & Xiaoqing Wang in the paper The First Administrative Regulation on Space Activities in China presented at the United Nations/International Institute of Air and Space law (IIASL) Workshop on Capacity Building in Space Law during November 18-21, 2002 in the Hague, the registration procedure include open end; possibility of being amended after certain period of implementation; and possibility of being upgraded into administrative law or regulation in the future.

[819] The Provisional Regulation on Liability for Damage Caused by Space Objects has been placed on the agenda.

3. NATIONAL REGIME FOR TELECOMMUNICATIONS SERVICES

3.1. Introduction

China's entry into the WTO on December 11, 2001 was recognized not only as a driving force for China to continue its pace along the settled open-door policy of the market economy, but also as the hopeful hero to the hovering economic recession around the world. This "win-win" situation has been the result of fifteen years of negotiation. It is perfectly understandable why both China and other WTO Members had high expectations for this milestone in economic development. After all, China now has the license to enter markets of other Members without structural or ideological barriers and the other WTO Members also benefit from officially obtaining the go-ahead to enter the vast market of China.

Commitments had been made even before China formally joined the WTO. These commitments were widely acknowledged as being able to exert substantial impact on the Chinese economy, especially on the traditionally sensitive areas like agriculture and telecommunications. The aim of this section, therefore, is to show how China's entry into the WTO has affected the telecommunications industry.

The telecommunications industry is developing rapidly in China with many improvements underway and plenty of plans in the pipeline. For example, China had 40 million cell phone users in a population of 1.4 billion—something must be done about this pathetic 3 percent market penetration after 2001. It is generally believed that the use of the telecom, both land-based and wireless, will grow at a rate of 50 percent or more in the coming years.[820] This rapid rate of course requires appropriate regulation and thorough planning.

Telecommunications services were considered as a monopolized branch due to its sensitiveness to national security.[821] China's telecommunications industry has long been listed as an area of prohibiting foreign investment in the previous Ministry of Foreign Trade and Economic Cooperation's (MOFTEC's).[822] Following the ongoing trend of liberalization in the world, this idea is finally facing evolution. Chinese government acknowledged this trend as inevitable and so had begun the reform as early as in the 1980s. However, this process was decided upon, whilst still under the illusion that the State played a strong role in telecommunications.

In the midst of the negotiations concerning China's entry, the WTO Members had successfully obtained formal promise from the Chinese government to liberalize telecommunications services.[823] The substantial commitments on telecommunications services that were made, speaks for itself: 50 percent ownership was permitted in some sectors within two years of entry (this is a huge advancement from a complete absence of

---

[820] The Impact of WTO on China's Telecommunications, available at <http://www.es123.com>.

[821] Foreign investment has been shielded in basic services since the very beginning. Limited competition in wireless sector was introduced only with the entry of Unicom in 1994. See further H. Chang, Lian Tong: A Quantum Leap in the Reform of China's Telecommunications, 18 *Telecommunications Policy*, 206-210 (1994).

[822] See China Ministry of Foreign Trade & Economic Cooperation, Catalogue for the Guidance of Foreign Investment Industries, available at <http://www.moftec.gov.cn>. Prior to 1994, China's telecommunications industry was a monopoly market dominated by the State run China Telecom.

[823] See for example, Historic USA-China Trade Agreement, available at <http://www.sinomania.com>; see also The U.S.-China WTO Accession Deal: A Clear Win for U.S. High Technology, Greater Openness and U.S. Interests, March 1, 2000, available at <http://clinton4.nara.gov>.

foreign ownership previously).[824] Even though such achievements were obtained only after a series of intensive negotiations and heated discussions, we should be careful not to simply accept the generally conceived idea that China has a reluctant and stubborn attitude towards foreign entry. In fact, the Chinese government has, to a certain extent, voluntarily agreed to open its telecommunications market while witnessing the benefits entailed in liberalization that joining the WTO brings.[825]

Once China had formally entered the WTO, it naturally began to carry out its obligations immediately, *i.e.* from December 12, 2001. It is important to take note of China's efforts to comply with the WTO and offer an analysis on its performance in the up-coming phase where we will witness several substantial implementations.

So far there are no national laws on telecommunications services in China. However, several regulations have been made by the State Council and relevant ministries. Regulations of the People's Republic of China on Telecommunications (Telecommunications Regulations) is the most important one promulgated by the State Council in September 2000 and since then, provides the most important guidelines for telecommunications services in China. However, with China's accession to the WTO, several new regulations have been made to meet China's commitments under the WTO framework.

Accordingly, this section is a timely work in offering tentative evaluation of China's performance. In Part two, there is a general discussion on the WTO framework for telecommunication services, followed by a simple description of China's commitments. This will constitute the basis for further discussions. Removing barriers to market entry based on the agreed schedule is the *prima facie* evidence of compliance. The purpose of the section is to focus on the Chinese government in producing a pro-competitive market, establishing an independent regulator and realizing other regulatory principles provided in the Reference Paper. Thus, after a short description of the opening of the telecommunications market, Parts three and four elaborate on China's commitments as required by the Reference Paper. Already we can see that the Chinese government is on the right track, but there is still much room for improvement.

3.2. China's Commitments in Telecommunications Services

The Uruguay Round of negotiations started with ambitious goals, extending the arena of liberalization to services. However, the negotiations on telecommunications services, or more specifically, basic telecommunications services, appeared to be one of the most difficult areas for negotiations.[826] After a period of 'ups and downs', an agreement set to be the Fourth Protocol to the GATS, was reached on February 15, 1997 and came into force on February 5, 1998. This created a complete framework for telecommunications services at that stage, with the prospect of further liberalization at the next round of negotiations.

---

[824] C. Chandler, China Clears Barrier to WTO, Washington Post, September 15, 2001, at D1; see also European Commission, EU-China WTO Accession Negotiations, Highlights of the EU-China Agreement on WTO, available at <http://europa.eu.int>.

[825] See further X. Fan, China's WTO Accession and Its Telecom Liberalization, available at <http://www.csis.org/ics/chinaswtoaccession.html>.

[826] See further G.C. Hufbauer & E. Wada (eds.), *Unfinished Business: Telecommunications after the Uruguay Round* 3-4 (Institute for International Economics, 1997).

The present framework of the WTO for telecommunications services includes the conclusions that were reached during the Uruguay Round and later period under the auspices of the Negotiation Group on Basic Telecommunications (NGBT) and the Group on Basic Telecommunications (GBT).

The General Agreement on Trade in Services (GATS) is the basic document for all the services defined in the articles, with no exception to telecommunications services.[827] One Annex was attached dealing specifically with value-added telecommunications services. It specifically addresses and ensures access to and use of public telecommunications transport networks and services on reasonable and non-discriminatory terms and conditions for the supply of a service included in its Schedule.[828]

Unlike the trade in goods, the barriers to trade in services may not be in the form of high tariffs or quotas but rather in the form and functioning of domestic regulation of a host country.[829] Basic telecommunications was targeted for sector-specific negotiation due to its complex domestic legal structures, highly regulated business environment, economic importance, capital-intensive nature, and national security importance within domestic infrastructure.[830] Acknowledging regulation as a significant barrier to services, the Reference Paper[831] was agreed upon at a later stage for regulatory principles in basic telecommunications, followed by the adoption of the Fourth Protocol at an even later stage. All the documents above constitute the basis for bilateral negotiations between China and other Member States. It is thus necessary to discuss China's obligation in view of the structures set by different documents.

3.2.1. The General Agreement on Trade in Services (GATS)

The GATS is an introduction, but not specifically, to telecommunications services. The only major obligation that a Member assumes with respect to trade in all services is the Most-Favored-Nation (MFN) Treatment.[832] Unless exceptions are stated in a Member's Schedule, the market access and national treatment provisions both afford foreign companies the same right of investment as a country's nationals may enjoy without the restriction of ownership. Generally speaking, the provisions contained in the GATS, function as guidance for Members to make detailed national commitments. China, while acceding to the WTO, naturally accepts the GATS as a whole. However, when we come to discuss the commitments undertaken by China, we actually need to look further into the detailed offer and concession made by China.

Telecommunications are generally categorized into basic and value-added services. China also follows this classification. Although this classification has, to a large extent, facilitated the negotiation, problems still exist for them where different countries might have different standards for classification. In this way, it is even more important to have a clear-cut list for

---

827 M. Mueller & Z. Tan, *China in the Information Age* 105 (1997).

828 Paragraph 5 (a) of the Annex on Telecommunications.

829 T. Warren & C. Findlay, Competition Policy and International Trade in Air Transport and Telecommunications Services, 21 *The World Economy* 445 (1998).

830 J.S. Thomas & M.A. Meyer, *The New Rules of Global Trade* 243 (1997).

831 For discussion of the Reference Paper, see generally M. Fredebeul-Krein & A. Freytag, The Case for a More Binding WTO Agreement on Regulatory Principles in Telecommunication Markets, 23 *Telecommunications Policy* 625-644 (1999).

832 Exemptions are granted subject to meeting the conditions of the GATS Annex on Article II Exemptions. For further discussion, see L.J. Spiwak, From International Competitive Carrier to the WTO: A Survey of the FCC's International Telecommunications Policy Initiatives 1985-1998, 51 *Federal Communication Law Journal* 169 (1998).

each category. China has successfully produced a document listing telecommunications services under these two categories. The list was initially publicized in the Telecommunications Regulation issued on September 25, 2000 and was further clarified at a later stage.

As listed in the Annex 9 to the Protocol on the Accession of China, value-added services include electronic mail, voice mail, on-line information and database retrieval, electronic data interchange, enhanced/value-added facsimile services (including stored and forward, store and retrieve), on-line information and/or data processing (including transaction processing); basic telecommunication services include paging services, mobile voice and data services analogue/digital/cellular services and personal communication services, voice services, packet-switched data transmission services, circuit-switched data transmission services, facsimile services, domestic private leased circuit services and international closed user group voice and data services.[833] The Ministry of Information Industry (MII) Order No. 429 issued on June 11, 2001 further defines Internet data centers and virtual private networks as value-added services, which are two significant areas omitted from the Telecommunications Regulation.

3.2.2. Commitments for Value-added Services

Most commitments made during the Uruguay Round were limited to value-added services. The negotiation on this area was comparatively easier since most States had opened certain parts of value-added services to competition from the inception of telecommunications. The situation is the same in China. Before acceding to the WTO, China had actually opened the door to foreign investors. The concessions made in this part were much less significant, compared to other Members.

Foreign Service suppliers were permitted to establish joint venture enterprises without quantitative restrictions and provide services in Shanghai, Guangzhou and Beijing. Foreign equity in joint ventures will not be more than 30 per cent. Within one year after the accession, the applicable geographical areas expanded and the percentage rose to 49. No geographical restriction existed after two years and foreign equity is allowed for no more than 50 per cent.

3.2.3. Commitments for Basic Telecommunications

It took almost three additional years to reach an agreement on basic telecommunications and substantial achievements were only obtained after an arduous series of bargaining. These commitments made by China on telecommunications services lie specifically in this area, where it can be time-consuming and lead to much public attention.

Basic telecommunications services are widely considered as sensitive to national economy and security. Moreover, many developing countries lag behind in this field, so opening markets to foreign investors could adversely retard the growth of indigenous capabilities. This problem is also true in China where the lengthy negotiations that have occurred, testify the above concerns. This is why, when foreign investors extolled the significance of China's accession, they realized the ensuing benefits they could enjoy in the

---

[833] See World Trade Organization, Negotiating Group on Basic Telecommunications, Note by the Chairman, Revision, Notes for Scheduling Basic Telecom Services Commitments, S/GBT/W/2/Rev.1, January 16, 1997, 36 I.L.M. 354, 371 (1997). According to the Basic Telecommunications Agreement, basic telecommunications includes local, long distance, and international services, for public and non-public uses, offered through any technology, such as cable, wireless, or satellite, on a facilities basis or by resale.

field of telecommunications, or more specifically, in basic telecommunications services. Accordingly, when we start to evaluate the performance of China in telecommunications, we aim to focus on its progress in liberalizing the market of basic services.

Ericsson, Nokia, Motorola and Qualcomm have had significant investments in China and under the agreement, these firms have more freedom to manufacture, distribute and market within the country.[834] To secure its control in the post-WTO era, the Chinese government has been careful about the foreign direct investment cap, [835] believing that ownership control by default equals management control.[836] China rejected concessions of foreign ownership at fifty-one percent as this figure was considered as politically unacceptable.[837] The carefully selected figures suggest that Chinese domestic law in many cases implies company control hinges on percentage ownership.

For paging services, foreign service suppliers are permitted to establish joint venture enterprises without quantitative restrictions and provide services in and between Shanghai, Guangzhou and Beijing. Foreign investment is limited to 30 percent. Within one year of entry, the applicable areas were extended and the investment was raised to 49 percent. No geographical restrictions existed after two years of entry and investment rates were raised further to 50 percent.

Mobile voice and data services are at approximately the same stage, but the difference lies in the percentage and the period needed to reach that percentage. Within one year after entry, the area permitted to establish joint ventures were expanded and foreign investment was allowed to no more than 35 percent. This number was further raised to 49 percent within three years after entry and no geographical restriction existed after five years.

As far as other basic services are concerned, nothing changed within the first three years after entry. China had three years' cushioning period to readjust and prepare for the approaching competition. It is thus paramount to look at how China had prepared for the challenges on the horizon.

3.2.4. Additional Commitments

The most remarkable feature of the Fourth Protocol is the acceptance of the Reference Paper by most Members. The six key principles are listed as follows: competitive safeguards, interconnection, universal service, public availability of licensing criteria, independent regulators, allocation and use of scarce resources. They are laid down for the redesign of national regulatory rules and institutions to ensure the compatibility with trade disciplines.

China has accepted the Reference Paper as additional commitments. However, the real problem resides not in whether to accept or not, but in how to implement the principles. Just as it has been pointed out by some scholars, although the rules are the same, the enforcement mechanisms, the way enforcement occurs, the norms of behavior, and the subjective models of the actors are not. In this way, both the real incentive structures and the perceived consequences of policies will differ too.[838] The Reference Paper has been consistently

---

[834] Qualcomm has recently licensed its CDMA (code division multiple access) technology to China Unicom.

[835] Remarks by Ambassador Charlene Barshefsky, United States Trade Representative, Nortel Network Policy Forum, China's WTO Accession: America's Choice, February 23, 2000, at 4.

[836] Y. Xu, A Special WTO Zone for Telecommunications?, available at <http://www.bm.ust.hk>.

[837] G. Winestock, China, EU Gain an Edge in WTO Deal: Three Major Concessions for U.S. Involve Retail, Insurance and Telecom, *Wall Street Journal*, May 22, 2000, at A30.

[838] D. North, *Institutions, Institutional Change, and Economic Performance* 101 (Cambridge University Press 1990).

criticized for its simplicity and many loopholes exist in further implementation of the principles. Different Members can have different interpretations for the principles and various justifications can be made to accommodate for any possible deviations. Thus, China's implementation of the principles rightly deserves attention from domestic and overseas observers.

3.3. Basic Regulations on Telecommunications Services

3.3.1. Licensing of Private Satellite Telecommunications Operators (Both National and Foreign)

China classifies the telecommunications business operation according to telecommunication business (basic services and value-added services) and implements the license system thereof.[839] The operators, in order to engage in the basic telecommunications services, or in the value-added telecommunications services with coverage of more than two provinces, autonomous regions, or municipalities directly under the Central People's Government, must be examined and approved by the administrative departments in charge of information industry of the State Council and obtain the License to Operating Basic Telecommunications Services or the License to Operating Trans-regional Value-added Telecommunications Services. The operator, in order to engage in trial telecommunications services that are not listed by the Catalogue of Telecommunications Business Classification with new technology, shall apply to the administrative departments in charge of telecommunications for records.[840]

The operator providing basic telecommunications services shall own the following qualifications: (a) the operator must be the specialized company engaging in the basic telecommunications business that is established according to law and the Chinese stock rights shall be no less than 51 percent; (b) having the feasibility study report and network construction scheme; (c) having the corresponding funds and professionals engaging in operation; (d) having places and corresponding resources engaging in operation; (e) having good reputation or capacity to provide long-term service for users; and (f) other qualifications as provided by the State.[841] The administrative departments in charge of information industry of the State Council shall complete the inspection and make the decision of approval or non-approval within 180 days upon the acceptance of the application.[842] The elements for consideration during the inspection include the State security, telecommunications network security, continuous use of telecommunications resources, environmental protection, competition of the telecommunications market.[843]

In order to operate value-added telecommunications services, the operator shall own the following qualifications: (a) the operator shall be the company established according to law; (b) having corresponding funds and professionals engaging in operation; (c) having good reputation or capacity to provide long-term service for users; and (d) other qualifications as

[839] Telecommunications Regulations, Article 7(1).
[840] Telecommunications Regulations, Article 9.
[841] Telecommunications Regulations, Article 10.
[842] Telecommunications Regulations, Article 11.
[843] Telecommunications Regulations, Article 12.

provided by the State.[844] The administrative departments in charge of information industry of the State Council or provinces, autonomous regions and municipalities directly under the Central People's Government, shall complete the inspection and make decision of approval or non-approval within 60 days upon the acceptance of the application.[845]

3.3.2. Rate Regulation

The telecommunications rate is primarily based on costs; other factors for consideration include the requirement of national economy and social development, development of telecommunications industry, the bearing capacity of users.[846] Telecommunications charges shall be divided into market adjusting price, governmental guidance price and rated price by the governments; only market adjusting price shall be applicable to the telecommunications services with full market competition; the administrative classification catalogue for telecommunications charges reflected by the above three types of charges shall be formulated and promulgated by the administrative departments in charge of information industry of the State Council based on asking for comments and suggestions of the administrative departments in charge of price control.[847] For the standard range of telecommunications charges with rated price by the governments or governmental guidance price, hearing and other manners shall be adopted for hearing comments of telecommunications business operators, telecommunications users and other relevant parties.[848]

3.3.3. Content Regulation (Including Privacy)

Any organization or individual shall not make, copy, distribute, and promulgate information with contents specified as follow by means of telecommunications network: (1) opposing basic principles confirmed by the Constitution of the People's Republic of China; (2) endangering state security, betraying state secret, subverting state political power, breaching state unification; (3) damaging state reputation and benefits; (4) instigating nationality enmity, nationality discrimination, and undermining the nationality solidarity; (5) undermining the state religious policy, preaching illegal religion and feudal superstition; (6) disseminating rumors, disrupting public order and social stability; (7) disseminating obscenity, eroticism, gambling, violence, homicide, horror or abetting crime; (8) humiliating or slandering others, and infringing legal rights and interests of others; and (9) other contents that are prohibited by laws or administrative regulations.[849] In the course of providing public information services, the telecommunications business operators, if discovering that the transporting information belongs to the above, shall immediately stop transporting such information, keep the record concerned, and report them to the relevant authorities.[850]

Any organization or individual shall not have any of the following acts endangering telecommunication network security and information security: (1) canceling or revising the function of the telecommunications network, data of storage, processing, and transporting, and the application program; (2) engaging activities of stealing or undermining information of

[844] Telecommunications Regulations, Article 13.
[845] Telecommunications Regulations, Article 14.
[846] Telecommunications Regulations, Article 23.
[847] Telecommunications Regulations, Article 24.
[848] Telecommunications Regulations, Article 26 (1).
[849] Telecommunications Regulations, Article 57.
[850] Telecommunications Regulations, Article 62.

others and damaging legal rights and interests of others; (3) intentionally making, copying, promulgating computer virus or attacking telecommunication networks and other telecommunications facilities by any means; and (4) other acts endangering telecommunications network security or information security.[851]

Anyone who has one of the above acts with serious circumstances shall have his License to Operating Telecommunications Business revoked by the original license-issuing authorities, which will notify the enterprise registration authorities later.[852]

It is emphasized that freedom of using telecommunications services according to law and communication secret shall be protected by laws. Any organization or individual shall not inspect the telecommunications contents by any reason, unless the public security organizations or state security organizations or the people's procuratorates inspect the telecommunications contents for the purpose of state security or investigating criminal offences according to proceedings as provided by law; telecommunications business operators and their staffs shall not provide the users' contents transported by telecommunications networks to others without approval.[853]

3.4. Evaluation and Comments

3.4.1. General Observation

It is for the first time that telecommunications liberalization is set to a multilateral arena. The positive results achieved so far show the way forward. With this background, it would be sensible for the Chinese government to follow this trend where while endeavor to protect national interests, they also try to absorb the benefits of the liberalization.

As mentioned previously, the GATS has no direct effect on the Members *per se*. The specific and additional commitments attached to the GATS are the direct obligations for the Members and China has made substantial commitments on value-added and basic services. Specific commitments, as shown by the terminology, have been made very specific by the clear definition of the applicable geographical location, percentage and period of time. The geographical scope of the commitments is in accordance with the longstanding preference of China for testing liberalization strategies in individual provinces before applying them to the country as a whole.

China's promising history of compliance with international obligations means that we should have no doubt that China will proceed as it has promised[854] especially since the Chinese government on various occasions has pledged to do so.[855] China even opened up some areas earlier than under the agreement[856] and this was revealed in the annual evaluation made by the WTO, which was rather impressed with China's performance in the first year.

---

[851] Telecommunications Regulations, Article 58.

[852] Telecommunications Regulations, Article 78.

[853] Telecommunications Regulations, Article 66.

[854] China's record, though mixed, is better than most detractors think. See D.H. Rosen, China and the World Trade Organization: An Economic Balance Sheet, available at <http://www, chinaonline.com>.

[855] The MII stated that administrative statutes, including the regulations on Computer Networks and Information Safety Management, would be adopted to facilitate China's entry into the WTO. See Beijing Urged to Reshape Telecom Policies, available at <http://www.chinaonline.com>.

[856] For example, China will open up mobile phone markets two years sooner than under the agreement, see <http://www.interlinkchina.com/wto.htm>.

The clear wording in the specific commitments leaves no room or grey area for evasion. Nevertheless, the understanding on geographical restrictions is disputed to negate the benefits accorded to foreign value-added service providers. The MII prohibits inter-regional service, based in one city but serving customers in another.[857] This practice will be examined to decide on its legality.

China has accepted the Reference Paper as additional commitments, but as discussed above, it has been disputed as being too ambiguous. Such ambiguity has led to various considerations during the implementation period, including national conditions, stage of national development and liberalization, and the understanding of certain terms. Whether China's performance is in compliance with the Reference Paper is difficult to determine, so an in-depth analysis of the document is required.

To start with, we must settle the basis for interpreting the Reference Paper. With no other documents for further clarification, we shall turn recourse to Vienna Convention on the Law of Treaties. Article 31 (1) provides that a treaty shall be interpreted in good faith in accordance with the ordinary meaning to be given to the terms of the treaty in their context, and in light of its object and purpose. Accordingly when we try to give an appropriate understanding to the Reference Paper, we should resort to the object and purpose of this document and further to the goal of the WTO: trade liberalization—developing an integrated, more viable and durable multilateral trade system.[858]

We shall now look at how China has performed in honoring the Reference Paper. There are three particular points which will be discussed: establishing an independent regulator; procuring a pro-competitive market; formulating regulations on foreign investment and licensing practices. The principles of interconnection, universal services, transparency, allocation and use of scarce resources can be achieved with the successful establishment of a fair market and an independent regulator. Since China has only been in the WTO for several years, it is perfectly reasonable to expect that all the principles are strictly conformed to, provided that a reasonable regulatory structure is established. However, measures to achieve a healthy market and regulator are big steps for China to move forward in its few years of entry.

3.4.2. Establishing an Independent Regulator

According to the suggestion of the International Telecommunications Union (ITU) and international practice, the transformation of telecommunications services regulation is directed to three aspects: the independence of telecommunications regulation; the separation of regulation and service provision; and the diversification of telecommunications services.[859] The telecommunications regulation policy in China has largely fallen behind the demands of market and technical development, which has become one of the bottlenecks restricting the development of the whole industry.

---

[857] See further G. Blue, China WTO Written Comments by Trade Policy Staff Committee, Office of the U.S. Trade Representative, September 10, 2002, available at <http://www.uscib.org>.

[858] Final Act Embodying Results of the Uruguay Round of Multilateral Trade Negotiations, April 15, 1994, Legal Instruments-Results of the Uruguay Round Vol. 1 (1994), 33 I.L.M. 1125, 1144 (1994). See also J.H. Jackson, GATT and Recent International Trade Problems, 11 *Maryland Journal of International Law & Trade* 8 (1987).

[859] Six Suggestions Posed by WTO Experts for Chinese Telecommunications Reform, available at <http://www.wtoinfo.net.cn/cgi-bin/search/read.php?id=654>.

Since 1998, when the State Council reorganized the administrative body, there has been much effort to alter this situation.[860] The Ministry of Information Industry (MII) was formed, replacing the Ministry of Post and Telecommunications (MPT), Ministry of Electronics Industry (MEI) and Ministry of Radio, Film, and Television (MRFT).[861] The purpose was simple: to establish a regulatory body in accordance with the international standard. Nevertheless, this reform also aimed at boosting the growth of national carriers in order to meet the competition ahead.

According to the Reference Paper, the regulatory body should be separated from service providers where the regulator should not have any interest in the telecommunications industry.[862] While market forces will play the fundamental role in the regulation of services, the regulatory body will undertake the task of preventing anti-competitive practices. Only when the regulator is separated from providing services, will fair and even-handed regulation be procured. This can build trust from actual service providers and further promote professional operations.

Formerly, the ministry was not simply a regulator; it also owned telecommunications corporation exclusively with its own investment.[863] Understandable enough, it is difficult for the ministry to take an objective stance with business at stake. This move to separate the new Ministry from business shows that they are heading in the right direction. The MII cannot directly involve itself in the network operation though and telecommunications corporations are detached from the MII with their own management strategy. The regulatory and operational function was thus nominally split off for the first time in nearly fifty years. This ministerial reorganization has formally paved the way for complete separation of the regulatory function from the service provider function.

The MII began to perform its task from the date of establishment and one of its most important tasks is to make regulations. Fortunately, an increasing amount of regulations are being placed on the Web, aiming at establishing the rules of market competition. This is a bright start and this task will be enhanced with further liberalization.

We should note that such a separation between the regulatory and operational functions is only a prerequisite, rather than an ambitious strategy to create a fair, transparent, pro-competitive, and independent regulatory institution in accordance with the Reference Paper. The MII is able to evolve into the independent regulator, though at the present stage, the benefactor of this role is yet unclear.[864] When we analyze further the management of the corporations, we can see that the connection between the MII and the corporations still exists.[865]

Historically, the MII has a deep-rooted and complicated relationship with China Telecom and other regulated carriers. The MII enjoys the power to appoint, promote and dismiss key officials of postal, telephone and telegraph branches, including China Telecom, China

---

860 Morrison & Foerster LLP, China's Telecommunications Industry: The New Ministry of Information Industry (MII) and Foreign Investment Opportunities, March 1, 1998, available at <http://mofo.com>.

861 For a discussion on the New Ministry, see generally Z. Tan, Regulating China's Internet: Convergence toward a Coherent Regulatory Regime, 23 *Telecommunications Policy*, 261-276 (1999).

862 B. Zhang & M.W. Peng, Telecom Competition, Post-WTO Style, *China Business Review*, May 1, 2000, at 5.

863 It is described as the mode of "twin status as both referee and player". See Y. Xu & D. Pitt, One Country, Two Systems: Contrasting Approaches to Telecommunications Deregulation in Hong Kong and China, 23 *Telecommunications Policy* 248 (1999).

864 M. Forney, China Gives Foreign Firms Telecom Access: New Rules May Open Sector, Maintain Regulatory Ties, *Asian Wall Street Journal*, June 7, 2000.

Mobile, and Unicom. For instance, the former Vice Minister of the MPT was transferred to the new position of Chairman of Board of China Telecom.[866] As a result, there is still doubt concerning the real independency of the regulator. The event of raising international interconnection fee unilaterally in November 2002 has further aroused doubts concerning the independence of the services and the functions of the regulator.

Considering the present political and economic situation in China, this phenomenon is unavoidable and since it is difficult to make drastic change within such a short period of time, we ought to accept the progress that has been made and recognize the correct direction we ought to be taking. We should maintain optimistic expectations and hopefully, with further implementation of the WTO commitments, a truly independent regulator will not be just a dream, but a reality.

3.4.3. Producing a Pro-Competitive Market

The WTO is an organization promoting liberalization of trade. This can be realized through different means--an important way has been constructing a competitive environment. In certain situations, competition and liberalization have been used interchangeably and in the present context, competition is believed to be a way to realize final liberalization.

As defined in the WTO Reference Paper, principles have been laid down to promote competition. Direct reference can be made to the first principle where the competitive safeguards exert less direct or indirect effects in establishing a competitive environment for telecommunications. Since China has formally committed to this Paper, measures should be undertaken to stay within the obligations. Just as the Minister of the MII stated, China would not only continue to reinforce regulatory efforts in the telecommunications industry by carefully examining the qualifications of all foreign investors, but would facilitate orderly competition according to the relevant regulations.[867]

The process began even before China's formal entry into the WTO; several structural modifications were carried out in February 1999 when the State Council passed the plan to restrict China Telecom;[868] three group corporations-China Mobile, China Telecom and ChinaSat, were constructed respectively in December 1999, January 2000 and June 2000. Meanwhile, Unicom was also reconstructed to include Paging Corporation. A competitive structure came into being with two or more corporations involved in each type of basic services.

However, with various connections between China Telecom and the MII, China Telecom has taken an advantageous position compared with other providers and is a monopoly in essence. It has a 90 percent market share while China Unicom holds less than 10 percent. Furthermore, China Railcom, another basic telecommunications service provider, is still in its infancy, in China's national telecommunications market. ChinaSat so far carries out business focusing mainly on Satellite-based communication and Internet services.[869] All of these

---

865 J. Leahy, China: Foreigners Eye the China Pie, *Financial Times*, November 13, 2000.

866 J. Wang, Breakup of China Telecom, U.S. & Foreign Commercial Service, May 2000.

867 See China's Net Czar Downplays WTO Effect on High Tech Industry, available at <http://www.chinaonline.com>.

868 C.B. Chuan *et al.*, Telecommunications and Information Technology, in J.J. Williams *et al.* (eds.), *Business Opportunities in Northeastern China* 244 (1999).

869 China to Open Up Its Basic Telecommunications Sector, available at <http://english.peopledaily.com.cn>.

magnificent developments can, to a large extent, actually restrict competition; thus, evidently the process of reform is far from completion.

Confronting the imminent deepening liberalization process, the intensive reform came only after the formal entry. On May 16, 2002, two Corporations finally came into being: China Telecom and China Netcom. This reconstruction was carried out on a territorial basis.[870] The former China Telecom was divided into two parts: the northern part was grouped as China Netcom and the Southern part retain the same name as China Telecom. Consequently, the former 7-big-power structure (including China Paging) turned into '5+1' structure, namely, China Telecom, China Netcom, China Mobile, China Unicom, China Railcom, plus ChinaSat.

The aim of this reform was crystal clear from the start: establishing a competitive environment and maintaining the character of a complete and harmonized network. The new China Telecom and China Netcom are approximately equal in strength; both have got their own nation-wide fixed-line backbone telecommunications network. Moreover, the government permits both of them to penetrate into the other's market. Accordingly, while removing the monopoly in basic services, this reform has maintained the characteristic of "a complete set of network for whole course of communications".[871]

It is obvious that this reform has substantially reformulated the competitive structure for basic services in China. Competition in the real sense has been introduced in the Chinese market, though such competition is carried out among the Chinese service providers themselves only. In order for extension to foreign providers to occur, it is necessary to formulate coherent telecommunications policy to safeguard competition, which will avoid cross-subsidy, distorted tariffs and highly concentrated markets.

Furthermore, three levels of competition should exist in the telecommunications services: competition between telecommunications expenses and other expenses of consumers; competition among service providers and competition among interconnection providers.[872] Only when these three platforms are totally open for competition can the telecommunications market experience full and true liberalization. The restriction on liberalization on any one platform will distort the logic of market economy. Thus, full liberalization of the telecommunications market will be the ultimate goal. With further liberalization, as shown in the agenda, foreign service providers can gain more and more access. The period in between creates a golden opportunity for Chinese providers to gain experience and prepare for the fierce international competition, not only in the Chinese market, but also in the foreign markets.

3.4.4. Formulating Regulations on Foreign Investment in Telecommunications Services and Licensing Practices

While the rest of the world retrenches, China continues to gear up for investing in the telecommunications infrastructure. In the past years, total investment in telecommunications infrastructure has registered an impressive annual increase of 62 percent.[873] During this

---

[870] L. Chang & M. Pottinger, China Telecom, Once Split, Will Service Separate Regions; IPO May Be Speeded, *Wall Street Journal*, October 17, 2001; H. Zhao, Telecom Needs Competition, *China Daily* June 10, 1999.

[871] Reconstruction ends monopoly in Telecommunications, available at <http://www.datacomit.com>.

[872] How to Greet the WTO Accession? A Tentative Analysis of Competitive Framework for Telecommunications, available at <http://www.wtoinfo.net.cn/cgi-bin/search/read.php?id=782>.

[873] Telecommunications Industry in China, available at <http://www.interliance.com>.

period, some of the largest telecom companies entrenched in the Chinese market through various means. China's WTO membership has no doubt led to upsurge in investment.

For foreign providers, joint venture (referred to as "localization" in the telecommunications industry) has been considered as one of the best ways to invest. They can take advantage of China's considerable low labor costs and bypass the tariff and non-tariff barriers. Formerly, to evade the prohibition of direct involvement of foreign providers in this field, the so-called "foreign-Chinese-Chinese" joint venture has been constructed.[874] Foreigner providers seeking to invest must negotiate a pre-determined rate of return with Unicom and then link with a local partner in a joint venture, which then funds Unicom.[875] However, after a drastic change in the attitudes of the Chinese government, this practice was considered in breach.[876] A statement was released stating that such contracts executed between Unicom and foreign investment enterprises were contrary to State policy and regulation.[877]

With WTO's commitments allowing for foreign investment, joint ventures could revive again in a more direct form: foreign-Chinese. Closely related with this development are the two regulations preventing foreign investment in telecommunications that were repealed on December 11, 2001. On the same date, the State Council promulgated the Provisions on the Administration of Foreign-Invested Telecommunications, permitting foreign investment in the telecoms sector in the form of a Chinese-foreign structure.

Moreover, while anticipating the incoming of foreign direct investment, the Ministry of Information Industry (MII) has introduced several regulations.[878] The regulation tightens the management strings to licensed joint-ventures carriers, acknowledging the legality of foreign direct investment.[879] It is stipulated that for joint ventures set up by basic telecom operators and other domestic State-owned firms; if the licensed carrier holds less than 51 percent of the shares, the joint venture should apply to the MII for a license before engaging in telecom business; if the licensed carrier holds more than 51 percent of the shares, the joint venture should register with the MII if it wishes to operate a telecom business.[880] It is clear from the regulations that investors are limited to high-profit foreign firms and high-profit Chinese firms, so this will narrow the pool of foreign firms qualified to enjoy China's market access commitments.[881]

---

874 M. O'Neill, Beijing May Scrap Unicom Foreign-Investment Formula, *South China Morning Post-Business Post*, September 23, 1998, at 4.

875 R. Janda, Benchmarking a Chinese Offer on Telecommunications: Context and Comparisons, 3 *International Journal of Communications Law & Policy*, 5 (Summer 1999).

876 For further discussion, see L.D. Chuang, Investing in China's Telecommunications Market: Reflections on the Rule of Law and Foreign Investment in China, 20 *Journal of International Law & Business* 516-522 (Spring 2000); see also M. Forney & S. Webb, China Phone Firm Remains Ensnared by Bureaucracy, *Wall Street Journal*, June 13, 2000.

877 China: Telecoms Firm Told to Abandon Foreign-Funded Joint Ventures, BBC Monitoring Asia Pacific-Political Supplied by BBC Worldwide Monitoring, February 4, 1999.

878 One set of rules, entitled Framework Regulations on Liberalizing Last Mile Broadband Access, targets the growing number of unlicensed broadband operators, who must reapply for a license. Another Regulation bans companies from extending their licenses to their joint-venture units without approval.

879 United States Department of Commerce, International Trade Administration, Office of Telecommunications Technologies, China/MII Submits Draft Telecom Regulations to Council, Asia Telecommunications Newsletter, September 8, 2000, available at <http://infoserv2.ita.doc.gov>.

880 China's Telecom Market, Legislation Undergoing Changes as Country Readies for Global Trade, available at <http://pulse.tiaonline.org/article.cfm?id=591>.

881 As provided, the select group of foreign firms must have telecom revenues greater than $10 billion during the last two years prior to applying to operate in China; Chinese partner should be appointed as chairperson of the

Some may argue such a regulation restricts the threshold requirements for qualified foreign firms. However, as long as all the foreign firms are treated under the same process, there should be no violation of Most-Favored-Nation (MFN) obligations.[882] Moreover, such restrictions are in line with international practice and thus cause no violation of national treatment obligations.[883]

Another change is that more and more telecommunications companies are publicly listed in the foreign stock markets.[884] This has been one efficient way of absorbing capital from international channels and benefiting from the experience of modern enterprise management. For foreign investors, public listing also presents a unique means to invest in China's telecommunications.[885] The amount of possible foreign investment shall comply with the progressive process of China's Commitments.

A new regulation has been adopted regarding foreign capital in the profitable sector.[886] This regulation was issued after China's formal entry and reiterated its commitments in the WTO. According to Article 6, 49 and 50 percent is the respective limit for foreign investment in basic and value-added telecommunications services. Applications should be made to responsible departments in the MII, who are required to examine and make decisions within 180 and 90 days for basic and value-added services respectively.[887] The provision of time limits for making decisions can successfully avoid former strategies of delay, to prevent the entry of foreign competitors.

Other new regulations include the Administrative Regulations on Operational Licenses for Telecom Business, [888] and the MII Rule on Management of Telecom Business Operating Licenses.[889] All the new regulations[890] have closely aligned foreign investment requirements with China's WTO commitments and allowed the MII to gradually lift equity and geographic restrictions in accordance with China's WTO telecommunications commitments.[891]

---

joint venture. See further Telecommunications Regulations of the People's Republic of China (Guowuling No. 291), September 25, 2000; see also M. Forney, Chinese Investors Offer Static on Telecom Rules: Smaller Foreign Investors May Get Shut Out, *Asian Wall Street Journal*, September 26, 2000; V. Bath & C. Chong, China's New Telecommunications Regulations, November 2000, available at <http://www.coudert.com/practice/chinanewtelecom.htm>.

882 L.B. Sherman, China After the WTO, What You Need to Know Now: The Impact of China's WTO Entry on the Telecommunications and IT Sectors, PLI Order No. A0-0095, at 230-231 (February 2001).

883 See further R. Abramson, Catching Flies with Chopsticks: China's Strategic Leap into Wireless Telecommunications, 11 *Minnesota Journal of Global Trade* 31 (Winter 2002).

884 For example, China Unicom sold more than a twenty percent share on the New York and Hong Kong stock exchanges, raising 5.65 billion dollars. See P. Wonacott, China Maps IPO to Gird for Foreign Telecom Invasion, *Wall Street Journal*, December 6, 2000.

885 See for example China Unicom's IPO Rings up $ 4.92 Billion, *Asian Wall Street Journal*, June 19, 2000, at 14; see also R. Lachica, China Unicom Gets Strong Welcome in First Session, *Asian Wall Street Journal*, June 22, 2000, at 2.

886 The Regulation on the Management of Foreign Investment in Telecommunications Enterprises was promulgated on December 11, 2001 and came into force on January 1, 2002.

887 Article 11 of the Regulation.

888 It is issued by the MII on December 26, 2001 and took effect on January 1, 2002.

889 See MII Order No. 19.

890 One exception is the Administrative Measures for International Gateway Facilities, which was issued on June 26, 2002 and took effect on October 1, 2002. This regulation restricts operation of gateway facilities to wholly state-owned telecommunications providers, thus was claimed not to be in accordance with the market access commitments.

891 G. Blue, China's WTO Written Comments by Trade Policy Staff Committee, Office of the U.S. Trade Representative, September 10, 2002, available at <http://www.uscib.org>.

3.4.5. Miscellaneous

To promote a competitive environment, the government is required to take more measures than those listed above. As shown in the Reference Paper, interconnection, universal service, licensing criteria, etc. shall be available to all the existing and potential providers.

First of all, the obligation of transparency is very important.[892] Chinese law has generally believed to be highly generalized and lacking in procedural guidelines.[893] Formerly there were quite a lot of internal regulations which were unknown or difficult to trace for providers thereof. Such a vague legal framework reflects a tension between encouraging foreign investment and maintaining state control over the economy.[894] The WTO requires a single access point for Chinese law and regulations, so China needs to streamline the multilayered complexity that plagues its present-day legal system. [895] Now, with the assistance of electronic facilities, the government can make the access to all those regulations easier and more systematic for the public. With the web site of the MII, the purpose of transparency can be easily achieved. However, continuous efforts will be maintained to provide updated information, guidance and efficient response.

Nevertheless, as described by one practitioner, the present regulatory structure is an odd mix of detailed regulations in certain areas but lacking in a comprehensive national telecoms law and governing regulations which address industry concerns.[896] The current absence of a Telecommunications Law has subjected telecommunications policy to the discretion of officials.[897] This means that it is even more important to pass the Telecommunications Law, which can work as the constitutional document for telecommunications services in China covering regulatory aspects of the telecommunications services.[898] It will define the government's role in the industry, allow deregulation of tariffs, outline rules for new entrants, and foster orderly competition.[899] This legislation is an urgent task for the government[900] and it is to be noted that China must take into account the rules-of-law of the WTO while making economic policies for telecommunications.[901]

Secondly, efficient interconnection will be vital to the entry of foreign providers. Formerly, China has been reluctant to mandate the interconnection[902] and various obstacles

---

892 S. Ostry, China and the WTO: The Transparency Issues, 3 *UCLA Journal of International Law & Foreign Affairs*, 11 (1998).

893 C.D. Lee, Legal Reform in China: A Role for Nongovernmental Organizations, 25 *Yale Journal of International Law* 368 (2000).

894 P.B. Potter, Foreign Investment in the People's Republic of China Dilemmas of State Control, in S. Lubman (ed.), *China's Legal Reforms* 155 (1996).

895 Ostry, *supra* note 153, 13; B. Bacon, The People's Republic of China and the World Trade Organization: Anticipating a United States Congressional Dilemma, *9 Minnesota Journal of Global Trade* 387 (2000).

896 J.P.L. Teoh, Sector Seeks Level Pathway between the Legal Potholes, *South China Morning Post*, June 11, 1998.

897 N. Ingelbrecht, The China Syndrome, *Communications Week International*, June 1, 1998.

898 In September 2000, China released the Telecommunications Administration Regulations as a preview of the anticipated comprehensive Telecommunications Law. See China Legal Change, The Regulations of the People's Republic of China on Telecommunications, September 25, 2000, available at <http://www.chinalegalchange.com>.

899 C. Chan, Unicom Document Reveals New Law's Intent, *South China Morning Post*, May 18, 2000.

900 China Online, China's Telecom Law to be Promulgated "Soon", available at <http://www.chinaonline.com>.

901 The most important characteristic of the WTO is that it is a rules-oriented organization. For discussion, see further G. Winham, The World Trade Organization: Institution-Building in the Multilateral Trade System, 21 *The World Economy* 362 (1998).

902 R.B. Chong & W. Chow, Financing Telecommunications Project in Asia: A Promising Regulatory Perspective, 52 *Federal Communications Law Journal* 14 (1999).

were created to delay or deny the interconnection of other providers. In this era of liberalization, we ought to try to figure out the crux of the problem--the reallocation of economic benefits.[903] "Temporary Regulation on Telecommunications Network Interconnection" has been issued earlier by the MII. However, this Regulation is considered as insufficient compared with the requirements of the Reference Paper. For example, the problem of sufficient unbundling requirement is missing; nothing in the Regulation touched on the issue of number portability.[904] Thus, it is necessary to obtain opinions from existing service providers and offer a complete legal framework for interconnection, meeting the requirement stated in the Reference Paper that competitors are permitted to interconnect with public telecommunications networks at any technically feasible point, under non-discriminatory terms.[905] The interconnection rates must be non-discriminatory, cost-oriented, transparent, reasonable, economically feasible, and sufficiently unbundled. Furthermore, the interconnection procedures and agreements must be made publicly available.[906]

Thirdly, universal service is of paramount importance to China. These policies are not regarded as anti-competitive *per se* if they are administered in a transparent, non-discriminatory and competitively neutral manner and are not more burdensome than necessary.[907] Deciding on how to provide services to the western part of China is a tough issue for the Chinese government.[908] The harsh natural conditions and sparse population has directly led to costly services. The "Grand Exploitation of Western Areas" Movement mobilized by the Chinese government can serve as an impetus to achieve this goal. Favorable policies are provided for investment in western areas but it is important in this regard to prevent cream-skimming and fairly allocate the universal service obligation among the targeted telecommunications service providers in accordance with the requirements of the Reference Paper.

Fourthly, technical considerations should be put in place to realize the real convergence of telecommunications in China. The resolution of all the issues concerning the entrance of foreign providers shall be based on technical consideration. This would mean that, implementing regulations will be well in place offering a clear guidance on technical factors. For example, the former administrative-oriented allocation of frequency system should be substituted by an objective, pro-competitive one.

Lastly, national security concerns for telecommunications are equally shared by Members. Luckily, Article XIV *bis* of the GATS provides the possibility of actions for the protection of essential security interests in time of war or other emergencies in international

---

903 Reform of Telecommunications with the Accession of WTO, available at http://www.wtoinfo.net.cn/cgi-bin/search/read.php?id=890>.

904 For discussion on number portability, see B. Petrazzini, *Global Telecom Talks: A Trillion Dollar Deal*, 64 (Washington D.C.: Institute for International Economics, 1996).

905 See Reference Paper to the Fourth Protocol to the General Agreement on Trade in Services, April 30, 1996, 36 I.L.M., at 2. Interconnection.

906 *Id.*, at 2.2 (a) (b); 2.3 and 2.4.

907 FCC Memo, Connecting the Globe: A Regulator's Guide to Building a Global Information Community, Universal Service, Part VI, June 16, 1999, available at <http://www.fcc.gov>.

908 J. Ure, China's Telecommunications: Options and Opportunities, in P.S.N. Lee (ed.), *Telecommunications and Development in China* 248 (1997); L. Ladany, *Law and Legality in China: The Testament of a China-Watcher* 17 (University of Hawaii Press, 1992); Z. He, A history of Telecommunications in China, Development and Policy Implications, in P.S.N. Lee (ed.), *Telecommunications and Development in China* 84 (1997).

relations.[909] Relevant provision can also be found in Article XIV where measures can be adopted or enforced to protect public morals or to maintain public order.[910] Thus, the loose wordings of "emergency" and "public order" offer the possibility of adopting measures out of national security considerations. These two terms are fully within the discretion of the Members.[911] The 1993 National Security Law of China has defined five classes of acts that endanger national security.[912] With the WTO entry, China should reconsider the list and clarify the application of the provision in telecommunications services. While striving to observe the WTO obligations, China should provide the justified legal framework for possible deviation.

3.5. Conclusion

The WTO Membership has had a tremendously positive impact on Members' national liberalization agenda, but such effects shall vary and mainly depend on the specific institutional endowments and regulatory stances of Members.[913] When studying the WTO's effects on a specific Member, it is necessary to note the institutions' objective within that specific Member.

The process of China's liberalization of telecommunications services has been accelerated by its entry into the WTO and it is believed that it has posed substantial influence on China's political and economic reforms. The World Bank predicts that China will be the world's second largest trader by 2020.[914] The growth of the Chinese economy combined with the development currently taking place in Chinese telecommunications will no doubt contribute to further increase of foreign investment.

Within a short period of time, great achievements have already been made and this has been recognized internationally. These developments have brought benefits not only to the WTO Members in gaining profits through entering the enormous Chinese market, but also to the Chinese residents who can directly benefit from the lower service fee and better service

---

909 It provides that nothing in this Agreement shall be construed to: (b) to prevent any Member from taking any action which it considers necessary for the protection of its essential security interests:...(iii) taken in time of war or other emergency in international relations: ... .

910 It provides, "subject to the requirement that such measures are not applied in a manner which would constitute a means of arbitrary or unjustifiable discrimination between countries where like conditions prevail, or a disguised restriction on trade in services, nothing in this Agreement shall be construed to prevent the adoption or enforcement by any Member of measures: (a) necessary to protect public moral or to maintain public order..."

911 D. Shapiro, Be Careful What You Wish for: U.S. Politics and the Future of the National Security Exception to the GATT, 31 *George Washington Journal of International Law & Economics* 97 (1997); M. Hahn, Vital Interests and the Law of GATT: An Analysis of GATT's Security Exception, 12 *Michigan Journal of International Law* 558 (1991).

912 Article 4 identifies the following five acts: plotting to subvert the government, dismember the state, or overthrow the socialist system participating in foreign intelligence organizations or accepting missions from such organizations or their agents; stealing, probing, purchasing or unlawfully providing state secrets; instigating, bribing, or luring state personnel to defect; and any other sabotage endangering state security. For a complete analysis of this legislation, see further H. Fu & R. Cullen, National Security Law in China, 34 *Columbia Journal of Transnational Law* 449 (1996).

913 See generally North, *supra* note 99.

914 Y. Huang, Director, World Bank China Program, Realizing China's Potential, Address at the Asian Investment Conference, March 2000, available at <http://www.worldbank.org.cn>; see also W. Martin & C. Bach, The Importance of State Trading in China's Trade Regime, in F.M. Abbott (ed.), *China in the World Trading System* 155 (1998).

quality. With the "win-win" situation, the accession itself has even brought further gains to the world as a whole: since the potential influence of telecommunications on national economic development is so great, the chances of this positive impact extending world-wide is extremely high, providing that the WTO commitments are further implemented by the Chinese government.

4. Space Legislation in Hong Kong

4.1. Introduction

Often claimed as the best example of "East meets West", Hong Kong is a region with an advanced economy. With strong financial backup, Hong Kong is able to actively take part in space activities. Considering the relatively small geographical area, Hong Kong has to a certain extent restricted its scope of space activities. One of the most important activities has been telecommunications. It is to be noted that all those activities basically serve the economic ends. This directly leads to the betterment of people's well-being, which the government has constantly proclaimed as its main target.

Along with the ongoing activities, relevant rules and regulations are put in place to offer valuable guidance and provide some order to their unfolding. This is vital to the legitimate exploitation of economic side of space resources. As space activities easily transcend national borders, thus international coordination is indispensable. Hong Kong, when acceding to these international agreements and treaties, shall certainly subject to the regulations. This is necessary to the harmonious development of space activities among the States. For example, one satellite company in Hong Kong, AsiaSat, [915] had "difficult negotiations with Thailand trying to coordinate satellites located at 77.5 and 78.5 degrees." Because the distance between the satellites was likely to cause "serious interference ...Asiasat [ ] tried to negotiate a technical solution even though it claimed first priority to the slot."[916] Bilateral negotiation could resolve the problem, but the existence of coordinating body shall be most meaningful in providing consistent resolution of the existing and future disputes. Accordingly an international centralized mechanism in making appropriate coordination is justified. Meanwhile, national rules are formulated to deal with issues with national concerns. Discussion of national regulation should not be left out. Consequently, the combination of national and international rules provides a complete legal framework for space activities in Hong Kong.

There are quite some papers on isolated issues, like telecommunications. However, no such work exists so far touching on space activities as a whole in Hong Kong. The isolated discussions fail to give a complete view of the whole structure, policy determination for space activities in Hong Kong. Furthermore, it leads to the false conception that space activities in Hong Kong refer exclusively to telecommunications. Accordingly, it is necessary to offer a platform to clarify the misconception.

---

[915] It is a wholly-owned subsidiary of Asia Satellite Telecommunications Holdings Limited, which is incorporated in Bermuda and listed on the New York and the Hong Kong Stock Exchanges.

[916] A. Copiz, Scarcity in Space: The International Regulation of Satellites, 10 *Common Conspectus* 208 (2002).

The present section tries to give an overview of space policy and programs in Hong Kong. Policy issues are discussed in Part two. Part three is devoted to both national and international rules in relation to space activities in Hong Kong, which shall form the basis for further discussion. The regulation of space activities deserves a complete examination, which shall include the licensing regime, liberalization process, etc. Two aspects: satellite launching activities and telecommunications services, have been singled out for elaboration respectively in Part four and five. A simple conclusion shall be followed in Part six identifying the way forward for further development of space law in Hong Kong.

4.2. Policy Orientation

Hong Kong is a small but highly populated city. The Hong Kong government is sensible to devote limited resources to regional economic development and the improvement of the people's livelihood. This attitude is in accordance with the policy of consumer protection. Making full use of the existing resources, the Government tries to bring more benefits to the consumers: better services and lower prices, etc. It is thus natural that economic consideration takes up a very important role in formulating detailed rules in Hong Kong. This is also justified by the status of Hong Kong as a financial and commercial center in Asia. The starting point for space activities is no exception.

In the era of technology, Hong Kong has alleged itself to be a telecommunications hub and a hub for modern technology. Correspondingly, the government has formulated policies encouraging and promoting the development and application of modern technology. This has most direct effect on space activities, which make intensive use of modern science and technology. The support from modern technology shall be indispensable to the success of space activities.

Hong Kong is known as a free port and one of the world's best examples of an "open market economy". The Government is committed to promoting competition to enhance economy efficiency and free trade, thereby also benefiting consumer welfare. The policy of competition applies to space activities. Competitive safeguards have been put in place by the regulatory authority to ensure that the incumbent does not leverage its market power to disadvantage foreign service providers in the Hong Kong market.[917] This is further exemplified in the provisions of telecommunications services and launching activities.

Liberalization is the main character for telecommunications services in Hong Kong for the time being. The competitive environment created by the sufficiently flexible licensing regime is a good example to show the achievements of liberalization. With the launch of the new round of negotiations, Hong Kong actively takes part in the negotiations and is ready to undertake further commitments realizing full open of telecommunications services.

[917] See further P.W. Kenefick, A Step in the Right Direction: The FCC Provides Regulatory Relief in International Settlements and International Services Licensing, 8 *CommLaw Conspectus* 46 (Winter, 2000).

4.3. Legal Framework for Space Activities in Hong Kong

4.3.1. National Framework

Before the return of Hong Kong to the People's Republic of China in July 1997, the Outer Space Act 1986 (Hong Kong) Order 1990 applied to Hong Kong. This Order implemented four treaties relating to outer space activities, namely, the Outer Space Treaty (610 UNTS 205); the Rescue Agreement (672 UNTS 119); the Liability Convention (961 UNTS 187); the Registration Convention (1023 UNTS 15). The four treaties were extended to Hong Kong on ratification by the United Kingdom.

China, having also ratified the four treaties, has agreed to their continued application to Hong Kong after June 30, 1997. China has further agreed to "localize" the Outer Space Act 1986 (Hong Kong) Order 1990, which forms the basis of the present Outer space Ordinance (Cap. 523).[918] This ordinance is the basic constitutional document with respect to the launching and operation of space objects and other activities in outer space.[919] Actually, no substantial change has been made to the old Order. The main modification has been the change of terminology, like replacing "Governor" and "Governor in Council" by "Chief Executive" and "Chief Executive in Council" respectively. Accordingly, the transfer of sovereignty did not change the outer space policies in Hong Kong.

Although the Outer Space Ordinance is the basic regulation applicable to space activities, several other ordinances that could also have a significant impact on the use of satellites and outer space activities also deserve consideration. The Telecommunications Ordinance (Cap. 106) is one of the most important. It provides rules on licensing and control of telecommunications, telecommunications services and telecommunications apparatus and equipment.[920]

The Broadcasting Ordinance (Cap. 562) likewise has also some application, but is less germane to the present discussion, since its main purpose is to regulate broadcasting services, and it only incidentally applies to space by virtue of the use of satellites for broadcast transmission. Similar statements can be made regarding the Submarine Telegraph Ordinance (Cap. 497) and the Telephone Ordinance (Cap. 269).

4.3.2. International Regime and Cooperation

International coordination and cooperation is vital to the success of space activities. In addition to the four conventions mentioned above, several other space documents also apply to Hong Kong. These include the International Agreement on the Use of INMARSAT Ship Earth Stations within the Territorial Sea and Ports (1985); the Agreement relating to the International Telecommunications Satellite Organization (1971); the Convention on the International Maritime Satellite Organization (1976); the Constitution and Convention of the International Telecommunications Union (1992); the Final Acts of Additional Plenipotentiary Conference of the ITU (1992); and the Final Acts of the Plenipotentiary Conference of the ITU (1994). Supported by the Office of the Telecommunications Authority (OFTA), the Telecommunications Authority (TA) was appointed to represent Hong Kong in implementing

---

918 Legislative Council Economic Services Panel Paper: Localization of Laws: Outer Space Bill, Economic Services Branch, April 1997.

919 Long Title of the Outer Space Ordinance (Cap. 523).

920 Long Title of the Telecommunications Ordinance (Cap. 106).

these treaties. Their implementation will bring Hong Kong well into line with international practice.

Meanwhile, Hong Kong participates in the activities of international and regional space organizations. As a member of the China delegation, Hong Kong is represented in conferences and meetings convened by the International Telecommunications Satellite Organization (INTELSAT) and the International Telecommunications Union (ITU). Furthermore, Hong Kong takes part in its own right in the meetings of the Asia-Pacific Telecommunity and the Telecommunications Working Group of the APEC. Hong Kong also took part in the initiative to implement the APEC Mutual Recognition Arrangement for Conformity Assessment of Telecommunications Equipment. The membership of those treaties and organizations places Hong Kong in a good position to cooperate with other members in space activities.

With its strategic geographical location, Hong Kong has also hosted several high level conferences on space policies. For example, the Inter-Union Satellite Operations Group Forum was held in November 1995; and five years later, the ITU TELECOM Asia was also held in Hong Kong, hosting over 50, 000 visitors and 500 companies in the field of telecommunications services from 167 countries.[921]

The active stance of Hong Kong has on the one hand facilitated the rapid development of space activities and services in Hong Kong, on the other hand improved the regulatory standard and complemented the legal framework for space activities in Hong Kong.

4.4. Satellite Launching Activities

Hong Kong is very active in launching activities. The ITU has an allocation scheme for Member States, which allows States to launch satellites into allocated areas. For example, the ITU allocated four broadcasting satellites service (BSS) channels for use by Hong Kong at the orbital position 122 degrees East.[922] However, Hong Kong has also, by agreement, launched satellites into areas allocated to other countries, [923] as in the case of the Asia Satellites.[924]

The Outer Space Ordinance is the basic document to be referred to when carrying out launching activities. Two companies incorporated in Hong Kong have been granted licences under the Ordinance: APT Satellite Company Limited (APT) and Asia Satellite Telecommunications Company Limited[925]. A healthy and competitive environment is in place in Hong Kong for launching activities. When launching activities are needed, the OFTA issues a guidance note to invite applications. The two companies above can then bid for the launching activities.[926]

---

921 Available at <http://www.info.gov.hk>.

922 Legislative Council Brief: The Licensing of Broadcasting Satellite Service, File Ref.: ITBB(CR) 9/2/14 (00) Pt.3.

923 S. Cahill, Give me My Space: Implications for Permitting National Appropriation of the Geostationary Orbit, 19 *Wisconsin International Law Journal* 246-247 (Spring, 2001).

924 J.C. Thompson, Comment, Space for Rent: The International Telecommunications Union, Space Law, and Orbit/Spectrum Leasing, 62 *Journal of Air Law and Commerce* 20 (1996).

925 The principal shareholder of this company is Bowenvale Limited which is owned by the China International Trust and Investment Corporation (CITIC) and Societe Europeenne des Satellites S.A. (SES), a European satellite service operator.

926 See Guidance Note for the Satellite Facility Provider and Those Interested in Making Use of Broadcasting-Satellite Service Channels to Provide Broadcasting Services in Hong Kong.

The OFTA also monitors the operation of the launched satellites. To date, these are AsiaSat's AsiaSat 1, AsiaSat 2, AsiaSat 3S, and Optus A2 satellites, as well as APT's Apstar-1, Apstar-1A, Apstar-IIR satellites (and their associated telemetry, tracking, control and monitoring earth stations), to ensure that their operation is in compliance with the respective licensing provisions.

To launch a satellite, two licences are required. First of all, an Outer Space Licence must be granted by Hong Kong's Chief Executive under section 5 of the Outer Space Ordinance for procuring the launch and the operation of the satellite. Section 5(2) states that the space activities should not jeopardize public health or the safety of persons or property; should be consistent with the international obligations of China and should not impair the national security of China or Hong Kong.[927] The Chief Executive has the power to issue an appropriate licence and to specify appropriate conditions.[928]

The licence may be transferred with the written consent of the Chief Executive. A licence may be revoked, varied or suspended with the consent of the licensee; or where the Chief Executive considers that the public interest [929] so requires, or where there has been a failure to comply with a condition of the licence or any regulation made under the Ordinance..[930]

Where the Chief Executive intends to grant or revoke a licence, he or she is required to give notice of such intention to the Central People's Government. When the Central People's Government issues an instruction with regard to the above licence, the Chief Executive must comply with that instruction.[931]

Secondly, a Telemetry, Tracking, Control and Monitoring (TTC & M) Licence shall be granted by the Chief Executive in Council under sections 7 and 34 of the Telecommunications Ordinance for the licensee to establish, maintain, possess, use and operate space stations on the satellite and an earth station in Hong Kong for telemetry, tracking, control and monitoring of the satellite.[932] Generally the term of the licence is 20 years, a period congruent with the expected life-span of most satellites.

While granting a licence, the Chief Executive in Council will take into account several other factors: the decision to grant a licence shall not conflict with the provisions of the Basic Law, including those with human rights implications; proper and adequate measures should be taken to safeguard the public against any electrical or radiation hazard.

From the financial and staffing part, the additional workload required in administering the licence conditions will be absorbed by the Office of the Telecommunications Authority Trading Fund; the relevant costs incurred will be fully recovered in the licence fee.

Subject to the satisfactory completion of all the relevant milestones in the performance bond submitted by the launching company, and the fulfillment of other necessary requirements, approval can be sought from the Chief Executive to grant the Outer Space Licence nearer the time of the launch of the satellite.

Aside from establishing the licensing regime for launching activities in Hong Kong, the Outer Space Ordinance contains the following provisions:

---

[927] Section 5 (2) of the Outer Space Ordinance (Cap. 523).

[928] See further Section 5 (3) of the Outer Space Ordinance (Cap. 523).

[929] It refers to the interests of public health or the national security of China or the security of Hong Kong or any international obligation of China.

[930] Section 7 of the Outer Space Ordinance (Cap. 523).

[931] Section 8 of the Outer Space Ordinance (Cap. 523).

[932] See for example, Legislative Council Brief: Telecommunication Ordinance (Cap. 106): Grant of Licence for ASIASAT 3S, ITBB, Government Secretariat, February 12, 1999.

- Maintenance of a register of space objects by the Chief Executive;[933]
- The power of the Chief Executive to give directions in case of contravention of the provision of the Ordinance or the conditions of a licence;[934]
- The power of a magistrate to issue a warrant authorizing direction action;[935]
- The obligation to indemnify the Hong Kong Government and the Central Government against any claims;[936]
- Offences and penalties for contraventions of the provisions of the Ordinance.[937]

As discussed earlier, space activities shall center on the economic consideration: the launching activity shall bring about economic benefits to Hong Kong by opening up service-based business opportunities and creating employment opportunities.

4.5. Telecommunications Services

4.5.1. Introduction

Telecommunications services are a heated topic for international society. The theme is how to well liberalize the services. Hong Kong, as one of the freest regions, has taken a lead to liberalize telecommunications in all aspects. The commitments were recorded in the WTO schedules. But the recorded schedule in the Uruguay Round is not a terminal point.

Hong Kong has developed an excellent and advanced telecommunications infrastructure with 100 percent full broadband coverage for commercial buildings; over 95 percent coverage for domestic households. There are 31 external connectivity operators are licensed, or about to be licensed , to operate satellite and cable facilities. In July 2002, Hong Kong has already had a cell phones penetration rate as high as 86 percent.[938]

The Telecommunication (Amendment) Ordinance 2000 has been the instrument directly regulating the licensing framework. Its aim is to respond to the rapid development of the telecommunications industry by enhancing competition safeguards for the industry; improving interconnection and access arrangements to telecommunications services; and clarifying the powers of the Telecommunications Authority (TA) over certain technical areas.

Hong Kong has a two-tier regulation system. The TA, an independent statutory body, oversees the regulation of the telecommunications sector, including the licensing of operators and the management of radio spectrum. The OFTA, the executive arm of the TA, was created in 1993 as the regulatory agency for telecommunications services.[939] Although the OFTA has in the past been accused of regulating "with a light hand, " and failing to take firm, proactive measures to prevent anticompetitive conduct by the former monopoly providers, recent measures taken by the OFTA have dispelled some of these concerns.[940]

---

[933] Section 9 (1) of the Outer Space Ordinance (Cap. 523).
[934] Section 10 of the Outer Space Ordinance (Cap. 523).
[935] Section 11 of the Outer Space Ordinance (Cap. 523).
[936] Section 12 (1) of the Outer Space Ordinance (Cap. 523).
[937] Section 14 of the Outer Space Ordinance (Cap. 523).
[938] Premier City for Business: Infrastructure, available at <http://www.business.gov.hk>.
[939] C.H. Kennedy & M.V. Pastor, *An Introduction to International Telecommunications Law* 169 (Artech House, 1996).
[940] See for example, OFTA, Telecommunications Authority Takes Regulatory Action against Anti-Competitive [sic] Practices of Hong Kong Telecom, available at <http://www.ofta.gov.hk/press/pr98.html#fm29>; see also

4.5.2. Licensing Regime

The pro-competition licensing regime[941] has established liberal ownership reforms that encourage foreign ownership. The Telecommunications Ordinance establishes the licensing regime for telecommunications in Hong Kong. As a result, the mobile communications market in Hong Kong is now among the most liberal in the world. Seven cellular companies are operating under four different cellular standards. More than 30 licences have been issued for paging operations. The licensing practice is technology neutral, generally consisting of a pre-qualification exercise followed by spectrum auction.

Competition was formally introduced into Hong Kong's local phone market in 1994 when three additional fixed-line operators were introduced: Hutchison Whampoa, Wharf Holdings and New World Telephone. The original provider, HK Telecom, still exists. Licensing for the provision of public telecommunications services now contains a condition prohibiting anti-competitive arrangements. In international voice service, the most important event was when the Cable and Wireless HK Telecom agreed to end its monopoly position eight years before the scheduled date (in 2006). Accordingly, the local and long distance services have now been effectively open for competition for some time. The process of liberalization reached its climax when Hong Kong committed to opening its basic telecommunications market on February 15, 1997.[942]

Hong Kong has also agreed to adopt the Reference Paper, which sets out six pro-competitive regulatory principles.[943] These safeguards were created to prevent monopolies of basic telecommunications from exploiting their dominant position to distort market forces and impede the ability of competitors to supply networks or services for which commitments would be made.[944]

Indeed Hong Kong has provided strong support for the principles stated in the Reference Paper. The OFTA takes an "objective cost-based approach" toward setting interconnection charges and requires that the incumbent and former monopoly provider interconnect "at charges which are based on reasonable relevant costs."[945] Hong Kong has also adopted a distributed approach to universal service obligations by requiring service providers to pay a percentage of revenues to the incumbent carrier for its universal service expenses.[946] Finally, certain regulations also promote competition. For instance, in order to avoid predatory

---

OFTA, Determination under Section 36A of the Telecommunication Ordinance for Interconnection Between Hong Kong Telephone Company Limited and New T&T Hong Kong Limited, Statement of the Telecommunications Authority, available at <http://www.ofta.gov.hk/ tas/interconnect/ta980821.html>.

941 General Trends in Telecommunication Reform 1998: Asia Pacific Volume V, ITU, compiled in General Trends in Telecommunication Reform 1998: World Report, at 86 tbl.5.4 (1998)

942 L.B. Sherman, "Wildly Enthusiastic" About the First Multilateral Agreement on Trade in Telecommunications Services, 51 *Federal Communications Law Journal* 62 n.3 (1998).

943 See World Trade Organization: Agreement on Telecommunications Services (Fourth Protocol to the General Agreement on Trade in Services) 36 I.L.M. 354 (1997).

944 See further T.L. McLarty, Liberalized Telecommunications Trade in the WTO: Implications for Universal Service Policy, 51 *Federal Communications Law Journal* 49 (1998).

945 Hong Kong Telecomms. (Pacific) Ltd., Application for Authority Pursuant to Section 214 of the Comms. Act of 1934, as Amended to Resell Int'l Private Lines for the Provision of Non-telephonic [sic] Serv. between the United States and Hong Kong, Order and Authorization, 13 F.C.C.R. 20050, para. 26, 14 Comm. Reg. (P & F) 50 (1998).

946 General Trends in Telecommunication Reform 1998: Asia Pacific Volume V, ITU, compiled in General Trends in Telecommunication Reform 1998: World Report, at 93, 5.6.2. (1998).

pricing, the incumbent operator must separate its services and ensure that there will be no cross-subsidization.[947]

No licensing restrictions apply to computer services and value-added services. International Value-Added Network Services (IVANS) were considerably liberalized when Hong Kong removed a requirement for bilateral government-to-government agreements to be in place prior to service rollout. In 1997, four local phone operators and 14 new operators were licensed to administer Virtual Private Networks (VPNs).[948] With the OFTA's support, four Hong Kong telecommunications operators obtained approval for direct access to the INTELSAT Satellite Systems.

Licensing for the provision of public telecommunications services contain a condition prohibiting anti-competitive arrangements. The Telecommunications Ordinance establishes the licensing regime for telecommunications in Hong Kong. Section 8 provides that:

> " Save under and in accordance with a licence granted by the Governor in Council or with the appropriate licence granted or created by the Authority, no person shall in Hong Kong or on board any ship, aircraft or space object that is registered or licensed in Hong Kong-
> a) establish or maintain any means of telecommunications; or
> b) possess or use any apparatus for radiocommunications or any apparatus of any kind that generates and emits radio waves notwithstanding that the apparatus is not intended for radiocommunications; or
> c) deal in the course of trade or business in apparatus or material for radiocommunications or in any component part of any such apparatus or in apparatus of any kind that generates and emits radio waves whether or not the apparatus is intended, or capable of being used, for radiocommunications; or
> d) demonstrate, with a view to sale in the course of trade or business, any apparatus or material for radiocommunications."

The term "governor in Council" here shall of course, be replaced by "Chief Executive in Council", who is empowered to exempt any person or class of persons from the requirement to obtain a licence.[949] The owner or user of apparatus connected to the public telephone system is exempted from the requirement to obtain a licence for the apparatus when it is not being used to provide a service to the public and similar exemptions apply in respect of apparatus used by the customers of other licensees under the Ordinance.[950]

Licences may be granted by Chief Executive in Council or the TA. The TA may grant licences specified in Part I of Schedule 1 to the Telecommunications Regulations, namely, Broadcast Relay Station Licence, Closed Circuit Television Licence, Public Non-Exclusive Telecommunications Service Licence, Hotel Television (Transmission) Licence, Public Radiocommunication Service Licence, Satellite Master Antenna Television Licence, Fixed Telecommunications Network Services Licence, Self-Provided External Telecommunications

---

[947] R.B. Chong & W. Chow, Financing Telecommunications Projects in Asia: A Promising Regulatory Perspective, 52 *Federal Communications Law Journal* 9-11 (December, 1999).

[948] G.C. Hufbauer & E. Wada (eds.), *Unfinished Business: Telecommunications after the Uruguay Round* 202-205 (Institute for International Economics, 1997)

[949] Section 39 of the Telecommunications Ordinance (Cap. 106).

[950] Para. 2 of the Telecommunications (Public Non-Exclusive Telecommunications Service Customers) (Exemption from Licensing) Order (Cap. 106J).

System Licence.[951] The Chief Executive in Council shall have the power to issue other licences.

The TA may attach special conditions to a licence.[952] Furthermore, a licence can be cancelled or withdrawn in case of contravention of the licence conditions or the Ordinance. In addition, Chief Executive in Council may cancel or suspend a licence at any time if he considers that the public interest so requires.[953]

4.6. Conclusion

Both the sophistication of space activities and the ease with which those activities cross national boundaries have advanced dramatically in recent years. These developments have been accompanied by a rapid evolution of the rules under which the space activities are provided. Among the States, commercial, scientific, and political arrangements are adjusting to the need to move information seamlessly around the globe. Within nations or regions, a growing trend toward competition and liberalization is accelerating the implementation of new technologies and increasing the frequency of space activities. Hong Kong, as one of the most important and developed regions in the world, is also at the forefront of the development.

As part of its space policy, Hong Kong has pursued a consistent path towards a competitive model with the three goal of competitive prices, state of the art infrastructure and service innovation. With Hong Kong entrenching its position as a pre-eminent telecommunications and broadcasting hub, more satellite operators and uplinkers base are likely to seek to base their operations in Hong Kong.[954] As a result, Hong Kong has one of the most vibrant telecommunications sectors in the world, given the size of its population.[955]

Thanks to the good technical and practical developments in Hong Kong, space law is able to proceed steadily in recent years. The Outer Space Ordinance is, however, largely restricted its application to the procuring and launching of satellites. Other relevant Ordinances are also limited to certain aspects. Space activities can include more than those that have been regulated. Disputes are therefore likely to arise more frequently with an increasing number of space activities taking place in the international background. How to well resolve these disputes shall be largely based on international rules. For example, when a Hong Kong company moved its satellite to 134 degrees east, a dispute erupted between that company and an Indonesian company that claimed rights to that orbital slot. In an act of defiance, the Indonesian operator jammed the signal to the Hong Kong Apstar 1A satellite. Although the Hong Kong operator has since tilted its antenna angle to prevent the jamming, the situation is by no means resolved.[956]

Space law is developing rapidly with technological development. Hong Kong should try to actively participate in more space activities. This would provide Hong Kong with

---

[951] See further Schedule 1 to the Telecommunications Regulations (Cap. 106A).

[952] Section 7A of the Telecommunications Ordinance (Cap. 106).

[953] C.D. Long, *Telecommunications Law and Practice* 450-452 (Sweet & Maxwell, 2nd ed., 1995).

[954] Satellite Applications in Hong Kong, Address by Director-General of Telecommunications, OFTA, Hong Kong, at the Inter-Union Satellite Operations Group Forum, November 7, 1995.

[955] I. Walden & J. Angel (eds.), *Telecommunications Law* 461 (2001).

[956] H. Wong, The Paper "Satellite" Chase: The ITU Prepares for its Final Exam in Resolution 18, 63 *Journal of Air Law and Commerce* 681-682 (May/June, 1998).

opportunities to go beyond its limited geographical resources, as well as provide a foundation for a balanced legal structure in Hong Kong as public international law and private domestic law develop in tandem.

Further rules on space law should be introduced. One potential improvement would be for Hong Kong to become more actively involved in international space projects and forums, whether acting by itself or as part of a delegation from China. Adopting relevant international space treaties should be the priority. Meanwhile, further education regarding space law is required. For the general public, they are currently at a loss when confronted with space law issues or they simply do not know what space law is. Only when society accepts and understands the concept of space law will a complete framework for space law arise. The present author optimistically expects that the work on space law shall be improved and well accommodated in Hong Kong as long as further communications and exchanges continue.

Chapter 7

INTERNATIONAL SPACE COOPERATION

1. INTRODUCTION

International space cooperation is a key factor for future exploration and utilization of outer space. Its supporters believe it should permeate all space endeavors and is a significant duty that will affect private industry.[957] The International Geophysical Year (IGY) of 1957-1958 marked the start of a cooperative and truly international effort in space activities. More than 60 States participated in the IGY, which resulted in a rapid increase in geographical studies and an invigoration of the whole field of solar-terrestrial physics.[958] Recent developments in international space cooperation signal the introduction of a new era in the rapidly developing field of space law.[959] The importance of international cooperation in outer space has been recognized by the space-faring countries. The International Space Year (ISY) in 1992, bringing about a global effort to establish a long-term comprehensive observation capability, was indeed an ambitious cooperative space endeavor undertaken by the world scientific community.[960] The adoption of the UN Declaration on International Cooperation (hereinafter referred to as "the UN Declaration") in 1996 has further pushed the development of space cooperation.

So far, several experience and lessons could be summarized as follows: (1) space activities are increasingly moving towards globalization and commercialization. Commercialization becomes the main theme and international cooperation cannot disregard this important trend. (2) space activities require international cooperation and coordination. Cooperation can provide excellent opportunities for the countries to exchange scientific views and concepts, share experiences and establish new base for making use of the achievements from space activities. (3) mutual trust is the most important element in securing the success of international cooperation. This kind of trust exists between and among the partner states in different levels and aspects: politically, economically, scientifically, socially and personally. Only with the above all-around trust can international cooperation achieve great success. (4)

---

[957] Freeman & Inadomi, Who's the Captain Kirk of this Enterprise?: Regulating Outer Space Industry Through Corporate Structures, 18 *U.C. Davis Law Review* 805-806 (1985); Trimble, The International Law of Outer Space and Its Effect on Commercial Space Activity, 11 *Pepperdine Law Review* 545-546 (1984).

[958] Sikandar Zaman, Building International Cooperation Through ISY, *IEEE Technology and Society Magazine*, 32-33 (Spring 1992).

[959] For further discussion, see T.S. Twibell, Space Law: Legal Restraints on Commercialization and Development of Outer Space, 65 *University of Missouri at Kansas City Law Review* 603-606 (Spring 1997).

[960] Zaman, *supra* note 2, at 36.

most States have realize the importance of international cooperation. The vital point now is how to implement and realize international cooperation. The present chapter will look into the issue. Section two offers a guide by using China-Brazil cooperation for purpose of illustration.

2. China-Brazil Space Cooperation

In fact, international space cooperation emerged far earlier than the adoption of the UN Declaration. China has undertaken extensive cooperation arrangements with other countries, *e.g.* the sharing of satellite technology.[961] The history of space cooperation between China and Brazil is symbolized by the China-Brazil Earth Resource Satellite (CBERS) set up in 1986, followed by the signature of the Protocol on Research and Production of the Earth Resource Satellite in 1988. This was China's first international cooperative space technology venture with another developing country.[962] In 2002, after 15 years' of successful joint creative work, the two sides were able to reach a new Protocol (hereinafter referred to as "the 2002 Protocol"), providing a more concrete framework for further cooperation in space projects.[963]

The 2002 Protocol, based on and in the spirit of the Protocols reached before, continues space cooperation between the two States. Besides developing a second generation of CBERS satellites, the Protocol also establishes that the two sides will examine the viability of jointly developing a geostationary meteorological and telecommunications satellite. It contains 19 articles of great innovation on the commercialization of outer space. This bilateral agreement has been herald as an authentic bilateral effort amplifying the so-called South-South relationship.

This section will evaluate the Protocol, highlighting its significance in promoting space cooperation. Part one provides a brief overview of the history of space cooperation between China and Brazil. Part two examines the 2002 Protocol and provides an evaluation of its principles. This part demonstrates how the 2002 Protocol promotes space cooperation and commercialization in outer space. Finally, Part three provides some observations that will pave the way to the infinite rewards which may be reaped from the commercialization of outer space.

2.1. History of Space Cooperation between China and Brazil

One of the major space powers, China strongly supports activities involving the peaceful use of outer space and maintains that international space cooperation be promoted and strengthened on the basis of equality and mutual benefit, mutual complementarity and

961 G. Milhollin & G. White, A New China Syndrome: Beijing's Atomic Bazzar, *Washington Post*, C1, May 12, 1991.

962 China, Brazil to Jointly Launch a 2nd Satellite, *China Daily*, March 5, 2002, available at <http://www.china.org.cn/english/2002/Mar/28110.htm> (viewed on December 21, 2004).

963 See further Brazil Expects to Further Space Tech Cooperation with China, *Xinhua News Agency*, October 22, 2003, available at <http://www.china.org.cn> (viewed on January 11, 2004).

common development.[964] China's participation in international space cooperation started in the mid-1970s. Since 1985, the country has signed many inter-governmental or inter-agency cooperative agreements, protocols and memorandums, and established long-term cooperative relations with a dozen countries, including the United States, Italy, Germany, the UK, France, Japan, Sweden, Argentina, Brazil, Russia, Ukraine and Chile.[965]

Brazil was among the earliest countries to undertake cooperative projects with China. The CBERS project, set up in 1986, was jointly financed by China and Brazil. And the Protocol on Research and Production of the Earth Resource Satellite was signed by both governments in 1988. However, the first consequence of the Protocol only occurred 11 years later, when the CBERS-1 was launched in 1999 from the Chinese base in Taiyuan. It is China's first generation transmission Earth resources satellite developed by China and Brazil. The satellite was officially delivered for service in 2002.[*] More than 230, 000 satellite data pictures have been received from CBERS-1 and these have been widely applied in various areas of social and economic development for both countries.

The successful launch of CBERS-1 showed that China and Brazil were beginning to use their indigenously developed satellite to obtain real-time remote data, ending China's long lack of a home-made resource satellite. It was the first time that China had developed an Earth resource satellite with remote sensors. It was also the first time it had obtained remote sensing imagery of remote areas of the western part of China. This made a certain contribution to the development of that part of the country. Experts world-wide believed that the successful development and launch of the CBERS-1 indicated that China's satellite development capability had reached a new stage.[966]

Another two cooperative protocols were concluded in 1994 and 2000, respectively. Both protocols deal with cooperation in space technology, or more specifically, in the development of Earth resources satellites. Thanks to their creative joint research and development, both parties were able to agree a further cooperative protocol in 2002. Soon after this, CBERS-2 was launched from Taiyuan in October 2003. With this satellite, Brazil became independent in remote sensing radar imaging. This means that the country no longer needs to purchase US Landsat imagery, or to rely on other satellites, which it had been doing for at least seven years.[967] CBERS-2 will monitor deforestation and forest fires in Brazil, as well as providing data to be used for harvest estimates.

Plans included in the 2002 Protocol to launch two more satellites in the future--the CBERS-3 (launch forecast for 2006) and CBERS-4 (launch sometime in 2007)—have been confirmed. These satellites will have more advanced cameras than the previous two.

---

[964] See White Paper on China's Space Activities, available at <http://english.people.com.cn/features/spacepaper/spacepaper5.html> (viewed on January 11, 2004).

[965] *Id.*

[*] CBERS-2 was launched in 2003 since CBERS-1 has exceeded its two-year expectancy.

[966] Y. Chen, CBERS and Its Applications, available at <http://www.cnsa.gov.cn/espacechina/v3n7.htm> (viewed on June 15, 2004).

[967] But in reality, Brazil still makes use of free EOS data from the US. Launch of the Sino-Brazilian Satellite Makes Brazil Self-Sufficient in Remote Sensing Radar, Agencia Brasil, Arab Brazilian Chamber of Commerce, available at <Http://www.anba.com.br/ingles/noticia.php?id=470> (viewed on December 21, 2004).

2.2. Understandings of the 2002 Protocol

The 2002 Protocol is a complementary Protocol to the 1994 Framework Agreement between the Government of the Federative Republic of Brazil and the Government of the People's Republic of China on Cooperation in the Peaceful Applications of Outer Space Science and Technology on the Continuity of the Joint Development of Earth Resources Satellites. It begins by recognizing several prior agreements. The basic purpose is to continue the cooperation between the two sides to develop a second generation of CBERS satellites (CBERS-3 and 4).[968] With 15 years of successful cooperation, the two sides were able to reach a higher level of cooperation. The 2002 Protocol, 19 articles in total, contains very important new dispositions.

2.2.1. Dispute Resolution

It is important to note that the Protocol contains clear rules on dispute resolution. Indeed, an appropriate dispute resolution mechanism is critical to the success of such cooperation, since various rules and principles will only protect commercial ventures to the extent that they are enforceable.[969] Thus the Protocol creates a Coordination Committee to solve problems during its implementation. The Protocol further establishes a Joint Project Committee as an executive body with wide competence.[970] Misunderstandings or disputes concerning the interpretation or application of the Protocol can be settled by mutual consultations between the parties within the framework of the Joint Project Committee. The second and final instance, at the request of either party, will be the Coordination Committee.[971] This Committee is different from a formal dispute resolution body. Because of their years of cooperation, the two parties have a trusting relationship. This informal dispute resolution mechanism can function well and maintain good relationships between the two parties.

2.2.2. Areas for Cooperation

Rules are provided for facilitating the entry and exit of equipment and materials required for the implementation of the Project in both countries, as well as for the provision of the appropriate documentation for citizens from each country to enter, exit and reside within the territory of the other country in order to carry out activities relating to the Project.[972] This is essential to its smooth operation. Free movement of facilities, information and personnel necessary for the project is the basis of cooperation.

Further facilitation is provided later on: both parties give priority to companies or institutions of the other party to provide the services, parts and components or equipment each party needs to complete its duties in fulfillment of the project.[973] This preference provided to the other party could promote both a friendly relationship and economic development. This arrangement is also in line with the global trend of economic development,

---

[968] Article 1 (1) of the 2002 Protocol.

[969] Bockstiegel, Proposed Draft Convention on the Settlement of Space Law Disputes, 12 *Journal of Space Law* 136-138 (1984).

[970] According to Article 4 of the 2002 Protocol, within 60 days of the entry into force of this Protocol, Brazilian Space Agency and the Chinese National Space Administration, designated to coordinate and manage the Project, shall establish the Joint Project Committee.

[971] Article 17 of the 2002 Protocol.

[972] Article 7 and 8 of the 2002 Protocol.

[973] Article 10 of the 2002 Protocol.

thus meaning more than merely providing a model for space cooperation—it provides a prelude and model for future trade liberalization between the two parties.[974]

2.2.3. Model of Cooperation

It is vital to note that the parties have agreed on an equal sharing of the total investment in the project.[975] This is different from the previous investment model, where China took up 70 percent of the cost. This means that activities concerning the launch of the CBERS-3 and 4 will be shared on an equal basis, with each sharing 50 percent of the costs.[976] It follows from this arrangement that both parties will have equal rights to utilize the products of CBERS-3 and 4 and that these products may be used by a third party only with the mutual consent of both parties.[977] This equal arrangement is a considerable improvement on the previous 70-30 model. Moreover, there are plans to launch the CBERS-3 from China, and the CBERS-4 from the Alcantara Rocket Center in Maranhao, Brazil.

There have clearly been great achievements from the previous cooperation, where Brazil provided scientists, engineers and a smaller percentage of investment capital in exchange for a smaller percentage of the profits. This rightly reflects the principle that space cooperation should be based on mutual benefits and common development.[978] But, after 15 years of cooperation, Brazil is now capable of taking greater control over this space project and is thus able to take on more responsibilities. This rightly accords with both the guiding principles of China's international cooperation and the UN Resolution.

2.2.4. Commercial Benefits from Cooperation

Commercialization is the final goal of the space project. Accordingly, several articles are devoted to this purpose. Since Brazil is in charge of the CBERS-4 launching, it will develop its Alcantara Launch Center as a competitive international center for commercial launches. The launch of the CBERS-4 will be a test of the viability of the Center as a future commercial launch site. This will have far-reaching effects on satellite launches among developing countries. Currently, launch activities have largely been monopolized by a few developed countries; the work of the center will no doubt add to the competition in launch services. Developing countries can be expected to enjoy favorable conditions from their "pal".

According to the 2002 Protocol, both parties enjoy equal benefits from the satellites. For each launch, each country will sign a contract with off-set and re-flight insurance clauses, according to the rules of international commercial launch services.[979] Meanwhile, the model of a joint venture is to be studied for the purpose of marketing and/or distributing CBERS images to third parties.[980] Furthermore, we should note that the issue of intellectual property

[974] Trade in goods and services can be largely facilitated by the arrangements for free movement of materials and personnel. Future liberalization in trade can follow this example by removing trade barriers and advocating trade facilitation.

[975] Article 9 of the 2002 Protocol.

[976] Article 11 of the 2002 Protocol. China is in charge of the CBERS-3 launching and Brazil is in charge of the CBERS-4 launching.

[977] Article 12 of the 2002 Protocol.

[978] See the UN Declaration on International Cooperation, G.A. Res. 51/122, U.N. Doc. A/AC.105/572/Rev. 1 (1996).

[979] Article 11 of the 2002 Protocol.

[980] Article 13 of the 2002 Protocol.

rights is included in the Protocol for the first time.[981] These two provisions touch on the most sensitive issue in space commercialization.

As a result of increasing international space cooperation and the future commercialization of prospective technical innovations in outer space, the protection of property rights in space activities, including issues regarding technology transfer is essential.[982] The ongoing multinational project on the International Space Station (ISS) provides one example of how to undertake space commercialization. The Inter-Governmental Agreement (IGA) of 1998, together with bilateral Memoranda of Understanding, defines the overall cooperative model for the partners. However, the situation is different when it comes to commercialization of the ISS. The IGA does not cover commercialization and, with 16 partners involved in the project, each having its own national commercialization plan, the commercial operation of the ISS therefore has to integrate a number of complicated factors. It is taking a long time to reach a consensus on the operational framework for commercialization of the ISS. However, the special relationship between China and Brazil has justified a different approach. We can expect that more and more space cooperation will be carried out in the future on a model like that of China and Brazil, especially when developed countries continue to maintain restrictions on technology transfer.

2.1. Evaluation and Recommendations

2.3.1. Establishing a Cooperation Mechanism

The principle of international cooperation is laid down in Article I (1) of the 1967 Outer Space Treaty. Two different standpoints existed during its formulation. The developed countries agreed that this principle set forth limitations and obligations on the use of outer space, but that it did not diminish their inherent rights to determine how they shared the benefits derived from their space activities. The developing countries, on the one hand, believed that this principle was not only an appeal to all States to conduct their space activities on a cooperative international basis, but it actually implies that they have an obligation to do so.[983] As a consequence of their standpoints, most developed countries are of the opinion that there is no formal mechanism to enforce the principle, while developing countries insist that there should be a requirement for a stricter and fully codified international legal instrument to ensure cooperation and access for all countries.[984]

The question of the need to establish a cooperation mechanism to carry out this principle has been a serious concern for the UNCOPUOS. After years of discussion, the UN Declaration was adopted, offering basic guidance in international cooperation, namely: (1) states are free to determine all aspects of their participation in international cooperation on an equitable and mutually acceptable basis; (2) international cooperation should be conducted in the modes that are considered most effective and appropriate by the countries concerned,

[981] According to Article 16 of the 2002 Protocol, aspects concerning intellectual property rights of the Cooperation Project, where they could be applied, shall be object of particular arrangements taking into account the national laws of each country and the international rules accepted by both countries.

[982] R. Moenter, The International Space Station: Legal Framework and Current Status, 64 *Journal of Air Law and Commerce* 1052 (Fall 1999).

[983] N. Jasentuliyana, Ensuring Access to the Benefits of Space Technologies for All Countries, *Space Policy* 8-9 (1994).

including, *inter alia*, governmental and non-governmental, commercial and non-commercial, global, multilateral, regional or bilateral; and international cooperation among countries at all levels of development.[985]

The international climate is conducive to laying the groundwork for international cooperation. The greatest impact the major space powers could have on space law is the formulation of bilateral or multilateral agreements governing cooperative space activities. Current and potential future commercial applications of outer space usage include remote sensing, direct television broadcasting, space tourism, mining mineral deposits and erecting solar panels for energy generation; further applications extend to the ISS, whose constitutive document has been viewed as a model for multilateral cooperation.[986] However, multilateral space cooperation requires long periods of negotiation and is more complicated when it comes to further implementation. Bilateral cooperation, largely based on mutual trust and more readily representing mutual interests, can be a prelude to further extension. Normally bilateral cooperation can provide a test-bed for a deeper level of cooperation and can entail outcomes beyond the purely economic elements. Furthermore, bilateral cooperation can be well formulated to suit the specific requirements of both parties. This is obvious from the China-Brazil activity, whose achievements can have a positive, reinforcing effect on political stability and states' political relations.[987] Bilateral cooperation is thus often adopted by many nations, avoiding tedious multi-sided negotiations.

2.3.2. Dual-use Issue and Cooperation among Developing Countries

In the past few years we have witnessed a tremendous growth of space applications to serve a wide range of activities. Moreover, many satellite systems are inherently of a dual-use nature, with both civilian and military applications. Remote-sensing, earth observation and surveillance satellites are the most important examples of such dual-use systems.[988] China and Brazil's cooperative development of Earth Resource Satellites clearly falls within the above examples.[989] While the intelligence provided by such satellites can be used to strengthen an early warning and crisis prevention system, it can also be used for military purposes. CBERS-2 has been described as a military version of a satellite jointly developed for remote sensing—evidence of how development of a civil program can have clear military benefit.[990] Nevertheless, China has in its public pronouncements on space activities always urged the

---

984 *Id.*, at 9.

985 UN Declaration, para. 2 and 4.

986 L.L. Manzione, Multinational Investment in the Space Station: An Outer Space Model for International Cooperation?, 18 *American University International Law Review* 515 (2002).

987 The US policy for meteorological and remote sensing data from space for Earth observations is (as a matter of policy and law) a public good—the cost to the developed world either is very small (e.g., COFUR with Landsat) or free (e.g., EOS data). It is in fact cheaper for the developing world to make use of this public good data rather than develop an indigenous national satellite system. However, political and longer-term technological and commercial benefits justify such indigenous development as CBERS represents—this is especially the case for Brazil.

988 Gerald M. Steinberg, Satellite Capabilities of Emerging Space-Competent States, available at <http://faculty.biu.ac.il/~steing/military/sat.htm> (viewed on December 21, 2004).

989 The CBERS is aimed at the development of a complete remote sensing system by developing countries which would be both compatible to and competitive with other systems produced and operational during the present decade. See Pericles Gasparini Alves, *Access to Outer Space Technologies: Implications for International Security* 16 (New York: United Nations, 1992).

990 Joan Johnson-Freese, China's Manned Space Program: Sun Tzu or Apollo Redux?, 56 *Naval War College Review*, No. 3, 56 (Summer 2003).

peaceful use of outer space. Concern over the possibility of dual use has been resolved by using the term "peaceful applications" in the title of the 2002 Protocol. The two nations have cooperated and will continue their cooperation in space activities following this Principle.

One of the most important ways of promoting the utilization of space science and technology for the benefit of all mankind is through space science and technology transfer to more countries. The establishment of an effective cooperation mechanism at global, regional, multilateral or bilateral level will play a pivotal role in guaranteeing access to space science and technology. Only through this mechanism can developing countries possess genuine capabilities in space science and technology for the purpose of fulfilling their specific needs.

While following the UN Declaration on International Cooperation, China has further specified the importance of simultaneously increasing the space development capability of all countries, especially developing countries, and enabling all countries to enjoy the benefits of space technology. With developed countries still setting limits in transferring relevant technologies, it is all the more meaningful that China is committed to supporting the use of its more developed space technology and space application technology to undertake cooperation with other developing countries and to provide services to these countries.[991] The China-Brazil cooperation, only one among various bilateral cooperative agreements which have been signed between China and other countries, is thus rightly considered an excellent example of "South-South Cooperation" in the high-tech field for developing countries.[992]

2.3.3. Prospects for Further Improvements

Unfortunately, the 2002 Protocol only offers simple principles without going further into detailed arrangements. For example, when we come to the issue of intellectual property rights, the protocol contains only simple wording, requiring specific arrangements in future. Protection of intellectual property is critical to the success of the project, especially for those involved in research and development efforts through collaborative relationships. Both parties should agree to respect proprietary rights in, and the confidentiality of, identified property and appropriately marked data and goods.[993]

Furthermore, the creation, use, transfer, ownership and protection of intellectual property are of utmost importance to both parties. A detailed set of rules concerning intellectual property rights should thus be in place, pulling together the different national laws of both parties. The efforts of the two parties should not be isolated from international society. It is important to note the attempts by the International Institute for the Unification of Private Law (Unidroit) to harmonize national space law in relation to space commercial activities.[994] In 2001 the Convention on International Interests in Mobile Equipment was opened for signature. Three different protocols were linked to the Convention, with one protocol on space assets. However, the question of incompatibilities between the Protocol on Space Assets and the current legal framework in existing space law was raised in the UNCOPUOS

[991] See further White Paper on China's Space Activities.

[992] See further China-Brazil Earth Resource Satellite (CBERS), available at <http://www.cast.ac.cn> (viewed on January 11, 2004).

[993] See for example, M.B. Broadwell, *Intellectual Property and the Economic Development of the International Space Station*, presentation at Space Technology and Applications International Forum (STAIF-2000), Albuquerque, NM, February 2000.

[994] See <http://www.unidroit.org>.

discussion.[995] The efforts of the Unidriot should generally be welcomed in view of the vacuum in space law; however, the organization should work closely with the UNCOPUOS, which remains the main body for harmonizing national space law. It is expected that issues concerning protection of intellectual property rights in relation to space commercial activities will be discussed in the near future. China and Brazil should actively participate in the process and concretize the 2002 Protocol in this aspect for better cooperation.

No provisions in the Protocol touch on the issue of liability. Reference might be made to the dispute resolution arrangement, through which disputes concerning the liability of each party can be resolved. However, this arrangement does not affect the situation when a third party is involved. It is thus helpful to refer to the 1972 Liability Convention for possible resolution.

The simple formulation of the Protocol—although understandable—could also be a problem for further implementation. At the time of the negotiations, space commercialization was still at the testing and developing stage. This is also true where development of a legal regime for space commercialization is concerned. Various discussions are still going on concerning the appropriate legal rules for space commercialization. Thus, while Chinese-Brazilian cooperation provides a good example for bilateral space commercialization, in future implementation, it will be necessary to study other existing commercial space projects and make the protocol a more concrete document.

It is to be noted that the Protocol will remain in force for five years and will be automatically renewed for equal and successive periods of five years, unless either party notifies the other party of the intention to terminate the protocol with at least six months' prior notice. Based on such an arrangement, we can reasonably expect that more detailed rules will be further negotiated and added to the existing Protocol for better coordination and performance.

Finally, for the purpose of coordination and the prevention of possible conflicts among the parties to various agreements, it is suggested that such agreements should be under the aegis of a space organization. As provided in the Vienna Convention on the Law of Treaties, treaties shall, after their entry into force, be transmitted to the Secretariat of the UN for registration or filing and recording, as the case may be, and for publication.[996] In the present case, the UNCOPUOS[997] may be one possible body to undertake this task, given its position within the UN system. Unfortunately, the UNCOPUOS may be unwilling to take on this task since it basically deals with multilateral aspects of space law and not bilateral ones. Nevertheless, the UN is widely considered to be well-suited for the regulatory and coordinating function as evidenced by its proven record of formalizing treaties regarding space activities[998] as well as resolving other international issues.[999] Moreover, once an agreement has proven itself to be of significance to future space activities, the UNCOPUOS

---

995 For further discussion, see Alvaro Fabricio dos Santos, Financing of Space Assets, 19 *Space Policy* 128-129 (2003).

996 Vienna Convention on the Law of Treaties, Article 80 (1).

997 The UNCOPUOS may be unwilling to take this task since it basically deals with multilateral aspects of space law and not bilateral ones.

998 N. Jasentuliyana, Treaty Law and Outer Space: Can the United Nations Play an Effective Role?, 11 *Annals of Air & Space Law* 226 (1986).

999 J.B. Ashe, III, Space Station Alpha: International Shining Star or Legal Black Hole?, 9 *Temple International & Comparative Law Journal* 353 (Fall 1995).

would be the appropriate body to push forward such practices and deepen future space cooperation.

2.4. Conclusion

Efforts towards international space cooperation are nothing new to the space countries[1000]: Space exploration is a tremendous undertaking requiring the resources, expertise, and efforts of many individuals from different nations throughout the world. Different nations need to work together for common goals.

Examples of multilateral space cooperation include INTELSAT, INMARSAT, EUTELSAT and ESA, which have laid a solid foundation for future endeavors. Bilateral cooperation has also developed rapidly, but mostly between developed countries. From the examples above, we can see that rules and principles can be accumulated and improved while better balancing various competing interests.[1001] Space cooperation between China and Brazil amplifies the so-called "South-South" relationship, especially in view of the present situation where developing countries are seen as potential clients for commercial remote sensing programs.

While developed countries are the main providers of satellite images, they tend to impose high charges, though assuring the required public services through subsidized prices. With the success of the CBERS program, this situation should largely change: such cooperation has the added benefit of ensuring that no one state monopolizes too many space resources. Additionally, the model of space cooperation can further extend to other developing countries, encouraging them to participate in ventures on a modest scale and contributing to common benefits for these nations.[1002]

A close examination of the 2002 Protocol has thus revealed that this document, while responding to the UN Declaration, has made a specific contribution and set a good example for space cooperation among developing countries. Witnessing the unstable legal environment created by the 1967 Outer Space Treaty, the China-Brazil cooperation model can mean more to international society. Placed against the background of the trend towards space commercialization, the success of this model can test the viability of existing space commercial rules and help create further improvements. No doubt the achievements from

---

1000 See for example, F. Kosmo, The Commercialization of Space: A Regulatory Scheme that Promotes Commercial Ventures and International Responsibility, 61 *University of Southern California Law Review*1086 (May 1988).

1001 L.B. Malagar & M.A. Magdoza-Malagar, International Law of Outer Space and the Protection of Intellectual Property Rights, 17 *Boston University International Law Journal* 364 (Fall 1999).

1002 L.M. Fountain, Creating Momentum in Space: Ending the Paralysis Produced by the "Common Heritage of Mankind" Doctrine, 35 *Connecticut Law Review* 1778 (Summer 2003).

such a model of cooperation will provide an excellent opportunity to exceed the "one small step for man, one giant leap for mankind."[1003]

[1003] Statement made by Neil Armstrong on July 20, 1969 when he became the first man to walk on the Moon.

REFERENCES

A. BOOKS

[1] P.G. Alves, Access to Outer Space Technologies: Implications for International Security, Vol. 16, (New York: United Nations; 1992).

[2] Marietta Benko & Kai-Uwe Schrogl (eds.), *International Space Law in the Making: Current Issues in the UN Committee on the Peaceful Uses of Outer Space* (1993).

[3] K.H. Bockstiegel, *Commercial Use of Space Stations—The Legal Framework of Transatlantic Cooperation* (1986).

[4] K.H. Bockstiegel (ed.), *Environmental Aspects of Activities in Outer Space* (1988).

[5] Antonio Cassese, *International Law*, 2nd Edition (Oxford University Press, 2005).

[6] Carl Q. Christol, *The Modern International Law of Outer Space* (Pergamon Press, 1982).

[7] Carl Q. Christol, *Space law: Past, Present, and Future* (Kluwer, 1991).

[8] I.H.Ph. Diederiks-Verschoor, An Introduction to Space Law, (Kluwer Law International, 2nd ed., 1999).

[9] Frans G. von der Dunk, *Private Enterprise and Public Interest in the European 'Spacescape': Towards Harmonized National Space Legislation for Private Space Activities in Europe* (1998).

[10] F.G. von der Dunk & M.M.T.A. Brus (eds.), *The International Space Station: Commercial Utilization from a European Legal Perspective* (Martinus Nijhoff: Leiden/Boston, 2006).

[11] Peter van Fenema, *The International Trade in Launching Services: The Effect of U.S. Laws, Politics and Practices on Its Development* (Leiden, The Netherlands, 1999).

[12] D.I. Fisher, *Prior Consent to International Direct Satellite Broadcasting* (1990).

[13] F. Francioni & T. Scovazzi (eds.), *International Responsibility for Environmental Harm* (Graham & Trotman, 1991).

[14] Nathan C. Goldman, *American Space Law: International & Domestic* (1996).

[15] S. Gorove (ed.), *United States Space Law: National & International Regulation (IV)* (1998).

[16] P.P.C. Haanappel, *The Law and Policy of Air Space and Outer Space: A Comparative Approach* (Kluwer Law International, 2003).

[17] Albert A. Harrison, *Spacefairing: The Human Dimension* (2001).

[18] Julian Hermida, *Legal Basis for a National Space Legislation* (Kluwer, 2004).

[19] G.J.H. van Hoof, *Rethinking the Sources of International Law* (1983).

[20] G.C. Hufbauer & E. Wada (eds.), *Unfinished Business: Telecommunications after the Uruguay Round* (Institute for International Economics, 1997).
[21] B.A. Hurwitz, *The Legality of Space Militarization* (1986).
[22] N. Jasentuliyana & R. Lee, *Manual on Space Law* (1981).
[23] N. Jasentuliyana (ed.), *Maintaining Outer Space for Peaceful Uses, Proceedings of a Symposium held at the Hague* (1984).
[24] N. Jasentuliyana (ed.), *Space Law: Development and Scope* (Praeger, 1992).
[25] N. Jasentuliyana (ed.), *Perspectives on International Law* (Kluwer, 1995).
[26] N. Jasentuliyana, *International Space Law and the United Nations* (Kluwer, 1999).
[27] C.H. Kennedy & M.V. Pastor, *An Introduction to International Telecommunications Law* (Artech House, 1996).
[28] M. Lachs, *The Law of Outer Space, An Experience in Contemporary Law Making* (Sijthoff Leiden, 1972).
[29] G. Lafferanderie & D. Crowther (eds.), *Outlook on Space Law over the Next 30 Years* (1997).
[30] C.D. Long, *Telecommunications Law and Practice* (Sweet & Maxwell, 2nd Edition, 1995).
[31] Francis Lyall & Paul B. Larssen (eds.), *Space Law* (Ashgate, 2007).
[32] P. Malanczuk, *Akehurst's Modern Introduction to International Law* (Routledge, 7th ed., 1997).
[33] V.S. Mani (ed.) *Recent Trends in International Space law and Policy* (1997).
[34] Moses Moskowitz, *The Roots and Reaches of United Nations Activities and Decisions* (1980).
[35] S. Mosteshar (ed.), *Research and Invention in Outer Space, Liability and Property Rights* (Martinus Nijhoff Publishers: Dordrecht, 1995).
[36] Charles C. Okolie, *International Law of Satellite Remote Sensing & Outer Space* 42 (Kendall/Hunt, 1989).
[37] Robert Rachlin, *Return on Investment Strategies for Decision-Making* (1987).
[38] B. Reijnen, *The United Nations Space Treaties Analyzed* (1992).
[39] Glenn H. Reynolds & Robert P. Merges, *Outer Space: Problems of Law and Policy* (Boulder: Westview Press, 1989).
[40] M.N. Shaw, *International Law* (Cambridge University Press, 4th ed., 1997).
[41] Kurt Siodmak, *Skyport* (Mass, 1959).
[42] H.L. van Traa-Engelman, *Commercial Utilization of Outer Space* (Martinus Nijhoff Publishers, 1993).
[43] Walden & J. Angel (eds.), *Telecommunications Law* (2001).
[44] Henri A. Wassenbergh, *Principles of Outer Space Law in Hindsight* (Martinnus Nijhoff Publishers, 1991).
[45] Gennady Zhukov & Yuri Kolosov, *International Space Law* (1984).
[46] T. Zwann (ed.), *Space Law: Views of the Future* (1988).

B. ARTICLES

[1] Recent Development: Commercialization of Space Commercial Space Launch Amendments Act of 2004, 17 *Harvard Journal of Law & Technology* 626 (Spring 2004).

[2] R.I.R. Abeyratne, The Use of Nuclear Power Sources in Outer Space and Its Effect on Environmental Protection, 25 *Journal of Space Law* 17 (1997).

[3] J.B. Ashe III, Space Station Alpha: International Shining Star or Legal Black Hole? 9 *Temple International & Comparative Law Journal* 353 (1995).

[4] Kurt Anderson Baca, Property Rights in Outer Space, 58 *Journal of Air Law & Commerce*, 1069 (1993).

[5] Anna Maria Balsano, Intellectual Property within Public International Research Organizations: The Example of the European Space Agency, *The Proceedings of the 36th Colloquium on the Law of Outer Space*, IISL 3 (1993).

[6] M. Benko, G. Gruber & K. Schrogl, The UN Committee on the Peaceful Uses of Outer Space: Adoption of Principles Relevant to the Use of Nuclear Power Sources in Outer Space, *Proceeding 36th Colloquium on the Law of Outer Space* 238 (1993).

[7] R. Berkley, Space Law Versus Space Utilization: The Inhibition of Private Industry in Outer Space, 15 Wisconsin International Law Journal 428 (1997).

[8] Berlin & L. I. Tennen, The Role of the United Unions in Colonization of Outer Space, or Chicken Little was Right, 19 *Colloquium on the Law of Outer Space* (1977).

[9] A.W. Blaser, The Common Heritage in Its Infinite Variety: Space Law and the Moon in the 1990s, 5 *Journal of Law & Technology* 93 (1990).

[10] K.H. Bockstiegel, Proposed Draft Convention on the Settlement of Space Law Disputes, 12 *Journal of Space Law* 136-138 (1984).

[11] K.H. Bockstiegel, The Terms 'Appropriate State' and 'Launching State' in the Space Treaties—Indicators of State Responsibility and Liability for State and Private Space Activities, *Proceedings 34th Colloquium on the Law of Outer Space*, 15 (1992).

[12] K.H. Bockstiegel, The Term "Appropriate State" in International Space Law, in *Proceedings 37th Colloquium on the Law of Outer Space* 77-79 (Jerusalem, 1994).

[13] K.H. Bockstiegel, Launching State in International Space Law, *Proceedings 37th Colloquium on the Law of Outer Space* 80-83 (Jerusalem, 1994).

[14] Joseph A. Bosco, International Law regarding Outer Space – An Overview, 55 *Journal of Air Law & Commerce* 614-620 (1990).

[15] Margaret A. Boulware, Jeffery A. Pyle & Frank C. Turner, An Overview of Intellectual Property Rights Abroad, 16 *Houston Journal of International Law*, 12 (1994).

[16] M. Bourely, Is It Necessary to Re-Negotiate the Convention on Registration?, *Proceedings 30th Colloquium on the Law of Outer Space*, 231 (Bangalore, 1988).

[17] Lea Brilmayer & Natalie Klein, Land and Sea: Two Sovereignty Regimes in Search of a Common Denominator, 33 *NewYork University Journal of International Law & Politics* 703, 706-07 (2001).

[18] Dan K. Burk, Application of US Patent Law to Commercial Activity in Outer Space, 6 *Santa Clara Computer & High Technology Law Journal* 307 (1991).

[19] Dan L. Burk, Protection of Trade Secrets in Outer Space Activity: A Study in Federal Pre-emption, 23 *Seton Hall Law Review* 563 (1993).

[20] S. Cahill, Give me My Space: Implications for Permitting National Appropriation of the Geostationary Orbit, 19 *Wisconsin International Law Journal* 246-247 (Spring 2001).

[21] J.I. Charney, The United States and the Revision of the 1982 Convention on the Law of the Sea, 23 *Ocean Development & International Law* 240 (1992).

[22] Yanping Chen, China's Space Commercialization Effort, 9 *Space Policy*, No. 1, 45 (February 1993).

[23] Bin Cheng, The Commercial Development of Space: The Need for New Treaties, 19 *Journal of Space Law* 17, 43 (1991).

[24] B. Cheng, Article VI of the 1967 Space Treaty Revisited: "International Responsibility", "National Activity" and "The Appropriate State", 26 *Journal of Space Law* 7-32 (1998).

[25] R.B. Chong & W. Chow, Financing Telecommunications Projects in Asia: A Promising Regulatory Perspective, 52 *Federal Communications Law Journal* 9-11 (December, 1999).

[26] C.Q. Christol, International Liability for Damage Caused by Space Objects, 74 *American Journal of International Law* 368 (April 1980).

[27] Carl Q. Christol, The Common Heritage of Mankind Provision in the 1979 Agreement Governing the Activities of States on the Moon and Other Celestial Bodies, 14 *International Lawyer* 429, 473 (1980).

[28] C.Q. Christol, The Moon Treaty Enters into Force, 79 *American Journal of International Law* 163, 164 (1985).

[29] Carl Q. Christol, Commercial Uses of Outer Space: Highlights of American Policies, 10 *Annuaire de Droit Maritime et Aerospatiale* 348 (1989).

[30] C.Q. Christol, Nuclear Power Sources (NPS) for Space Objects: A New Challenge for International Law, *Proceedings 35th Colloquium on the Law of Outer Space*, 250 (1993).

[31] J.C. Clayton, Nuclear Power Sources for Outer Space: Political, Technical and Legal Considerations, *Proceedings 31st Colloquium on the Law of Outer Space*, 287 (1989).

[32] A.A. Cocca, The Advances in International Law through the Law of Outer Space, 9 *Journal of Space Law* 13, 16 (1981).

[33] A.A. Cocca, Are the Principles on the Use of Nuclear Power Sources in Outer Space a Progress in Space Law?, *Proceedings 36th Colloquium on the Law of Outer Space* 258 (1993).

[34] S. de Cordoba, Changing Basic Space Laws: Popularity, Pragmatism and Historical Lessons, *Proceedings 36th Colloquium on the Law of Outer Space* 330 (1993).

[35] A.F. Cohen, Cosmos 954 and the International Law of Satellite Accidents, 10 *Yale Journal of International Law* 80 (1984).

[36] Kevin V. Cook, The Discovery of Lunar Water: An Opportunity to Develop a Workable Moon Treaty, 11 *Geo. Int'l. Envtl. Rev.* 647, 648 (1999).

[37] A. Copiz, Scarcity in Space: The International Regulation of Satellites, 10 *Common Conspectus* 208 (2002).

[38] Paul G. Dembling & Daniel M. Arons, The Evolution of Outer Space Treaty, 33 *Journal of Air Law & Commerce* 456 (1967).

[39] DeSaussure & P. Haanappel, A Unified Multinational Approach to the Application of Tort and Contract Principles to Outer Space, in *Proceedings of 21st Colloquium on the Law of Outer Space* 138 (1978).

[40] M.C. Devlin & W.G. Schmidt, Legal Issues Continue to Surround the International Space Station, 8 *USAFA Journal of Legal Studies* 248 (1997/1998).

[41] Frans G. von der Dunk, Towards a European Space Agency, Mark II?, in Proceedings 35th Colloquium on the Law of Outer Space 172 (1992).

[42] Frans G von der Dunk, Heeding the Public-Private Paradigm: Overview of National Space Litigation around the World, 2004 *Space Law Conference Paper Assemble*, Beijing, China April 25-27, 2004, China Institute of Space Law.

[43] F.G. von der Dunk, The Illogical Link: Launching, Liability and Leasing, *Proceedings 35th Colloquium on the Law of Outer Space*, 351 (Graz, 1993).

[44] F.G. von der Dunk, The Moon Agreement and the Prospect of Commercial Exploitation of Lunar Resources, 32 *Annals of Air and Space Law* 91 (2007).

[45] James E. Dunstan, Is Launching a Rocket Still an Ultra-Hazardous Activity? Toward a Negligence Theory for Launching Activities, 9 *Space Manufacturing the High Frontier: Accession, Development & Utilization* 226, 229 (1993).

[46] R. Dusek, Lost in Space?: The Legal Feasibility of Nuclear Waste Disposal in Outer Space, 48 *William and Mary Environmental Law and Policy Review* 213 (Fall 1997).

[47] J.I. Edelstein, Anonymity an International Law Enforcement in Cyberspace, 7 *Fordham Intellectual Property Media & Entertainment Law Journal* 284-286 (1996).

[48] Mahdi El-Baghdadi, The Seabed's Mineral Resources and the Conditions Affecting the Regime to Regulate Their Exploitation, 26 *Journal of World Trade* 88 (1992).

[49] Andre Farand, Commercialization of International Space Station Utilization: The European Partner's Viewpoint, 28 *Air & Space Law* 85 (2003).

[50] Peter van Fenema, The Unidroit Space Protocol, the Concept of 'Launching State', Space Traffic Management and the Delimitation of Outer Space: The 41st Session of the UNCOPUS Legal Subcommittee, Vienna, 2-12 April 2002, 28 *Air & Space Law* 277-279 (September 2002).

[51] Anthony R. Filiato, The Commercial Space Launch Act: America's Response to the Moon Treaty?, 10 Fordham International Law Journal 763, 772 (1987).

[52] Michael J. Finch, Limited Space: Allocating the Geostationary Orbit, 7 *Nw. J. Int'l L. & Bus.* 788, 789 (1986).

[53] E.R. Finch, Jr., Heavenly Junk II: Recent Developments in Space Debris, 8 *Air & Space Law*, 9 (1994).

[54] M.S. Firestone, Problems in the Resolution of Disputes Concerning Damage Caused in Outer Space, 59 *Tulane Law Review* 764 (January 1985).

[55] W.F. Foster, The Convention on International Liability for Damage Caused by Space Objects, *Canadian Yearbook of International Law* 143 (1972).

[56] Lynn M. Fountain, Creating Momentum in Space: Ending the Paralysis Produced by the "Common Heritage of Mankind" Doctrine, 35 *Conn. L.Rev.* 1753, 1774-75 (2003).

[57] Frankle & Steptoe, Legal Considerations Affecting Commercial Space Launches from International Territory, *Proceedings of the Workshop on "Legal Framework for Commercial Launch and Associated Activities"*, Bremen, January, 2000 (Project 2001).

[58] Inadomi Freeman, Who's the Captain Kirk of This Enterprise?: Regulating Outer Space Industry through Corporate Structures, 8 *U.C. Davis Law Review* 805-806 (1985).

[59] C.E. Fumarola, Stratospheric Recovery: Recent and Forthcoming Changes in International Air Disaster Law and Its Effect on Air Terrorism Recovery, 36 *Suffolk University Law Review* 835-836 (2003).

[60] E. Galloway, United Nations Consideration of Nuclear Power for Satellites, *Proceedings 22nd Colloquium on the Law of Outer Space 135* (1979).

[61] M.A. Gary, The International Crime of Ecocide, 26 *California Western International Law Journal* 247 (1996).

[62] M.B. Gerrard, Asteroids and Comets: U.S. and International Law and the Lowest Probability, Highest Consequence Risk, 6 *New York University Environmental Law Journal* 44 (1997).

[63] L. F. E. Goldie, A Note on Some Diverse Meaning of 'The Common Heritage of Mankind', 10 *Syracuse Journal of International & Comparative Law* 69, 81 (1983).

[64] L. F. E. Goldie, Title and Use (and Usufruct) – An Ancient Distinction Too Oft Forgot, 79 *American Journal of International Law* 689 (1985).

[65] A. Gorbiel, Large Space Structures: The Need for a Special Treaty Regulation, *Proceedings 26th Colloquium on the Law of Outer Space*, 247-250 (Lausanne, 1984).

[66] S. Gorove, *Studies in Space Law: Its Challenges and Prospects* 105 (1977); H.A. Baker, *Space Debris: Legal and Policy Implications* 62 (1989).

[67] P.P.C. Haanappel, Some Observations on the Crash of the Cosmos 954, 6 *Journal of Space Law* 148 (1978).

[68] P.P.C. Haanappel, A Competitive Environment in Outer Space, 32 *Journal of Space Law* 1 (2006).

[69] Michael Hardy, The Law of the Sea and the Prospects for Deep Seabed Mining: The Position of the European Community, 17 *Ocean Development & International Law Journal* 309, 314 (1986).

[70] Qizhi He, The Problem of Definition and Delimitation in Outer Space, 10 *Journal of Space Law* 157-163 (1982).

[71] Barbara Ellen Heim, Exploring the Last Frontiers for Mineral Resources: A Comparison of International Law Regarding the Deep Seabed, Outer Space and Antarctica, 23 *Vanderbilt Journal of Transnational Law*, 819, 827 (1990).

[72] Stephen Hobe, Adequacy of the Current Legal and Regulatory Framework Relating to the Extraction and Appropriation of Natural Resources in Outer Space, 32 *Annals of Air and Space Law* 115 (2007).

[73] B.M. Hoffstadt, Moving the Heavens: Lunar Mining and the "Common Heritage of Mankind" in the Moon Treaty, 42 *UCLA Law Review* 581 note 30 (1994).

[74] Roger K. Hoover, Law and Society in Outer Space from the Viewpoint of Private Industry, 11 *Journal of Space Law* 115, 122-24 (1983).

[75] M. Hoskova, The Notification Principle in the 1992 NPS Resolution, *Proceedings 35th Colloquium on the Law of Outer Space*, 308-309 (Graz, 1993).

[76] Barry J. Hurewitz, Non-Proliferation and Free Access to Outer Space: The Dual-Use Conflict between the Outer Space Treaty and the Missile Technology Control Regime, 9 *High Technology Law Journal* 220 (1994).

[77] Eric Husby, Comment, Sovereignty and Property Rights in Outer Space, 3 *J. Int'l L. & Prac.* 362 (1994).

[78] Atsuyo Ito, Issues in the Implementation of the International Charter on Space and Major Disasters, 21 *Space Policy* 141-142 (2004).

[79] N. Jasentuliayana, Treaty Law and Outer Space: Can the United Nations Play an Effective Role? 11 *Annals of Air & Space Law* 226 (1986).

[80] N. Jasentuliyana, An Assessment of the United Nations Principles on the Use of Nuclear Power Sources in Outer Space, *Proceedings 36th Colloquium on the Law of Outer Space* 316 (Graz, 1993).

[81] N. Jasentuliyana, Ensuring Access to the Benefits of Space Technologies for All Countries, *Space Policy* 8-9 (1994).

[82] N. Jasentuliyana, Regulation of Space Salvage Operations: Possibilities for the Future, 22 *Journal of Space Law* 5-21 (1994).

[83] J. Johnson-Freese, China's Manned Space Program: Sun Tzu or Apollo Redux? 56 *Naval War College Review* (2003).

[84] Christopher C. Joyner, Legal Implications of the Concept of the Common Heritage of Mankind, 35 *International Law & Comparative Law Quarterly* 198 (1986).

[85] H. Keefe, Making the Final Frontier Feasible: A Critical Look at the Current Body of Outer Space Law, 11 *Computer & High Technology Law Journal* 357-358 (1995).

[86] P.W. Kenefick, A Step in the Right Direction: The FCC Provides Regulatory Relief in International Settlements and International Services Licensing, 8 *CommLaw Conspectus* 46 (Winter 2000).

[87] A. Kerrest, Launching Spacecraft from the Sea and Outer Space Treaty: the Sea Launch Project, 23 *Air & Space Law* 16-21 (1998).

[88] Kerrest, Remarks on the Notion of Launching State, *Proceedings 41st Colloquium on the Law of Outer Space*, 310 (1999).

[89] V. Kopal, The Use of Nuclear Power Sources in Outer Space: A New Set of United Nations Principles?, *Proceedings 34th Colloquium on the Law of Outer Space* 128 (1991).

[90] V. Kopal, Some Remarks on Issues Relating to Legal Definitions of "Space Object", "Space Debris" and "Astronaut", *American Institute of Aeronautics and Astronautics, Inc.*, 1 (1994).

[91] F. Kosmo, The Commercialization of Space: A Regulatory Scheme that Promotes Commercial Ventures and International Responsibility, *Southern California Law Review*, Vol. 61, 1069 (May 1988).

[92] James P. Lampertius, The Need for an Effective Liability Regime for Damage Caused by Debris in Outer Space, 13 *Michigan Journal of International Law* 456 (1992).

[93] P.B. Larsen, Future Protocol on Security Interests in Space Assets, 67 *Journal of Air Law & Commerce* 1091-1092 (Fall 2002).

[94] H. Lauterpacht, Sovereignty over Submarine Areas, *British Yearbook of International Law*, 376 & 394 (1950).

[95] R.J. Lee, Reconciling International Space Law with the Commercial Realities of the Twenty-First Century, 4 *Singapore Journal of International & Comparative Law* 230-231 (2000).

[96] Stephanie Lee-Miller, Licensing and Regulating U.S. Commercial Space Launches, 4 *Journal of Law & Technology* 45 (1989).

[97] John S. Lewis & Christopher F. Lewis, A Proposed International Legal Regime for the Era of Private Commercial Utilization of Space, 37 *George Washington International Law Review* 751 (2005).

[98] P.T. Limperis, Orbital Debris and the Spacefaring Nations: International Law Methods for Prevention and Reduction of Debris, and Liability Regimes for Damage Caused by Debris, 15 *Arizona Journal of International and Comparative Law*, 338 (Winter 1998).

[99] Y. Lodico, Developing Legal Principles for the Safe Use of Nuclear Power Sources in Outer Space, *Proceedings 34th Colloquium on the Law of Outer Space* 134 (1991).

[100] Leo B. Malagar & Marlo Apalisok Magdoza-Malagar, International Law of Outer Space and the Protection of Intellectual Property Rights, 17 *Boston University International Law Journal* 363-364 (Fall 1999).

[101] P. Malanczuk, Space Law as a Branch of International Law, *Netherlands Yearbook of International Law*, 147 (1995).

[102] James L. Malone, The United States and the Law of the Sea, 24 *Va.J. Int'l L.* 785, 786 (1984).

[103] L.L. Manzione, Multinational Investment in the Space Station: An Outer Space Model for International Cooperation?, 18 *American University International Law Review* 519-520 (2002).

[104] Mariorsky, A Few Reflections on the Meaning and the Interrelation of "Province of All Mankind" and "Common Heritage of Mankind Notions", 29 *Colloquium on the Law of Outer Space* 58-61 (1986).

[105] T.L. McLarty, Liberalized Telecommunications Trade in the WTO: Implications for Universal Service Policy, 51 *Federal Communications Law Journal* 49 (1998).

[106] Sean R. Mikula, Blue Helmets in the Next Frontier: The Future is Now, 29 Ga. J. Int'l & Comp. L. 531, 556-57 (2001).

[107] Partricia Minola, The Moon Treaty and the Law of the Sea, 18 *San Diego law Review* 455, 459-60 (1981).

[108] R. Moenter, The International Space Station: Legal Framework and Current Status, 64 *Journal of Air Law & Commerce* 1051-1052 (Fall 1999).

[109] E. Molodtsova, Nuclear Accidents on Space Objects with Nuclear Power Sources: Applicable International Law, *Proceedings 34th Colloquium on the Law of Outer Space* 142-144 (1991).

[110] Roscoe M. Moore, Risk Analysis and the Regulation of Reusable Launch Vehicles, 64 *Journal of Air Law & Commerce* 245, 251 (1998).

[111] Richard A. Morgan, Military Use of Commercial Communication Satellites: A New Look at the Outer Space Treaty and "Peaceful Purposes", 60 *Journal of Air Law & Commerce* 300 (1994).

[112] K.F. Nagel, Das neue Regierun sab kommenuber die Internationale Raum Station, 47 *Zeit Schrift fur Luft-und Weltraumrecht (ZLW)* 149-163 (2002).

[113] P.D. Nesgos, The Challenges Facing the Private Practitioner: Liability and Insurance Issues in Commercial Space Transportation, 4 *Georgetown University Law Review* 24 (Winter 1989).

[114] P. D. Nesgos, *Commercial Space Law: Practical Examples Relating to Contracts, Insurance and Finance*, United Nations Committee on the Peaceful Uses of Outer

Space/International Institute of Space Law Symposium on Commercial Activities in Space, Vienna, Austria, 22 March 1994.

[115] R. Oosterlinck, Intellectual Property and Space Activities, *The Proceedings of the 26th Colloquium on the Law of Outer Space*, IISL (1983).

[116] L. Perek, Scientific Criteria for the Delimitation of Outer Space, 5 *Journal of Space Law* 111-124 (1977).

[117] L. Perek, The 1976 Registration Convention, 47 *German Journal of Air and Space Law*, 351-360 (1998).

[118] C.M. Petras, "Space Force Alpha": Military Use of the International Space Station and the Concept of "Peaceful Purposes", 53 *Air Force Law Review* 165-166 (2002).

[119] Alejandro Piera, Intellectual Property in Space Activities: An Analysis of the United States Patent Regime, 29 *Air & Space Law*, No. 1, 50-51 (February 2004).

[120] M.C.W. Pinto, The Developing Countries and the Exploitation of the Deep Seabed, 15 *Columbia Business Law Review* 30 (1980).

[121] Virgiliu Pop, Appropriation in Outer Space: the Relationship between Land Ownership and Sovereignty on the Celestial Bodies, 16 *Space Policy*, No. 4, 275-282 (2000).

[122] Richard A. Posner, The Material Basis of Jurisprudence, 69 *Ind. L.J.* 1, 10 (1993).

[123] Grier C. Raclin, From Ice to Ether: The Adoption of a Regime to Govern Resource Exploitation in Outer Space, 7 *Nw. J. Int'l L. & Bus.* 727, 739 (1986).

[124] R.A. Ramey, Armed Conflict on the Frontier: The Law of War in Space, 48 *Air Force Law Review*, 93 (2000).

[125] Harminderpal Singh Rana, The "Common Heritage of Mankind" & The Final Frontier: A Revaluation of Values Constituting the International Legal Regime for Outer Space Activities, 26 *Rutgers L.J.* 225, 250 (1994).

[126] R. Thomas Rankin, Space Tourism: Fanny Packs, Ugly T-Shirts, and the Law in Outer Space, 36 *Suffolk University Law Review* 695 (2003).

[127] James L. Reed, "The Commercial Space Launch Market and Bilateral Trade Agreements in Space Launch Services", 13 *American University International Law Review* 175 (1997).

[128] E.J. Reinstein, Owing Outer Space, 20 *Nw. J. Int'l L. & Bus.* 62 (1999).

[129] Reis, Some Reflections on the Liability Convention for Outer Space, 6 *Journal of Space Law* 127 (1978).

[130] G.H. Reynolds, Outer Space and Peace: Some Thoughts on Structures and Relations, 59 *Tenn. Law Review* 731 (1992).

[131] G.H. Reynolds, International Space Law: Into the Twenty-First Century, 25 *Vanderbilt Journal of Transnational Law* 225 (1992).

[132] Lawrence L. Risley, An Examination of the Need to Amend Space Law to Protect the Private Explorer in Outer Space, 26 *W. St.U.L. Rev.* 47 (1998-1999).

[133] L.R. Roberts, Orbital Debris: Another Pollution Problem for the International Legal Community, 11 *Florida Journal of International Law*, 622 (1997).

[134] I.H.Ph. de Rode-Verschoor, Observations on Comparing the Responsibility for Damage Caused by Space Craft and that Caused by Nuclear Installations and Nuclear-Powered Ships, *Proceedings 4th Colloquium on the Law of Outer Space* 329 (Washington, 1961).

[135] Charity Trelease Ryabinkin, Let there be Flight: It's Time to Reform the Regulation of Commercial Space Travel, 69 *Journal of Air Law and Commerce* 129 (Winter 2004).

[136] A.F. dos Santos, Financing of Space Assets, 19 *Space Policy* 128-129 (2003).

[137] Rosanna Sattler, US Commercial Activities aboard the International Space Station, 28 *Air & Space Law* 70-71 (2003).

[138] Oscar Schachter, Philip Jessup's Life and Ideas, 80 *American Journal of International Law* 878, 894 (1986).

[139] K.U. Schrogl & C. Davis, A New Look at the "Launching State": The Result of the UNCOPUOS Legal Subcommittee Working Group "Review of the Concept of the Launching State" 2000-2002, *Proceedings 44th Colloquium on the Law of Outer Space*, 286-301 (Huston, 2002).

[140] Schwartz & M.L. Berlin, After the Fall: An Analysis of Canadian Legal Claims for Damage Caused by Cosmos 954, 27 *McGill Law Journal* 676 (1982).

[141] Jennifer M. Seymour, Containing the Cosmic Crisis: A Proposal for Curbing the Perils of Space Debris, 10 *Georgetown International Environmental Law Review* 899-900 (1998).

[142] G.C. Sgrosso, International Legal Aspects of Commercialization of Private Enterprise Space Activities, *Proceedings 30th Colloquium on the Law of Outer Space* 251-262 (Brighton, 1987).

[143] A.L. Shapiro, The Disappearance of Cyberspace and the Risk of Code, 8 *Seton Hall Constitutional Law Journal 703* (1998).

[144] L.B. Sherman, "Widely Enthusiastic" About the First Multilateral Agreement on Trade in Telecommunications Services, 51 *Federal Communications Law Journal* 62 n.3 (1998).

[145] Jocelyn H. Shoemaker, The Patent in Space Act: Jedi Mind Trick or Real Protection for American Inventors on the International Space Station, 6 *Journal of Intellectual Property* 395 (1999).

[146] Delbert D. Smith, The Technical, Legal, and Business Risks of Orbital Debris, 6 *New York University Environmental Law Journal* 55 (1997).

[147] M.S. Smith, Legal Aspects of Using Nuclear Reactors on the Moon, *Proceedings 35th Colloquium on the Law of Outer Space* 312 (1992).

[148] Henry Spkplski, U.S. Satellites to China. 27 *International Defense Review* (April 1994).

[149] Bruce Stackfish, Space Transportation and the Need for New International Legal and Institutional Regime, 17 *Annals of Air & Space Law* 359 (1992).

[150] Stott, Making Space Profitable: the Role of Law and Policy, 2004 Space Law Conference Paper Assemble 119-123 (Beijing, 2004).

[151] Mark J. Sundahl, Unidentified Orbital Debris: The Case for a Market-Share Liability Regime, 24 *Hastings International & Comparative Law Review* 137-138 (2000).

[152] S. Tai & T. Bissett, 2000 Manfred Lachs Space Law Moot Court Competition: Winning Briefs: Respondent Brief, 13 *Georgetown International Environmental Law Review* 328-329 (Fall 2000).

[153] David Tan, Towards a New Regime for the Protection of Outer Space as the "Province of All Mankind", 25 *Yale Journal of International Law* 145, 193 (2000).

[154] Nina Tannenwald, Law Versus Power On the High Frontier: The Case for a Rule-Based Regime for Outer Space, 29 *Yale Journal of International Law* 363, 419 (2004).

[155] A.D. Terekhov, The 1986 IAEA Conventions on Nuclear Accidents and the Consideration of the Use of Nuclear Power Sources in Outer Space in the Legal Subcommittee of COPUOS, *Proceedings 30th Colloquium on the Law of Outer Space* 403 (1987).

[156] A.D. Terekhov, International Responsibility for Using Nuclear Power Sources in Outer Space – Reflections on the text adopted by COPUOS, *Proceedings 34th Colloquium on the Law of Outer Space* 147-149 (1991).

[157] A.D. Terekhov, Review and Revision of the Principles Relevant to the Use of Nuclear Power Sources in Outer Space, *Proceeding 36th Colloquium on the Law of Outer Space* 340 (1993).

[158] A.D. Terekhov, U.N.G.A. Resolutions and Outer Space Law, *Proceedings of the 4oth Colloquium on the Law of Outer Space 101* (1998).

[159] Jonathan C. Thomas, Spatialis Liberum, 7 *Florida Coastal Law Review* 579 (Summer 2006).

[160] J.C. Thompson, Comment, Space for Rent: The International Telecommunications Union, Space Law, and Orbit/Spectrum Leasing, 62 *Journal of Air Law and Commerce* 20 (1996).

[161] James S. Trimble, The International Law of Outer Space and Its Effect on Commercial Space Activity, 11 *Pepp. L.Rev.* 521, 530 (1984).

[162] T.S. Twibell, Space Law: Legal Restraints on Commercialization and Development of Outer Space, 65 UMKC Law Review 589, 591 (1997).

[163] T.S. Twibell, Circumnavigating International Space Law, 4 ILSA Journal of International & Comparative Law 259 (1997).

[164] Vladlen S. Vereshchetin & Gennady M. Danilenko, Custom as a Source of International Law of Outer Space, 13 *Journal of Space Law* 32 (1985).

[165] V. Vereschetin & E. Kamenetskya, On the Way to a World Space Organization, 12 *Annals of Air & Space Law* 337 (1987).

[166] H.A. Wassenbergh, A Launch and A Space Transportation Law, Separate from Outer Space Law?, 21 *Air & Space Law* 28 (1996).

[167] H.A. Wassenbergh, International Space Law: A Turn of the Tide, 22 *Air & Space Law* 334 (1997).

[168] A.D. Watson & W.G. Schmidt, Legal Issues Surrounding the International Space Station, 1 *USAFA Journal of Legal Studies* 159 (1996).

[169] A.D. Watson & W.G. Schmidt, Legal Issues Surrounding the International Space Station, 7 *USAFA Journal of Legal Studies* 172 (1996/1997).

[170] Allen Duane Webber, Extraterrestrial Law on the Final Frontier: A Regime to Govern the Development of Celestial Body Resources, 71 *Geo. L.J.* 1427, 1453-54 (1983).

[171] Edith Brown Weiss, International Environmental Law: Contemporary Issues and the Emergence of a New World Order, 81 *Geo. L.J.* 675, 704 (1993).

[172] C.D. Williams, Space: The Cluttered Frontier', *Journal of Air Law & Commerce*, Vol. 60, 1148 (1995).

[173] M. Williams, Perceptions on the Definition of a "Launching State" and Space Debris Risks, *Proceedings 44th Colloquium on the Law of Outer Space*, 285 (Huston, 2002).

[174] H. Wong, The Paper "Satellite" Chase: The ITU Prepares for its Final Exam in Resolution 18, 63 *Journal of Air Law and Commerce* 681-682 (May/June, 1998).

[175] Sylvia Maureen Williams, The Law of Outer Space and Natural Resources, 36 *International Law & Comparative Law Quarterly* 142, 145 (1987).

[176] D.L. Willson, An Army View of Neutrality in Space: Legal Options for Space Negation, *Air Force Law Review*, Vol. 50, 191 (2001).

[177] S. Zaman, Building International Cooperation through ISY, *IEEE Technology and Society Magazine* 32-33 (1992).

[178] K.M. Zullo, The Need to Clarify the Status of Property Rights in International Space Law, 90 *Georgetown Law Journal* 2413-2444 (July 2002).

C. Newspaper Reports

[1] Walter Sullivan, Course Recorded – Navy Picks Up Radio Signals – 4 Report Sighting Device, New York Times, 5 October 1957, A1.

[2] John Noble Wilford, A Powdery Surface Closely Explored, New York Times, 20 July 1969, A1.

[3] Andrew Lawler, U.S. to Confront China on Launch Sales, Space News, No. 26, Vol. 1, at 29, 9-15 July 1990.

[4] G. Milhollin & G. White, A New China syndrome: Beijing's Atomic Bazzar, Washington Post, C1; 12 May 1991.

[5] James H. Andrews, US Changes Tack on Ocean Treaty, Christian Science Monitor, 8 May 1994.

[6] Janet Guyong, Satellite Venture Seeks Shortcut to Space: Global Partners to Fire Rockets from Sea Along Equator, The Wall Street Journal, 20 March 1996.

[7] SS/Loral Inks Multimillion Dollar Launch Deal with Arianespace, Satellite News, 6 May 1996.

[8] Satellite Owners Get Big Price Break from New Launch Suppliers, Space Business News, 8 January 1997.

[9] Is Cassini Risky? Look to Facts, Not Emotion, 147 Aviation Week & Space Technology, No. 13, 29 September 1997.

[10] Eilene Galloway, Status of the Moon Treaty, Space News, 3-9 August 1998.

[11] Craig Covault, Policy and Technology Shape Manned Spaces Ops, Aviation Week & Space Techology, 8 January 2001.

[12] Anna Badkhen, US Tourist Arrives at Space Station: Tito is Greeted by Russians After Weekend Flight, Boston Global, 1 May 2001, C4.

[13] Peter Baker, U.S., Russia Agree to Allow "Space Tourists", Washington Post, 10 August 2001, A20.

[14] P. Pae, NASA Seeks $1 Billion for Nuclear Propulsion Plan, Los Angeles Times, 7 February 2002.

[15] South African Tourist Docks at Space Station, Los Angeles Times, 28 April 2002, A10.

[16] Russia Out to Retain Quarter of Space Market-Koptev, ITAR-TASS News Agency, 1 November 2004.

[17] Julie Blondeau, Launchers: Competing for Customer Satisfaction, 20 Via Satellite, No. 3, 1 March 2005.

[18] China's Fourth Satellite Launching Center Likely to be Built in Southernmost Province, Xinhua News Agency, Xinhua General News Services, 11 March 2005.

[19] China to Export First Chinese Satellite, Xinhua General News Service, Xinhua News Agency, 12 April 2005.

[20] China Launches New Commercial Communication Satellite, Beijing, Agency France Press, 12 April 2005.

[21] China to Launch Another Satellite for Hong Kong Firm: Space Firm, Xinhua General News Service, Xinhua News Agency, Beijing, 13 April 2005.

D. INTERNET RESOURCES

[1] Office of Technology Licensing, University of Florida, Invention and Inventorship to Potential Inventors, <http://www.rgp.ufl.edu/otl/inventorship.html>

[2] A.M. Balsano, ESA Legal Affairs, Paris, Intellectual Property Rights and Space Activities, <http://esapub.esrin.esa.it/ecsl/ecsl15/ecsl15ba.htm>

[3] African Space Tourist Ends $20 Million Odyssey, 5 May 2002, <http://edition.cnn.com/2002/TECH/space/05/04/africa.tourist>

[4] Alexander Witze, Here Comes the Space Competition, *The Dalla Morning News*, 7 September 2003, <http://www.globalsecurity.org/org/news/2003/030907-space01.htm>

[5] Anders Lindskold, Space Tourism and Its Effects on Space Commercialization, Master of Space Studies Program 1998/99, <http://www.spacefuture.com/pr/archive/space_tourism_and_its_effects_on_space_commercialization.shtml>

[6] Andre Farand, Head of new initiatives, ESA legal department, Astronauts' behaviour onboard the International Space Station: Regulatory Framework, <http://portal.unesco.org/shs/en/file_download.php/785db0eec4e0cdfc43e1923624154cccFarand.pdf>.

[7] B. Behrhorst, *Nuclear Rocket Power in Space: Generational Legacy*, <http://www.nuclearspace.com>

[8] Brazil Expects to Further Space Technology Cooperation with China, Xinhua News Agency, 22 October 2003, <http://www.china.org.cn>

[9] Bryan E. Erickson & Gary C. Fisher, Mars Society Steering Committee, Mar Foundation, Treasurer & Design Team, Space Patents: Intellectual Property in Outer Space, presentation at the 8th Mars Society Convention, 12 August 2005, <http://www.marshome.org/files2/SPACE –PATENTS-MS2005.ppt>

[10] China, Brazil to Jointly Launch a 2nd Satellite, *China Daily*, 5 March 2002, <http://www.china.org.cn/english/2002/Mar/28110.htm>

[11] China's Space Industry Flying High, 23 November 2000, Xinhua News Agency, <http://www.chinagate.com.cn>

[12] Chinese Launch could Signal New Space Race: Nation's First Taionaut Blasts Off Early Wednesday, <http://edition.cnn.com/2003/TECH/space/10/14/space/race/index.html>

[13] Decision Paper on Russian Aviation and Space Agency (Rosaviakosmos) Request for MCB Approval of Exemption to Fly Mr. Dennis Tito Abroad the April 2001 Soyuz 2

Taxi Flight to the International Space Station, April 24, 2001, <<http://ftp.hq.nasa.gov/pub/pao/reports/2001/tito<uscore>decision.pdf>>

[14] First Chinese to have Space Travel, <http://news.creaders.net/headline/newsPool/30A220050.html>

[15] Foreign Launch Vehicles, US Centennial of Flight Commission, <http://www.centennialofflight.gov/essay/SPACEFLIGHT/foreign_launch_vehicl…>

[16] Franceska O. Schroeder, Developments in Agreements on International Trade in Commercial Launch Services, ECSL News No. 16, May 1996, <http://esapub.esrin.esa.it/ecsl/ecsl16/schr16.htm>

[17] Clark, *Will Nuclear Power Pull Humans on Mars?*, <http://www.space.com>

[18] G.M. Steinberg, Satellite Capabilities of Emerging Space-competent States, <http://faculty.biu.ac.il/~steing/military/sat.htm>

[19] House Floor Debate on Commercial Space Launch Act of 2004, House of Representatives, 19 November 2004, <http://www.spaceref.com/news/viewsr.html?pid=14565>

[20] H.R. 3752, 108th Congress, 2nd Session, Report No. 108-429, <http://www/theorator.com/bills108/hr3752.html>

[21] Intellectual Property and the Internet Space Station: Creation, Use, Transfer, and Ownership and Protection, <http://www.hq.nasa.gov/ogc/iss/index.html>

[22] *International Seabed Authority: From Wikipedia, The Free Encyclopedia*, <http://en.wikipedia.org/wiki/International _Seabed_Authority>

[23] *International Space Station Framework*, <http://www.esa.int/esaHS/ESAH700VMOC_iss_0.html>

[24] International Space Station—Introduction, <http://www.estec.esa.nl/spaceflight/issintro.htm>

[25] Jim Banke, Space Tourist Pays His Full Fare, <http://www.msnbc.com/news/509288.asp>

[26] Jonathon N. Goodrich, Jerry Haar & Manuel A. Mindreau, Third World Activities in Space Commercialization: A Note, April 1996, <http://www.docentes.uo.edu.pe/Mnindreau/docs/Space%20Commercialization.PDF>

[27] Launch of the Sino-Brazilian satellite makes Brazil self-sufficient in remote sensing radar, Agencia Brasil, Arab Brazilian Chamber of Commerce, <http://www.anba.com.br/ingles/noticia.php?id=470>

[28] Leonard David, What Next for China? Friendly Competition or New Cold War?, 17 October 2003, <http://www.space.com/missionlaunches/china_future_031017.html>

[29] Linda A. Williams, Launch Vehicles Price Elasticity of Demand, Space Technology and Application International Forum. 13 February 2001, Futron Corporation, <http://www.futron.com/pdf/STFELST.PDF>

[30] Marco Caceres, Near-Team Outlook for Satellite Launches, *Aerospace America*, 2005年4月, <http://www.rsicopyright.com/ics/prs_request.html>

[31] Marjorie Ann Browne, *Law of the Sea: the International Seabed Authority – Its Status and U.S. Participation Therein*, 1996年9月16日, <http://www.ncseonline.org/NLE/CRSreports/Marine/mar-22.cfm?&CFID=16587223&CFTOKEN=99935987>

[32] K. Grossman, Plutonium in Space (Again!), Global Network Against Weapons and Nuclear Power in Space, Covert Action Quarterly, No. 73, Summer 2002, <http://www.globenet.free-online.co.uk/articles/morenukesinspace.htm>

[33] L. David, *NASA to Seek Nuclear-Powered Spaceflight Alternatives*, 1 February 2002, <http://cndyorks.gn.apc.org>

[34] Marco Caceres, Launch Market Takes a Wrong Turn, Industry Insights, at 12, *Aerospace America*, America Institute of Aeronautics and Astronautics, Inc., February 2005, <http://www.rsicopyright.com/ics/prc_main/prs_request.html>

[35] Michael Cabbage, China Finds Launches Lucrative, Taiwan Security Research, 10 December 2001, <http://www.orlandosentinel.com>

[36] Michael Wollersheim, Considerations towards the Legal Framework of Space Tourism, 2nd International Symposium on Space Tourism, Bremen, April 21-23, 1999, <http://www.spacefuture.com/archive/considerations_towards_the _legal_framework_of_space_tourism.shtml>

[37] NASA Administrator Honaorable Sean Okeefe, *NASA Biography of Okeefe*, <http://www.nasa.gov/bios/okeefe.html>

[38] Normal Space Commercial Cooperation Between China and US Must Not be Jeopardized, 7 January 1999, <http://www.fas.org/news/china/1999/990107-prc-lv.htm>

[39] NPC Deputies Push for New Satellite Launch Center, *People's Daily Online*, <http://english.people.com.cn/200303/06/print20030306_112787.html>

[40] OFTA, Determination under Section 36A of the Telecommunication Ordinance for Interconnection Between Hong Kong Telephone Company Limited and New T&T Hong Kong Limited, Statement of the Telecommunications Authority, <http://www.ofta.gov.hk/tas/interconnect/ta980821.html>

[41] OFTA, Telecommunications Authority Takes Regulatory Action against Anti-Competitive [sic] Practices of Hong Kong Telecom, <http://www.ofta.gov.hk/press/pr98.html#fm29>

[42] Patent Perspectives, <http://www.ladas.com/patents/patpers.html>

[43] Patrick Collins, The Regulatory Agenda for the Era of Passenger Space Transportation, Proceedings of 20th ISTS, Paper No. 96-f-13, <http://www.spacefuture.com/archive/the_regulatory_reform_agenda_for_the_era_of_passenger_space_transportation.shtml>

[44] Patrick Collins & Koichi Yonemoto, Legal and Regulatory Issues for Passenger Space Travel, *Proceedings 49th Colloquium on the Law of Outer Space*, <http://www.spacefuture.com/pr/archive/legal_and_regulatory_issues_for_passenger_space_travel.shtml>

[45] Premier City for Business: Infrastructure, <http://www.business.gov.hk>

[46] Richard D. Fisher, JR., Commercial Space Cooperation Should Not Harm National Security, No. 1198, The Heritage Foundation, 26 June 1998, <http://www.heritage.org>

[47] Satellite Launches in the PRC-Loral, the Robinson Rojas Archive: China's Intelligence on US Nuclear Arsenal, <http://www.rrojasdatabank.org>

[48] Space Law: China's Regulations, World Security Institute, China-US Dialogue on Space, <http://www.wischina.org/subprogram.cfm?subprogramid=2&charid=1#00008>

[49] Space Tourism in Science Fiction, <http://www.spacefuture.com/tourism/sciencefiction.shtml>

[50] Statement by the Board of Directors of the International Institute of Space Law (IISL) on Claims to Property Rights Regarding the Moon and Other Celestial Bodies, <http://www.iafastro-iisl.com/downloads/statement_moon_2004.doc>

[51] Stephaniel Paul, *Joint Ownership of Patents: A to Z*, <http://www.legalzoom.com/articles/article_content/article14005.html >

[52] Stephen Clark, China Launches First Commercial Spacecraft in Six Years, *Spaceflight Now*, 13 April 2005, <http://www.space.com/missionlaunches/sfn_longmarch_apstar6_050413.html>

[53] STS-107: Columbia Disaster, 1 February 2003, <http://www.space.com/columbiatragedy>

[54] The First Chinese Tourist Expected to Explore in Space Next Year, 28 February 2005, <http://tour.huash.com/gb/tour/2005-02/28/content_1668183.htm>

[55] The First Cosmonaut in the World is in Space, 1 April 1998, <http://news.bbc.co.uk/1/hi/special_report/1998/03/98/gagarin/72182.stm>

[56] The Protection of Intellectual Property Rights in Outer Space of the EU and Thailand, <http://www.thailawforum.com/articles/ipspacenoichim.html>

[57] The Return of Space Nuclear Reactors, Secrecy News from the FAS Project on Government Secrecy, Vol. 2002, 31 January 2002, <http://cndyorks.gn/apc.org>

[58] World Intellectual Property Organization, Model Law for Developing Countries on inventions, <http://www.wipo.int/eng/general/ipc/manual/manual1.htm>

[59] World Wide Pritt – Space Proof Quality, <http://www.prittworld.com/space_proof/index_hau.htm>

[60] Y. Chen, *CBERS and its Application*, <http://www.cnsa.gov.cn/espacechina/v3n7.htm>

[61] Yasuaki Hashimoto, The Space Plane and International Space Law, <http://www.spacefuture.com/pr/archive/the_space_plane_and_international…>

E. TREATIES AND OTHER INSTRUMENTS

[1] Commercial Space Launch Act 1984 (US).

[2] Convention Establishing the World Intellectual Property Organization, 14 July 1967, Art. 2, para Viii, 21 U.S.T. 1770, 828 U.N.T.S. 3.

[3] ESA/C/290, rev. 5.

[4] Final Environmental Impact Statement for the Cassini Mission, National Aeronautics and Space Administration, Solar System Exploration Division, Office of Space Science, June 1995.

[5] G.A. Res. 1348, 12 U.N. GAOR Supp. (No. 18) at 5, U.N. Doc. A/4090 (1958).

[6] Guidance Note for the Satellite Facility Provider and Those Interested in Making Use of Broadcasting-Satellite Service Channels to Provide Broadcasting Services in Hong Kong.

[7] ICAO Doc. 7838, 9201 (1929).

[8] International Law Association Resolution 1/2002: Space Law (2002).

[9] Law of the Russian Federation on Space Activities.

[10] Legislative Council Brief: The Licensing of Broadcasting Satellite Service, File Ref.: ITBB(CR) 9/2/14 (00) Pt.3.

[11] Legislative Council Economic Services Panel Paper: Localization of Laws: Outer Space Bill, Economic Services Branch, April 1997.

[12] Marcia Smith, 93062: Space Launch Vehicle: Government Requirements and Commercial Competition, Congressional Research Service Issue Brief for Congress, 2 July 1998.

[13] Marguerite B. Broadwell, ISS Commercial Development Manager, National Aeronautics and Space Administration, Intellectual Property and the Economic Development of the International Space Station, Presentation on the Space Technology and Applications International Forum (STAIF-2000), Albuquerque, NM, February 2000.

[14] National Aeronautics & Space Administration, NASA Safety Standard: Guidelines and Assessment Procedures for Limiting Orbital Debris A-1 & A-2 (August 1995).

[15] New Solar Cells with Record Efficiency, ESA Press Information Note No. 0794, 29 April 1994.

[16] North Sea Continental Cases, 1969 ICJ 3.

[17] Outer Space Act 1986 (UK).

[18] Patent Ordinance (Cap. 514) (HK).

[19] Proceedings of the United Nations/Republic of Korea Workshop on Space Law: United Nations Treaties on Outer Space: Actions at the National Level, Office for Outer Space Affairs, United Nations Office at Vienna, ST/SPACE/22, 137-139 (New York, 2004).

[20] *SmithKline Beecham Corp. v. Apotex Corp.*, Fed. Cir., No. 04-1522.

[21] Statement of Gary R. Bachula, Acting Undersecretary for Technology, US Department of Commerce, US Commercial Space Launch Industry: Hearing before the Subcommittee on Science, Technology and Space of the Senate Committee on Commerce, Science, and Transportation, 105th Congress (1998).

[22] The Manual of Patent Examining Procedure of the U.S. Patent and Trademark Office, s. 2113, quoting *In Re Thorpe*, 777 F.2d 695, 698, 227 USPQ 964, 966 (Fed.Cir. 1985).

[23] UN Doc. A/AC.105/787, at 10 (2002).

[24] White House Fact Sheet, Presidential Directive on National Space Policy (19 September 1996).

[25] World Trade Organization: Agreement on Telecommunications Services (Fourth Protocol to the General Agreement on Trade in Services) 36 I.L.M. 354 (1997).

APPENDIX

REGULATIONS OF THE PEOPLE'S REPUBLIC OF CHINA ON TELECOMMUNICATION

Chapter 1. General Principles

Article 1

In order to standardize the order of the telecommunication market, to maintain the legal rights and interests of the telecommunication users the telecommunication business operators, to safeguard the telecommunication network and information security, and to promote the healthy development of the telecommunication industry, these Regulations are hereby formulated.

Article 2

Engaging in telecommunication activities or activities related to the telecommunication with in the territories of the People's Republic of China must abide by these Regulations.

The "telecommunication" as referred to herein shall mean activities of transmitting, transporting, or receiving sound, words, data, image, and other information through wireless or cable electromagnetic system or photoelectric system.

Article 3

The administrative departments in charge of information industry of the State Council shall implement the supervision over and administration of the national telecommunication industry in the light of these Regulations.

The administrative departments in charge of information industry of all provinces, autonomous regions, and municipalities directly under the Central People's Government shall implement the supervision over and administration of telecommunication industry within their respective administrative regions under the guidance of the administrative departments in charge of information industry of the State Council according to these Regulations.

Article 4

Supervision over and administration of telecommunication shall abide by the principles of separating governmental functions and enterprise management, uprooting the monopoly, encouraging competition, accelerating the development, publicity, equity, and fairness.

Telecommunication business operators must operate according to law, abide by commercial morals, and accept the legal supervision and inspection.

Article 5

Telecommunication business operators shall provide prompt, accurate, safe, and convenient telecommunication service with reasonable price to the telecommunication users.

Article 6

Security of telecommunication network and information shall be protected by laws. Any organization or individual shall not engage in activities that imperil the state security, social public benefits or legal rights and interests of others by means of telecommunication network.

Chapter 2. Telecommunication Market

Section 1. License to Telecommunication Business

Article 7

The State classifies the telecommunication business operation according to telecommunication business and implements the license system thereof.

In order to operate the telecommunication business, the operators must obtain in advance the license to operating telecommunication business issued by the administrative departments in charge of information industry of the State Council or the administrative departments in charge of telecommunication of all provinces, autonomous regions, and municipalities directly under the central People's Government in the light of these Regulations.

Any organization or individual shall not engage in telecommunication business activities without the license to operating telecommunication business.

Article 8

The telecommunication business is divided into basic telecommunication business and value-added telecommunication business.

The basic telecommunication business shall mean the business of providing the public network infrastructures, the public data transmission, and the basic sound communication service. The value-added telecommunication business shall mean the business of telecommunication and information service by means of the public network infrastructures.

The detailed classification of the telecommunication business is listed into the attached Catalogue of Telecommunication Business Classification. The administrative departments in charge of information industry of the State Council may adjust partially the items as listed by the aforesaid catalogue and make second proclamation according to practical conditions.

Article 9

The operators, in order to engage in the basic telecommunication business, must be examined and approved by the administrative departments in charge of information industry of the State Council and obtain the License to Operating Basic Telecommunication Business.

The operators, in order to engage in the value-added telecommunication business with coverage of more than two provinces, autonomous regions, or municipalities directly under the Central People's Government, must be examined and approval by the administrative departments in charge of information industry of the State Council and obtain the License to Operating Trans-regional Value-added Telecommunication Business. The operator, in order to engage in the value-added telecommunication business with coverage of just one province, autonomous regions, or municipalities directly under the Central People's Government, must be examined and approved by the administrative departments in charge of telecommunication of all provinces, autonomous regions, and municipalities directly under the central People's Government and obtain the License to Operating Value-added Telecommunication Business.

The operator, in order to engage in trial telecommunication business that is not listed by the Catalogue of Telecommunication Business Classification with new technology, shall apply to the administrative departments in charge of telecommunication of all provinces, autonomous regions, and municipalities directly under the central People's Government for records.

Article 10

In order to operate the basic telecommunication business, the following qualifications must be owned by the operator:

(1) The operator must be the specialized company engaging in the basic telecommunication business that is established according to law and the Chinese stock rights shall be no less than 51%;
(2) Having the feasibility study report and network construction scheme;
(3) Having corresponding funds and professionals engaging in operation;
(4) Having places and corresponding resources engaging in operation;
(5) Having good reputation or capacity to provide long-term service for users; and
(6) Other qualifications as provided by the State.

Article 11

Application for operating the basic telecommunication business with the relevant documents as specified by Article 10 herein shall be filed to the administrative departments in charge of information industry of the State Council. The administrative departments in charge of information industry of the State Council shall complete the inspection and make the decision of approval or non-approval within one hundred and eighty days upon the acceptance of the application. The License to Operating Basic Telecommunication Business shall be issued to the qualified applicant, and written notice with explanation shall be given to the unqualified applicant.

Article 12

When inspecting the application for operating the basic telecommunication business, the administrative departments in charge of information industry of the State Council shall take consideration of the state security, telecommunication network security, continuous use of telecommunication resources, environmental protection, competition of the telecommunication market, and so on.

The License to Operating Basic Telecommunication Business shall be issued by means of bidding according to the relevant provisions of the State.

Article 13

Qualifications specified as follows shall be owned by the operator in order to operate the basic telecommunication business:

(1) The operator shall be the company established according to law;
(2) Having corresponding funds and professionals engaging in operation;
(3) Having good reputation or capacity to provide long-term service for users; and
(4) Other qualifications as provided by the State.

Article 14

Application for operating the value-added telecommunication business with the relevant documents as specified by Article 13 of these Regulations shall be filed according to provisions as specified by Article 9 Paragraph 2 of these Regulations to the administrative departments in charge of information industry of the State Council or the administrative departments in charge of telecommunication of all provinces, autonomous regions, and municipalities directly under the central People's Government. If the value-added telecommunication business is required to be examined and approved by the relevant administration, the approval document of the same administration shall be also submitted. The administrative departments in charge of information industry of the State Council or the administrative departments in charge of telecommunication of all provinces, autonomous regions, and municipalities directly under the central People's Government shall complete the inspection and make the decision of approval or non-approval within sixty days upon the acceptance of the application. The License to Operating Trans-regional Value-added Telecommunication Business or License to Operating Value-added Telecommunication Business shall be issued to the qualified applicant, and written notice with explanation shall be given to the unqualified applicant.

Article 15

In the course of operating telecommunication business, in order to alter the operation principal or business scope or to stop business, an application must be filed to the original license-issuing departments ninety days in advance and the corresponding procedures must be completed. If the operation is stopped, the aftermath work shall be completed according to the relevant provisions of the State.

Article 16

The operator engaging in the telecommunication business shall obtain the License to Operating Telecommunication Business according to law and shall complete the registration procedures with the enterprise registration authorities.

The special telecommunication network operation unit, if engaging in the telecommunication business within his location, shall file an application in the light of provisions as specified by this Article. Upon obtaining the License to Operating Telecommunication Business under approval, this unit may complete the aforesaid registration procedures.

Section 2. Telecommunication Inter- Connection between Networks

Article 17

Thė telecommunication networks shall be connected one another according to principles of feasible technology, economy, equity, justness, and mutual coordination.

The leading telecommunication business operators shall not refuse the request on inter-connection between networks as raised by other telecommunication business operators and special network operation units.

The leading telecommunication business operators as referred herein shall mean the operators who control necessary basic telecommunication infrastructures, take relatively large share of the telecommunication market, and can affect other telecommunication business operators for entering the telecommunication business market substantially.

The leading telecommunication business operators shall be defined by the administrative departments in charge of information industry of the State Council.

Article 18

The leading telecommunication business operators shall formulate the inter-connection regulations, including programming, time limit, non-binding element catalogues, and so on according to the principles of non-discrimination and openness. The inter-connection regulations shall be reported to the administrative departments in charge of information industry of the State Council for examination and approval. The leading telecommunication business operators shall be bounded by these inter-connection regulations.

Article 19

The inter-connection between the public telecommunication networks, or between the public telecommunication network and the special telecommunication network shall be based on the inter-connection negotiation between both parties according to administrative rules of the administrative departments in charge of information industry of the State Council on inter-connection between networks. The inter-connection agreement therout shall be entered into by both parties of inter-connection.

The inter-connection agreement shall be reported to the administrative departments in charge of information industry of the State Council for records.

Article 20

If the inter-connection parties do not reach an inter-connection agreement according to negotiation, any party may apply for coordination to the administrative departments in charge of information industry of the State Council or the administrative departments in charge of telecommunication of all provinces, autonomous regions, and municipalities directly under the central People's Government according to the coverage of the inter-connection agreement within sixty days upon the raising date of the inter-connection request. The departments receiving the application shall coordinate them according to the principles as specified by Article 17 Paragraph 1 and urge both parties to reach an agreement. If there is no agreement according to coordination within forty-five days upon the application date for coordination, the coordinating departments may invite telecommunication technology experts and other experts at random to demonstrate the relevant matters in public and lodge inter-connection scheme. The coordinating departments shall make decision in the light of the conclusion and inter-connection scheme of these experts to realize the mandatory inter-connection between networkss

Article 21

Both parties of inter-connection shall realize the inter-connection between networks within the time limit as stipulated by the agreement or as provided by the decision. Any party shall not disconnect the inter-connection between networks without approval of the administrative departments in charge of information industry of the State Council. The technological breakdown to the inter-connection between networks shall be settled by both parties through immediate and effective measures. Disputes to the inter-connection between networks shall be settled according to procedures and measures as specified by Article 20 of these Regulations.

The quality of inter-connection between networks shall comply with relevant standard as provided by the State. If the leading telecommunication business operators provide the inter-connection between networks, the service quality thereof shall not be lower than that of like business within their own network or the like business provided to their subsidiary companies or branches.

Article 22

The settlement and apportion of expenses for inter-connection between networks shall be transacted according to the relevant rules of the State. No additional charges are allowed.

The technical standard, expense settlement measures, and detailed administrative rules on inter-connection between networks shall be formulated by the administrative departments in charge of information industry of the State Council.

Section 3. Telecommunication Charges

Article 23

The price making principle based on costs is applicable to the standard of telecommunication charges. Meanwhile, when making price, the requirement of national economy and social development, development of telecommunication industry, the bearing capacity of users and so on shall be taken consideration of.

Article 24

Telecommunication charges shall be divided into market adjusting price, governmental guidance price and rated price by the governments.

The rated price by the governments, governmental guidance price or market adjusting price are applicable to the basic telecommunication business and the market adjusting price or governmental guidance price is applicable to the value-added telecommunication business.

Only market adjusting price shall be applicable to the telecommunication business with cruel competition.

The administrative classification catalogue for telecommunication charges reflected by the rated price by the governments, governmental guidance price, and market adjusting price shall be formulated and promulgated by the administrative departments in charge of information industry of the State Council based on asking for comments and suggestions of the administrative departments in charge of price control.

Article 25

The scheme for the major telecommunication charges that are rated by the governments shall be lodged by the administrative departments in charge of information industry of the State Council based on asking for comments and suggestions of the administrative departments in charge of price control and shall take effect upon the approval by the State Council.

For the standard range of the telecommunication charges with governmental guidance price shall be formulated and promulgated by the administrative departments in charge of information industry of the State Council shall lodge a scheme based on asking for comments and suggestions of the administrative departments in charge of price control and report it to the State Council. Within the standard range of charges, the telecommunication operators may determine their own charge standards and report them to the administrative departments in charge of telecommunication of all provinces, autonomous regions, and municipalities directly under the central People's Government for records.

Article 26

For the standard of telecommunication charges with rated price by the governments or governmental guidance price, hearing and other manners shall be adopted for hearing comments of telecommunication business operators, telecommunication users and other relevant parties.

The telecommunication business operators shall provide accurate and complete business cost data and other relevant data and documents according to requirements of the administrative departments in charge of information industry of the State Council or the administrative departments in charge of telecommunication of all provinces, autonomous regions, and municipalities directly under the central People's Government.

Section 4. Telecommunication Resources

Article 27

The State implements the involuntary use system to plan uniformly, administer collectively, and distribute reasonably the telecommunication resources.

The telecommunication resources as referred to herein shall mean the limited resources such as radio frequency, satellite orbit location and telecommunication network serial number that are used to realize functions of telecommunication.

Article 28

The telecommunication business operators, when using the telecommunication resources, shall pay telecommunication charges. The detailed charging measures shall be formulated by the administrative departments in charge of information industry of the State Council jointly with the administrative departments in charge of finance an in charge of price control, and shall be promulgated upon the approval of the State Council.

Article 29

The distribution of the telecommunication resources shall take the planning of the telecommunication resources, purposes, and estimated service capacities for consideration.

The distribution of the telecommunication resources may be by means of appointment or auction.

The operator, when obtaining the telecommunication resource use right, shall star using the distributed resources within the specified time limit to reach the specified minimum use scale. The operator shall not use, transfer, lease telecommunication resources or change the purpose of telecommunication resources without approval by the administrative departments in charge of information industry of the State Council or the administrative departments in charge of telecommunication of all provinces, autonomous regions, and municipalities directly under the central People's Government.

Article 30

When the telecommunication resources users obtain the telecommunication network serial number, the leading telecommunication business operators and other relevant units have the obligation to adopt necessary technical measures to help users to realize the function of the telecommunication network serial number.

The special provisions, if any, on the administration of the telecommunication resource, shall be abided by.

Chapter 3. Telecommunication Service

Article 31

The telecommunication business operators shall provide service to the users according to the service standard as stipulated by the relevant provisions of the State. The variety, scope, charging standard, and time limit of service provided by the telecommunication business operators shall be proclaimed to the public and shall be reported to the administrative departments in charge of telecommunication of all provinces, autonomous regions, and municipalities directly under the central People's Government for records.

The telecommunication users have option to select and use various telecommunication services.

Article 32

If the telecommunication users apply for installing or transferring telecommunication terminal equipment, the telecommunication business operators shall ensure the completion and success of the installation or transfer. If the telecommunication business operators cannot complete the installation or transfer, they shall pay the liquidated damages at the rate of one percent of installation charges, transfer charges, or other expenses collected by the operators per day to the telecommunication users.

Article 33

The telecommunication business operators shall repair or modulate the drawback of telecommunication service put forward by the telecommunication users within forty-eight hours for cities and seventy-two hours for rural areas upon the receipt of such application. If the operators cannot repair or debug aforesaid drawback in time successfully, they shall notify the telecommunication users immediately and shall exempt the month-rent charges during the period of drawback. However, the telecommunication service drawback caused by the telecommunication terminal equipment shall be excluded.

Article 34

The telecommunication business operators shall provide convenience for the telecommunication users to pay charges and inquire of relevant information. The lists of charges on domestic long distance, international long distance, mobile communication, and information service, etc., if any required by the telecommunication users, shall be provided by the telecommunication business operators free of charge.

For abnormal enormous amount of telecommunication expenses, the telecommunication business operators shall notify the telecommunication users and take necessary measures upon the discovery of such condition.

The enormous amount of telecommunication expenses as referred herein shall mean the expenses that are five times of the average amount of the previous three months and arise suddenly.

Article 35

Telecommunication users shall pay the telecommunication expenses to the telecommunication business operators with a full amount timely within the stipulated time and by stipulated means. If telecommunication users do not pay telecommunication expenses within the stipulated time, the telecommunication business operators have the right to claim an overdue payment and impose liquidated damages of 3/1000 of the arrears per month to the users.

For the telecommunication users who do not pay their telecommunication expenses thirty days beyond the stipulated time limit, the telecommunication business operators may suspend their telecommunication service. For the telecommunication users who do not pay their telecommunication expenses sixty days beyond the stipulated time limit, the telecommunication business operators may terminates telecommunication service to them and may recourse the overdue charges and liquidated damages.

The operators engaging in mobile telecommunication business may stipulates with the telecommunication users the time limit and means of telecommunication expense payment without being restricted by the time limit as specified by the preceding article.

The telecommunication operators shall resume the suspended telecommunication service to the telecommunication users within forty-eight hours upon the receipt of the complement payment or payment for the deferred telecommunication expenses by the telecommunication users.

Article 36

In case of project construction, network construction, and other causes that will affect or are possible to affect the normal telecommunication service, the telecommunication business operators shall timely notify users within the specified time and report them to the administrative departments in charge of telecommunication of all provinces, autonomous regions, and municipalities directly under the central People's Government.

If the telecommunication service suspends on account of the cause as specified by the preceding paragraph, the telecommunication business operators shall reduce or exempt the expenses related to the suspension period accordingly.

Under the situation as specified by Paragraph 1 of this article, the telecommunication business operators, if failing to notify users, shall compensate for the losses suffered by users thereout.

Article 37

The mobile phone operators engaging in local phone business shall provide fire alarm, robbery alarm, medical emergency alarm, transportation accident alarm, and other public welfare telecommunication service, and keep the smoothness of the communication lines free of charge.

Article 38

The telecommunication business operator shall timely provide equal and reasonable connection service for the group user that needs to be connected into its telecommunication network through trunk lines.

The telecommunication business operator shall not disconnect the connection service without approval.

Article 39

The telecommunication business operators shall build healthy internal quality management system and may formulate and promulgate the enterprise standard that is higher than the national telecommunication service standard.

The telecommunication business operators shall hear comments and suggestions of telecommunication users, accept the social supervision, and improve the telecommunication service quality ceaselessly.

Article 40

If the telecommunication service provided by the telecommunication business operators cannot reach the national telecommunication service standard or their own enterprise standard proclaimed by them, or the users hold demurral to the payment of telecommunication expenses, telecommunication users have the right to claim the settlement by telecommunication business operators. In case telecommunication business operators refuse to settle such matters or telecommunication users do to satisfied with the settlement, telecommunication users have the right to appeal to the administrative departments in charge of information industry of the State Council or the administrative departments in charge of telecommunication of all provinces, autonomous regions, and municipalities directly under the central People's Government or other relevant departments. The department that accepts the appeal shall transact the appeal timely and shall make a reply to the appellant within thirty days upon the receipt of the appeal.

If the telecommunication user holds demurral to the local phone expenses, the telecommunication business operator shall provide local phone bills free of charge upon the request of the user and shall take necessary measures to assist the user to search for causes.

Article 41

The following acts shall be rejected by the telecommunication business operator in the course of operating telecommunication service:

(1) To restrict the telecommunication user to use its designated business by any means;
(2) To restrict the telecommunication user to purchase its designated telecommunication terminal equipment or to refuse to let the user self-prepared telecommunication terminals with license to connection to network;
(3) In violation of provisions of the State to change or change with a disguised form the charging standard, increase or increase with a disguised form the charging items without approval;
(4) To refuse, delay, or stop the telecommunication service to the user without appropriate reasons;
(5) Not to perform its commitment made by it in public or to make false publicity with misleading content; and
(6) To obstruct the user deliberately or to retaliate the user who complain about the telecommunication service.

Article 42

The following acts shall be rejected by the telecommunication business operator in the course of operating telecommunication service:

(1) To restrict the telecommunication user to select the telecommunication service which is established by other telecommunication business operators according to law;
(2) To subsidize different business unreasonably and mutually; and
(3) To conduct illicit competition for squeezing out the competitor by providing telecommunication business or service which is lower than the cost.

Article 43

the administrative departments in charge of information industry of the State Council or the administrative departments in charge of telecommunication of all provinces, autonomous regions, and municipalities directly under the central People's Government shall within their authorities supervise and inspect the telecommunication service quality and operation activities of the telecommunication business operators and proclaim the results of the supervision and inspection.

Article 44

The telecommunication business operators must perform obligations of the corresponding general telecommunication service according to the relevant provisions of the State.

The administrative departments in charge of information industry of the State Council may determine the obligations of general telecommunication service that shall be borne by the telecommunication business operators by means of appointment or bidding.

The cost compensation measures of the general telecommunication service shall be formulated by the administrative departments in charge of information industry of the State Council jointly with the administrative departments in charge of finance and in charge of price control, and shall be implemented upon the approval of the State Council.

Chapter 4. Telecommunication Construction

Section 1. Telecommunication Facility Construction

Article 45

The construction of public telecommunication network, special telecommunication network and radio and television transportation network shall be under the uniform planning and industry administration of the administrative departments in charge of information industry of the State Council.

National information network projects, or the public telecommunication network, special telecommunication network, and radio and television transportation network shall be under the approval by the administrative departments in charge of information industry of the State Council before reporting them for examination and approval according to examination and approval procedures of the national infrastructure projects.

The telecommunication infrastructure projects shall subject to the general plan of city construction, town construction, and village construction of local people's government at various levels.

Article 46

The telecommunication facilities shall be assorted to the city construction, town construction, or village construction. The tubing and lines and distribution within the buildings and the telecommunication tubes covered by the construction projects shall be listed into the design documents and shall be checked and accepted simultaneously with construction projects. Needed outlay thereout shall be counted into the construction project budgetary estimate.

If wishing to plan and construct roads, bridges, tunnels or underground railways and so on, the relevant units or departments shall notify the administrative departments in charge of telecommunication of all provinces, autonomous regions, and municipalities directly under the central People's Government and the telecommunication business operators in advance, and negotiate with them the pre-installation of telecommunication tubes and lines and other related matters.

Article 47

The basic telecommunication business operators may set up the telecommunication lines, small antenna, mobile communication base station and other public telecommunication facilities on the civil buildings. However, they shall notify the owners of these buildings in advance or the users of these buildings, and pay the use charges to the owners or other obligees of these buildings according to the standard as provided by the people's governments of all provinces, autonomous regions, or municipalities directly under the Central People's Governments.

Article 48

The marks for the telecommunication facilities in the water or under the ground and in high altitude shall be set up according to the relevant rules of the State.

In order to construct submarine telecommunication cables, the basic telecommunication business operators shall obtain approval from the administrative departments in charge of information industry of the State Council and complete the relevant procedures according to law based on asking for comments and suggestions of the relevant departments. The submarine cables shall be marked on the marine chart by the relevant department of the State Council.

Article 49

Any unit or individual shall not change or transfer the telecommunication lines and other telecommunication facilities of others. If these lines or facilities must be shifted or transferred in case of special situations, the consent of the owner of the telecommunication facilities shall be obtained in advance, and all expenses for the change or transfer and the economic loss caused thereout shall be borne by the unit or individual who has lodged the request of such change or transfer.

Article 50

Engaging in construction, manufacture, and planting, etc. shall not endanger the security of telecommunication lines or other telecommunication facilities and the smoothness of the lines. In case of endangering the telecommunication security, a notice in advance shall be given to the relevant telecommunication operators, and the unit or individual who engages in this activity shall adopt necessary security measures.

Anyone who, in violation of the preceding provisions, causes damage to the telecommunication lines and other telecommunication facilities, or hinders the non-block of telecommunication lines, shall repair or resume these facilities or non-block of the lines and compensate for economic loss caused thereout.

Article 51

Construction of telecommunication lines shall keep necessary safe distance from the telecommunication lines that have been built up. If the construction cannot avoid or must pass through them or needs to use the built telecommunication tubing, negotiation with the owners of the built telecommunication lines shall be conducted and an agreement shall be entered into with them. If the agreement cannot be reached through negotiation, the administrative departments in charge of information industry of the State Council or the administrative departments in charge of telecommunication of all provinces, autonomous regions, and municipalities directly under the central People's Government shall be responsible for the coordination and settlement according to practical conditions.

Article 52

Any organization or individual shall not obstruct or hinder the basic telecommunication business operators to engage in the telecommunication facility construction and providing public telecommunication service to telecommunication users. However, the special districts that are prohibited from entering or restricted to enter by the State shall be excluded.

Article 53

Telecommunication vehicles executing duties of special communication, emergent communication, rush repair, and emergency dealing may not be restricted by the transportation marks for motor vehicles under the precondition of keeping non-block and security of traffic upon approval of the administrative departments in charge of communications.

Section 2. Connection to the Network

Article 54

The State implements the license system of connection to the network for the telecommunication terminal equipment, wireless telecommunication equipment, and equipment concerning the connection between networks.

Telecommunication terminal equipment, wireless telecommunication equipment and equipment concerning the connection between networks that join up the public telecommunication network must accord with the standard as provided by the State and for them the License to Joining up Network shall be obtained.

The telecommunication equipment catalogues under the license system of connection to the network shall be formulated and promulgated by the administrative departments in charge of information industry of the State Council jointly with the supervisory departments in charge of production quality.

Article 55

For obtaining the license to joining up network for telecommunication equipment, an application shall be to filed to the administrative departments in charge of information industry of the State Council with the inspection report issued by the supervisory departments in charge of production quality of the State Council or the production quality attestation certificate issued by the relevant attestation authorities.

The administrative departments in charge of information industry of the State Council shall complete the examination to the application, telecommunication equipment inspection report or the production quality attestation certificate within sixty days upon the receipt of the application for joining up the network. The License to Joining up Network shall be issued to the qualified applicant, and the written reply with explanation shall be given to the unqualified applicant.

Article 56

Telecommunication equipment manufacturers must ensure that the quality of telecommunication equipment with License to Joining up Network is stable and reliable and they shall not reduce quality and function of products.

Telecommunication equipment manufacturers shall affix the joining-up-network mark on the telecommunication equipment with License to Joining Up Network.

The supervisory departments in charge of production quality of the State Council jointly with the administrative departments in charge of information industry of the State Council shall supervise, and selectively inspect telecommunication equipment with License and proclaim the results of selective inspection.

Chapter 5. Telecommunication Security

Article 57

Any organization or individual shall not make, copy, distribute, and promulgate information with contents specified as follow by means of telecommunication network:

(1) Opposing basic principles confirmed by the Constitution of the People's Republic of China;
(2) Endangering state security, betraying state secret, subverting state political power, breaching state unification;
(3) Damaging state reputation and benefits;
(4) Instigating nationality enmity, nationality discrimination, and undermining the nationality solidarity;
(5) Undermining the state religious policy, preaching illegal religion and feudal superstition
(6) Disseminating rumors, disrupting public order and social stability;
(7) Disseminating obscenity, eroticism, gambling, violence, homicide, horror or abetting crime;
(8) Humiliating or slandering others, and infringing legal rights and interests of others; and
(9) Other contents that are prohibited by laws or administrative regulations.

Article 58

Any organization or individual shall not have any of the following acts endangering telecommunication network security and information security:

(1) Canceling or revising the function of the telecommunication network, data of storage, processing, and transporting, and the application program;
(2) Engaging activities of stealing or undermining information of others and damaging legal rights and interests of others;

(3) Intentionally making, copying, or promulgating a computer virus to attack telecommunication networks and other telecommunication facilities by any means; and
(4) Other acts endangering telecommunication network security or information security.

Article 59

Any organization or individual shall not have any of the following acts of disturbing telecommunication market:

(1) Operating international telecommunication business or telecommunication business to Hong Kong, Macao, and Taiwan by renting international telecommunication lines, privately building transfer equipment or by other means without approval;
(2) Illegally connecting telecommunication lines of others, copying telecommunication serial numbers of others, and using aforesaid telecommunication facilities or serial number intentionally;
(3) Falsifying, altering telephone card and other value vouchers of telecommunication service; and
(4) Completing the joining-up-network procedures with the false national identity card or national identity cards of others and using mobile phone.

Article 60

Telecommunication business operators shall build up the internal security safeguard system and implements the security safeguard responsibility system according to provisions of the State on telecommunication security.

Article 61

In the course of design, construction and operation, telecommunication business operators shall be in strict accordance with requirements of the state security and telecommunication network security.

Article 62

In the course of providing public information service, the telecommunication business operators, if discovering that the transporting information belongs to contents as listed by the Article 57 herein, shall immediately stop transporting such information, keep the record concerned, and report them to the relevant authorities.

Article 63

The telecommunication users shall be responsible for the contents of the telecommunication network information and the consequences thereof.

The telecommunication users, if discovering that the used information belongs to state secret, shall take necessary measures in the light of the provisions of the Law on State Secret.

Article 64

In case of serious natural calamities and other emergencies, the administrative departments in charge of information industry of the State Council may transfer various telecommunication facilities to ensure the un-block of major communication upon approval of the State Council.

Article 65

International communication business in the territory of the People's Republic of China shall be transacted through the international communication entrance and exit established upon approval of the administrative departments in charge of information industry of the State Council.

Communication between the Mainland of the People's Republic of China and the Hong Kong Special Administrative Region, Macao Special Administrative Region, and Taiwan Province shall refer to the preceding paragraphph.

Article 66

Freedom of using telecommunication service according to law and communication secret shall be protected by laws. Any organization or individual shall not inspect the telecommunication contents by any reason, unless the public security organizations or state security organizations or the people's procuratorates inspect the telecommunication contents for the purposes of state security or investigating criminal offenses according to proceedings as provided by laws.

Telecommunication business operators and their staffs shall not provide the users' contents transported by telecommunication networks to others without approval.

Chapter 6. Penalty Provisions

Article 67

Anyone who, in violation of provisions of Article 57 and Article 58 herein, commits a crime shall be prosecuted for his criminal liability according to law. If he does not commit a crime, he shall be given punishment by the public security organization, state security organ according to the relevant laws and administrative regulations.

Article 68

Anyone who, committing one or more acts as specified by Paragraph (2), (3), and (4) of Article 59 herein, disturbs the telecommunication market and commits a crime therefore shall be prosecuted for his criminal liability according to law. If the offence does not constitute a crime, the offender shall be ordered to make corrections by the administrative departments in charge of information industry of the State Council or the administrative departments in charge of telecommunication of all provinces, autonomous regions, and municipalities directly under the central People's Government. The illegal gains, if any, shall be confiscated, and the offender shall be subject to a fine of more than three times but less than five times of the illegal gains. If there are no illegal gains or the illegal gains are less than RMB10, 000, the offender shall be imposed upon a fine of not less than RMB10, 000 but not more than RMB100, 000.

Article 69

Anyone who, in violation of these Regulations, falsifies or transfers the License to Operating Telecommunication Business, License to Joining-up-Network, takes others'

License to Operating Telecommunication Business, License to Joining-up-Network, or fabricates the joining-up-network serial number, shall be imposed a fine of more than three times but less than five times of illegal gains and their illegal gains shall be confiscated by the administrative departments in charge of information industry of the State Council or the administrative departments in charge of telecommunication of all provinces, autonomous regions, and municipalities directly under the central People's Government. If there are no illegal gains or the illegal gains are less than RMB10, 000, the offender shall be subject to a fine of not less than RMB10, 000 but not more than RMB100, 000.

Article 70

Anyone who, in violation of these Regulations, has one of following acts shall be ordered to make corrections by the administrative departments in charge of information industry of the State Council or the administrative departments in charge of telecommunication of all provinces, autonomous regions, and municipalities directly under the central People's Government. The illegal gains hereof, if any, shall be confiscated and a fine of more than three times but less than five times of illegal gains. If there are no illegal gains or the illegal gains are less than RMB50, 000, the offender shall be subject to a fine of not less than RMB100, 000 but not more than RMB1, 000, 000. If the circumstances are serious, the offender shall be ordered to suspend and rectify his business:

(1) Operating telecommunication business or operating telecommunication business beyond the specified business scope in violation of Article 7 Paragraph 3 herein or Article 59 Paragraph 1 herein;
(2) Establishing international communication entrance and exit to operating international communication without approval by the administrative departments in charge of information industry of the State Council;
(3) Using, transferring, or lending telecommunication resources or changing the purpose of telecommunication resources without approval;
(4) Suspending inter-connection between networks or joining-up-network service; or
(5) Refusing to perform general service obligation.

Article 71

Anyone who, in violation of these Regulations, has one of following acts shall be ordered to make corrections by the administrative departments in charge of information industry of the State Council or the administrative departments in charge of telecommunication of all provinces, autonomous regions, and municipalities directly under the central People's Government. The illegal gains hereof, if any, shall be confiscated and a fine of more than one time but less than three times of illegal gains. If there are no illegal gains or the illegal gains are less than RMB10, 000, the offender shall be subject to a fine of not less than RMB10, 000 but not more than RMB100, 000. If the circumstances are serious, the offender shall be ordered to suspend and rectify his business:

(1) Adding charges for inter-connection between networks in violation of the relevant provisions;
(2) Not taking effective measures to avoid drawbacks in case of inter-network communication;

(3) Providing contents that belongs to the telecommunication users and are transported by the telecommunication network to others without approval; or
(4) Refusing to pay expenses for using telecommunication resources according to relevant provisions.

Article 72

Anyone who, in violation of provisions of Article 42 herein, engages in illicit competition in the courses of operating telecommunication business, shall be ordered to make corrections by the administrative departments in charge of information industry of the State Council or the administrative departments in charge of telecommunication of all provinces, autonomous regions, and municipalities directly under the central People's Government. A fine of not less than RMB10, 000 but not more than RMB1, 000, 000 shall be imposed. If the circumstances are serious, the offender shall be ordered to suspend his business for rectificationn.

Article 73

Anyone who, in violation of these Regulations, has one of following acts shall be ordered to make corrections by the administrative departments in charge of information industry of the State Council or the administrative departments in charge of telecommunication of all provinces, autonomous regions, and municipalities directly under the central People's Government. A fine of not less than RMB50, 000 but not more than RMB100, 000 shall be imposed. If the circumstances are serious, the offender shall be ordered to suspend and rectify his business:

(1) Refusing the request of inter-connection raised by other telecommunication business operators;
(2) Refusing to execute the inter-connection decision of the administrative departments in charge of information industry of the State Council or the administrative departments in charge of telecommunication of all provinces, autonomous regions, and municipalities directly under the central People's Government; or
(3) Providing inter-connection service to other telecommunication business operators with inferior quality than that of service to his own network or his subsidiary companies or branches.

Article 74

Any telecommunication business operator who, in violation of Article 34 Paragraph 1 and Article 40 Paragraph 2 herein, refuses to provide the charge lists of domestic long distance, international distance, mobile communication, and information service free of charge to telecommunication users, or refuses to provide local phone bills free of charge in case the telecommunication users lodge demurral to local phone expenses, shall be ordered to make corrections by the administrative departments in charge of information industry of the State Council or the administrative departments in charge of telecommunication of all provinces, autonomous regions, and municipalities directly under the central People's Government, and extend a formal apology to users. If the offender refuses to make corrections or extend a formal apology, he shall be subject to a warning and a fine of not less than RMB5, 000 but not more than RMB50, 000.

Article 75

Any telecommunication business operator, in violation of Article 41 herein, shall be ordered to make corrections by the administrative departments in charge of telecommunication of all provinces, autonomous regions, and municipalities directly under the central People's Government, extend a formal apology to users, and compensate for losses to users. If the offender refuses to make corrections, extend a formal apology, or compensate loss to users, he shall be subject to a warning and a fine of not less than RMB10, 000 but not more than RMB100, 000. If the circumstances are serious, the offender shall be ordered to suspend and rectify his business.

Article 76

Anyone who, in violation of these regulations, has one of the following acts shall be ordered to make corrections by the administrative departments in charge of telecommunication of all provinces, autonomous regions, and municipalities directly under the central People's Government, extend a formal apology to users, and compensate for losses to users. A fine of not less than RMB10, 000 but not more than RMB100, 000 shall be imposed to the offender:

(1) Selling telecommunication terminal equipment without License of Hooking-up-Network;
(2) Illegally preventing or hindering telecommunication business operators to provide public information service to telecommunication users; or
(3) Shifting or transferring telecommunication lines and other telecommunication facilities of others without approval.

Article 77

Anyone who, in violation of these Regulations, reduces quality and functions products after obtaining License to Joining-up-Network, shall be punished by the supervisory departments in charge of production quality according to relevant laws or administrative regulations.

Article 78

Anyone who has one of acts as specified by Article 57, Article 58, and Article 59 with serious circumstances shall have his License to Operating Telecommunication Business revoked by the original license-issuing authorities.

Upon revocation of License to Operating Telecommunication Business, the administrative departments in charge of information industry of the State Council or the administrative departments in charge of telecommunication of all provinces, autonomous regions, and municipalities directly under the central People's Government shall notify the enterprise registration authorities.

Article 79

Any staff member of the administrative departments in charge of information industry of the State Council or the administrative departments in charge of telecommunication of all provinces, autonomous regions, and municipalities directly under the central People's Government who abuses his power of office, neglect his duties, practices irregularities for personnel gains shall be prosecuted for his criminal liability according to law if the offence constitutes a crime, or shall be subject to disciplinary sanctions according to law if the offence does not constitute a crime.

Chapter 7. Supplementary Rules

Article 80

Detailed measures for foreign organizations or individuals to invest and operate telecommunication business in the territory of the People's Republic of China, and organizations or individuals of Hong Kong Special Administrative Region, Macao Special Administrative Region, and Taiwan Province to invest and operate telecommunication business in the Chinese Mainland shall be formulated by the State Council separately..

Article 81

These Regulations shall take effect as of the date of promulgation.

RULES ON THE CONTROL OF FOREIGN INVESTED TELECOMMUNICATION ENTERPRISES

Decree No. 333 of the State Council of the People's Republic of China

Rules on the Control of Foreign invested telecommunication Enterprises were adopted by the 49th Executing Meeting of the State Council on 5th December 2001. We hereby issue these Rules, which shall take effect as of 1st January 2002.

Premier: Zhu Rongji
Dated the 11th day of December 2001

Article 1

In order to be adapted to the need for the telecommunication industry's opening to the outside world, and to boost the telecommunication industry's development, these Rules are hereby enacted in accordance with the laws and administrative regulations on the foreign investment and the Telecommunication Regulations of the People's Republic of China (hereinafter referred to as the "Telecommunication Regulations").

Article 2

Foreign invested telecommunication enterprises mean enterprises that are established jointly by foreign investors and Chinese investors in the form of China-foreign equity joint venture within the territory of the People's Republic of China to operate the telecommunication services.

Article 3

Foreign invested telecommunication enterprises, when engaging in the telecommunication business operations, must abide by not only these Rules, but also the Telecommunication Regulations, and other relevant laws and administrative regulations.

Article 4

Foreign invested telecommunication enterprises may engage in the basic telecommunication services, the value-added telecommunication services, and the specific classification of services shall be based on the relevant provisions of the Telecommunication Regulations.

The territorial scope for services of foreign invested telecommunication enterprises shall be determined by the administrative department in charge of information industry under the State Council according to the relevant provisions.

Article 5

The registered capital of the foreign invested telecommunication enterprise shall fulfill the following provisions:

(1) If the enterprise operates the basic telecommunication services nationwide or beyond a province, autonomous region, or municipality directly the Central People's Government, its minimum registered capital shall be RMB 2 billion; if it operates the value-added telecommunication services, its minimum registered capital shall be RMB 10, 000, 000; and

(2) If the enterprise operates the basic telecommunication services within a province, autonomous region, or municipality directly the Central People's Government, its minimum registered capital shall be RMB 200, 000, 000; if it operates the value-added telecommunication services, its minimum registered capital shall be RMB 1, 000, 000.

Article 6

The capital subscription proportion of the foreign investors to the foreign invested telecommunication enterprise operating the basic telecommunication services (the wireless pager service excluded) shall not exceed 49% finally.

The capital subscription proportion of the foreign investors to the foreign invested telecommunication enterprise operating the value-added telecommunication services (including the wireless pager service in the basic telecommunication services) shall not exceed 50% finally.

The administrative department in charge of information industry under the State Council shall determine the capital subscription proportion for the Chinese investors and foreign investors to the foreign invested telecommunication enterprise within different periods.

Article 7

The foreign invested telecommunication enterprise, if desiring to operate the telecommunication services, shall fulfill not only conditions as specified in Article 4, Article 5, and Article 6 herein, but also conditions that should be satisfied to operate the basic telecommunication services or value-added telecommunication services as provided for by the Telecommunication Regulations.

Article 8

The principal Chinese investors to the foreign invested telecommunication enterprise operating the basic telecommunication services shall fulfill the following conditions:

(1) They must be companies established according to law;
(2) They shall have funds and professional personnel adapted to the development of business operations; and
(3) They shall satisfy the requirements of the administrative department in charge of information industry under the State Council on the circumspectness and special industries.

"Principal Chinese investors to the foreign invested telecommunication enterprise" as referred to in the preceding Paragraph mean capital subscribers whose amount of subscribed capital is more than that of other Chinese investors, and covers 30% or more of the total amount of capital subscribed by all Chinese investors respectively.

Article 9

The principal foreign investors to the foreign invested telecommunication enterprise operating the basic telecommunication services shall fulfill the following conditions:

(1) They shall have the legal person's status;
(2) They shall have obtained the basic telecommunication service operation licenses in the countries or regions they have registered;
(3) They shall have funds and professional personnel adapted to the development of business operations; and
(4) They shall have the favorable achievements and operation experience in the basic telecommunication services.

"Principal foreign investors to the foreign invested telecommunication enterprise" as referred to in the preceding Paragraph mean capital subscribers whose amount of subscribed capital is more than that of other foreign investors, and covers 30% or more of the total amount of capital subscribed by all foreign investors respectively.

Article 10

The principal foreign investors to the foreign invested telecommunication enterprise operating the value-added telecommunication services shall have favorable achievements and operation experience in the value-added telecommunication services.

Article 11

In order to establish a foreign invested telecommunication enterprise operating the basic telecommunication services, or operating the value-added telecommunication services beyond a province, autonomous region, or municipality directly under the Central People's

Government, the principal Chinese investors thereof shall file an application, and submit the following documents to the administrative department in charge of information industry under the State Council:

(1) The project proposal;
(2) The feasibility research report;
(3) The certification for qualifications, or the relevant affirmation documents for all investors to the enterprise as specified in Article 8, Article 9, and Article 10 herein; and
(4) Certification or affirmation documents for qualifications that shall be fulfilled for operation of the basic telecommunication services or value-added telecommunication services as specified in the Telecommunication Regulations.

The administrative department in charge of information industry under the State Council shall examine the relevant documents as specified in the preceding Paragraph as of the date of the receipt of the application. If the enterprise operates the basic telecommunication services, the examination of the relevant documents shall be completed, and the decision shall be made whether to approve the application within 180 days. If the enterprise operates the value-added telecommunication services, the examination of the relevant documents shall be completed, and the decision shall be made whether to approve the application within 90 days. It shall, in case of approval, issue the Approval Opinion for the Foreign Investment in the Telecommunication Services, or shall, in case of disapproval, notify in writing the applicant with reasons.

Article 12

In order to establish a foreign invested telecommunication enterprise operating the basic telecommunication services or operating value-added telecommunication services beyond a province, autonomous region, or municipality directly under the Central People's Government, the principal Chinese investors to the enterprise, when filing an application according to the provisions of Article 11 herein, may, according to the practical conditions, submit documents other than the feasibility research report preliminarily, and submit the feasibility research report subsequently upon the examination, approval, and written notification of the administrative department in charge of information industry under the State Council. However, it shall not exceed 1 year from the date of notification to the date of submission of the feasibility research report, and this period shall be excluded from the specified examining and approving period.

Article 13

In order to establish a foreign invested telecommunication enterprise operating the value-added telecommunication services within a province, autonomous region, or municipality directly under the Central People's Government, the principal Chinese investors thereof shall file an application, and submit the following documents to the administrative department in charge of telecommunication of the province, autonomous region, or municipality directly under the Central People's Government:

(1) The feasibility research report;

(2) The certification for qualifications, or the relevant affirmation documents as specified in Article 10 herein; and
(3) Certification or affirmation documents for qualifications that shall be fulfilled for operation of the value-added telecommunication services as specified in the Telecommunication Regulations.

The administrative department in charge of telecommunication of the province, autonomous region, or municipality directly under the Central People's Government shall introduce its remarks within 60 days upon the receipt of the application. It shall, in case of consent, transfer the application to the administrative department in charge of information industry under the State Council, or shall, in case of dissent, notify in writing the applicant with reasons.

The administrative department in charge of information industry under the State Council shall, within 30 days as of the date of receipt of application documents consented by the administrative department in charge of telecommunication of the province, autonomous regions, or municipality directly under the Central People's Government, complete the examination, and make a decision on whether or not to approve the application. It shall, in case of approval, issue the Approval Opinion for the Foreign Investment in the Telecommunication Services, or shall, in case of disapproval, notify in writing the applicant with reasons.

Article 14

The project proposal of the foreign invested telecommunication enterprise shall mainly cover: names and background of all parties to the joint venture, the total amount of investment in the enterprise to be established, the registered capital, the capital subscription proportion of all parties concerned, the category of services under application, the joint venture period, etc.

The feasibility research report of the foreign invested telecommunication enterprise shall mainly cover: the background of the enterprise to be established, the service items, the business forecast and development planning, the investment results analysis, the estimated business hours, etc.

Article 15

If, in respect of the establishment of a foreign invested telecommunication enterprise, its investment projects must be examined and approved by the administrative department in charge of planning or the administrative department in charge of comprehensive control of economy under the State Council according to the relevant provisions of the state, the administrative department in charge of information industry under the State Council shall, before issuing the Approval Opinion for the Foreign Investment in the Telecommunication Services, transfer the application documents to the administrative department in charge of planning or the administrative department in charge of comprehensive control of economy under the State Council for examination and approval. Where the application is transferred to the administrative department in charge of planning or the administrative department in charge of comprehensive control of economy under the State Council for examination and approval, the examining and approving time limit as specified in Article 11 and Article 13 herein may be extended for 30 days.

Article 16

In order to establish a foreign invested telecommunication enterprise operating the basic telecommunication services or value-added telecommunication services beyond a province, autonomous region, or municipality directly under the Central People's Government, the principal Chinese investors thereof shall submit the contracts and articles of association of the enterprise to be established to the administrative department in charge of foreign trade and economic cooperation under the State Council depending on the Approval Opinion for the Foreign Investment in the Telecommunication Services. If the enterprise operates the value-added telecommunication services within a province, autonomous region, or municipality directly under the Central People's Government, the principal Chinese investors thereof shall submit the contracts and articles of association of the enterprise to be established to the administrative department in charge of foreign trade and economic cooperation of the people's government of the province, autonomous region, or municipality directly under the Central People's Government depending on the Approval Opinion for the Foreign Investment in the Telecommunication Services.

The administrative department in charge of foreign trade and economic cooperation under the State Council or the administrative department in charge of foreign trade and economic cooperation of the people's government of the province, autonomous region, or municipality directly under the Central People's Government shall, within 90 days as of the date of receipt of the contracts and articles of association of the enterprise to be established, complete the examination, and make a decision on whether or not to approve them. It shall, in case of approval, issue the Certificate of Approval for the Foreign Investment Enterprise, or shall, in case of disapproval, notify in writing the applicant with reasons.

Article 17

The principal Chinese investors to the foreign invested telecommunication enterprise shall go through formalities for the License for Operation of Telecommunication Services with the administrative department in charge of information industry under the State Council depending on the Certificate of Approval for the Foreign Investment Enterprise.

The principal Chinese investors to the foreign invested telecommunication enterprise shall go through formalities for registration of the enterprise with the administration for industry and commerce depending on the Certificate of Approval for the Foreign Investment Enterprise and the License for Operation of Telecommunication Services.

Article 18

The foreign invested telecommunication enterprise that desires to operate the multinational telecommunication services must be approved by the administrative department in charge of information industry under the State Council, and shall transact such services via the international telecommunication gateway set up upon approval of the same department.

Article 19

Anyone in violation of the provisions of Article 6 herein shall be ordered to make corrections within a specified time limit, and be imposed a fine of more than RMB 100, 000 but less than RMB 500, 000 by the administrative department in charge of information industry under the State Council. If it fails to make corrections within the specified time limit, the administrative department in charge of information industry under the State Council shall revoke its License for Operation of Telecommunication Services, and the administrative department in charge of foreign trade and economic cooperation originally issuing the Certificate of Approval for the Foreign Investment Enterprise shall revoke its Certificate of Approval for the Foreign Investment Enterprise.

Article 20

Anyone in violation of the provisions of Article 18 herein shall be ordered to make corrections within a specified time limit, and be imposed a fine of more than RMB 200, 000 but less than RMB 1, 000, 000 by the administrative department in charge of information industry under the State Council. If it fails to make corrections within the specified time limit, the administrative department in charge of information industry under the State Council shall revoke its License for Operation of Telecommunication Services, and the administrative department in charge of foreign trade and economic cooperation originally issuing the Certificate of Approval for the Foreign Investment Enterprise shall revoke its Certificate of Approval for the Foreign Investment Enterprise.

Article 21

If an applicant applying for establishing a foreign invested telecommunication enterprise provides false or forged certification for qualifications or affirmation documents to defraud of the approval, the approval shall be invalid, and the administrative department in charge of information industry under the State Council shall impose a fine of more than RMB 200, 000 but less than RMB 1, 000, 000 on the offender, and revoke its License for Operation of Telecommunication Services, and the administrative department in charge of foreign trade and economic cooperation originally issuing the Certificate of Approval for the Foreign Investment Enterprise shall revoke its Certificate of Approval for the Foreign Investment Enterprise.

Article 22

Any foreign invested telecommunication enterprise, if violating the Telecommunication Regulations and other relevant laws or administrative regulations in the course of operating the telecommunication services, shall be punished by the relevant authority according to law.

Article 23

A domestic telecommunication enterprise that desires to be listed out of this country must pass the examination of the administrative department in charge of information industry under the State Council, and shall be approved according to the relevant provisions of the state.

Article 24

These Rules shall be applicable with reference to the investment in the telecommunication services in the Mainland China by companies and enterprises from the Hong Kong Special Administrative Region, the Macao Special Administrative Region, and Taiwan Province.

Article 25

These Rules shall take effect as of 1st January 2002.

INTERIM MEASURES ON THE ADMINISTRATION OF PERMITS FOR CIVIL SPACE LAUNCH PROJECTS

Order No. 12 of the Commission of Science, Technology, and Industry for National Defense of the People's Republic of China

The "Interim Measures on the Administration of Permits for Civil Space Launch Projects" are hereby promulgated, and shall come into force on December 21, 2002.

Director General: Liu Jibin
November 21, 2002

Interim Measures on the Administration of Permits for Civil Space Launch Projects

Chapter I*. General Provisions*

Article 1

The present measures are formulated with a view to regulating the administration of civil space launch projects, promoting the healthy development of civil space industry, maintaining the state security and the public benefits, and performing the obligations of China as a contracting state to the international outer space convention.

Article 2

Civil space launch projects mentioned in the present measures shall refer to the entry of such spacecrafts as satellites inside the territory of China into the outer space not for military purpose, and the entry of such spacecrafts as satellites, etc. over which the natural persons, legal persons or other organizations of the People's Republic of China have had property or have property by means of on-orbit delivery into the outer space from outside of the territory of China.

Article 3

The system of permit administration shall apply to the civil space launch projects. Any natural person, legal person or other organization undertaking civil space launch projects shall, in accordance with the present measures, apply for examination and approval, and shall not carry out the civil space launch projects until he/it is found to be qualified upon examination and has obtained for the permit for civil space launch projects (hereinafter referred to as the permit).

Article 4

The Commission of Science, Technology, and Industry for National Defense (hereinafter referred to as the Commission of STIND) shall apply uniform planning and administration to civil space launch projects, and be responsible for examining, approving and supervising civil space launch projects (hereinafter referred to as projects).

***Chapter II**. Procedures of Application, Examination and Approval*

Article 5

The general project contractor shall be the applicant for the permit. Where there is no a domestic general project contractor, the final owner of the satellite or other spacecraft shall be the applicant for the permit.

The applicant for the permit shall meet the following conditions:

(a) he/it shall abide by the laws and regulations of the state, and maintain the state secrets;
(b) the project under application shall not endanger the state security, damage the benefits of the state, violate the state's diplomatic policies or the international conventions which have been concluded and become effective;
(c) the project under application will not cause irremediable danger to the health, safety or properties of the public due to major negligence or intentional acts;
(d) he/it shall have the relevant permission documents for carrying out the project under application, which are issued by the relevant departments of the state;
(e) he/it shall have the technical strength, economic strength and complete technical documents for carrying out the project under application;
(f) other conditions provided for in laws, regulations or rules.

Article 6

The applicant shall, 9 months before the prearranged month for the launch of the project, submit the following documents (in triplets) to the Commission of STIND:

(a) the application letter for the permit for the civil space launch project and the materials on examination of the qualification of the applicant for the permit;
(b) the relevant materials proving that the project conforms to the laws and regulations of the state on environmental protection;
(c) for a project in the stage of a domestic executive launching site, the prearranged time for launch, the technical requirements on the satellite, the carrier rocket and the communication system for launch, observation and control, the detailed orbital parameters of the carrier rocket, the survey report on the landing area or recovering place, and the documents on detailed orbital parameters of the satellite and use of frequency resources shall be provided;
for a project in the stage of a foreign executive launching site, copies of the legally binding documents on orbital parameters, etc. of the carrier rocket and the satellite, and copies of the permission documents on the use of the relevant frequency resources shall be submitted;
a Chinese satellite launcher shall provide a copy of the "Radio Station License of the People's Republic of China" issued by the Ministry of Information Industry for the space station;
(d) the safety design report relating to the project and materials on guaranty of the public security; supplementary materials on the reliability of key safety system, on affects of the normal state and malfunction of the carrier rocket during the launch to the property and personal safety near the launching site and within the scope of the

launch track, on how to avoid pollution and space debris, and on other relevant safety; for a foreign-related project, the materials on policy evaluation and confidentiality and safety evaluation must also be submitted.

Article 7

The Commission of STIND shall, within 30 days as of receipt of the application documents, organize the examination of the project under application, and shall issue a permit to the applicant of a project found to be qualified upon examination, or shall not issue the permit to the applicant of a project examined to be unqualified, and shall notify the applicant and the relevant departments in writing.

Article 8

Where the applicant has any objection to the conclusion from examination, it may apply to the Commission of STIND for re-examination or apply for administrative reconsideration in accordance with the law.

Article 9

The relevant matters of a foreign-related project must be organized by a foreign trade company designated by the Chinese government, and the contract on such a project shall not become effective until it is approved by the Commission of STIND.

Chapter III. *Supervision and Administration*

Article 10

The permit shall mainly include the following contents:

(a) the applicant and its legal representative;
(b) the registration address (the applicant's domicile);
(c) main contents of the project;
(d) the prearranged time for launch;
(e) validity period of the permit;
(f) the organ issuing the permit and the time of issuance.

Article 11

The permit shall only be limited to the purpose for an approved project, and shall, after the ending of the project, be automatically invalidated.

Article 12

A permit shall not be altered or transferred.

Article 13

Where any content in a permit needs to be modified, the permit holder shall, 90 days before the expiry of the validity period of the permit, file an application for modification to the Commission of STIND, and shall not modify the permit until it has been approved upon examination.

Article 14

With respect to a project under planned cancellation, the permit holder shall, 90 days before the expiry of the validity period of the permit, apply to the Commission of STIND for cancellation, and the permit shall be nullified upon approval.

Article 15

With respect to a project unable to be accomplished due to inappropriate management of the permit holder, the Commission of STIND shall nullify the permit for the project.

Article 16

Where a permit holder is under any of the following circumstances, the Commission of STIND shall order it to get right within a time limit; if case is severe, its permit shall be suspended:

(a) It violates the relevant laws or regulations of the state, or the agreement between states on maintaining confidentiality during execution of the project;
(b) It has, during execution of the project, any act endangering the state security, damaging the benefits of the state, violating the state's diplomatic policies or the international conventions which have been concluded and become effective;
(c) It does not carry out activities of civil space launch within the scope approved by the permit;
(d) Other acts in violation of the present measures.

Article 17

With respect to a project for which the permit is suspended, the applicant for the project shall not, within two years as of the suspension, file a second application for the permit regarding the same project.

Article 18

Where, due to the reason of the permit holder, any content of the project is changed, or the project is delayed or cancelled, thus resulting in expenses in the relevant aspects, the corresponding liability and the expenses to be borne shall be clarified in the contract by the permit holder and the relevant parties.

Article 19

The permit holder must comply with the relevant provisions of the state to purchase the third party liability insurance and other relevant insurances for launching a space object.

Article 20

For a project in the stage of a domestic executive launching site, the permit holder shall, 6 months before the prearranged month for launch, report the launching plan of the project to the Commission of STIND.

The permit holder shall, before entering the stage of a launching site, file an application to the Commission of STIND for approval of the project to leave the factory, and submit the following materials:

(a) documents on technical state of the carrier rocket, documents on quality state control, flight test outline, documents on security and confidentiality, and other documents to be issued;
(b) copies of the policy of the third party liability insurance effective for the project and copies of the relevant documents (in triplets), copies of the policies of the relevant effective insurances (in triplets). Under particular circumstances, the permit holder shall provide the Commission of STIND with written materials, which shall be dealt with specifically.

The project shall not enter the stage of the launching site before approved.

Article 21

For a project in the stage of a foreign executive launching site, the permit holder shall, 60 days before the prearranged day for launch, file an application to the Commission of STIND for approval of the project to leave the factory, and attach copies of the effective final documents (in triplet) legally binding in respect of the third party liability insurance, the relevant insurances, security, confidentiality, etc., and shall not continue carrying out the project before approved.

Article 22

The permit holder must, within one month after the launch of a project is ended, report to the Commission of STIND in writing on the accomplishment of the project.

Article 23

The Commission of STIND shall irregularly supervise and inspect the carryout of the approved projects, and its authorized functionaries shall have the right to inspect the relevant activities during the carryout of the projects on the spot.

***Chapter IV**. Legal Liabilities*

Article 24

A permit holder who conceals the truth, practices frauds or damages the benefits of the state during application or carryout shall be imposed upon administrative penalties in accordance with the law. If he commits a crime, he shall be subject to criminal liabilities in accordance with the law.

Article 25

Any natural person, legal person or other organization without the permit who undertakes projects unauthorizedly shall be ordered by the Commission of STIND to cease the illegal activities, and the parties involved shall be imposed upon administrative penalties in accordance with the law. If he/it commits a crime, he/it shall be subject to criminal liabilities in accordance with the law.

Article 26

An approving institution or any of its functionaries who neglects its/his duties or abuses its/his powers during the examination and approval of the permits, thus causing loses to the state, shall be imposed upon administrative sanctions. If it/he commits a crime, it/he shall be subject to criminal liabilities in accordance with the law.

***Chapter V**. Supplementary Provisions*

Article 27

The power to interpret the present measures shall remain with the Commission of STIND.

Article 28

The present measures shall come into force on December 21, 2002.

REGULATIONS OF THE PEOPLE'S REPUBLIC OF CHINA ON EXPORT CONTROL OF MISSILES AND MISSILE-RELATED ITEMS AND TECHNOLOGIES

2002-08-22

Article 1

These Regulations are formulated for the purposes of strengthening export control of missiles and missile-related items and technologies, and safeguarding the State security and social and public interests.

Article 2

The export of missiles and missile-related items and technologies referred to in these Regulations means the export for trade of missiles and missile-related equipment, materials and technologies listed in "The Missiles and Missile-related Items and Technologies Export Control List" (hereinafter referred to as the Control List) attached to these Regulations, and the gift to, exhibition in, scientific and technological cooperation with, assistance to, provision of service for as such and other forms of technological transfer thereof to foreign countries and regions.

Article 3

The State shall exercise strict control on the export of missiles and missile-related items and technologies so as to prevent the proliferation of missiles and other delivering systems listed in the Control List that can be used to deliver weapons of mass destruction.

Article 4

The State shall practice a licensing system for the export of missiles and missile-related items and technologies. Without being licensed, no unit or individual shall export missiles and missile-related items and technologies.

Article 5

The export of items and technologies listed in Part I of the Control List shall be subject to the Regulations of the People"s Republic of China on Administration of Arms Export and other relevant provisions.

To export items and technologies listed in Part II of the Control List (hereinafter referred to as missile-related items and technologies), the exporter shall follow the examination and approval procedures provided for in Articles 7 to 13 of these Regulations; however, the export of missile-related items and technologies for military purpose shall be subject to the provisions of the preceding paragraph.

Article 6

The receiving party of missile-related items and technologies shall guarantee not to use missile-related items and technologies supplied by China for purposes other than the declared end-use, nor to transfer missile-related items and technologies supplied by China to any third party other than the declared end-user without the consent of the Chinese Government.

Article 7

Exporters of missile-related items and technologies shall register themselves with the competent department in charge of foreign economic relations and trade of the State Council (hereinafter referred to as the competent foreign economic and trade department of the State Council). Without such registration, no unit or individual shall export missile-related items and technologies. The specific measures for such registration shall be formulated by the competent foreign economic and trade department of the State Council.

Article 8

Anyone who intends to export missile-related items and technologies shall apply to the competent foreign economic and trade department of the State Council, fill in the export application form for missile-related items and technologies (hereinafter referred to as the export application form), and submit the following documents:

(1) identification of the applicant"s legal representative, chief managers and the persons handling the deal;
(2) duplicates of the contract or agreement;
(3) technical specifications of the missile-related items and technologies;
(4) certificates of the end-user and end-use;
(5) documents of guarantee as defined in Article 6;
(6) other documents as may be required by the competent foreign economic and trade department of the State Council.

Article 9

An applicant shall truthfully fill in the export application form.

Export application forms shall be uniformly produced by the competent foreign economic and trade department of the State Council.

Article 10

The competent foreign economic and trade department of the State Council shall, from the date of receiving the export application form and the documents set forth in Article 8 of these Regulations, examine the application, or examine the application jointly with other relevant departments of the State Council and relevant departments of the Central Military Commission, and make a decision of approval or denial within 45 working days.

Article 11

Where the export of missile-related items and technologies entails significant impact on the State security, social and public interests, the competent foreign economic and trade department of the State Council shall, jointly with relevant departments, submit the case to the State Council and the Central Military Commission for approval.

Where the export of missile-related items and technologies is submitted to the State Council and the Central Military Commission for approval, the timing restriction set forth in Article 10 of these Regulations shall not be applied.

Article 12

Where an application for the export of missile-related items and technologies is examined and approved, the competent foreign economic and trade department of the State Council shall issue a licence for the export of missile-related items and technologies (hereinafter referred to as an export licence), and notify the Customs in writing.

Article 13

An export licence holder who intends to change the missile-related items and technologies originally applied for export shall return the original export licence and file a new application to obtain a new export licence according to relevant provisions of these Regulations.

Article 14

While exporting missile-related items and technologies, the exporter shall present the export licence to the Customs, complete the customs procedures and accept supervision and control of the Customs in accordance with the provisions of the Customs Law.

Article 15

Where the receiving party contravenes the guarantees made according to the provisions of Article 6 of these Regulations or there is a risk of proliferation of missiles and other delivering systems listed in the Control List that can be used to deliver weapons of mass destruction, the competent foreign economic and trade department of the State Council shall suspend or revoke the export licence granted and notify the Customs in writing.

Article 16

Where the exporter knows or should know that the missile-related items and technologies to be exported will be used by the receiving party directly in its program for developing missiles and other delivering systems listed in the Control List that can be used to deliver weapons of mass destruction, the export shall be subject to the provisions of these Regulations even if the items or technologies are not listed in the Control List.

Article 17

Upon approval by the State Council and the Central Military Commission, the competent foreign economic and trade department of the State Council may, jointly with relevant departments, temporarily decide to exercise export control on specific items and technologies other than those listed in the Control List in accordance with the provisions of these Regulations.

Article 18

Those who export missile-related items and technologies without being licensed, or export missile-related items and technologies beyond the scope of the export licence without authorization, shall be investigated for criminal liability in accordance with the provisions of the criminal law on the crime of smuggling, the crime of illegal business operations, the crime of divulging State secrets or other crimes; if such acts are not serious enough for criminal punishment, by distinguishing different circumstances, they shall be punished in accordance with relevant provisions of the Customs Law, or be given a warning, confiscated of their illegal income, and fined not less than one time but not more than five times the illegal income by the competent foreign economic and trade department of the State Council; the competent foreign economic and trade department of the State Council may concurrently suspend or even revoke the licensing for their foreign trade operations.

Article 19

Those who forge, alter, buy or sell the licence for the export of missile-related items and technologies shall be investigated for criminal liability in accordance with the provisions of the criminal law on the crime of illegal business operations or the crime of forging, altering, buying or selling official documents, certificates or seals of a State organ; if such acts are not serious enough for criminal punishment, they shall be punished in accordance with relevant provisions of the Customs Law, and the competent foreign economic and trade department of the State Council may concurrently revoke the licensing for their foreign trade operations.

Article 20

Where a license for the export of missile-related items and technologies is obtained by fraud or other illegal means, the competent foreign economic and trade department of the State Council shall revoke such an export license, confiscate the illegal income, impose a fine of not more than the illegal income, and suspend or even revoke the licensing for their foreign trade operations.

Article 21

Where, in violation of Article 7 of these Regulations, the export of missile-related items and technologies is operated without registration, the competent foreign economic and trade department of the State Council shall ban such illegal activities according to law, and relevant competent departments of the State shall impose punishment thereon in accordance with relevant laws and administrative regulations.

Article 22

Where the State functionaries in charge of control on the export of missile-related items and technologies abuse their powers, neglect their duties or extort or accept money or properties from others by taking advantage of their positions, they shall be investigated for criminal liability in accordance with the provisions of the criminal law on the crime of abuse of power, the crime of neglect of duties, the crime of accepting bribes and other crimes; if such acts are not serious enough for criminal punishment, they shall be given administrative sanctions according to law.

Article 23

In light of actual situations, the competent foreign economic and trade department of the State Council may, jointly with relevant departments, amend the Control List and submit it to the State Council and the Central Military Commission for approval before implementation.

Article 24

These Regulations shall be effective as of the date of promulgation.

Annex. The Missiles and Missile-related Items and Technologies Export Control List

1. Introduction

(1) Part 1 of this List includes missiles and other delivery systems (including ballistic missiles, cruise missiles, rockets and unmanned air vehicles) as well as their specially designed items and technologies. Part 2 includes items and technologies related to Item 1 of Part 1.

(2) If a Part 1 item is included in a system, that system will also be considered as a Part 1 item, except when the incorporated item cannot be separated, removed or duplicated and the system is designed for civilian uses, where the item will be considered as a Part 2 item.

(3) All items listed in this List include their directly related technologies.

2. Definitions

For the purpose of this List, the following definitions apply:

(1) "Technology" means specific information which is required for the "development", "production" or "use" of a product. The information may take the form of "technical data" or "technical assistance". But "technology" does not include technology "in the public domain" nor "basic scientific research".

(a) "In the public domain" as it applies to this List means technology which has been made available without restrictions upon its further dissemination. (Copyright restrictions do not remove technology from being "in the public domain".)

(b) "Basic scientific research" means experimental or theoretical work undertaken principally to acquire new knowledge of the fundamental principles of phenomena and observable facts, not primarily directed towards a specific practical aim or objective.

(2) "Development" is related to all phases prior to "production" such as:

(a) Design

(b) Design research

(c) Design analysis

(d) Design concepts

(e) Assembly and testing of prototypes

(f) Pilot production schemes

(g) Design data

(h) Process of transforming design data into a product

(i) Configuration design

(j) Integration system design

(k) Layouts

(3) "Production" means all production phases such as:

(a) Production engineering

(b) Manufacture

(c) Integration

(d) Assembly

(e) Inspection

(f) Testing

(g) Quality assurance

(4) "Use" means:

(a) Operation

(b) Installation (including on-site installation)

(c) Maintenance

(d) Repair

(e) Overhaul

(f) Refurbishing

(5) "Technical data" may take forms such as:

(a) Blueprints

(b) Plans

(c) Diagrams

(d) Models

(e) Formulae

(f) Engineering designs and specifications

(g) Manuals and instructions written or recorded on other media or devices such as disk, tape, read-only memories.

(6) "Technical assistance" may take forms such as:

(a) Instruction

(b) Skills

(c) Training

(d) Working knowledge

(e) Consulting services

(7) "Production facilities" means equipment and specially designed software therefor integrated into installations for "development" or for one or more phases of "production".

(8) "Production equipment" means tooling, templates, jigs, mandrels, moulds, dies, fixtures, alignment mechanisms, test equipment, other machinery and components therefor, limited to those specially designed or modified for "development" or for one or more phases of "production".

Part I

1. Complete ballistic missiles, space launch vehicles, sounding rockets, cruise missile and unmanned air vehicles that can be used to deliver at least a 500 kg payload to a range of at least 300 km as well as the specially designed production facilities therefor.

2. The following items usable in the systems in Item 1:

(1) Individual stages of a ballistic missile;

(2) Individual stages of a rocket;

(3) Reentry vehicles of missiles;

(4) Heat shields and components fabricated of ceramic materials used in Subitem (3);

(5) Heat shields and components fabricated of ablative materials used in Subitem (3);

(6) Heat sinks and components fabricated of light-weight, high heat capacity materials used in Subitem (3);

(7) Electronic equipment specially designed for Subitem (3);

(8) Storable liquid propellant rocket engines, having a thrust force of 90 kN or greater;

(9) Solid propellant rocket engines, having a total impulse capacity of 1100 kN??猫s or greater;

(10) Guidance sets capable of achieving system accuracy of 10 km or less (CEP) for ballistic missiles with a range of 300 km;

(11) Thrust vector control sub-systems;

(12) Warhead safing, arming, fuzing, and firing mechanisms;

(13) Production facilities and equipments designed for Subitems (1) to (12).

3. Interstage mechanisms for space launch vehicles and the specially designed production equipment therefor.

4. Rocket motor cases and the specially designed production equipment therefor.

5. Hydraulic, mechanical, electro-optical, or electro-mechanical flight control systems specially designed or modified for the systems in Item 1 of Part I.

6. Attitude control equipment specially designed or modified for the systems in Item 1 of Part I.

7. Design technology for integration of air vehicle fuselage, propulsion system and lifting control surfaces to optimize aerodynamic performance throughout the flight regime of an unmanned air vehicle.

8. Design technology for integration of the guidance, flight control, and propulsion data into a flight management system for optimization of trajectory of ballistic missiles or space launch vehicles.

9. Passive interferometer equipment usable in the systems in Item 1.

10. Apparatus and devices designed or modified for the handling, control, activation and launching of the systems in Item 1.

11. Vehicles designed or modified for the transport, handling, control, activation and launching of the systems in Item 1.

12. Gravity meters, gravity gradiometers, and specially designed components therefor, for airborne or marine use, and having a static or operational accuracy of one milligal or better, with a time to steady-state registration of two minutes or less;

13. Precision tracking systems:

(1) Tracking systems which use a translator installed on the rocket system or unmanned air vehicle in conjunction with either surface or airborne references or navigation satellite systems to provide real-time measurements of in-flight position and velocity;

(2) Software which processes post-flight, recorded data, enabling determination of vehicle position throughout its flight path.

14. Structure specially designed for reduced radar reflectivity.

15. Structural material specially designed for reduced radar reflectivity.

16. Coatings specially designed for reduced radar reflectivity.

17. Coatings specially designed for reduced optical reflectivity or emissivity.

18. Production equipment, technology and specially designed software usable in Items 14 to 17 above.

19. Technology and specially designed software for reduced radar reflectivity, ultraviolet/infrared signatures or acoustic signatures.

Part II

1. Reentry Vehicle Components and Technology Thereof

(1) Design and manufacturing technology for ceramic heat shields;

(2) Design and manufacturing technology for ablative heat shields;

(3) Design and manufacturing technology for heat sinks and components thereof;

(4) Structure for protection against electromagnetic pulse (EMP) and X-rays and shock wave and combined blast and thermal effects:

(a) Radiation-hardened microcircuits and detectors;

(b) Hardened radome structure designed to withstand a combined thermal shock greater than 418 J/cm2 accompanied by a peak over pressure of greater than 50 kPa.

(5) Design technology for radiation hardenning;

(6) Design technology for hardened structure.

2. Propulsion Components and Technology Thereof

(1) Lightweight turbojet engines that are small and fuel efficient;

(2) Lightweight turbofan engines that are small and fuel efficient;

(3) Lightweight turbocompound engines that are small and fuel efficient;

(4) Ramjet engines;

(5) Scramjet engines;

(6) Pulse jet engines;

(7) Combined cycle engines;

(8) Devices to regulate combustion for the above Subitems (4) to (7);

(9) Liquid and slurry propellant control systems, and specially designed components thereof, designed or modified to operate in vibration environments of more than 10 g (RMS) between 20 Hz and 2, 000 Hz:

(a) Servo valves designed for flow rates of 24 liters per minute or greater, at an absolute pressure of 7, 000 kPa or greater, that have an actuator response time of less than 100 microseconds;

(b) Pumps, for liquid propellants, with shaft speeds equal to or greater than 8, 000 RPM or with discharge pressures equal to or greater than 7, 000 kPa.

(10) Production facilities specially designed for the above Subitems (1) to (9).

3. Liquid Propellants

(1) Hydrazine with a concentration of more than 70 percent;

(2) Unsymmetric dimethylhydrazine (UDMH);

(3) Monomethylhydrazine (MMH);

(4) Mixed amine;

(5) Dinitrogen tetroxide;

(6) Red Fuming Nitric Acid.

4. Solid Propellant and Propellant Constituents

(1) Metal fuels with particle sizes less than 500 mm, whether spherical, atomized, spheroidal, flaked or ground, consisting of 97 percent by weight or greater of any of the following metal and alloys of these:

(a) Zirconium;

(b) Boron;

(c) Magnesium;

(d) Titanium;

(e) Uranium;

(f) Tungsten;

(g) Zinc;

(h) Cerium.

(2) Ammonium perchlorate with particle sizes less than 500 mm;

(3) Spherical aluminum powder meeting the following requirements:

(a) With particle of uniform diameter;

(b) With aluminum content of 97 percent or greater;

(c) With diameter of less than 500 mm.

(4) Boron Slurry, having an energy density of more than 40 x 106 J/kg;

(5) Nitro-amines:

(a) Cyclotetramethylene-tetranitramene (HMX);

(b) Cyclotrimethylene-trinitramine (RDX).

(6) Composite Propellants:

(a) Molded colloid propellants;

(b) Propellant including nitrate bonding agents and with an aluminum (particle) content of 5 percent or greater.

(7) Polymeric substances:

(a) Carboxl-terminated polybutadiene (CTPB);

(b) Hydroxy-terminated polybutadiene (HTPB).

(8) Triethylamine as an igniting agent.

5. Guidance and Control Set, Components and Related Technologies

(1) Gyro-astro compasses and other devices which derive position or orientation by means of automatically tracking celestrial bodies or satellites;

(2) Flight control software and related test software;

(3) Gyro stability platform;

(4) Automatic pilots for UAV;

(5) Gyros with a rated drift rate stability of less than 0.5 degree per hour;

(6) Test table for inertial platform (including high-accuracy centrifuges and rotating table);

(7) Inertial Measurement Unit (IMU) tester;

(8) Inertial Measurement Unit (IMU) stable element handling fixture;

(9) Inertial Measurement Unit (IMU) platform balance fixture;

(10) Tester for gyro tuning;

(11) Tester for gyro dynamic balance;

(12) Gyro run-in/motor test station;

(13) Gyro evacuation and filling station;

(14) Centrifuge fixture for gyro bearings;

(15) Rectangular scatterometer for ring laser gyro production;

(16) Polarity scatterometer for ring laser gyro production;

(17) Reflectometer for ring laser gyro production;

(18) Surface profilometer for ring laser gyro production;

(19) Accelerometers with a proportional error of 0.25 percent or less;

(20) Accelerometer test station;

(21) Accelerometer axis align station;

(22) Specially designed test, calibration, and alignment equipment for gyro or accelerometer.

6. Target Detection System and Related Electronics

(1) Radar systems;

(2) Altimeters;

(3) Terrain contour mapping equipment;

(4) Scene mapping and correlation (both digital and analog) equipment;

(5) Imaging sensor equipment;

(6) Processors and software specially designed for processing navigation information;

(7) Electronic devices and components removed of conductive heat;

(8) Radiation-hardened electronic devices and components;

(9) Electronic assemblies and components operating at temperatures in excess of 125 ??C for a short period of time;

(10)Electronic devices and components with specially designed integrated support;

(11) Telemetry equipment and related technologies;

(12) Telemetering and telecontrol ground equipment;

(13) Analogue computers and digital computers having either of the following characteristics:

(a) Rated for continuous operation at temperatures from below minus 45 ??C to above plus 55 ??C;

(b) Designed as ruggedized or radiation hardened.

(14) Analogue-to-digital converter having one of the following characteristics:

(a) Rated for operation at temperatures from below minus 54 ??C to above plus 125 ??C, and

(b) Designed to meet military specifications for ruggedized equipment; or

(c) Designed or modified for military use or designed as radiation hardened, and having one of the following characteristics:

<1> Converting at a rate of over 200000 times (complete conversion) per second under rated accuracy;

<2> With accuracy exceeding 1/10000 of the whole range in the rated temperature scope;

<3> With quality factor of over 1??108 (complete conversion times per second divided by accuracy);

<4> The inbuilt microcircuits having the following characteristics:

(A) The maximum converting time is less than 20 microseconds under maximum resolution, and

(B) The rated nonlinearity is better than 0.025 percent of the range in rated temperature scope.

(15) Design technology for protection of avionics and electrical subsystems against electromagnetic pulse and electromagnetic interference hazards from external sources:

(a) Design technology for shielding systems;

(b) Design technology for the configuration of hardened electrical circuits and subsystems;

(c) Determination of hardening criteria for the above.

7. Material

(1) Structural composites, including composite structures, laminates, and manufactures thereof, and resin impregnated fibre prepregs and metal coated fibre preforms therefor, made with either organic matrix or metal matrix utilizing fibrous or filamentary reinforcements having a specific tensile strength greater than 7.62 x 104 m and a specific modulus greater than 3.18 x 106 m:

(a) Polyimide composite;

(b) Polyamide composite;

(c) Polycarbonate composite;

(d) Quartz-fibre-reinforced composite;

(e) Carbon-fibre-reinforced composite;

(f) Boron-fibre-reinforced composite;

(g) Magnesium matrix composite;

(h) Titanium matrix composite.

(2) Ceramic composite materials with dielectric constant less than 6 at frequencies from 100 Hz to 10, 000 MHz;

(3) Fine grain bulk artificial graphites having the following features measured at 20 ??C:

(a) With a bulk density of at least 1.72 g/cm3;

(b) With a tension rupture strain of at least 0.7 percent;

(c) With a heat expansion coefficient of at least 2.75??10-6 (measured at temperatures from 20 ??C to 982 ??C).

(4) Resaturated pyrolized carbon-carbon materials;

(5) Special Steel:

Titanium-stabilized duplex stainless steel (Ti-DSS) having the following characteristics:

(a) Containing 17.0 to 26.5 weight percent chromium and 4.5 to 7.0 weight percent nickel;

(b) Having a ferritic-austenitic microstructure (also referred to as a two-phase microstructure) of which at least 10 percent is austenite by volume;

(c) Having any of the following forms:

<1> Ingots or bars having a size of 100 mm or more in each dimension;

<2> Sheets having a width of 600 mm or more and a thickness of 3 mm or less;

<3> Tubes having an outer diameter of 600 mm or more and a wall thickness of 3 mm or less.

(6) Ceramic heat shielding material;

(7) Ablative heat shielding material.

8. Design and Test Equipment and Technologies Related to Ballistic Missiles and Rockets

(1) Specially designed software, or analogue and digital computers thereof, for modeling, simulation, or design integration of the systems;

(2) Vibration test systems capable of providing a force of 100kN or more and incorporating a digital controller, as well as specially designed vibration test auxiliaries and software;

(3) Wind-tunnel for supersonic (Mach 1.4 to 5) or hypersonic (Mach 5 to 15) speeds except those specially designed for teaching and those with the test area dimensions smaller than 25 cm (measured internally);

(4) Test benches which have the capacity to handle solid or liquid propellant rocket motors of more than 90 kN of thrust, or which are capable of simultaneously measuring the three axial thrust components.

9. Production Equipment and Production Technology

(1) Equipment for production of solid propellants listed in Item 4 of Part II:

(a) Batch mixers having:

<1> A total volumetric capacity of 110 litres or more; and

<2> At least one mixing/kneading shaft mounted off centre.

(b) Continuous mixers having:

<1> Two or more mixing/kneading shafts; and

<2> Capability to open the mixing chamber.

(c) Equipment for the production of atomized or spherical metallic powder in a controlled environment;

(d) Fluid energy mills;

(e) Handling equipment for production of solid propellant;

(f) Curing equipment for production of solid propellant;

(g) Casting equipment for production of solid propellant;

(h) Pressing equipment for production of solid propellant;

(i) Acceptance testing equipment for production of solid propellant;

(j) Machining equipment for production of solid propellant;

(k) Extruding equipment for production of solid propellant.

(2) Equipment for producing liquid propellant in Item 3 of Part II:

(a) Handling equipment for production of liquid propellant;

(b) Production equipment for liquid propellant;

(c) Acceptance testing equipment for production of liquid propellant.

(3) Pyrolytic deposition and densification equipment and technology

(a) Technology for producing pyrolytically derived materials formed on a mould, mandrel or other substrate from precursor gases which decompose at temperatures from 1,

300 ??C to 2, 900 ??C and at pressures of 130 Pa to 20 kPa, including technology for the composition of precursor gases, flow-rates and process control schedules and parameters;

(b) Specially designed nozzles for the above processes;

(c) Isostatic presses having all of the following characteristics:

<1> Maximum working pressure of 69 MPa or greater;

<2> Designed to achieve and maintain a controlled thermal environment of 600 ??C or greater, and

<3> Possessing a chamber cavity with an inside diameter of 254 mm or greater.

(d) Chemical vapor deposition furnaces for the densification of carbon-carbon composites;

(e) Pyrolytic deposition and densification process controls equipment and specially designed software therefor.

(4) Equipment and technology for production of composite component:

(a) Filament winding machines coordinated and programmed in three or more axes, and specially designed computers and software thereof;

(b) Tape-laying machines coordinated and programmed in two or more axes, and specially designed software thereof;

(c) Adapters and modification kits of weaving machines for fibre structure composites;

(d) Technical data and procedures for the regulation of temperature, pressures or atmosphere in autoclaves or hydroclaves;

(e) Equipment for converting polymeric fibres (such as polyacrylonitrile, rayon or polycarbosilane) including special provision to strain the fibre during heating;

(f) Equipment for the vapor deposition of elements or compounds on heated filament substrates;

(g) Equipment for the wet-spinning of refractory ceramics (such as aluminium oxide);

(h) Equipment for special fibre surface treatment;

(i) Equipment for producing prepregs and preforms;

(j) Moulds, mandrels, dies, fixtures and tooling for the preform pressing, curing, casting, sintering or bonding of composite structures, laminates and manufactures thereof.

1. China's Space Activities in 2006 (White Paper)

by Information Office of the State Council of the People's Republic of China

October 2006, Beijing

Table of Contents

III. Development Targets and Major Tasks for the Next Five Years
IV. Development Policies and Measures
IV. International Exchanges and Cooperation

Preface

Space activities around the world have been flourishing in the first few years of the 21st century. Leading countries in the area of spaceflight have formulated or readjusted their development strategies, plans and goals in this sphere. The role of space activities in a country's overall development strategy is becoming increasingly salient, and their influence on human civilization and social progress is increasing.

It has been 50 splendid years since China embarked on the road to develop its space industry, starting in 1956. For half a century, China has worked independently in this field. It has made eye-catching achievements, and ranks among the world's most advanced countries in some important fields of space technology. China is unflinching in taking the road of peaceful development, and always maintains that outer space is the common wealth of mankind. While supporting all activities that utilize outer space for peaceful purposes, China actively explores and uses outer space and continuously makes new contributions to the development of man's space programs.

China has set the strategic goal of building itself into a well-off society in an all-round way, ranking it among the countries with the best innovative capabilities in the first 20 years of the 21st century. The development of the space industry in China now faces new opportunities and higher requirements. In the new stage of development, China will adhere to the scientific outlook on development as guidance, center its work on the national strategic goals, strengthen its innovative capabilities and do its best to make the country's space industry develop faster and better.

China's space industry has made great progress since the Chinese government issued the white paper China's Space Activities in 2000. In order to give people around the world a better understanding of the development of China's space industry over the past five years and its plans for the near future, we hereby offer an expanded introduction to some related issues.

I. Aims and Principles of Development

The aims of China's space activities are: to explore outer space, and enhance understanding of the Earth and the cosmos; to utilize outer space for peaceful purposes, promote human civilization and social progress, and benefit the whole of mankind; to meet the demands of economic construction, scientific and technological development, national security and social progress; and to raise the scientific quality of the Chinese people, protect China's national interests and rights, and build up the comprehensive national strength.

When developing the space industry, China will follow the principles guiding the development of the country's scientific and technological programs, namely, making innovations independently, making leapfrogging development in key areas, shoring up the economy and leading future trends. In the new development stage, the principles of development for China's space industry are as follows:

- Maintaining and serving the country's overall development strategy, and meeting the needs of the state and reflecting its will. China considers the development of its space industry as a strategic way to enhance its economic, scientific, technological and national defense strength, as well as a cohesive force for the unity of the Chinese people, in order to rejuvenate China. Since the space industry is an important part of the national overall development strategy, China will maintain long-term, stable development in this field.

- Upholding independence and self-reliance policy, making innovations independently and realizing leapfrogging development. China relied completely on itself when it developed its space industry from scratch, and has made constant progress through making independent innovations. Therefore, increasing the capability for independent innovation is a strategic basis for developing the space industry. In light of the country's actual situation and needs, China will focus on certain areas while ignoring less-important ones. It will choose some limited targets, concentrate its strength on making key breakthroughs and realize leapfrogging development.
- Maintaining comprehensive, coordinated and sustainable development, and bringing into full play the functions of space science and technology in promoting and sustaining the country's science and technology sector, as well as economic and social development. China will strengthen strategic planning, making overall plans for the development of space technology, space application and space science. It will encourage progress in space science and technology to promote the development of high technology and industry, as well as the trans-formation and upgrading of traditional industries. Meanwhile, it will protect the space environment, and develop and utilize space resources in a rational manner.
- Adhering to the policy of opening up to the outside world, and actively engaging in international space exchanges and cooperation. China supports all activities that utilize outer space for peaceful purposes. It will strengthen exchanges and cooperation in this field with other countries on the basis of the principles of equality, mutual benefit, peaceful utilization of outer space and common development.

II. Progress Made in the Past Five Years

From 2001 to 2005, China's space industry has developed rapidly, making many achievements. A group of research and development and testing bases of the advanced world level has been built, and the system of research, design, production and testing has been further improved, markedly enhancing the country's basic capabilities in space science and technology. With breakthroughs in important key technologies, the overall level of China's space technology has been improved remarkably. Having made a historic breakthrough in manned spaceflight, China has embarked on a comprehensive lunar exploration project. Space application systems have taken shape, the range of application has been further expanded, application benefits have been noticeably enhanced, and important achievements have been made in space scientific experiments and research in this regard.

Space Technology

1. Man-made Satellites

Over the past five years, China has independently developed and launched 22 different types of man-made satellites, upgrading its overall level in this field markedly. On the basis of the four satellite series initially developed, China has developed two more satellite series, to bring the total to six -- the recoverable remote-sensing satellites, "DFH" (Dongfanghong, or The East is Red) telecommunications and broadcasting satellites, "FY" (Fengyun, or Wind and Cloud) meteorological satellites, "SJ" (Shijian, or Practice) scientific research and technological experiment satellites, "ZY" (Ziyuan, or Resources) Earth resource satellites, and "Beidou" (Plough) navigation and positioning satellites. In addition, the oceanic satellite series will come into being soon. China has speeded up the implementation of the plan to establish "a constellation of small satellites for environment and disaster monitoring and forecasting." Research and development of the payload of some new, high-performance satellites have been successful, and many application satellites have begun regular operation. The Fengyun Iand Fengyun II meteorological satellites have been listed by the World Meteorological Organization in the international satellite series for meteorological services. Important breakthroughs have been made in key technologies related to the common platform for big geostationary orbit satellites. Periodical achievements have been made in the research and development of large-capacity telecommunications and broadcasting satellites. Substantial progress has been made in the research and development, and application of small satellites.

2. Launching Vehicles

Over the past five years, "Long March" rockets independently developed by China have made 24 consecutive successful flights, and their major technological functions and reliability have been notably upgraded. From October 1996 to the end of 2005, "Long March" rockets made 46 consecutive successful flights. Important breakthroughs have been made in key technologies of the new-generation launching vehicles. Research and development of the 120-ton thrust liquid-oxygen/kerosene engine and the 50-ton thrust hydrogen-oxygen engine are proceeding smoothly.

3. Launching Sites

The construction of three launching sites at Jiuquan, Xichang and Taiyuan, has made new progress, and their comprehensive test and launch capabilities have been enhanced. Various launching vehicles, man-made satellites, unmanned experimental spacecraft and manned spacecraft have been successfully launched from the three launching sites many times.

4. Telemetry, Tracking and Command (TT&C)

The overall performance of the country's TT&C network has been improved and expanded. It has provided TT&C support to man-made satellites traveling in different orbits, and to unmanned experimental spacecraft and manned spacecraft during launch, operation in orbit, return and landing.

5. Manned Spaceflight

On November 20 and 21, 1999, China launched and retrieved the first "Shenzhou" unmanned experimental spacecraft. It then launched three more "Shenzhou" unmanned experimental spacecrafts not long afterwards. On October 15 and 16, 2003, it launched and retrieved the "Shenzhou V" manned spacecraft, China's first of its kind. Having mastered the basic technologies for manned spacecraft, China became the third country in the world to develop manned spaceflight independently. From October 12 to 17, 2005, the "Shenzhou VI" manned spacecraft completed a five-day flight with two astronauts on board. This was the first time for China to have men engage in experiments in space, another major achievement in the sphere of manned spaceflight.

6. Deep-space Exploration

Advance studies and engineering work of the lunar-orbiting project has been conducted, making important progress.

Space Application

1. Satellite Remote-sensing

The fields and scale where satellite remote-sensing is used have been constantly expanded. Breakthroughs have been made in a large number of key application technologies; infrastructure facilities have been strengthened; the technological level and operational capabilities of the application system have been notably improved; and a national satellite remote-sensing application system has taken shape. China has built and improved the National Remote-Sensing Center, National Satellite Meteorology Center, China Resources Satellite Application Center, National Satellite Oceanic Application Center and China Remote-Sensing Satellite Ground Station, as well as satellite remote-sensing application and certification institutes of relevant state departments, provinces and cities. An optical remote-sensing satellite radiation calibration station has also been completed and put into operation. Many remote-sensing products and services are provided by using data resources obtained from observation of the Earth by both Chinese and foreign satellites of multiple wavelengths of wide scope and long duration. Satellite remote-sensing application systems have been put into regular operation in many important fields, particularly in meteorology, mining, surveying, agriculture, forestry, land mapping, water conservancy, oceanography, environmental protection, disaster mitigation, transportation, and regional and urban planning. They are playing an important role in the nationwide land resources survey, ecological construction and environmental protection, as well as in major state projects, such as the South-North Water Diversion Project, the Three Gorges Project and the Project to Transmit Natural Gas from West to East.

2. Satellite Telecommunications and Broadcasting

Satellite telecommunications and broadcasting technologies are developing rapidly, their application is becoming more extensive and an application industry in this field has taken initial shape. By the end of 2005, China had more than 80 international and domestic telecommunications and broadcasting Earth stations, and 34 satellite broadcasting and TV link stations. Dozens of departments and some large corporations have established altogether some 100 satellite specialized communication networks and more than 50, 000 Very Small Aperture Terminals (VSAT). The development and application of satellite radio and TV broadcasting services has increased the coverage and improved the quality of the programs all over China, particularly in the vast countryside. Satellite telecommunications and broadcasting technologies play an irreplaceable role in the projects "to give every village access to broadcasting and TV" and "to give every village access to telephones." A satellite tele-education broadband network and a satellite tele-medicine network have been established. As a member of the International Maritime Satellite Organization, China has established a maritime satellite communication network covering the whole world, ranking it among the advanced countries in the application of international mobile satellite communication.

3. Satellite Navigation and Positioning

China has implemented several major related projects, one of which is called "industrialization of satellite navigation and positioning applications." By employing domestic and foreign navigation and positioning satellites, China has made great progress in the development, application and services of satellite navigation and positioning technologies. The range and fields where satellite navigation and positioning are applied are being continuously expanded and the size of the national market for satellite navigation and positioning doubles every two years. Satellite navigation and positioning technologies have been widely used in transportation, basic surveying and mapping, project surveys, resources investigation, earthquake monitoring, meteorological exploration, oceanic surveys, and so forth.

Space Science

1. Sun-Earth Space Exploration

In cooperation with the European Space Agency (ESA), China has carried out the Double Star Satellite Exploration of the Earth's Space Plan. Together with the four space exploration satellites of the ESA, China's satellites completed the world's first joint, synchronous six-point exploration of the Earth's space, obtaining important data. Advance research into exploration of the lunar and the solar systems was also conducted.

2. Micro-gravity Scientific Experiments and Space Astronomical Observation

China has carried out many items of experimental research in such fields as space life science, space materials science and micro-gravity science by using the "Shenzhou" spacecraft and recoverable satellites. It has also conducted trial tests of mutant crop breeding and high-power astronomical observation in space, and scored important achievements.

3. Space Environment Research

China has conducted research into space environment monitoring and forecasting, and made important progress in the observation, reduction and forecasting of space debris. It now has the ability to make forecasts of the space environment on a trial basis.

III. Development Targets and Major Tasks for the Next Five Years

"The Outline of the 11th Five-Year Program for National Economic and Social Development" and "The National Guideline for Medium- and Long-term Plans for Science and Technology Development(2006-2020)" formulated by the Chinese government in 2006 put the space industry in an important position. Based on the above two documents, the Chinese government has drawn up a new development plan for China's space industry, defining development targets and major tasks for the next five years or more. According to this plan, the country will launch and continue key space projects, including manned spaceflight, lunar exploration, high-resolution Earth observation, new-generation carrier rockets, and a group of priority projects in key sectors. It will also strengthen basic research, make arrangements ahead of schedule, develop frontier space technology, and accelerate progress and innovation in space science and technology.

Development Targets

To remarkably improve the country's capabilities and reliability of carrier rockets in space; to build a long-term, stably operated Earth observation system, and a coordinated and complete national satellite remote-sensing application system; to set up a relatively complete satellite telecommunications and broadcasting system, and remarkably enhance the scale and economic efficiency of the satellite telecommunications and broadcasting industry; to establish a satellite navigation and positioning system step by step to meet the demand, and bring into being China's satellite navigation and positioning application industry; and to achieve the initial transformation of applied satellites and satellite application from experimental application type to operational service type.

To enable astronauts to engage in extravehicular activities, and achieve spacecraft rendezvous and docking; to realize the lunar-orbiting probe; and make important and original achievements in space science research.

Major Tasks

- To develop nontoxic, pollution-free, high-performance, low-cost and powerful thrust carrier rockets of the new generation, eventually increasing the carrying capacity of near-Earth orbiters to 25 tons, and that of geostationary orbiters to 14 tons; develop in an overall way the 120-ton thrust liquid-oxygen/kerosene engine and the 50-ton thrust hydrogen-oxygen engine; and increase the reliability and adaptability of the present "Long March" carrier rockets.
- To start and implement a high-resolution Earth observation system; develop and launch new-type sun synchronous orbit and geo-stationary-orbit meteorological satellites, oceanic satellites, Earth resources satellites, small satellites for environmental protection and disaster mitigation monitoring and forecasting; and to start research into key technologies of new-type remote-sensing satellites, including stereo mapping satellites. To form an all-weather, 24-hour, multi-spectral, differential-resolution Earth observation system for stable operation, and achieve stereoscopy and dynamic monitoring of the land, atmosphere and sea.
- To make an overall plan for the development of a satellite remote-sensing ground system, and an application system; to integrate and improve the present satellite remote-sensing ground system, establish and improve a national satellite remote-sensing data center, and set up and improve supporting facilities for quantitative application, including a remote-sensing satellite radiation calibration station, and preliminarily materialize the common sharing of remote-sensing data to serve the public good; to set up a satellite environmental application institute and a satellite

disaster-mitigation institute, forming several important application systems; and to make breakthroughs in major satellite remote-sensing application fields.

- To develop and launch geostationary orbit telecommunications satellites and direct TV broadcasting satellites with long operating life, high reliability and large capacity; and to develop satellite technologies for live broadcast, broadband multi-media, emergency telecommunications, and telecommunications and broadcasting for public service. To continuously develop and improve the service functions of satellite telecommunications and broadcasting, and increase value-added services in the field of satellite telecommunications and broadcasting. To actively accelerate the commercialization of satellite telecommunications and broadcasting, and expand the industrial scale of telecommunications and broadcasting satellites and applications.
- To improve the "Beidou" navigation satellite test system, and launch and implement the "Beidou" navigation satellite system project. To independently develop application technologies and products in applying satellite navigation, positioning and timing service, and set up a standard positioning service supporting system and popular application terminus related to satellite navigation and positioning, expanding the application fields and market.
- To develop and launch new-technology test satellites, conduct more spaceflight experiments of new technologies, materials, apparatus and equipment, enhance the independent research and development level, and increase product quality and reliability.
- To develop and launch the "breeding" satellite, and promote integration of space technology and agricultural breeding technology and expand the application of space technology in the field of agricultural science research.
- To develop scientific satellites, including space telescope and new-type recoverable satellites; to conduct basic research in the fields of space astronomy, space physics, micro-gravity science, and space life science, and make important and original achievements in these fields; and to strengthen the ability to monitor the space environment and space debris, and initially set up a space environment monitoring and warning system.
- To enable astronauts to engage in extravehicular operations and conduct experiments on spacecraft rendezvous and docking; and to carry out research on short-term manned and long-term autonomously orbiting space laboratories, which is of certain application scale, and carry out follow-up work of manned spaceflight.
- To realize lunar-orbiting probe, make breakthroughs in developing basic technologies for lunar exploration, and develop and launch China's first lunar probe satellite "Chang'e I" for lunar science and lunar resources exploration; and to carry out final-period work for the lunar exploration project.
- To increase the comprehensive experimental ability and returns of spacecraft launching sites, optimize the layout, and enhance the reliability and automation level of the facilities and equipment of the sites.
- To advance the technology and capability of TT&C network, enlarge the coverage rate of the network, and acquire the ability to satisfy the basic demand for deep-space exploration.

IV. Development Policies and Measures

The Chinese government, under the guidance of the scientific out-look on development, has made overall plans in the three fields of space technology, space application and space science to promote independent innovations in space science and technology, make space activities create more economic and social benefits, ensure the orderly, normal and healthy development of space activities, and achieve the set goals.

The major policies and measures for China's space industry at present and in the near future are as follows:

- To make overall plans for and deploy rationally space activities. To give priority to the development of applied satellites and satellite applications, develop in a proper way manned spaceflight and deep-space exploration, and give active support to space science exploration.
- To muster strength in implementing key space scientific and technological projects, strengthen basic research and make plans for frontier technologies in advance. To muster superior forces to make leapfrogging development in space science and technology by making breakthroughs in core technologies and resources integration. To increase the sustainable innovative ability of space science and technology through strengthening basic research in the space field and developing several frontier technologies in advance.
- To promote space application and accelerate the industrialization of space activities. To strengthen the development of space application technologies, promote resource sharing and expand the scope of application. With emphasis on telecommunications satellites, satellite telecommunications, satellite remote-sensing, satellite navigation and carrier rockets, to vigorously construct a comprehensive chain of space industry covering satellite manufacturing, launching services, ground equipment production and operational services. To strengthen the spread, transformation and secondary development of space technology, and transform and upgrade the traditional industries.
- To attach importance to the infrastructure construction of the space science, technology and industry. To strengthen the building of infrastructure facilities for developing, producing and experimenting with spacecraft and carrier rockets. To give support to key laboratories and engineering research centers of space science and technology, strengthen the work on informatization, intellectual property rights and standardization of space activities.
- To promote the building of a space technology innovation system. To guide the reform, restructuring, transformation and updating of the space science, technology and industry, and accelerate the building of world-class large space corporations. To actively construct a space technology innovation system integrating production, education and research with space science and technology enterprises and national scientific research institutes at the core.
- To improve the scientific management of space activities. To adapt to the progress of the socialist market economy, actively make innovations in the system and mechanisms of scientific management, improve the sense of quality and profit among personnel, apply system engineering and other modern management tools to promote

scientific management, increase system quality, minimize system risks and enhance comprehensive benefits.

- To strengthen legislation work. To formulate laws, regulations and space industrial policies for guiding and regulating space activities, increase the level of administration by law, and create a legislative environment favorable for the development of space activities.
- To guarantee input of funds for space activities. The Chinese government will increase input to the space industry, and at the same time encourage the establishment of a diverse, multi-channel space funding system, so as to guarantee the sustainable and stable development of the space industry.
- To encourage people of all walks of life to participate in space-related activities, including encouraging industrial enterprises, scientific research institutes, commercial corporations, institutions of higher learning and social organizations, under the guidance of national space policies, to give full play to their advantages, take an active part in space activities, and participate in international space-related exchanges and cooperation. To encourage satellite operation enterprises and application units to use Chinese satellites and satellite-application products.
- To strengthen the fostering of talented people for the space industry. To spare no efforts for the education and cultivation of personnel, give attention to whetting their sense of innovation through practice. In particular, it is necessary to pay more attention to fostering a rationally structured contingent of young and highly qualified space scientists and engineers. To make efforts to publicize space knowledge and culture, and attract more outstanding personnel into the space industry.

The Chinese government continues to strengthen its administration and macro-guidance concerning space activities. The China National Space Administration (CNSA) is the country's governmental organization responsible for the management of space activities for civilian use and international space cooperation with other countries, and responsible for implementing corresponding governmental functions.

V. International Exchanges and Cooperation

The Chinese government holds that outer space is the common wealth of all mankind, and each and every country in the world enjoys equal rights to freely explore, develop and utilize outer space and celestial bodies; and that all countries' outer space activities should be beneficial to the economic development, social progress of nations, to security, subsistence and development of mankind, and to friendly cooperation between people of different countries.

International space cooperation should adhere to the fundamental principles stated in the "Declaration on International Cooperation in the Exploration and Use of Outer Space for the Benefit and in the Interest of All States, Taking into Particular Account the Needs of Developing Countries." China maintains that international space exchanges and cooperation should be strengthened on the basis of equality and mutual benefit, peaceful utilization and common development.

Fundamental Policies

The Chinese government has adopted the following policies with regard to developing international space exchanges and cooperation:

- Adhering to the principle of independence and taking the initiative in our own hands, carrying out active and practical international cooperation in consideration of the overall, rational utilization of domestic and international markets and resources to meet the needs of the national modernization drive.
- Supporting activities regarding the peaceful use of outer space within the framework of the United Nations. Supporting all inter- governmental activities for promoting the development of space technology, space application and space science as well as those conducted between non-governmental space organizations.
- Attaching importance to space cooperation in the Asia-Pacific region, and supporting other regional space cooperation around the world.
- Reinforcing space cooperation with developing countries, and valuing space cooperation with developed countries.
- Encouraging and endorsing the efforts of domestic scientific research institutes, industrial enterprises, institutions of higher learning, as well as social organizations to develop international space exchanges and cooperation in different forms and at different levels under the guidance of relevant state policies, laws and regulations.

Over the past five years, China has developed bilateral space cooperation with a host of countries. It has successively signed 16 international space cooperation agreements and memorandums with13 countries, space agencies and international organizations, and propelled multilateral cooperation in space technology and its application in the Asia-Pacific region and the process of establishing a space cooperation institution for the region. China has joined relevant activities sponsored by the United Nations and other relevant international organizations, and supported international space commercial activities. These measures have yielded positive results.

1. Bilateral Cooperation

Over the past five years, China has signed cooperation agreements on the peaceful use of outer space and space project cooperation agreements with Argentina, Brazil, Canada, France, Malaysia, Pakistan, Russia, Ukraine, the ESA and the European Commission, and has established space cooperation subcommittee or joint commission mechanisms with Brazil, France, Russia and Ukraine. It has signed space cooperation memorandums with space organizations of India and Britain, and has conducted exchanges with space-related bodies of Algeria, Chile, Germany, Italy, Japan, Peru and the United States.

China continues to collaborate with Brazil on the Earth resources satellite program. Following the successful launch of the Sino-Brazilian Earth Resources Satellite 02 in October 2003, the Chinese and Brazilian governments signed supplementary protocols on the joint research and manufacturing of satellites 02B, 03 and 04, and on cooperation in a data application system, maintaining the continuity of data of Sino-Brazilian Earth resources satellites and expanding the application of such satellites' data regionwide and worldwide.

China and France have developed extensive space exchanges and cooperation. Under the mechanism of the Sino-French Joint Commission on Space Cooperation, the exchanges and cooperation between the two countries have made important progress in space science, Earth science, life science, satellite application, and satellite TT&C.

The space cooperation between China and Russia has produced marked results. Within the framework of the Space Cooperation Sub-Committee of the Committee for the Regular Sino-Russian Premiers' Meeting, a long-term cooperation plan has been determined. In addition, exchanges and cooperation in the sphere of manned spaceflight have been carried out, including astronaut training.

China has unfolded space exchanges and cooperation with Ukraine. Under the mechanism of the Sino-Ukrainian Joint Commission on Space Cooperation, the two countries have determined cooperation plans.

China and the ESA have carried out the Sino-ESA Double Star Satellite Exploration of the Earth's Space Plan. China's relevant departments and the ESA have implemented the "Dragon Program, " involving cooperation in Earth observation satellites, having so far conducted 16 remote-sensing application projects in the fields of agriculture, forestry, water conservancy, meteorology, oceanography and disasters.

2. Multilateral Cooperation

In October 2005, the representatives of China, Bangladesh, Indonesia, Iran, Mongolia, Pakistan, Peru and Thailand signed the Asia-Pacific Space Cooperation Organization (APSCO) Convention in Beijing, and in June 2006 Turkey signed the Convention as well. APSCO will be headquartered in Beijing. This marks a significant step toward the official establishment of APSCO.

China continues to promote the Asia-Pacific Region Multilateral Cooperation in Small Multi-Mission Satellites Project. Together with Bangladesh, Iran, the Republic of Korea, Mongolia, Pakistan and Thailand, China has started the joint research, manufacture and application of small multi-mission satellites, to be launched in 2007.

China takes a positive part in activities organized by the United Nations Committee on the Peaceful Uses of Outer Space (UN COPUOS) and its Scientific and Technical Subcommittee and Legal Subcommittee. China has acceded to the "Treaty on Principles Governing the Activities of States in the Exploration and Use of Outer Space, Including the Moon and Other Celestial Bodies, " "Agreement on the Rescue and Return of Astronauts, and on the Return of Objects Launched into Outer Space, " "Convention on International Liability for Damage Caused by Space Objects, " and "Convention on the Registration of Objects Launched into Outer Space, " and strictly fulfils its responsibilities and obligations. China actively participates in the relevant activities organized by the UN COPUOS to implement the recommendations made by the Third United Nations Conference on the Exploration and Peaceful Uses of Outer Space (UNISPACE III). In particular, China, alongside Canada and France as co-chairs, has propelled the work of the space-system-based disaster mitigation and disaster management of the Action Team (AT-7) joined by 40 member states of COPUOS and 15 international organizations, and has actively taken part in the work of an ad hoc expert group to study the possibility of creating a coordination mechanism for disaster mitigation and management. China has acceded to a disaster mitigation mechanism consisting of space organizations from different countries in the light of the Charter on Cooperation to Achieve the Coordinated Use of Space Facilities in the Event of Natural or Technological Disasters. In cooperation with the UN, China has hosted UN/ESA/China basic space science workshops and a UN/China workshop on tele-health development in Asia and the Pacific. China has also hosted, in collaboration with the Multilateral Cooperation Secretariat of the Asia-Pacific Space Cooperation Organization and the UN Economic and Social Commission for Asia and the Pacific, training courses and symposia on space technology applications, and has provided financial support for these activities. China has also taken part in a program promoting the application of space for sustainable development in Asia and the Pacific organized and implemented by the UN Economic and Social Commission for Asia and the Pacific.

China has actively participated in activities organized by the Inter-Agency Space Debris Coordination Committee, started the Space Debris Action Plan, and strengthened international exchanges and cooperation in the field of space debris research. It has participated in the relevant activities organized by the Committee on Earth Observation Satellites (CEOS), and hosted the 18th CEOS plenary and 20th anniversary activities in Beijing in November 2004. In May 2005, China officially became a member of the ad hoc inter-governmental Group on Earth Observations (GEO), and an executive committee member as well. In July 2006, China held in Beijing the 36th COSPAR (Committee on Space Research) Scientific Assembly and the 8th International Lunar Exploration Working Group(ILEWG) International Conference on the Exploration and Utilization of the Moon. In addition, China has taken part in the relevant activities of the International Telecommunications Union (ITU), World Meteorological Organization (WMO), International Astronautical Federation (IAF), and Committee on Space Research (COSPAR).

3. Commercial Activities

China launched a communications satellite "APSTAR VI" into orbit in April 2005. In December 2004, China signed a commercial contract for a communications satellite with Nigeria, providing in-orbit delivery service to that country. In November 2005, China signed a commercial contract for a communications satellite with Venezuela, providing in-orbit delivery service and associated ground application facilities.

Priority Cooperation Areas

The Chinese government continuously renders support to international exchanges and cooperation in space technology, space application and space science, with priority given in the next five years to cooperation in the following areas:

- Scientific research into space astronomy, space physics, micro-gravity science, space life science, lunar exploration and planet exploration;
- Data sharing and services of Earth observation satellites, and application and research in the areas of resources investigation, environment monitoring, prevention and mitigation of disasters, and global climate change monitoring and forecasting;
- Sharing of space TT&C network resources, and mutual provision of space TT&C assistance;
- Design and manufacture of communications satellites and Earth observation satellites;
- Manufacture of ground facilities and key components of satellite communications, remote sensing, and navigation and positioning;

- Application of satellite communications and broadcasting in tele-education and tele-medicine, and expansion of application scope of satellite broadcasting and TV, and related services for satellite navigation and positioning;
- Commercial satellite launching services, export of satellites and their components and parts, and construction and services of satellite ground TT&C and application facilities;
- Exchanges and training of personnel in various fields of space activities.

INDEX

A

F

I

N

Q

R

S

T

U

V

W

X

Z